BRAZIL: THE FORGING OF A NATION, 1798-1852

BRAZIL

THE FORGING OF A NATION, 1798-1852

RODERICK J. BARMAN

STANFORD UNIVERSITY PRESS   1988
STANFORD, CALIFORNIA

This book has been published with the
help of a grant from the Social Science
Federation of Canada, using funds
provided by the Social Sciences and
Humanities Research Council of Canada.

Stanford University Press
Stanford, California
© 1988 by the Board of Trustees of the
Leland Stanford Junior University
Printed in the United States of America

CIP data appear at the end of the book

Preface

This work, which has been far too long in the making, is indebted for its existence to a great many people and institutions. First and foremost, the financial assistance granted since 1973 by the Social Sciences and Humanities Research Council and by its predecessor, the Canada Council, has been both generous and indispensable. I am particularly beholden to the SSHRC for its award, through the agency of the Social Science Federation of Canada, of a publication subsidy. Naturally the views here expressed in no way reflect those of any of the granting agencies.

My interest in Brazilian history dates from my first days as a graduate student in a seminar given by Engel Sluiter, who also showed me the path to good prose writing. Over the years, Dauril Alden has provided much information and sound advice, including his comments on this manuscript in its penultimate form. Orde Morton generously lent his dissertation, which is, alas, still unpublished, and Harold Livermore kindly gave access to his copies of the *Correio Braziliense*. To the members of the interlibrary loan staff at the University of British Columbia and to the editorial staff of the *Handbook of Latin American Studies* in the Library of Congress my debts are multiple and long-standing.

In Brazil, indispensable help on research was given to me, as to so many other foreign scholars, by José Gabriel da Costa Pinto of the Arquivo Nacional. My thanks are also due to, among many others, Adelaide Alba and her assistants at the Instituto Histórico e Geográfico Brasileiro; Maria Amélia de Porto Migueis at the Arquivo Imperial; and Maria Marta Gonçalves at the Arquivo Histórico do Itamaratí. Research in Brazil not only was rewarding for itself but has provided much good company, including Victor of the *bigodes*.

Researched and written within the context of an intellectual and personal partnership of almost twenty-five years' standing, this book has benefited from, to adapt the words of an eminent writer, "one who has constantly encouraged, whose mind and judgement have ever guided these pages, the most severe of critics, but—a perfect spouse!" Rodza and Emily have valiantly adapted to being children of not one but two academics and have endured innumerable disputations on matters historical. Finally, since the machines invented by Messrs. Amdahl and Jobs alone made possible the completion of this work, it is only honest that I acknowledge what is a considerable if impersonal debt.

Belonging as I do to a country which both patronized and exploited Brazil during most of the period this work covers, I am conscious that the book contains ideas and opinions that may, to some Brazilians perhaps, seem both derogatory to their nation's identity and disdainful of their country's achievements. Such was not my intent in writing. The persistence, fortitude, and resource which Brazilians displayed in creating a nation-state against formidable obstacles can only arouse admiration and a desire to know more about Brazil's past.

R.J.B.

Contents

Illustrations

BRAZIL: THE FORGING OF A NATION, 1798-1852

Introduction

During the last two hundred years the world has developed within the matrix of the nation and its formal embodiment, the nation-state.[1] From its origins in Europe, the concept of the nation has expanded to engulf the entire globe and to become the standard and unavoidable form of political and social organization. We cannot, in all truth, envisage a viable model of political and social existence other than the nation-state, a polity admitting no external control or authority over its actions and possessing immediate and untrammeled power over a contiguous territory occupied, in theory, by a population homogeneous in speech, culture, and ethnicity.[2]

As the concept of "nation building" attests, the nation as an ideal possesses an allure and a potency which enable it to triumph even in areas where it did not previously exist and conditions do not favor its establishment. The principal goal of new states is and has long been to create those conditions, welding at no matter what cost the territories and peoples being governed into that one and indivisible entity we call a nation. No better testimony exists to the appeal and the vitality of the nation during the past two centuries than the lack of a rival concept disputing its dominance. Even Marxism, in other respects so deadly to the existing order, has been, if not vanquished, at least obliged to accommodate itself to the nation.

This significant, even central, element in the development of the modern world has not received a degree of scholarly attention commensurate with its importance.[3] The reasons for this indifference are various, not all of an academic nature or germane to this study. A principal factor is certainly what Louis Snyder has called "the tantalizing ambiguity" of the word "nation," for, as Charles Tilly remarked, " 'nation' remains one of the most puzzling and tendentious items in the political lexicon."[4] If the nature and so the existence of a state can be determined by independent criteria, such is not possible for a nation, in its essence a normative concept. A nation "exists" if a sufficient body of individuals agrees that it does, even though it lack the structure of a state or acceptance by the majority of inhabitants within its envisaged boundaries. It is, in Benedict Anderson's apt phrase, "an imagined community."[5] In its ability to create identity and to arouse loyalty, no matter what the external, objective realities may be, lies the enduring strength of the nation as a political ideal, and perhaps the principal reason for its worldwide success. In other words, support for a nation—"nationalism"—is emotional and subjective, not rational and objective, even though the nation ideal has a proven capacity to express itself in and so harness to its service most intellectual systems.[6]

These characteristics of the nation have served to hinder and undermine study of the evolution of the nation-state and its rise to global dominance, because academic research (particularly in the social sciences) proceeds upon the assumption that topics for investigation are amenable to analysis according to rational, objective criteria, with the researcher remaining external to the topic. The standard techniques of analysis, which proceed from identifying and abstracting principal characteristics out of a range of case studies through to formulating a general theory of explanation, are not usefully applied to the study either of the nation as a type or of specific nations. The outcome is, all too often, simply shallow and descriptive.

Furthermore, in studying the nation, the scholar does not stand detached from the topic: the researcher's own attitude towards the nation or nations under investigation affects the outcome of the whole analysis. As David M. Potter nicely expressed the point some twenty years ago, "when the [researcher] attributes nationality to any group, he establishes a presumption in favor of any acts involving an exercise of autonomy that group may commit; when he denies nationality, he establishes a presumption against any exercise of autonomy."[7] The basis for such "evaluative judgments," to use Potter's term, is not necessarily intellectual. Researchers live in a world of functioning nation-states, to which they cannot be emotionally indifferent, so that when undertaking research on the nation ideal or on specific nations their attitudes to the topic chosen cannot but be influenced, and possibly motivated, by perceptions derived from the current scene.[8]

Although their concern for the vanished past might seem to shield historians from contemporary influences, one characteristic of the nation ideal makes them peculiarly liable to such motivations. The legitimacy and strength of nations have long been perceived as best demonstrated by longevity. Research into the history of any nation cannot be a neutral process, for its findings will inevitably impinge, if no more than obliquely, on the reality of that nation's claims to longevity and so to legitimacy. Historical research undertaken specifically into the origins of a nation usually does serve to affirm that nation's antiquity and continuity because, as Potter has pointed out, the tendency of historians to exhaust all the evidence means that, in such investigations, "they will usually find some indications of separateness, however limited."[9] Although common in the nineteenth century, a deliberate, explicit employment of historical research to affirm national identity and to arouse nationalism is now unusual, in part because it is no longer necessary. The hegemony of the nation-state has become by now so well established and so accepted that it requires no more than maintenance. All that is needed of historians is for them to make the nation-state a principal focus of their studies and to give tacit support to the perception of their own particular nation as historically necessary, inevitable, and beneficent.

Formidable as the conceptual problems bedeviling research into the nation-state are, they do not prohibit investigation into the topic, provided that certain precautions are taken. Given that research cannot be neutral or impartial in motivation, the soundest course is to maintain, constantly replenished, a very high degree of skepticism, amounting to incredulity, in respect to the claims by the nation or nations under study to historical inevitability, legitimacy, efficacy, and beneficence. Such skepticism is indispensable, because otherwise the nation's formation and development, instead of constituting the topic for analysis, become untested and incontrovertible assumptions which are built into the fabric of the analysis, rendering the actual investigation nothing more than a self-fulfilling demonstration of predetermined conclusions.[10] The danger of that approach lies in its encouragement of a perception of the past which Eric Hobsbawm has characterized, in another context, as "writ[ing] history backwards and eclectically."[11] History becomes simple hindsight, nothing more than a recording of the inexorable and justifiable flowering of the nation into its present form. Research based on such secular predestination seriously biases the interpretation of both evidence and causation.

Since nations are subjective, normative entities, springing from and existing within particular social, economic, and cultural settings, a second necessary precaution is to study both the nation and the nation-state as strictly historical phenomena, rather than as universal, abstract concepts existing independent of spatial and temporal constraints. The need for this precaution can best be illustrated by the following two points. In semantic terms, the words "nation" and "nation-state" carry in the vernacular of each and every nation a range of distinctive and particular elements and connotations. Some of the elements' meanings are similar in different vernaculars, but such a similarity does not mean that they can be detached from their associated elements and connotations, to be analyzed as a single type. Secondly, the processes by which individual nations and nation-states have emerged, during the last two centuries, have often displayed great similarities, the gaining of national independence being often inspired and sometimes directly guided by precedents. The formation of each individual nation and nation-state was, nonetheless, the outcome of a particular conjunction of social, economic, and cultural factors, so that comparison and classification, although not impossible, should be undertaken with great caution.

For historians to achieve an understanding of the nature of the nation and the nation-state, the causes of their appeal, and the reasons for their success, a fruitful approach is to concentrate on specific cases occurring in the era of the nation-states' first establishment, on the period when they were oddities rather than the norm for political organization and when their functioning did not follow standard patterns but entailed trial and error. As might be anticipated, such an approach has its own problems.

It is generally accepted that the nation-state first took form in Europe. No such agreement exists among scholars about the precise date of that emergence, a dispute in large part caused by two specific difficulties. In some countries, such as England and France, the nation evolved out of, and a national identity formed within, a monarchical state existing since the Middle Ages. There was, in other words, no decisive moment of discontinuity which marked the change from traditional polity to nation-state.[12] In other countries, particularly those of Eastern Europe, the problem is quite the reverse. There, most of the nation-states did not emerge until the nineteenth century, but these considered themselves to be "revivals" of vanished polities, nations which although long deprived of political autonomy had not on that account ceased for one moment to exist.[13] The lack of any objective criteria for establishing whether a nation exists precludes any definite judgment on these claims to continuity and so to longevity as nations.

These difficulties do not complicate research on the formation of nation-states in the Western Hemisphere. The United States, which emerged as a single national polity between 1776 and 1788, has been aptly and accurately termed "the first new nation," and the countries of continental Latin America antedate those of Eastern Europe as independent nation-states.[14] Rejection of a colonial status resulted of necessity in a moment of institutional discontinuity, although the new nations in the Americas did not differ in language and culture from the polities they had rejected. The prevailing attitudes towards the original peoples of the New World ensured that identification by the new nations with the pre-Columbian states and cultures was, if not absent, minimal.[15] Accordingly, the emergence of what indisputably were new nations and the formation of their respective national identities can be studied in as close an approximation to laboratory conditions as historical realities permit. Analysis of the experience of the new American nations makes it possible to identify the basic imperatives behind and the internal dynamic within the nation-state in the phase of its first expansion outside its European heartland.

Brazil, which achieved political independence in 1822, displays characteristics that render it distinctive among the nations of the Americas and make it highly suited for such study.[16] Since the Portuguese Crown prohibited, prior to 1808, both printing and higher education in its New World possessions, the formation of a separate and autonomous identity was, as Chapters 1 and 2 make clear, delayed until very late. That the subsequent

emergence of that identity after 1808 occurred in an accelerated and concentrated form facilitates analysis. In 1822 and 1823 the actual struggle for
political independence took a swift, uninterrupted course that was little
affected by extraneous factors, as is shown in Chapter 3. In contrast to the
outcome in British North America and Spanish America, all the colonies
of Portuguese America were incorporated into a single nation-state. The
monarchical form of government adopted by the nation at independence
not only distinguished Brazil from the United States and Spanish America
but represented, as demonstrated in Chapters 4 and 5, a distinctive form
of conservative nationhood owing much to Napoleonic France.[17]

Even more significant for the understanding of the dynamics of the
nation-state's formation was Brazil's development during the 30 years following the achievement of independence. Because of its geographic loca-
tion, effectively isolated by ocean and tropical forests, the new nation
developed largely unaffected by the course of international affairs.[18] The
impact of conflicting concepts of nationhood and the effect of nation-
statehood upon the peoples and territories therein incorporated—topics
discussed in Chapters 5 through 8—can therefore be precisely identified.

Analysis of the transformation of the colonies of Portuguese America
into the nation-state called Brazil during the half century between 1798
and 1852 suggests some of the factors lying behind the success of the
nation-state concept in its first phase of expansion. As indicated by the
Porto rising of 1820 in Portugal and the independence movement in Brazil
itself two years later, the nation ideal appealed to individuals and groups
who held grievances against the political status quo and for whom the
existing forms of identity and loyalty had become, psychologically and
intellectually, either insufficient or irrelevant. Particularly attracted were
those who felt their standing in the existing polity to be incommensurate
with their culture and capacities. The replacement of the existing polity
by a nation-state offered them the prospect of enhanced status, even the
chance to rule. The nation-state appealed in part because it could and did
serve as a vehicle not just for self-advancement but for dominance and
control by specific interests, as the conduct of the central bureaucracy in
Rio de Janeiro during 1822 makes clear. A basic, probably universal, cause
of the nation-state's success both then and thereafter was that it promised
to its rulers, acting in the name of the nation, complete yet licit control
over the process of "who gets what, when, and how." The appeal of the
nation-state was the appeal of power.

Power, when exercised, inevitably involves a considerable element of
coercion. As the Brazilian experience attests, the formation of a new
nation-state may entail a degree of compulsion to secure the obedience
of peoples and territories, no matter what their preferences, which are
deemed to belong to the new nation. In 1822 and 1823, the rulers of Brazil, believing that the new Empire rightfully and naturally inherited the
boundaries of the former Kingdom of Brazil, did not hesitate to secure by

force of arms the inclusion of the provinces of Maranhão and Pará in the far north and the Banda Oriental (modern Uruguay) in the far south.

Conditions in Brazil in the early nineteenth century show further that the formation of a nation-state did not necessarily depend upon the active participation of the mass of the people. In Brazil a plurality of the population were slaves, deprived of all rights. Among the free only a small minority were literate, and since the campaign for independence as a nation predominately employed the printed word, it appealed directly to a very limited section of Brazilians. Popular backing for the cause was generated mainly by presenting the nation ideal in terms compatible with existing group loyalties (such as offering an emperor in the place of the king) and by harnessing suspicion and fear of outsiders (who in the Brazilian case were those born in Portugal). Neither approach was capable of generating enduring and positive attachment to the new nation-state. The establishment and the continuance of Brazil as a nation-state depended principally upon the activities of a small stratum of educated men deeply affected by Enlightenment thought, whose familiarity with the medium of print gave them a mastery both of communications and of the new participatory politics. Although the nation-state was, in this first phase of its expansion, often justified as embodying the popular will, as the American Declaration of Independence did in 1776, it must be questioned whether mass support was, in this period, indispensable for the successful creation of a nation-state.

As pointed out above, the claims of the nation-state to authority and to obedience by its citizens were, as they still are, absolute and exclusive. Anyone disputing those claims has ultimately to choose between submission and total rejection, which is only viable if followed by the creation of an opposing nation-state.[19] The claims to authority and obedience which the inhabitants of Portuguese America had been willing to accept from the king were not, to influential elements in Brazil, licit or tolerable when asserted by the Lisbon Cortes, an elected government in Portugal set up after the Porto rising of 1820. The consequence was the emergence of the new nation-state known as Brazil. The formation of that nation-state in turn generated movements within its boundaries protesting its claims to absolute authority and obedience, most notably the Confederation of the Equator of 1824 and the revolt in the Banda Oriental of 1825. Since only the latter was willing to replace the Brazilian nation by another, it alone was successful.

What the Brazilian experience in 1822 and in subsequent years suggests is that the actual gaining of political independence was not necessarily coterminous with the creation of nationhood, that is, of a homogeneous community sharing a common identity and purpose. The change in the control of power did not, of itself, automatically transform existing attitudes and ambitions of the peoples included within the boundaries of the new state. Even in long-established nation-states, as Potter has pointed out, "the various elements of the population must vary in the extent to which they share the sense of group identity and the commitment to group purpose."[20] It should not be assumed on the basis of events in Brazil from 1822 to 1852 that the consolidation of the nation-state was necessarily perceived by much of the population as serving their needs or as designed for their benefit. Indeed, the exclusive authority and absolute obedience exacted by the nation-state, once created, inevitably restricted the options for subsequent development open to the constituent peoples and territories. In Brazil, for example, national consolidation meant that the needs of the capital Rio de Janeiro and its hinterland took precedence over those of all other regions.

Even when nation-states failed to provide the security and prosperity promised at their creation, they were not likely on that account to collapse.[21] Nation-states have always had a vested interest in their own survival, no matter how scanty their achievements. Nation-states have possessed considerable means of ensuring that survival, as the outcomes of the Farroupilha revolt (1835–45), the Minas Gerais and São Paulo rising of 1842, and the Praieira revolt (1848–49) attest in the case of Brazil. Moreover, the simple passage of time endowed the status quo with a familiarity that discouraged experimentation, and dissatisfaction was further checked by fears of the social disorder it might provoke. By 1852, an entire generation of Brazilians had reached maturity without knowing anything but the existing polity. By that date the nation-state had become so much the norm on both sides of the Atlantic as to undermine all alternative ideals. The original phase of nation-state expansion was, in short, completed.

In studying the transformation of the colonies of Portuguese America into the nation-state of Brazil, the purpose of this work is to elucidate three principal themes: (1) the growth of an autonomous identity from the late eighteenth century onwards, (2) the process of state formation from 1808 to 1852, and (3) the exercise of politics and the formulation of policy at the national level (that is, at the center) during the three decades after 1822. This book has a second purpose: to provide what has previously been lacking in the English language—a comprehensive and analytical narrative of the history of Brazil during the crucial period when it was forged as a nation-state. In this respect the work is traditional political history, and unashamedly so. It is so not merely because a comprehension of the political evolution of what had been the colonies of Portuguese America is central to understanding the emergence of modern Brazil, but because economic and social developments took place within and were profoundly influenced by the political context. The efforts made by Brazilians after 1852 to bring their country to fully functioning nationhood by modifying the dominant economic and social structures so that they fit the mold of an orthodox nation-state—efforts finally abandoned in the first decade of this century—will form the subject of a second volume.

1

Portuguese America: Diversity Against Unity, 1798-1808

As the year 1797 drew toward its close, an important meeting took place in the city of Lisbon, as the ministers and chief advisers of Her Most Faithful Majesty the Queen of Portugal gathered to hear a long exposition presented by the minister of the navy and overseas dominions, D. Rodrigo de Sousa Coutinho.[1] For Portugal the final years of the eighteenth century were a time of constant danger. The war between revolutionary France and its satellites on the one hand and Great Britain and its allies on the other had engulfed the whole of Europe and reached every corner of the world. Portugal, traditionally an ally of the British, fought briefly on their side but since 1795 had sought to maintain neutrality. Peace with France had not been restored, in part because that republic required, as a precondition for a peace treaty, that Portugal break with Great Britain, and in part because Spain, since 1796 allied to France, worked for its own ends to prevent a settlement. Portugal, which had belonged to the Spanish Crown from 1580 to 1640, still aroused the territorial ambitions and cupidity of its neighbor.[2]

It was paradoxical that at this moment of stress and danger the economy of the Portuguese world was booming as never before. The nascent industries of Great Britain and the needs of the war economies in most of the European states created a huge market for raw materials of every kind. Further, the French colony of Saint Domingue, the principal sugar and coffee producer in the New World, had been ravaged by a race war following the slave insurrection of 1791; its collapse caused rising prices and a seller's market, to the profit of the other producers. Exports from Portugal and its possessions were to quadruple between 1789 and 1807. By the middle of the 1790's the Portuguese balance of payments had moved decisively into surplus, with Lisbon prospering as a major entrepôt for trade.[3]

The exposition presented by D. Rodrigo de Sousa Coutinho in October 1797 and the plans it contained for the management of Portugal's overseas

possessions were therefore a matter of considerable interest to the assembled ministers and advisers of the Portuguese Crown.[4] In his speech the
minister outlined thirteen specific proposals for the reform of the fiscal
system in the New World colonies.[5] The recommendations included the
abolition of the salt tax and the reduction of all customs duties levied in
Portuguese America to a uniform 4 percent. The head tax on slaves imported from Africa was also to be lowered. All taxes were to be directly
collected by the Crown, and the fiscal accounting system reformed. The
royalties received by the Crown on all gold mined were to be halved and
the mining of diamonds thrown open to all. The consequent shortfall in
revenues was to be recouped in part by new taxes. Those of the measures
that merited royal sanction would, the minister hoped, be then "executed,
to the advantage of the Royal Treasury and the benefit of the peoples."[6]

Prior to discussing his fiscal proposals, D. Rodrigo asked that he might
"be allowed to touch lightly on the political system most suitable for
adoption by our Crown for the preservation of its boundless dominions,
especially those of America, which in fact provide the basis for the greatness of our August Throne." There followed a sweeping, detailed, and
frank evaluation of the nature of the Portuguese Empire and its immediate needs. For the minister, the "dominions in Europe are no more than
the capital and center of the Portuguese Empire. Portugal reduced to itself alone would shortly be only a province of Spain, but as the point of
union and seat of the Monarchy," with possessions in America, Africa,
and Asia, "it has within it all the means of figuring conspicuously and
brilliantly among the first powers of Europe." For D. Rodrigo, Portugal's geographic position rendered it the entrepôt for trade not just between northern and southern Europe but between Europe and the outside
world. Consequently, the "bond between the Portuguese overseas dominions and the metropolis [is] as natural as that between other motherlands
and their recently separated colonies scarcely was." "Without this fortunate bond uniting our possessions," D. Rodrigo asserted, "they either
could not achieve the degree of prosperity made possible by our situation
or would be obliged deliberately to create the links which today happily
unite the Monarchy."[7]

D. Rodrigo thereby dismissed a matter of concern during the past
twenty years to the more percipient among the Crown's advisers: the rebellion of the thirteen colonies against Great Britain and their consolidation into the new United States of America. The problem which even
the minister, generally so blunt in his approach, did not directly tackle
was the possibility that Portugal's American colonies might follow the
precedent set by their British counterparts. Yet D. Rodrigo, by maintaining that "the inviolable and sacred principle of unity, the first basis of the
monarchy, . . . ought to be preserved with the utmost devotion, so that the
Portuguese born in every part of the world will perceive himself solely as
Portuguese and think only of the glory and grandeur of the Monarchy to

which he has the honor to belong," was in fact acknowledging the possibility of disaffection among the overseas colonies and of their separation from Portugal. To preserve the existing system, Portugal had to serve as "the common entrepôt" for the overseas dominions, each of which in its relations ought to be "more active and productive with the metropolis than with each other." "These two principles ought to apply especially," D. Rodrigo stressed, "to the most essential of our overseas dominions, which are without question the provinces of America, known under the generic name of Brazil."[8]

The speech of D. Rodrigo de Sousa Coutinho thus constituted official acknowledgment of a crucial historical development: the strength of the Portuguese Empire lay not in Europe but in the New World. The Crown's policies could be effective only if they recognized the primacy of the American colonies in the royal dominions and their growing economic and social maturity. It is tempting to go one stage further and to conclude, as Caio Prado Júnior, a leading Brazilian historian, has done, that "Brazil had, by that time, reached a stalemate. The colonial regime had accomplished all that it had to accomplish; the work of the mother country was felt to be complete." Since political independence came to Brazil 25 years after D. Rodrigo's speech, it is easy to view what did occur as part of an inexorable process, and so perceive the period around 1800 as being what Caio Prado Júnior termed "the moment when the elements that make up Brazilian nationhood—the basic institutions and energies— organized and stored up from the outset of colonization, finally came to flower and reached maturity."[9]

The future course of Portuguese America was not so ordained: in no way was the emergence of the nation-state of Brazil inevitable or predestined. The question should rather be, Given the conditions and perspectives of the late 1790's, what was the path most likely to be taken henceforth by the "provinces of America, known under the generic name of Brazil"? Four factors may be identified as of critical importance in shaping that course: (1) the environmental, economic, and human conditions then existing in the American colonies; (2) the attitude and policies of the Portuguese Crown toward its New World colonies; (3) the frame of mind and accustomed behavior prevailing among the inhabitants of those possessions; and (4) the goals and social composition of the disaffected elements among the colonial population. A careful evaluation of these factors reveals—as the real meaning of the phrase "generic name of Brazil" attests—that the future course of Portuguese America was by no means preordained.

I

"Brazil [is] without doubt the leading possession," D. Rodrigo asserted in 1797, "of all those founded by the Europeans outside their continent, due not to what it currently is but to what it can be if we derive all the advantages that Nature offers from its extent, situation, and fertility."[10] Portuguese America, as defined by the Treaty of San Ildefonso signed with Spain in 1777, encompassed territories of nearly three million square miles, stretching from just north of the equator to the river Chuí at latitude 30° south, and extending westwards from the Atlantic coasts to the forests edging the Andes. This sprawling vastness defied the feeble means of transportation and communication then available—sailing ship and canoe, horse and mule, and human feet—and worked against the integration of the Portuguese New World. The variety of geographic and climatic conditions existing across these territories reinforced their fragmentation and centrifugence.

Communication by land was at best slow and difficult, for nature conspired to separate, not link, the constituent parts of Portuguese America. Along much of the eastern Atlantic coast, the Serra do Mar rose almost vertically to two thousand feet or more and so blocked easy access to the interior. In that interior the course of the rivers seemed designed more to hinder than to assist any westward advance. Only in the south, in the captaincy of São Paulo, did the tributaries of the great Paraná River make it comparatively easy for the traveler to move inland by canoe, but even there the journey from the Atlantic coast to the gold mines of Mato Grosso took some five to seven months of paddling and portage, not to mention the danger of Indian attacks on the west side of the Paraná River.[11]

Despite its considerable risks, travel by sea was perforce the preferred form of communication between the different parts of Portuguese America. Yet even the sea divided and did not unite. The Southern Equatorial Current, which with its accompanying winds sweeps westwards along Brazil's northern coast from Cabo São Roque to the mouth of the Amazon, made direct sea communication nearly impossible between the far north and the east coast: it was easier and swifter for the far northern captaincies of Pará and Maranhão to communicate with Portugal than with the rest of Portuguese America.[12] The hostile and drought-ridden lands lying between the far north and the eastern seaboard formed a further barrier discouraging land communication between the two regions. Accordingly, almost nothing held together the ranchers on the rolling pasturelands of Rio Grande do Sul in the far south, the miners grubbing for gold and diamonds in the cold streams of Minas Gerais, the black slaves working in the humid cane fields of Pernambuco in the northeast, the mulattoes and mestizos herding cattle through the thornbush and cacti of Piauí in the northern interior, and the Amerindians forced to gather the forest products of the unending Amazon basin.

Moreover, what the labors of these working folk produced on plantation, mine, and ranch was, as a rule, not even consumed or used in Portuguese America itself. Their output was more commonly transported to the port city of the region and there shipped abroad, mostly to Portugal, but in small part to Africa and in lesser amounts to other markets. By the last decade of the eighteenth century, products from its New World colonies furnished over half the exports from Portugal itself to Europe, North Africa, and the United States.[13] Trade within the Portuguese New World was principally in animals on the hoof, dried meat, other foodstuffs, and imported goods moving from the port cities into the interior. The commercial economy within each region was powered by the production of raw materials for export.

Consequently, Portuguese America was not a single economy but rather six principal economic regions, all but one of them dominated by a single port city and relating more to the Atlantic market than to the other five. Of these economies, the most dependent on Portugal was that of the far north, the immense but thinly populated Amazon basin. This land of rivers and tropical forests yielded an infinity of *drogas,* as the Portuguese termed the harvest of the forest. Most valuable were cacao, coffee, rare woods, sarsaparilla, and spices such as cinnamon. Gathered by forced Indian labor, these products were brought down by canoe to the port of Belém do Pará, whence they were shipped to Portugal.[14]

To the east of the Amazon lay the burgeoning economy of Maranhão. On its rich coastal plains were grown both cotton and rice. Cotton planting had spread rapidly inland, so that by the end of the century its center of production was at Caxias, almost two hundred miles from the sea. Since the late 1760's output had risen eightfold, impelled by the insatiable demand of English and French textile mills. Exports of rice and cotton were dispatched to Portugal through the port of São Luís do Maranhão.[15]

The interior of the northeast, covering the captaincy of Piauí, most of Ceará, western Pernambuco, and northern Goiás, was in the 1790's still a frontier area, dominated by ranching and some subsistence farming. Never very fertile, and since the 1770's ravaged by repeated droughts, these lands had lost their importance as suppliers of meat on the hoof to the neighboring economies.[16] As a consequence, the interior northeast did not at the end of the century constitute a separate region but was an area economically subordinate to the coastal regions to its north and east.

Pernambuco and, farther south, Bahia not only were the oldest zones of settlement in Portuguese America but continued to be the two most productive economic regions. Sugar was the staple crop grown on the fertile coastal plains, with Bahian production exceeding that of its competitor to the north. Both regions were major exporters of other crops. In Pernambuco cotton production equaled that of Maranhão. The Recôncavo da Bahia, the hinterland surrounding the port city of Salvador, grew 90 percent of the tobacco produced in the Portuguese New World. Tobacco was the main item in the goods which the merchants of Salvador exchanged in West Africa for slaves. As a center of external commerce Salvador had for long outdistanced not only Recife, the port city of Pernambuco, but all other ports in Portuguese America.[17]

BAHIA Captaincy
- - - - Captaincy boundary
- - · - · Internatioanl boundary

Negro River

Barra

AMAZON RIVER

Javari River

RIO NEGRO

GRÃO
PARÁ

Tapajós River

Xingu River

Guaporé River

MATO GROSSO

Mato Grosso

Cuiabá

Goiás

GOIÁS

·Belém

São Luís

MARANHÃO
Cáxais

Oeiras·

PIAUÍ

Tocantins River

São Francisco River

FERNAMBUCO

Fortaleza

CEARÁ

RIO GRANDE
DO NORTE

C. de São
Roque

·Natal

PARAÍBA
Paraíba·
·Olinda
·Recife

BAHIA

·Salvador

MINAS
GERAIS
Vila Rica·

ESPÍRITO SANTO
Vitória

São Paulo
Sorocaba·

SÃO PAULO

·Santos

Rio de Janeiro

RIO DE JANEIRO

PACIFIC OCEAN

Paraguay River

Paraná River

SANTA
CATARINA
RIO
GRANDE
DO SUL

·Destêrro

·Porto Alegre

ATLANTIC OCEAN

Uruguay River

MISSION
DISTRICT

N

Rio de la Plata

0   100 200 300 400   500 miles

0   200   400   600   800 km

MAP 1. Portuguese America Circa 1800. (All boundary lines are approximations only.)

Of all the economic zones in Portuguese America, the region which had its outlet in the port city of Rio de Janeiro was probably the most variegated and the least dependent on external commerce. The axis on which the region turned was trade between Rio city and the mining zones in Minas Gerais, southern Goiás, and Mato Grosso to the far west. Output of gold and diamonds in all these areas had slumped since the middle of the century, but production still sufficed to fund a considerable importation of manufactured goods through the port of Rio. At the same time, the economy of the traditional mining areas in Minas Gerais had largely shifted to agriculture and artisan production, since the mountain ranges separating the captaincy from the coast made these local products fairly competitive with imported goods. There thus existed in Minas Gerais, with its growing population, something resembling a consumer market. In the immediate hinterland of Rio de Janeiro city new sugar and coffee plantations were springing up during the 1790's, stimulated by the rising prices and open markets following on the elimination of Saint Domingue. Sugar also became the main commercial crop in São Paulo, a subsidiary zone of this economic region.[18]

To the far south lay a sixth economic region, Rio Grande do Sul. During the last quarter of the eighteenth century its growth, based on cattle, mules, and wheat, was rivaled only by that of Maranhão. As the most exposed part of the Portuguese New World, having been invaded by the Spanish in 1762 and 1777, the region merited the particular attention of the Portuguese Crown, which sought to foster settlement and economic development. Rio Grande do Sul was exceptional in that most of its exports went not to Portugal but to the rest of Portuguese America. Horses and mules bred on its plains went north overland to be sold at the great animal fair at Sorocaba in São Paulo. Although Rio Grande do Sul lacked a good port on the Atlantic coast, it did export both *charque* (dried meat) and wheat by sea to Rio de Janeiro and Salvador, a trade which boomed in the last years of the century.[19]

The geographic and economic fragmentation of Portuguese America was not offset or even balanced by racial or linguistic unity among its two to three million inhabitants in the late eighteenth century.[20] Population figures for this period are partial and far from precise, but it is clear that the principal racial and cultural group was neither European nor Indian, but rather African. Near the very end of the colonial period, two-fifths of the population were slaves, and so colored, while a further quarter consisted of free blacks and mulattoes.[21]

If most blacks, both slave and free, lived on the coastal plains containing the large towns and plantations, they were to be found in the work force in all parts of Portuguese America as both menial and skilled labor, despised but indispensable. Whereas slave owners scorned their captives' cultures and sought to prevent slaves of the same origin from congregating together, African habits were already influencing the masters' ways of living in the coastal regions of Portuguese America.[22] A rapidly growing element in the late eighteenth century were the *gente de côr*, the mulattoes and blacks who were not only free and New World–born but Portuguese in language, culture, and religion. Lacking only the right skin color, they sought integration and acceptance. Even more numerous were the freed blacks and urban slaves, who by surviving in a hostile world managed to create a way of life that drew upon both Portuguese and African cultures.[23]

That a majority of the inhabitants of Portuguese America were black or mulatto did not in any way foster unity. The divisions between the free-born, freed, and slaves were profound, as were those generated by differing shades of color. Added to these rivalries were the differences caused by unequal assimilation into Portuguese culture. Among African-born slaves, a profound division separated those long resident and acculturated from the captives newly imported from Africa. Even among the latter no common identity existed, since Africa contained many tongues, religions, and cultures—and slaves were imported from many parts of Africa. Although fluctuating, the volume of the slave trade with Africa in the last quarter of the eighteenth century never dropped below 13,000 a year, sufficient to ensure that the differences—and divisions—persisted.[24]

Far less numerous in the population of Portuguese America were the Indian peoples. Most Indians probably still lived outside the limits of Portuguese settlement. Their influence was nonetheless considerable. The prejudices existing among the Portuguese against free and open mixing with blacks—covert relationships being another matter—did not apply with such force to relations with the Indians, who had since the time of first contact with Europeans provided what may be termed bed and board. Indeed, in 1755 the Crown, anxious to increase the population of its American dominions, had issued a decree officially sanctioning and encouraging marriage with Indians.[25] Many long-settled families had Indian ancestors. This mixing was most visible and important in social and economic terms in the areas where the Indians had most effectively resisted the devastation caused by Old World disease and Portuguese rapacity, in effect the arc of territory running from the Amazon basin in the north to the backlands of the south. In the Amazon region the process of assimilation and acculturation was by the 1790's far advanced, with the result that by the middle of the next century foreign travelers commented on the mestizo culture of the ordinary population, a culture characterized by such traits as use of manioc instead of wheat flour, the hammock instead of the bed, and Tupi as the vernacular instead of Portuguese.[26]

The missionary orders of the Catholic Church, acting as agents of the Portuguese Crown, had long tried to make the "wild" (bravo) Indian tribes of the interior settle in villages where they would adopt agriculture, Catholicism, and civilization, so becoming "tame" (manso). Such villages of índios mansos offered, however, too easy and tempting a target for Portuguese slavers. Raids on mission villages combined with disease and neglect to cripple the system. The abolition by the Crown in 1757 of the missionary orders' control of the Indians and their labor had accelerated the destruction. In sum, the Indians' presence in the population of Portuguese America was essentially compelled, not voluntary. Their influence was exerted more through individual Indians, often female, than through the interplay of one cultural group with another.[27]

The third racial group, smaller than the African and similar in size to the Indian, was the Portuguese. In the hands of the Portuguese lay dominance—control of the structures of rule, mastery of the economy, and possession of the official language and culture. What reinforced the Portuguese advantage over the other two groups was their being an off-shoot of the small, compact, and—by contemporary standards—remark-ably homogeneous society that was Portugal itself in the late eighteenth century. Notwithstanding marked regional differences between the north and south of Portugal, the existence of strong local loyalties, and some linguistic variation, Portugal was unusual in Europe of the period in re-spect to its sense of nationhood and its unity of culture. This unity was strengthened in the later eighteenth century by the spread of literacy and the first beginnings of a national infrastructure.[28]

Homogeneity of culture and sense of national identity were maintained in the New World in the face of several unfavorable factors. A novel and testing environment imposed a style of life very different from that in Por-tugal. The long Atlantic crossing, a voyage of several weeks, prevented close contact with the mother country. A considerable portion of the Por-tuguese population in the New World was by the 1790's American-born and bred, with no personal acquaintance of their ancestral land and its culture. Between the New World–born, known as *brasileiros* or *ameri-canos,* and the Portuguese-born, known as *europeus* or *reinóis,* consider-able tensions existed.[29] The American-born often regarded the *europeus* as arrogant and over-privileged intruders and resented their dominance. The latter tended to view the *americanos* as lazy, ignorant, presumptuous, and too often of tainted ancestry.[30] However, only rarely in the past had these tensions erupted into open hostilities, as in the "War of the Mas-cates" at Pernambuco in 1710. Even then the New World–born had not been shaken in their loyalty as Portuguese and in their allegiance to the Crown.[31]

Surprising as this lack of division within the Portuguese minority might seem in view of the contrary experience in British North America, it is explained by several factors. Identification with Portugal was in fact maintained and strengthened by a continued and considerable inflow of migrants. The discovery of gold and diamonds in the central interior dur-ing the early eighteenth century had triggered a massive rush across the Atlantic, and migration continued high thereafter, totaling by the end of the century several hundred thousand immigrants, perhaps as many as half a million.[32] Since these newcomers found themselves in a land where the bulk of the population was alien in color, language, and customs, the immigrants' loyalty to Portugal itself was naturally enhanced. Regional distinctions, previously so significant, were discounted, especially since settlements in the New World did not usually attract migrants solely from any one region of Portugal.[33] Males often migrated as young bachelors, and their decision to settle permanently was customarily marked by mar-riage to a local girl, a practice which blunted the distinction between *americanos* and *europeus.* At the same time, networks of kinship across the Atlantic were constantly maintained by the arrival of relatives seeking their fortunes in the New World.[34] The upper ranks of government, church, and commerce in the colonies were filled with Portuguese-born, whether permanent settlers or merely sojourners, and the New World–born tended to absorb their ideas and their outlook.[35] Above all, the harsh reality of living in the midst of an exploited and enslaved majority forced unity upon the Portuguese, no matter what their place of birth. Necessity and close bonds of blood and culture kept together the third and ruling racial group and tied it to the motherland.

The basic environmental, economic, and human factors existing in the Portuguese New World in the late eighteenth century formed a conjunction in which the internal structures were fragmented, distinct, and generally centrifugal. In contrast, external linkages exerted a powerful influence upon the constituent regions, orientating them away from each other and toward the outside world. Unification and integration of the royal colonies in America demanded a consistent implementation by the Crown of settled and coherent policies designed to achieve those ends.

II

Throughout the eighteenth century the governance of the New World territories had centered upon Lisbon. Ever since the ouster in 1777 of the marquess of Pombal as ruling minister and virtual dictator, the Crown's affairs had lacked a firm, directing hand. D. Maria I, who had ascended the throne in that year, was well intentioned but lacked both intelligence and experience of government. Her deteriorating psychological condition had by 1792 lapsed into madness, forcing her son, D. João, to conduct the business of government in her name. Only in July 1799, when all hope of the queen's recovery was gone, would D. João assume formal authority as prince regent. Since he was a timorous soul, adept at avoiding unpleasant decisions through procrastination, the affairs of the Crown did not greatly benefit from the change.[36]

The central government in Lisbon accordingly functioned as a congeries of rival bureaucratic fiefdoms, each seeking to extend its own power and influence while thwarting the ambitions and schemes of its competitors.[37] As minister of the navy and overseas dominions, a post to which he had been named late in 1796, D. Rodrigo de Sousa Coutinho controlled but one of these fiefdoms: he did not even enjoy unfettered control over all colonial affairs, so that the program of fiscal reforms proposed in his speech of October 1797 could not immediately be enacted.[38] Implementation depended upon his ability to persuade, placate, and circumvent his rivals at Lisbon, especially those who resented any tampering with the colonies' traditional role of supplying the Crown with a constant source of revenue and serving as a tied market for exports from Portugal. In the telling phrase of D. João IV, who founded the Bragança dynasty in 1640, the American colonies were "the milch cow" of Portugal.[39]

Although D. Rodrigo assigned to the colonies a much more exalted role, "as Provinces of the Monarchy awarded the same honors and privileges as those granted to" Portugal, his plans for fiscal reforms did not impinge to any significant extent upon the existing structures which made the overseas territories no more than suppliers of revenue, raw materials, and markets to the mother country.[40] This subordination the minister admitted in the very words he used to deny its existence: "The interests of the Empire are thus so usefully and wisely combined that what at first sight might seem a deprivation provides not only a mutual advantage but those who appear to gain less are the very ones to derive the greatest benefit from it."[41] In other words, D. Rodrigo's plans did not involve reforms in the sense of structural modifications to the system, but rather improvements which would render the system more coherent and more efficient.

The minister did not propose to alter the routing of nearly all colonial commerce through Portugal. Foreign vessels would still be prohibited from calling at the overseas ports, and the ban on foreign merchants' participation in colonial trade continued. Manufacturing in the overseas territories was discouraged, and where it competed directly with that of Portugal was forbidden.[42] Even D. Rodrigo's proposed concessions on this score were, as his own words revealed, more apparent than real: "It would not be contrary to the system of . . . the overseas dominions if the establishment of manufactures in them were permitted, but for many centuries agriculture will continue to be more profitable to them than industries, which ought to be encouraged in the metropolis in order to assure and to tighten the common bond."[43] As far as possible, the Portuguese dominions were meant to continue as a closed economic world.

In terms of cultural life, largely ignored in the minister's speech, the existing system was designed to keep the overseas territories isolated, dependent, and so incapable of establishing any intellectual independence from Portugal. The Crown's refusal to permit the establishment of printing in the New World epitomized the policy. In 1749 the setting up of a press in Rio de Janeiro by an enterprising Lisbon printer, with the tacit consent of the local governor, had rapidly become known to the authorities in Lisbon, who reiterated the ban on printing and ordered immediate confiscation of the press.[44] Publication of information about the New World colonies, particularly about their wealth, had been tightly controlled in the first decades of the century, but licenses to publish works on Portuguese America were thereafter more freely granted.[45] The export of books to the colonies was strictly regulated.

No official sanction, much less encouragement, was given to the creation of a cultural and technical infrastructure in Portuguese America. The development of schooling in the colonies had owed everything to the Jesuits and other clerical orders and nothing to the Crown. The expulsion of the Jesuits from the Portuguese dominions in 1759, at the behest of the marquess of Pombal, closed their *colégios* and primary schools. The *aulas régias,* or royal classes, decreed to replace the Jesuit system existed largely on paper until 1772, when the Crown imposed a new tax, the *subsídio literário,* to pay for salaries and costs of education. Even then the 40 teachers of basic literacy and the 15 "royal instructors" of Latin, Greek, and philosophy appointed to serve the New World colonies were patently insufficient to supply the educational needs of Portuguese America.[46] Reports by royal governors at the end of the century indicated that revenues from the new tax were as often peculated as applied to their intended purpose.[47] Although some unofficial classes were offered by the religious orders and by private individuals, they in no way offset the inadequacies of the state system. Only well-to-do families could afford to employ a personal chaplain who also instructed the younger generation. That the mass of the population lacked even the rudiments of literacy was not surprising.

In respect to institutions of higher education, the Crown was resolute in prohibiting their establishment in its New World colonies. Prior to 1759, the Jesuits' proposals to turn their *colégio* (essentially an advanced high school) at Salvador into a university had been consistently rejected.[48] The Crown believed that those of its subjects in the New World who desired higher education should cross the Atlantic and enroll at the University of Coimbra, even though the cost was far beyond the means of all but a tiny minority of the population.[49] No bars were ever placed in the way of men from the colonies who sought an advanced education in Portugal, nor was the Crown averse to employing them, after graduation, in its service.[50] Close to six hundred students born in the New World enrolled at Coimbra between 1772 and 1808, and nearly three hundred and fifty graduated in those same years.[51] Although immigrants from Portugal did include some Coimbra graduates, Portuguese America contained at the end of the eighteenth century a very small number of *letrados* (men of letters), as university graduates were known.

For men who could not afford or did not wish to cross the Atlantic, a possible alternative to Coimbra were the diocesan seminaries, of which eight had existed in Portuguese America at mid-century. No fewer than six of these had been created and staffed by the Jesuits, and they vanished after the order's expulsion. The only seminaries to survive were both at Rio de Janeiro. Not until 1799 were they supplemented by a new diocesan seminary at Olinda, near the port city of Recife.[52] Most of those preparing for holy orders, and all laymen desiring culture and knowledge, had therefore to resort to self-education or seek private instruction, often from among the clergy. The intellectual community in the New World was thus formed of *letrados,* priests, and self-taught laymen. The harsh reality was that Portuguese America possessed only the rudiments of the effective educational system indispensable for the creation of an integrated society.

Just as the Crown's economic and cultural policies ensured the isolation of Portuguese America, so its administrative system perpetuated and reinforced the fragmentation natural to its New World possessions. In his speech of October 1797, D. Rodrigo commented on "the necessity that exists of forming two great centers of strength, one in the North and the other in the South, under which there will be grouped the territories which Nature has so providently divided by the great rivers, to the point of making this administrative approach much more natural than artificial."[53] The existing Estado do Brasil (State of Brazil) was composed of the fourteen captaincies of southern, central, and northeastern Portuguese America. The state was headed by a viceroy, or royal delegate, who resided first at Salvador and then, from 1763, at Rio de Janeiro. In 1652 the Estado do Brasil had been provided with its own *relação*, or court of second instance, which sat at Salvador and decided appeals not only from the lower courts in the Estado but from those in Angola and the island of São Tomé. A second *relação* was created in 1751 at Rio de Janeiro, in belated response to the increase in business caused by the gold and diamond booms of the early eighteenth century.[54]

The four captaincies of the far north had originally been grouped together as the Estado do Maranhão, which was in 1751 reorganized as the Estado do Grão Pará e Maranhão, with its capital at Belém. Although the Estado was dissolved in 1772, its constituent territories continued totally separate from the Estado do Brasil, being ruled more directly from Lisbon than had previously been the case.[55] No *relação* was created in the far north, all appeals being taken directly to Lisbon. In 1797, D. Rodrigo advocated a return to the former system: "The governments of Goiás, Mato Grosso, the Rio Negro, Maranhão, and Piauí are destined by Nature and policy to depend on a viceroy residing at Pará, and to form with it a common league to defend the frontier of our possessions extending from the upper Paraguay to the Amazon."[56]

The same division was apparent in the affairs of the Catholic Church. In the ecclesiastical reorganization approved by the Holy See in 1676, an archdiocese was created in Portuguese America. The new archbishop of Bahia was not, however, given jurisdiction over the newly formed diocese of Maranhão, which continued subordinate to the patriarchal see of Lisbon. On the other hand, the archbishop was given authority over the African sees of Angola and São Tomé.[57]

The viceroy's high-sounding title and dignities of office could not disguise the fact that he had long been little more than governor of the most important captaincy in the Estado do Brasil. After 1763, when the viceroy moved from Salvador to Rio de Janeiro, he also held real authority over Santa Catarina and Rio Grande do Sul, the two frontier captaincies in the far south. Over the remaining captaincies of the Estado the viceroy possessed what is best termed oversight. Although the governors were in theory his subordinates, he could rebuke and cajole but not order and control. Only in time of conflict, as during the war with Spain in 1777, did the viceroy assume a central role in directing military operations and organizing supplies. Even then, his effectiveness was limited by royal orders prohibiting him from being absent from the viceregal capital.[58]

The governance of Portuguese America therefore depended upon the individual captaincies which varied greatly in size, population, and wealth. Some, like Bahia and Pernambuco, were worlds unto themselves, others no more than satellites. The nine major captaincies were each ruled by an official entitled "governor and captain general."[59] Despite the titular authority of the viceroy within the Estado do Brasil, all the governors received orders directly from and reported directly to the Crown in Lisbon.[60]

"The security and defense of these same captaincies," D. Rodrigo declared in his speech of October 1797, constituted the first principle which ought to direct "the internal regime" of government in the New World.[61] The governors and captains general were invariably military officers. Among the array of functionaries who surrounded the governors, composing what may be termed "the official world," the most important were certainly the professional military men who commanded the forts, the few units of regular troops, and the local militia. Although pay was poor and often in arrears, a career as an officer in the regular military conferred status as a noble, thus explaining the flood of applicants for commissions.[62] It was, however, on the local militia units that the defense of the captaincies depended. While the units' commanders were professionals, the ordinary militia officers were part-time, amateur soldiers drawn from the local "notables," or as they were aptly termed, "homens bons e melhores da terra acostumados a andar na governança dela," that is, "good men and among the best of the land accustomed to undertake its government." A third line of defense was provided by the ordenanças, or home guard, officered totally by local notables.[63]

One of the principles which D. Rodrigo believed should guide "the internal regime" of the captaincies was "the equal distribution of justice, which is the prime basis for securing the internal tranquillity of states."[64] The judiciary in the New World was headed by the elite desembargadores who heard the appeals sent to the relações of Bahia and Rio de Janeiro; below them were 24 ouvidores (superior judges), who heard cases and dispensed justice in vast comarcas (judicial districts), and a dozen juizes de fora (external judges), residing in the principal towns.[65] Upon the energy and the rectitude of these judges depended the effectiveness of royal administration, since justice in the Portuguese tradition was not confined to the passive judgment of cases but required the active enforcement of the characteristics of a just society. The ouvidores, for example, were ordered to carry out an annual "correction" (corregimento) of their comarcas, seeing that the laws were obeyed, municipal codes enforced, and society working as it ought.[66] One of the reforms urged by D. Rodrigo in 1797 was the separation of "the administration of justice from the collection of revenues," and to this end he urged the appointment in every comarca of an intendant responsible for all fiscal matters.[67]

The Catholic Church formed the third, and junior, branch of governance in the colonies. D. Rodrigo's speech referred to the role to be played by the established religion: since "religion . . . is so essential for the preservation of states," its priests "ought to warrant a special attention."[68] In the nine major captaincies the governor and captain general was flanked by a bishop, a figure of competing prestige. Next in social standing came the canons, who composed the official staff or chapter of the cathedral (if there were one), and the regular clergy of the monastic orders such as the Benedictines. Below these stood the ordinary clergy in the towns. The country clergy ranked lowest in status. In the eyes of the Crown, priests were expected to use their spiritual powers and privileged position to keep the laity in due reverence and proper obedience to God's appointed, El Rei Nosso Senhor, and to the monarch's chosen deputies.[69] The clergy ought also "to direct all their efforts to civilizing the wild Indians," not merely for pious reasons but because it was "indecorous" that "so many men should be allowed to exist without useful employment, and without increasing and promoting cultivation in the dominions."[70]

Officials named directly by the Crown, and in particular the governors, military commanders, and lower judiciary, were usually appointed for a fixed but renewable term and—if American-born—generally did not serve in their native captaincy. The Crown sought to prevent its agents from establishing ties with the population they governed. This policy, although not conspicuously successful, did prevent a massive undermining of the Crown's authority in the New World. Conscious of the weakness of its administrative machinery and jealous of its prerogatives, the Crown sought systematically to check the creation in the New World of formal, acknowledged institutions that embodied legitimate sources of power and authority independent of and thus potentially alternative to its own.[71]

In Portuguese America there existed few elective rather than appointive institutions, and in no case did their jurisdiction stretch beyond the borders of a single municipality. The most important of the bodies which could claim to rest upon an authority other than the king's were the town councils (câmaras municipais). These councils were not representative in any modern sense, since they were exclusively drawn from the local notables—the men of property, wealth, and influence in the community. In the eyes of the eighteenth century, the town councils so elected represented all that was worthy of representation. The council usually had six members (vereadores), of whom the most influential were the two local magistrates (juizes ordinários). In Salvador, Rio de Janeiro, Recife, and other leading towns, the Crown had replaced these elected magistrates with its own nominee, a juiz de fora who also acted as president of the city council and guardian of the royal interests.[72]

During the seventeenth century, the câmaras municipais in the overseas dominions did possess a certain independence and initiative, even though they represented a fairly narrow range of social and economic interests. By the end of the following century, however, if the comments on the câmara of Salvador by a local observer can be generalized, the councils had lost much of their effectiveness as a result of systematic interference in their proceedings by the Crown and of the *vereadores'* practice of preferring their own personal and familial interests to those of the town itself.[73]

The rural areas lying outside the municipalities formed *julgados* (districts of justice), each having an elected *juiz ordinário* whose role was strictly limited and local. At the start of the eighteenth century, efforts had been made to ensure that a *julgado* existed every five leagues in the countryside, but the reality remained that the administration of Portuguese America was concentrated in the towns and that the farther from them one traveled the more feeble became the Crown's authority.[74]

No one in any captaincy, not even one of the notables, was permitted to supplement this meager system of administration by creating voluntary lay associations.[75] To the Portuguese Crown, voluntary organizations were no less subversive of its authority than were elective institutions—and perhaps more so. At Salvador in the late 1750's, the local board of merchants had been summarily dissolved by the viceroy for being unable to produce a royal order authorizing its existence.[76]

The efforts of the Portuguese Crown to keep its American colonies free of all such "political" activities were, however, successful only in appearance. The existing system of governance and control could not enforce the ban, the royal officials being too few, too isolated, and too poorly remunerated. Although officials' salaries often consumed half the revenues collected, as in the captaincy of Bahia, their stipends were so modest and so often in arrears as to render most officials incapable of resisting the temptations that beckoned on every side: the proffering of lavish gifts and rich hospitality, the dangling of profitable business deals before them and their relatives, and the parading of their eligible daughters by leading local families. Nor was the impossible requested in return. By deliberate inattention, covert favoritism, and conspiracies of silence, royal officials could protect dubious undertakings and condone infractions of the law from which they stood to benefit.[77]

Outside the coastal towns the situation was even more intractable because the Crown's rule in the backlands, or *sertões*, depended upon the *juizes ordinários*, a few militia units, and the older *ordenanças*, all institutions dominated by local potentates.[78] These notables, usually large landowners, could not be coerced by the Crown into doing what they did not want: unwelcome policies were resisted not by open rebellion but by simply being ignored. Fortunately for the Crown, such individuals did not normally aspire to control more than local affairs and possessed little interest, knowledge, or understanding of the larger world. Since they valued official recognition of their local status, they could be placated by the bestowal of minor honors and offices.

Portuguese rule in the New World was, in sum, characterized by a limited ability to implement the Crown's chosen policies and by the lack of any considerable means of coercion to back its authority. As the marquess of Pombal had advised the new governor of Mato Grosso in 1767, "do not alter anything with force or violence," but "act with much prudence and moderation, a method that achieves more than power."[80] Royal officials who did attempt to enforce the letter of the law or to carry out novel or unpopular policies soon found themselves caught in a web of passive resistance and covert obstruction. Their dispatches, passionate with denunciations, exposés, and pleas for radical action, were usually written in vain. Only open affronts and defiance of its authority would arouse the Crown to decisive action. It usually preferred to deal with the situation by shifting the official to another post.[81] Although the Crown never abated by one iota its assertion of absolute authority in the colonies, its agents in the New World often found that the most effective and rewarding course lay in maintaining a discreet balance between the orders of the Crown and the interests of the governed.[82]

Schemes for wide-ranging reforms, such as that presented by D. Rodrigo de Sousa Coutinho in October 1797, thus faced two basic drawbacks: they both exceeded the administrative capacities of the Portuguese Crown in its overseas possessions and ran counter to the basic imperatives of Portuguese policy toward the colonies. Throughout the eighteenth century, in marked contrast to the Spanish monarchy, the Crown never seemed entirely confident that on the far side of the Atlantic its rule was secure and its subjects trustworthy.[83] D. Rodrigo's plans for Portuguese America failed to reckon with these two basic realities and were thereby seriously flawed. The minister lacked, moreover, the cunning, circumspection, and administrative skill needed to turn blueprints into reality. Although D. Rodrigo continued to rise in the royal service, being named in 1800 president of the royal treasury and so senior minister, few of the reforms he had advocated in October 1797 would actually be implemented. Late in 1803 the prince regent referred the decree reforming mining legislation, the key to the reform package, to the new minister of the colonies. D. Rodrigo, his position already weakened by his identification with Great Britain and its interests, treated D. João's action as a public gesture of royal disfavor, resigned, and withdrew to his country estates.[84] With his departure, the reforms he espoused lay forgotten. Colonial affairs resumed their accustomed course. The impetus for action would have to come from the inhabitants of Portuguese America themselves.

III

The social and human conditions existing in Portuguese America at the end of the eighteenth century make it difficult to postulate the existence of any common frame of mind, or *mentalité,* or to seek any single sense of identity among the population. For a majority of the inhabitants, exploited and often enslaved, the task of surviving from one day to the next dictated the terms of their existence. Many were ignorant of the official language and hostile to its culture; in any case, independent thought and initiative among this majority were deterred by ingrained habits of deference and brutal methods of control. In practice, only those who were Portuguese in language and culture and were deemed to be Portuguese by descent could aspire to influence and independent standing.[85] Even among this minority, the hierarchical ordering of existence and the concentration of property and wealth in the hands of a few meant that life in Portuguese America was dominated and usually directed by the *homens bons,* the men of substance and standing in their local communities.[86]

Given the ability of the privileged few to impose their will on the majority, their outlook and behavior dominated local society. Accordingly, in an analysis of the forces shaping the future of Portuguese America, it is the *mentalité* of the privileged few which must be studied. If the status quo in the New World were to be overturned, simple disaffection among the privileged minority would not suffice; there would have to exist a consensus about the desired alternative. Rejecting the existing objects of devotion and obedience, the minority would have to find fresh ideals, a new concept that could command their common loyalty and through which they could achieve a common identity. Existing patterns of thought and behavior among the privileged few did not, however, favor such a change.

In 1802 the royal teacher of Greek at Salvador remarked that he had had "the honor to serve Your Royal Highness and the Pátria in these States of Brazil."[87] From this phrase it is possible to deduce what were the concepts that provided the Portuguese on both sides of the Atlantic with a focus of loyalty, a sense of place, and so their sense of identity. Of the terms used by Luís dos Santos Vilhena, the *pátria,* perhaps best translated as homeland, was the most significant. In the captaincies of the New World, and probably also in Portugal itself, the *pátria* signified the visible, physical community in which an individual was born, brought up, married, pursued a living, and raised a family.[88] A man was loyal to and identified with his *pátria* within the context of his obedience to El Rei Nosso Senhor and his membership in the Portuguese *nação,* which was perceived as the totality of those owing allegiance to the monarch, regardless of their place of residence.[89] A poem written by a priest born in the New World reveals the intense devotion commanded by the *pátria:* "He who is not grateful to the *pátria* is base and uncouth of soul."[90]

The concept of *pátria,* when used in this manner, was essentially part of a visual, preliterate *mentalité.* Consequently, the word *pátria* could hold different meanings for men living in the same physical place. In the port city of Salvador at the end of the 1790's, for example, the word signified to the artisan groups, Portuguese in culture but often mulatto, the city of Salvador itself, while to a Salvador-born priest the word encompassed the entire captaincy. To one of the wholesale merchants, most of them *europeus,* or to the royal teacher of Greek, the *pátria* continued to be Portugal, or a community within it.[91]

As a rule of thumb, it can be said that for the New World–born among

the dominant minority, the *pátria* was synonymous with the captaincy of
their domicile. Where a captaincy was very large and fragmented into distinct areas, as was the case with Minas Gerais, the *pátria* would usually be
perceived as one area within the captaincy. Thus, a well-educated bureaucrat, writing after Independence in an official capacity to his monarch,
referred to "the *comarca* of Serro Frio, my Pátria," being the diamond
region in the north of Minas Gerais.[92] How strong a sense of locality and
community underlay the concept of *pátria* is evident from the practice of
referring to those born and raised in the same captaincy as *filhos da terra,*
or "natives of the land," in distinction to the *filhos da fora,* the "outsiders,"
born and raised everywhere else.

When the New World–born considered the totality of the royal dominions either as "Brazil" or as "Portuguese America," they did so through
the prism of the *pátria,* the larger concept having reality and relevance
solely as a magnification of and extrapolation from the individual's own
pátria. Thus Sebastião da Rocha Pita's *História da América Portuguesa,*
published at Lisbon in 1730, ostensibly covered all of the New World, but
in fact almost the entire book is devoted to the author's native captaincy of
Bahia.[93] The broader territorial entities, whether "Brazil" or "Portuguese
America," possessed validity and aroused interest only as they impinged
upon the *pátria,* the fundamental object of loyalty and identity.

Thus the term "o Brasil," in common use during the eighteenth century,
did not then bear its modern meaning. As textual analysis confirms, the
term did not yet denote a discrete society, one with a distinctive culture
and separate identity existing within clearly defined territorial boundaries—in short, a potential nation-state.[94] In the late colonial period the
term could be used to convey several different meanings. In its precise
sense, "o Brasil" referred to the Estado set up in 1549 containing the captaincies of the northeast, center, and south, those under the oversight of
the viceroy at Rio de Janeiro. In contrast, "América Portuguesa," or simply "América," referred to the totality of the New World colonies, so
that there was no logical contradiction in a reference by the minister of
the colonies in 1788 to the captaincies "which compose the dominions
of Brazil *and* [emphasis added] Portuguese America."[95] Since the Estado
do Brasil made up the predominant part of the Portuguese New World,
"o Brasil" was also frequently employed as a rough synonym for "América
Portuguesa" as when the royal teacher of Greek referred in 1802 to "os
Estados do Brasil," the States of Brazil.[96] Finally, the term was frequently
employed as no more than a vague spatial indicator, as in *o continente
do Brasil,* or "the land mass lying west of the Atlantic." In contrast to
"América Portuguesa," the meaning of which is almost always clear from
the textual context, which meaning of "o Brasil" an author intended is all
too often uncertain from the context.[97]

That the term did not bear its modern sense is also apparent from
the meaning then carried by the adjective deriving from it, *brasileiro.* The

change was noted as early as 1823: "The name that we then had of *bra-sileiros* did not signify as it does today a quality in the political sphere, it indicated only the place of birth."[98] The word as used in the eighteenth century lacked any connotation of collective identity, not just political but cultural or social as well. On the rare occasions when people did need an adjective to express a New World social and cultural identity, they never employed the word *brasileiro,* since it was equated with birthplace, but used the root *brasil* with some other suffix.[99]

The terms "América Portuguesa" and "o Brasil" were in common use during the late colonial period. Their usage did not mean, however, that they constituted spatial concepts encompassing the totality of the Portuguese New World and capable of attracting loyalty or providing a focus of identity. What did exist was a host of loyalties to lesser, limited entities, the *pátrias,* which did not challenge the common and broader allegiance to the king and to the Portuguese heritage. What reinforced among the notables in the New World captaincies this primary identification with the *pátria* was the nexus of property and privilege binding them to the particular community from which they drew their living and in which they enjoyed influence and status. In this respect the *pátria* was a magnification and extrapolation of the individual and his personal world, in the same fashion as "Brazil" or "Portuguese America" was of the specific *pátria.*[100]

The freeing of Portuguese America from its colonial status would, accordingly, have to begin as a series of discreet, individual movements in the different *pátrias,* that is to say, the captaincies. To be successful in the individual captaincies each movement would have to mobilize the local notables in support of the cause of independence. The question was whether existing patterns of behavior among the notables and their attitudes toward cooperative action were such as to presage success for any such movement.

Although almost all forms of independent association and initiative were forbidden, the notables, both urban and rural, had throughout Portuguese America developed a remarkable capacity for circumventing the ban while ostensibly obeying it. They did so by infiltrating existing (and so approved and "apolitical") institutions, which they then subverted to their own ends. Most commonly co-opted were the religious associations for laymen—brotherhoods (*irmandades*) and third orders—linked to the Catholic Church. Especially important were the "holy houses of mercy" (*santas casas de misericórdia*), which existed in the major towns, providing relief and shelter for the sick, helpless, and dying.[101] Particular bodies were used as the institutional cover for different networks of power and influence, as the brotherhood of Santo Antônio da Barra at Salvador was by the merchants of that city. Not only did membership in such a body advertise the individual's participation in a particular network, but the common membership and the distinctive rituals of the institution gave form and substance to that network. The precedence held by such bodies on public occasions, as, for example, the order in which *irmandades* marched in a religious procession on a feast day, served as a means of giving open recognition to the standing and influence within the local community both of the different networks and of individual notables.[102]

Two sacraments of the Church, baptism and marriage, were employed to create in acceptable form linkages otherwise illicit. *Compadrio,* the spiritual relationship joining together parents, sponsors, and child through baptism, established between those involved in the ceremony perpetual bonds of mutual obligation and support. The great advantage of *compadrio* ties was that they could link social superiors and social inferiors without loss of status to the former, an indispensable advantage in a hierarchical society.[103] Of almost equal importance was the sacrament of marriage, which signified more than the joining of two individuals. Marriage permitted influential families lacking mature males to co-opt as offspring young men of proven ability. Through judicious marriages, alliances between different family groupings could be created and the scope of existing *parentelas,* or kinship networks, extended or reinforced. The Church's sacraments thus legitimized networks of obligation and influence which in more open societies would have been embodied in voluntary associations, political and economic.[104]

Since such networks existed in the shadows and were not meant to leave evidence of their existence or influence, it is not easy for the historian to study their operation. That they existed and functioned effectively is shown by the fate of zealous officials who attempted to carry out the letter of the law or to implement new or unpopular measures. In conflicts between networks and officials, it was usually the latter who lost and were transferred to other posts. Lax or zealous, skilled or inefficient, officials came and went, but the networks endured.

Influential as these networks were, their power was essentially negative, their capacity for action being impeded by their particularism, their conservatism, and their lack of overt aims. To the extent that they were political, they were so in a most limited and circumscribed way. Further, these traits served to prevent the notables acquiring broader, more impersonal conceptions of society, the polity, and the political process. The interests of the individual notable, of his immediate family, and of his larger *parentela* took precedence within the context of his local community and of his *pátria*. Identification with the *pátria* similarly kept notables from forming broader links laying first claim upon their loyalties. The *pátria* was indeed a world unto itself, resisting external influences—although solidarity inside the *pátria* was not, it must be emphasized, complete, for within that world familial feuds and competition for status and wealth flourished.

The one object of identity and loyalty that did command allegiance across Portuguese America was El Rei Nosso Senhor, who in this patriarchal society served as the supreme father figure. The pomp and fervor with which local communities celebrated the solemnities marking the life cycle of the monarchy—accession to the throne, and birth, death, and marriage in the royal family—attested to the reality of this common loyalty. Moreover, the visible symbols of royal authority, such as the judges' staves of office, the royal coat of arms hung on public buildings and churches, and even portraits of the monarch, constituted the institutional backbone for the corpus of hierarchical privilege upon which the notables' dominance of the local community depended.

Although recognizing the king as the supreme source of authority, the notables did not expect him to meddle in matters which they perceived to relate only to the *pátria,* just as they did not believe that ordinary mortals had any right or business to demand a say in the handling of the higher affairs which were the prerogative of El Rei Nosso Senhor. Accordingly, failure to carry out the royal wishes within the *pátria* was not deemed by the notables to connote any lack of loyalty to the king as the supreme authority. However, disobedience to the royal orders, should it be necessary, must avoid any form of public disrespect for the vital symbols of royal authority.[105]

In sum, the *mentalité* and accustomed behavior prevailing among the notables in the captaincies of Portuguese America not only inhibited their acquiring new perceptions of the polity and society but deprived them of any consciousness of mutual interest and identity, in terms of belonging to a common class.[106] Given this lack of vision and solidarity, it was not likely that the notables would, as their counterparts in the thirteen colonies had done, produce from within their own ranks either a novel ideology or the leadership for an anti-colonial movement. Indeed, although the notables had cause for complaint against the status quo, they had evolved methods for coexisting with it, and it provided them with the means, both ideological and material, for exploiting the mass of the population. For most notables, the overthrow of the colonial regime would bring more risk than advantage.

I V

Although the conjunction of social and human conditions in Portuguese America in the late eighteenth century offered no immediate threat to the Crown's authority, cause for complacency did not exist. As the course of events in British North America had shown, discontents could breed and overt disaffection erupt with remarkable speed. In 1754 the legislatures of the thirteen colonies, although facing an urgent need for common defense against the French and Indians, had unanimously scorned the scheme for a loose confederation drafted at Albany by their appointed delegates. Twenty years later, in 1777, those same colonies joined in common revolt against the mother country and were, as the newly drafted Articles of Confederation showed, contemplating a permanent union.[107] In 1783

Great Britain was forced, by the Peace of Paris, to acknowledge the independence of its former colonies, and five years later the Philadelphia Convention created a viable nation-state.

The American Revolution appealed to the notables of the Portuguese New World in two respects. Its ideology—and indeed the philosophy of the Enlightenment in general—asserted the inalienable liberties of the individual citizen and his right to do anything not specifically prohibited by the law, theories that both expressed and stimulated the notables' self-interest.[108] What also attracted the notables was the Revolution's achievement of sweeping political change without disrupting a social order that included slavery and racial discrimination. Indeed, the war for American independence had not incited the blacks to rebellion. The transformation of the thirteen colonies into the United States had required no fundamental change to the existing social structures.

The only sedition in colonial Portuguese America inspired by the American Revolution was a movement in 1788–89 known as the Inconfidência Mineira. Confined to the captaincy of Minas Gerais, the sedition had been provoked by the bungling intervention of the Portuguese Crown. Refusing to accept that mining output had fallen precipitously since 1750, the minister of the colonies early in 1788 ordered the levying of a special tax to make up the shortfall in revenues, and he demanded the immediate collection of the massive debts owed to the Crown. These measures threatened ruin to the leading merchants and notables in Minas Gerais.[109] The ensuing conspiracy was a minor affair, involving less than twenty people, of whom only six or seven were active participants. Rapidly formed and poorly organized, the movement sought no more than the independence of Minas Gerais as a republic, although other captaincies, it was envisaged, would follow the lead. The conspiracy was soon betrayed and the participants rounded up without difficulty.[110] That the American Revolution spawned only this single movement and that the sedition occurred in Minas Gerais are not remarkable. The urban culture and the mining economy of the captaincy made it distinctive in Portuguese America. In no other captaincy was the royal treasury a creditor of the leading notables. Also unusual were the close ties which in Minas Gerais knit together notables and intellectuals: all save one of the conspirators in the Inconfidência Mineira came from these two groups.[111]

The prominent role played by intellectuals in the conspiracy of 1788–89 is not surprising, since they alone among the dominant minority possessed the frame of mind and the cohesion required to conceive and to organize a movement for political independence. The isolation imposed on the Portuguese New World meant that knowledge about the American Revolution and the new United States was not acquired directly but by way of Europe, most commonly from French-language sources. In the transmission of this information and of knowledge about Enlightenment ideas the small intellectual community played an essential role.[112]

A certain ambiguity characterized the position held by the intellectuals within the dominant minority. The prestige and influence which their knowledge and culture gave them did not always correspond to their actual social standing. Many priests and self-educated laymen were of humble origins and modest means. A study of the students at Coimbra from Bahia concludes that they were generally offspring of "small landowners, professional men, officers and officials," which suggests that many, perhaps most, of the American-born *letrados* did not belong to the top ranks of the notables.[113] The *letrados* were, in addition, psychological outsiders. The very process of being dispatched across the Atlantic to be educated in an unfamiliar environment alienated them from the culture of their homeland. In Portugal itself the American-born were a minority both exotic and out of place. In 1718 the overseas students at Coimbra organized a festival in honor of Nossa Senhora do Desterro, Our Lady of Exile, and alienation and deprivation were the themes dominating the sermon preached at the closing ceremonies.[114]

What reinforced the intellectuals' position as outsiders were the demands for intellectual conformity made by church and state. Because they were naturally interested in novel ideas and often owned the works of the Enlightenment, *letrados* inevitably aroused the suspicions of the Portuguese Inquisition, curbed by the marquess of Pombal but still a redoubtable institution. Membership in the Freemasons, which several students from the New World joined while at Coimbra, was regarded by the Inquisition as conclusive evidence of heterodoxy.[115] The case of Hipólito José da Costa, an American-born student who graduated from Coimbra in 1797, is instructive. A protégé of D. Rodrigo de Sousa Coutinho, the young *letrado* was sent on missions first to the United States, where he joined a Masonic lodge, and then to England. During the latter mission, Hipólito José openly consorted with the English Masons. In July 1802, on his return to Lisbon, he was arrested by the Inquisition and held without trial. Only in 1805 was Hipólito José's escape and flight to England successfully arranged.[116]

Powerful as were these influences, a majority of the intellectuals, particularly among the *letrados,* did not become disaffected. Acceptance of Enlightenment ideas did not necessarily entail support for political nonconformity. Most *letrados* were loyal subjects of the Crown, believing that the status quo needed no more than what were termed improvements. During the last quarter of the eighteenth century, Enlightenment ideas did, indeed, exert a strong influence, particularly upon the economic policies of the Portuguese Crown.[117] For most *letrados* potential feelings of alienation and rejection were outweighed by a desire for acceptance and advancement. Employment in the Crown's service provided the most certain route to social standing and personal wealth. What has been observed about the Bahians enrolled at Coimbra applies to all the students from the New World: the university served "as a stepping-stone to higher status for a handful of middle-class white families."[118]

No one alienated from the status quo was likely to make the considerable emotional and financial sacrifice that crossing the Atlantic and spending five years studying at Coimbra demanded. Almost two-thirds of the students from the New World did persist until graduation. Much may be inferred from the subjects in which they took their degrees, primarily civil and canon law, and the careers that they chose to follow. A significant proportion of the graduates did enter the royal service, either in the bureaucracy or the institutions of higher education, or as judges, who formed the core of the administrative apparatus in the Portuguese possessions. By the start of the nineteenth century, American-born *letrados* were to be found, if in small numbers, on the staffs of the government ministries in Lisbon, as judges on the appellate and royal courts on both sides of the Atlantic, and as professors at Coimbra and the technical academies in Portugal.[119]

The shared outlook and culture acquired through attendance at Coimbra, from a common training in law, and through similar experiences in their administrative careers made, as already noted, the *letrados* the logical leaders of any organized opposition to the status quo. In the event of political independence, they could provide the cadres needed to run a new state or states in Portuguese America. However, their shared qualities were precisely what in practice ensured that they would not form the leadership of an independence movement. They were both too assimilated into the ruling circles of Portugal and too scattered across the Portuguese possessions to exist as a coherent, self-conscious, and—above all—alienated group. Yet their existence was important. Their American birth and their preference for Enlightenment ideas meant that rather than accepting the colonies as simple hewers of wood and drawers of water, they conceived of the Empire as a mutually beneficial partnership, of which Portugal naturally formed the economic and trading center. In them D. Rodrigo found enthusiastic supporters for his reform measures.[120]

The outlook and expectations of the *letrados* do much to explain why the New World captaincies failed to follow the example of the thirteen colonies and why the Inconfidência Mineira did no more than ruffle the surface of events. What is much more remarkable was the lack of impact upon the Portuguese New World of the French Revolution. If a sense of separate identity were emergent and a desire "to seek liberty" did exist, they should both have, upon the face of it, been strongly stimulated by the doctrines of the French Revolution, powerfully expressed in the Declaration of the Rights of Man and of the Citizen in 1789, in the proclamation of the French Republic in 1792, and in the offer by the National Convention in that year to aid all peoples struggling to be free. In Europe the Revolution toppled thrones and annihilated ancient states. In Portuguese America, however, it generated no more than four incidents requiring judicial investigation. Of the four, only one, the "Tailors' Conspiracy" of 1798 at Salvador, involved an organized movement and required trial and punishment.

The failure of the French Revolution to subvert the Portuguese colonies was due in part to three countervailing influences—administrative, economic, and intellectual. The first was the vigilance of the Crown both in Portugal and the New World.[121] Its agents watched for the least signs of dissent and stopped at nothing to root them out.[122] Nor did the Crown remain on the defensive. It sought to forestall trouble: *americanos* educated in France during the Revolution were often prevented from recrossing the Atlantic.[123] An active propaganda campaign was carried on, stressing the risks of disloyalty. The slave rising of 1791 in the French colony of Saint Domingue, bringing destruction and death to all whites unable to escape abroad, provided an excellent object lesson, as the Crown tirelessly reminded its subjects.[124]

The second countervailing influence was the economic boom in the 1790's caused by the collapse of Saint Domingue and the demands of the European war economies. The ensuing prosperity in Portuguese America kept the notables fully occupied, mollified their discontents, made taxes more bearable and debts less onerous, and by swelling revenues, strengthened the fiscal position of the Crown.

The third factor was the program of reforms sponsored by D. Rodrigo de Sousa Coutinho and others in the second half of the 1790's.[125] Although D. Rodrigo did not propose to tamper with the traditional organization of the Crown's possessions as a closed economic system, his plans as presented in October 1797 did not perceive Portugal as being its indispensable center. The system would function satisfactorily no matter where the monarch chose to reside within his dominions. Such a belief in *ubi rex, ibi patria* (where the king is, there is the homeland) held a natural appeal for the American-born *letrados*. The minister entrusted several of them with key positions in the implementation of his reforms.[126] By so doing, D. Rodrigo was acting in the Crown's best interests: he was conciliating and co-opting individuals who, if alienated, might have turned against the status quo.

Significant as were the contributions of government vigilance, economic prosperity, and intellectual co-optation, the fundamental cause for the failure of the French Revolution to succeed in Portuguese America lay in its basic philosophy and the social groups to which it therefore appealed. As the slogan "Liberté, Fraternité, Egalité" proclaimed, revolutionary doctrine emphasized the rights of the individual citizen and denounced all distinctions and privileges not founded upon merit. All authority derived from the people alone, so that only those they elected had any right to rule. In consequence, any man of talent and ability, no matter how humble his social origins, could aspire to direct the affairs of state.

Whereas these ideas could only offend the royal officials, notables, and most of the *letrados,* they appealed strongly to the members of a social stratum which, although Portuguese in language and culture, was kept subordinate to the privileged few. This stratum was aptly termed by the

French *le menu peuple*, the small folk. Although many of the "small folk" were of Portuguese descent, their ranks incorporated the *gente de côr*, the freeborn and freed mulattoes and blacks, who formed a rapidly growing sector of the New World population.[127]

As was the case in France, most small folk in Portuguese America, whatever their color, resided in the towns. There they pursued trades and vocations which required skills and knowledge, giving them a certain independence of outlook and, for a minority, control over their own work. In social rank and remunerativeness, these occupations ranged from goldsmith, druggist, and legal agent down to tailor, shoemaker, and carpenter. At the top, the callings meshed with the most minor posts in the official world, whereas the humbler occupations and indeed many of the skilled trades could be and were carried on by slaves. In general, among the small folk lightness of skin tended to correspond to the social ranking of their occupation.[128] Whatever their complexion and calling, the small folk shared one trait that distinguished them sharply from the mass of the population: increasingly, they had learned to read and write.

The small folk of Portuguese descent, far more than the *gente de côr*, possessed some hope of upward mobility, though more for their sons than themselves. In the 1780's a master mason in Rio de Janeiro managed to send his son first to Coimbra and then to study medicine at Montpellier.[129] In general, however, the small folk born in the New World and of Portuguese descent found themselves caught in a position of deference to and dependence on the privileged minority, while also facing in their occupations strong competition from both skilled slaves and immigrants from Portugal. The latter were, by reputation, ruthless and grasping, faults exacerbated by their pretensions to superiority.

Among the small folk, the *gente de côr* had especial reason to resent the colonial regime. Although as a group they identified completely with Portugal and its culture and by serving in special militia units bore arms in its defense, they were systematically humiliated by the royal officials, barred from all posts and offices of profit within the official world, and treated as social pariahs.[130] Discrimination against the *gente de côr*, universal as it was, seems to have been particularly virulent among immigrants from Portugal.[131] Political independence as a republic promised an end to this intolerable denial of identity and self-respect. In a nation-state the very traits which now made them so despised might become the quintessence of national identity: to be a mulatto would be synonymous with being Brazilian. A movement for political independence would find popular backing —or at least what constituted in Portuguese America popular support— among the small folk in general, and the *gente de côr* in particular, since it promised them social and economic advancement.

The "Conspiracy of the Tailors," a movement for independence inspired by the doctrines of the French Revolution, challenged the existing position of the privileged minority—the notables, *letrados*, and government functionaries—by disputing their right to exploit the mass of the people. In August 1798, there appeared posted in the squares and on the public buildings of Salvador handwritten placards couched in the rhetoric of the French Revolution, which called on the people of the city to seize independence and to enforce social and racial equality.[132] Such an expression of sedition, and the existence of an organized network of subversion implied by the placards, caused the governor to order an immediate judicial investigation. Helped by delation, the authorities soon rounded up the conspirators and snuffed out the plot. Thirty-two men were arrested and brought to trial.[133]

The origins, legal status, ethnicity, and occupations of the accused, and the goals they advocated, make clear the reasons why the notables, *letrados,* and functionaries of Portuguese America did not rally to the cause of political independence. Almost all the accused were natives of Bahia and most had been born in the city itself. Among those tried, almost half were slaves or freedmen and two-thirds were mulatto.[134] While four of those charged belonged by their profession to the official world, the great majority were small folk, no less than ten being tailors.[135] The conspiracy was therefore essentially a local movement of small folk, by its very membership subversive of the social, racial, and occupational status quo.

Although officially described as "a rebellion and rising, planned in this city, to establish a Democratic government in this continent of Brazil," the goal of the movement, for most of the plotters, was limited to the city itself, with the expectation that the captaincy would follow in the city's steps. The movement's ideas were shaped by various printed works of the French Revolution which had reached Salvador illegally and which were either read by the small folk or retailed to them.[136] What especially appealed was the social element in the revolutionary doctrine. As José Felix da Costa admitted, upon his "inquiring what benefit would come from making this Brazil into a Republic, . . . Lucas Dantas replied, 'it is so that we can breathe free, since we live oppressed, and because we are mulattoes we are not admitted to any posts; with a Republic there will be equality for all.'" Another conspirator, João de Deus do Nascimento, asserted that "it is necessary for all to become Frenchmen," so that "everything being leveled in a popular revolution, all would be rich, released from the misery in which they were living, discrimination between white, black, and mulatto being abolished; because all occupations and jobs would be open and available without distinction to each and every one."[137] Such sentiments predictably outraged the Crown. Exemplary punishment was authorized by D. Rodrigo, as minister of the colonies, so that "the poison of their false principles may never contaminate its Vassals."[138]

Far more significant were the implications of the sedition for the privileged few in the Portuguese New World. The appeal of the American Revolution, such as it was, had been its promise that sweeping political change could be achieved without disrupting the existing social order. The philosophy of the French Revolution, or rather the doctrines of Jacobin nationalism, offered no such assurance. While the idea of political independence possessed an undeniable attraction, the dominant minority faced an insoluble dilemma. Since overthrowing the colonial regime meant rejecting monarchical rule, the new independent state had to be a republic. However, if the creation of a republic necessarily entailed, as João de Deus do Nascimento and others asserted, a popular revolution which would abolish all social, racial, and economic distinctions, then political independence offered no advantage to the privileged few whose entire way of life and very existence would be in jeopardy. That most of those involved in the "Conspiracy of the Tailors" were mulatto increased the cause for concern. In Saint Domingue it had been the bitter strife between whites and people of color, arising out of the latter's claims to political and legal equality, that had enabled the slaves to launch their rising and so destroy the colony.[139] A dread of what was termed *haitianismo*, political movements deliberately appealing to the *gente de côr* by harping on their grievances, would haunt the ruling circles in independent Brazil until the middle of the nineteenth century.[140]

That the French Revolution did not, however, expunge all desires for independence from the minds of the notables is clear from the incident known as the "Conspiracy of the Suassunas." In May 1801 a leading Pernambuco planter, discussing in private with a friend a letter from Lisbon reporting the Crown's demands for yet another loan from its subjects, rather wistfully suggested "that it was necessary to seek liberty," to which the friend gave an evasive reply: "Only with the concurrence of all of [Portuguese] America." The planter then compounded his indiscretion by retorting, "Not even with the aid of some foreign nation such as France?"[141] Some days later this and a previous conversation were denounced by the friend to the authorities.[142] From the evidence amassed by the ensuing judicial inquiry can be deduced the prevailing *mentalité* among the dominant minority in Portuguese America at the start of the nineteenth century.

Portugal was not regarded by the notables of Pernambuco with any particular awe or deference.[143] Their appreciation of its political position in the deepening European conflict was shrewd and sophisticated, though they eschewed displaying to the outside world any interest in "gazettes and public affairs."[144] Loyalty to the Crown was for them a matter of both habit and calculated self-interest. They preferred a condition of dependence to the risks of political innovation, heeding the precept so vividly phrased by Hilaire Belloc in another context: "Always keep ahold of Nurse for fear of finding something worse."

The notables were not free agents in the matter. By the start of the new century, government vigilance and the economic prosperity had renovated the Crown's control over its American colonies. The Crown's prestige in the New World captaincies was increased in 1801 when during war with Spain the valuable Missões district, lying to the east of the Uruguay River and adjacent to Rio Grande do Sul, was conquered, to be retained in the ensuing peace. Portuguese America had become not just the wealthiest but the most secure of the dominions of Her Most Faithful Majesty. In August 1803, just three months before his fall from office, D. Rodrigo de Sousa Coutinho submitted a political memorandum to the prince regent which expressed what more prudent men left unstated: "Portugal is not the best and most essential part of the monarchy," and were it lost, nothing prevented "its Sovereign and its peoples from leaving to create a powerful Empire in Brazil." [145]

V

In the final quarter of the eighteenth century, the relationship between Portugal and its American colonies was subject to major strains and underwent considerable change. In the economic sphere the onset of industrialization in both Great Britain and France was starting to transform the commercial and financial relationships that bound together the Atlantic world.[146] However, at no time during the late eighteenth century did changes in the Atlantic system ever come close to disrupting the Portuguese Empire, either politically or economically. The one brief moment of crisis, that of the Inconfidência Mineira in 1788–89, was the result of the blundering initiative of the Portuguese Crown itself, not external forces.[147] External dangers, essentially political, did threaten Portugal after 1795, but in that same period the commerce of the Portuguese Empire prospered to an unprecedented extent.

If the economic relationship between Portugal and the New World colonies did not undergo any fundamental change during the late eighteenth century, what did alter was their intellectual and psychological relationship. The American and French revolutions were in this respect decisive, since it was during those years that the Portuguese Americans, or rather the dominant minority among them, fell from a state of political innocence. They became familiar with other models of governance, grew more sophisticated in their political outlook, and saw themselves as an integral part of a larger world. As a British visitor to Rio de Janeiro in 1792 noted, its inhabitants seemed "to enquire, with an uncommon degree of interest, into the progress of the French Revolution, as if they foresaw the possibility of a similar event applying to themselves." [148] Yet only two concerted attempts to overthrow the status quo occurred—and both failed lamentably because of the narrowness of their spatial and social support. Both focused on the *pátria,* not on the nation. If the Inconfidência Mineira of 1788–89 was a sedition totally of notables and intellectuals, the "Conspiracy of the Tailors" of 1798 voiced mainly the grievances of the mulatto small folk. For an independence movement to succeed, it had to attract support across the social spectrum—notables, intellectuals, functionaries, and small folk. It also needed to appeal, if possible, to the Portuguese-born who had settled in the New World.

In the aftermath of the French Revolution, in particular after the Terror of 1793–94 and the rising in Saint Domingue, the status quo recouped much of the intellectual and psychological ground it had lost. The French Revolution had destroyed for the moment all belief that change in forms of government could be moderate, unaccompanied by social upheaval. Political independence, thus linked to social and racial disruption, ceased to be practical. By the first decade of the new century, what may be termed coexistence had been restored between the Crown and its American subjects. The traditional system was still in place and functioning with tolerable efficiency.

During the last decades of the eighteenth century, geographic, economic, and human realities persisted in keeping Portuguese America fragmented. The Crown's policies during this period never swerved from the essential object of preserving the New World colonies as divided, isolated, and dependent. The existing forms of identity, bonds of community, and means of common action among the notables in the New World did not during these years generate any encompassing vision of a single nation and a united future. Discontents and disaffections, especially among the *letrados* and the small folk, did cause some alienation from traditional ways and loyalties. The doctrines of the American and French revolutions proved attractive in part because they indicated new paths to follow. Nonetheless, the new ideologies failed because they appealed mainly to those for whom an end to the colonial regime implied destruction of the existing socioeconomic order within Portuguese America.

Even if the political and economic conditions which from the 1790's favored the continuance of colonial rule in the Portuguese New World had not persisted, it must be doubted whether their disappearance would have generated any major challenge to the colonial system. The qualities which had characterized the thirteen colonies of British North America in 1776—political self-government, social cohesion, cultural self-confidence, freedom of information, and a considerable degree of economic integration and diversification—were still markedly lacking in Portuguese America. It should not be forgotten that the thirteen colonies, even enjoying the advantages they did, required seven years of warfare and considerable foreign aid to achieve not the freedom of all the British colonies on the North American continent but only that of the areas where the revolt had started.

Postulating a chain of events in which a revolt against the colonial regime was successfully begun in some part of Portuguese America, there is nothing to indicate that the rebels would have achieved more than did their North American counterparts. Just as the British navy served to keep loyal the colonies of Newfoundland, Nova Scotia, and Quebec, so the Portuguese navy might have secured the three captaincies of the far north, particularly since their economies were booming and they shared a strong sense of separate identity. If the wars of independence from 1810 to 1825 in Spanish America which produced fifteen new republics are any guide, it is

MAP 2. Portuguese America That Might Have Been

unlikely that the captaincies of Portuguese America would upon winning political independence by force have proved any more capable than the Spanish colonies of forming a single state.

Just how many republics might have been formed is an intriguing speculation. Certainly around the axis of Minas Gerais and Rio de Janeiro, with their complementary economies, one state would probably have taken shape. A second state might well have been formed by a union of Bahia and Pernambuco. However, their competitive economies along with the unwillingness of each to take second place suggests that such a state in the northeast would have shared the fate of Simón Bolívar's Gran Colombia—fragmentation into its constituent parts. In any event, the overriding factors of loyalty to the *pátria*, the centrifugal effect of communication and geography, and the economic rivalries between regions made it most probable that had colonial rule been overthrown in Portuguese America in the late eighteenth or early nineteenth century the outcome would not have been a single nation encompassing all the former captaincies.

None of this occurred. The political destiny of Portuguese America was to be determined neither by its own inhabitants nor by events within its own borders or even the Western Hemisphere. Twice in twenty years—with the Napoleonic invasion of Portugal in 1807 and the Porto uprising of 1820—the fate of Portuguese America was to be controlled by developments in Europe.

2

A State, Not a Nation, 1808-1820

The Portuguese dominions had long been influenced by the course of events in Europe, because Portugal itself was in strategic terms caught between the great powers, a pawn in their maneuverings. Lisbon was exposed to attack by sea, while on land the border with Spain lay but six days' march away. Twice in the eighteenth century Portugal faced invading Spanish armies. The British navy appeared most often as an ally, although back in 1650 Admiral Blake had blockaded Lisbon, capturing the incoming fleet loaded with that year's sugar harvest.

An obvious remedy for this strategic weakness—and one suggested as early as 1580—was to move the capital of the Portuguese dominions to the New World. However, until the last decade of the eighteenth century the idea remained as visionary as human settlement on the moon is in our own time.[1] Then, as Portugal increasingly found itself embroiled in the wars between revolutionary France and Great Britain, the idea entered the realm of practical but radical policy, equivalent to moving the capital of the United States to San Francisco or Seattle. An audacious statesman such as D. Rodrigo de Sousa Coutinho did suggest to the Crown, shortly before his fall from power in November 1803, that it could leave Lisbon and "create a powerful Empire in Brazil."[2] To carry out such a move was not, however, as easy as D. Rodrigo asserted.

The wealth of the captaincies of Portuguese America had long made them the "milch cow" of Portugal; by the first years of the nineteenth century the economic supremacy of the American colonies within the royal dominions had become indisputable.[3] To transfer the seat of government to the economic heartland would, however, entail a radical reshaping of the formal structures of power, an alteration both offensive to traditionalists and inimical to the vested interests surrounding the Crown. Moving the seat of government would, moreover, mean abandoning any pretense to neutrality and all hope of conciliating both France and Great Britain. To leave Lisbon would be to range the Crown so firmly on the British side as to risk not only the loss of independence and initiative but the conquest and possible absorption of Portugal by France and its satellite, Spain. The "War of the Oranges" with Spain in the spring of 1801, which revealed Portugal's military weakness and ended in its loss of the frontier town of Olivença, confirmed these fears.

The expansion of the conflict between Great Britain and Emperor Napoleon of France from the military to the economic sphere doomed Portugal's policy of neutrality and conciliation. The Continental System decreed by Napoleon in 1806 excluded all British goods from the mainland of Europe. If the Portuguese Crown conformed to the System, it would see trade with its New World colonies interdicted by the British navy, and if it rejected the System, it would face the armies of Napoleon. Despite earnest appeals and desperate subterfuges, the dilemma could not be avoided. In the end, Napoleon decided to dispense with Portugal as an independent state and in October 1807, with the complicity of Spain, sent an army to invade Portugal.[4]

Although faced with the certainty of defeat and the prospect of dethronement, the prince regent of Portugal, D. João, equivocated until the French were but five days' march from Lisbon. Only then did he accept a plan prepared in the final weeks of the crisis by his more percipient advisers—the transfer of the entire royal court and government "to the States of America."[5] In the space of three days, the royal family and several thousand—perhaps as many as ten thousand—people were herded on board some 30 vessels, which were also loaded with the essential records of government. On the morning of November 29, 1807, just hours before the first French troops entered Lisbon, the fleet raised anchor and, escorted by warships from the British squadron watching Lisbon, sailed out into the Atlantic.[6]

After a stormy, difficult voyage, this dramatic migration reached the shores of the New World on January 22, 1808. The royal flight is customarily seen by historians as the single decisive step in the emergence of Brazil as a nation, even by some as the true beginning of Brazilian independence.[7] The long-term consequences of the transfer of the royal government were indeed momentous, but the Crown did not at the time desire or intend the changes that ultimately took place. Indeed, the ensuing development of Portuguese America was profoundly affected by the almost haphazard nature of the innovations effected after 1808.

What was achieved in this period should not be underestimated or disparaged. Between 1808 and 1820 the Crown created in Rio de Janeiro the institutions of a functioning state, and it expanded the existing fiscal and judicial infrastructure of the captaincies. Schooling at the primary level was encouraged, and three institutions of professional studies, a military and two medical schools, were founded. Portuguese America was thrown open to direct trade with all friendly nations, ending economic dependence on Portugal. The restrictions on manufacturing were revoked. Printing presses were finally introduced and two newspapers established. Although the local press was kept under tight censorship, the importation of works printed abroad was not much impeded. Consequently, the periodicals most widely read during these years were monthly journals in Portuguese published at London.

In December 1815 these and other innovations were recognized, and in a sense made permanent, by the Crown's grant of formal unity to its New World possessions, constituting them the Kingdom of Brazil, equal to and united with the Kingdom of Portugal. D. Rodrigo de Sousa Coutinho's plan for creating "a powerful Empire in Brazil" had in substance been achieved, although his death, in 1812, came before he could see its fulfillment.[8]

In this new status quo, fashioned out of the necessities of 1808, Brazil held both political and economic primacy among the royal dominions, with Portugal itself relegated to the margin. A sense of pride in and identification with the new system grew, not only among the Brazilians whom it directly benefited but also among readers of the new periodical press, which, in the words of a contemporary, gave those readers a "more just knowledge of themselves and the world."[9] As a consequence of these developments the political socialization among the literate minority which had begun during the latter years of the eighteenth century intensified and accelerated. From their reading, most absorbed a frame of mind in which the nation-state was the exemplar of political organization. The creation of the Kingdom of Brazil gave concrete reality to a spatial concept broader than the local *pátria*. The new political status of Portuguese America provided a fresh focus of solidarity and loyalty, creating in "the public mind a sense of independence, a proper consciousness of its own importance, and a determination to support the new dignity."[10] As a consequence, a third facet of identity was now added to a sense of being Portuguese and a loyal subject of the Crown.

Notable as were the innovations made from 1808 onwards, their significance and benefits should not be overestimated. The changes introduced by the Crown were designed to serve its own convenience and meet its own needs; it had no intention of, much less a coherent plan for, transforming its New World possessions into what amounted to a nation-state. Nothing was done to rationalize and unify the system of governance existing outside of Rio de Janeiro or to adapt traditional European formulas to the specific needs and conditions of the New World. Similarly, nothing was done to consolidate the three institutions of professional studies into a system of advanced education. To attend university, men still had to cross the Atlantic. The opportunities for economic development offered by the opening of the ports and the freeing of manufacturing in 1808 were stultified by the grant two years later of special commercial privileges to Great Britain. The creation of the Kingdom of Brazil was little more than a paper measure, designed to refurbish Portugal's claim to be a first-class power and to justify the Crown's unwillingness to return to Lisbon.

Important as was the new focus of identity, which the innovations crystallized and made overt, it did not replace, or even predominate over, established identities—the sense of being Portuguese and loyalty to the Crown. Nor did the innovations, symbolized by the elevation of Brazil to a kingdom, necessarily promote a sense of solidarity among the Brazilian-born, for the royal migration wrought a profound change in the relationship between the economic regions that made up Portuguese America. If, prior to 1808, Rio de Janeiro had been no more than the leading port city in the Portuguese New World, it now established, as the capital of the royal dominions, a political, economic, and cultural hegemony which reduced the other five regions of Portuguese America to dependence and subservience. This unequal relationship was in effect legitimized when all eighteen of the captaincies in Portuguese America were united as the kingdom of Brazil. Resentment against exploitation by Rio de Janeiro, with a yearning for a renewed local autonomy, was one cause for the revolt which in 1817 broke out in the northeast of Brazil. From 1808 to 1820 there was no coherent movement from diversity to integration, from fragmentation to unity, in the territories of the new Kingdom of Brazil.

I

At the time of its departure from Lisbon, the Portuguese Crown did not envisage either leaving that city permanently or altering the existing status of Portuguese America. The decision "to reside in the city of Rio de Janeiro until a General Peace" was an emergency measure, to last only as long as the crisis that compelled the move.[11] No accommodation was to be made to conditions in the New World, nor was it intended that crossing the Atlantic should modify the twin goals of royal policy: the maintenance of Portugal as the center of the empire, and the avoidance of dependence upon either of the great powers, France and Great Britain.

These intentions proved vain. The move to the New World under British protection inevitably brought back into office D. Rodrigo de Sousa Coutinho, who had always advocated a close alliance with England. The likelihood of a speedy return to Lisbon was slight, if the experience of the monarch of Savoy were any guide. By 1807 that king had spent nine years on the island of Sardinia, his capital Turin and mainland territories having been annexed by France. With Portugal in the hands of Napoleon and his armies, the Crown's American colonies patently could not continue to exist as a closed economy dependent on Portugal and trading exclusively through her. Further, with few or no revenues to be expected from an occupied Portugal, the Crown, if it were to meet the expenses both of government and of war with France (formally declared on May 28, 1808), would have to increase the revenues and mobilize the resources of its remaining dominions. The flight from Lisbon left the Crown in such financial straits that in 1809 it was forced to borrow £600,000 (U.S. $3,000,000) from the British government in order to cover indispensable expenditures.[12]

Consequently, it is not surprising that on January 28, 1808, within a week of landing in the New World and even before reaching Rio de Janeiro, the prince regent issued a decree opening the trade of his American colonies to all friendly nations, thus abolishing the existing monopoly of Portugal. The sweeping nature of the change, while certainly reflecting the ideas of Adam Smith and the new "science of political economy," was also designed to forestall demands by the British for exclusive trading privileges with Portuguese America.[13] The opening of the ports was soon followed on April 1, 1808, by its natural corollary—the revocation of the existing ban on certain types of manufacturing in the American colonies.[14] By these two measures the economy of Portuguese America was placed on a war footing.

The war with France also shaped the policies followed by the Portuguese Crown after its arrival in Rio de Janeiro on March 25, 1808. With the royal family had come most of the personnel and materials necessary for governing the royal dominions. However, virtually none of the actual institutions of governance had been moved to the New World.[15] The Council of Regency established in Lisbon could not function without them. Moreover, their removal to the New World would have been an open acknowledgment that the Crown's transfer of residence was not a temporary measure.

In less urgent circumstances improvisations and expedients might have sufficed until the Crown's return to Lisbon. The demands of war and the needs of the imperial system impelled the creation of a strong administrative apparatus in the New World. The Crown had no choice but to establish in Rio de Janeiro duplicates of the institutions of government still existing in Lisbon. Not surprisingly, the first duplicate bodies to be established were the Conselho Supremo Militar (Supreme Military Council) and the Arquivo Militar (the Military Archives), charged with gathering and guarding maps and other military intelligence. During the rest of 1808, six more institutions were created. Nearly all of them, including the Desembargo do Paço (Tribunal of the Palace), with combined judicial and administrative duties, and the Junta do Comércio, Agricultura, e Indústria do Brasil (Board of Trade, Agriculture, and Industry of Brazil), were entirely new bodies. Only the Casa da Suplicação do Brasil (Supreme Court of Appeals of Brazil) was formed out of an existing body, the Rio de Janeiro relação, or court of appeals.[16]

More than a simple duplication of the organs of government existing in Lisbon was required if the Crown were to create an administration capable of undertaking the tasks assigned to it. The technical and social infrastructure of a state at war had to be created in Portuguese America.

Among the changes made by the Crown on its arrival was the establishment of printing presses, first in Rio de Janeiro and then at Salvador, used
not only to print government documents but to produce an official newspaper in Rio de Janeiro (and later in Bahia) for the communication of
essential information. Another innovation made in 1808 was the creation
of schools of surgery in Bahia and Rio de Janeiro, intended to provide the
medical personnel and hospital services required by the armed forces.[17]
Finally, in an attempt to increase royal revenues and mobilize the wealth of
Portuguese America, in 1808 and 1809 the Crown imposed six new taxes,
and in October 1808 it set up the Banco do Brasil, which was authorized
to issue notes and make loans to the Crown.[18]

The fleet that brought the Crown to the New World had lacked space
for any troops. The royal army in Portugal was virtually destroyed as a
result of the French invasion. After a British expedition compelled the
French to evacuate Portugal in 1809, a new force was raised, commanded
by a British general, William Carr Beresford, and paid with British funds.[19]
These 40,000 men fought alongside the British in the Peninsular War that
lasted until 1814. Unable to transfer any troops from Portugal, the Crown
had to make a separate army in the New World out of the regular troops
already stationed in Portuguese America, supplemented by local recruits.
In order to train the necessary officers, particularly in the artillery and
engineering corps, the Crown created the Royal Military Academy (Real
Acadêmia Militar) at Rio de Janeiro in December 1810. The conquest of
the French colony of Cayenne in 1810 and an armed intervention into the
affairs of the Banda Oriental (modern Uruguay) in 1811 attested to the
effectiveness of the newly created armed forces.[20]

A necessary corollary of all these measures was a general reshaping and
expansion of the existing fiscal and administrative machinery in the provinces, as the captaincies were now increasingly called. The Crown's record
of achievement in this task was distinctly limited, although between 1808
and 1811 it did create three new *comarcas* and nineteen new *juizes de
fora*.[21] Although the system of administration at the provincial level was
left unchanged, decision making was increasingly concentrated in Rio de
Janeiro. The governors of the provinces did not lose their importance, but
the Crown was far more able than it had been prior to 1808 to meddle
in the affairs of the *pátrias*. Given the Crown's established style of governance, centralization upon Rio de Janeiro was probably inevitable, but
it meant, paradoxically, that the transfer of the Crown to the New World
resulted in less flexibility and effectiveness of government in the *pátrias*.
The ability of the local notables to influence decision making was reduced
and their overall influence proportionately lessened. This decline in local
autonomy was one innovation that did not find favor within the provinces
outside Rio de Janeiro.

Infinitely more damaging was the signing on February 19, 1810, of three
treaties with Great Britain which threatened to reduce the Portuguese do-

minions to a state of vassalage to the British. In particular, the British were granted sweeping, entrenched commercial rights in Portuguese America, including a maximum tariff of 15 percent on their goods. These commercial concessions rendered the development of manufacturing in the New World extremely difficult, if not impossible. What compensated somewhat for the harm wrought by the treaties was the guarantee they contained that even if D. João "should again establish the seat of the Portuguese Monarchy in the European Dominions of the Crown" the rights held by the British would not be abrogated. This provision effectively precluded any attempt to restore the colonial economy which had existed before 1808.[22]

The defects of the 1810 treaties were not immediately apparent. Direct trade with the outside world, stimulation of production by the demands of warfare, and increased government expenditures brought renewed prosperity to the economies of Portuguese America.[23] The climate of well-being and success had its effect. By the end of 1812, what had begun five years before as a temporary, emergency venture was becoming the status quo, as a minor bureaucrat with entry at court pointed out to his father in Lisbon: "The Baron of Rio Seco is constructing a superb palace . . . , and various other individuals are putting down roots in this country."[24]

II

The year 1812 brought significant changes in the affairs of the Portuguese world. In January the death of D. Rodrigo de Sousa Coutinho deprived the British of their warmest advocate in the inner councils of the Crown.[25] The final ejection in 1811 of the French armies from Portugal and in 1812 their defeat by the Anglo-Portuguese forces at Salamanca had the paradoxical effect of reducing British influence, because the victories lessened Portuguese dependence on its ally and permitted the Crown to revert to its traditional policy of avoiding a close identification with any of the great powers. The freeing of Portugal inevitably raised the question of when the Crown would fulfill its promise, made in its proclamation of November 26, 1807, to return to Lisbon.[26]

The question was debated with increasing intensity during the next two years. The royal adviser who described it as being "without doubt one of the greatest political problems that any sovereign has ever had to resolve" perceived that the dispute concerned the very nature of the Portuguese empire.[27] On the one side were the advocates of restoring the empire as it had existed prior to 1808, with its center of power in and its worldview concentrated upon Portugal. Naturally, pressure from Portugal in favor of this view was intense. The traditionalists who out of loyalty or necessity had accompanied the court saw no merit in prolonging the stay in Rio de Janeiro. "I am so sick of this country that I want nothing of it and when I leave I will not forget to clean my boots at the quayside so as not to take with me the least speck of dirt."[28] Others, more rational, had a personal interest in the restoration of the original economic supremacy of Portugal within the imperial system.[29] The British exerted their remaining influence to the same end, wishing to see the Crown living once more in close proximity to England and under the protection of an army led by British officers.[30]

These very considerations were also used as arguments on the other side, in favor of delaying the departure from Rio, "delaying" because the Crown never formally reneged on its commitment to return. The capacity of the foreign powers to interfere, and in particular the constant threat of invasion by Spain, was largely negated so long as the Crown remained at Rio de Janeiro.[31] By staying in the New World the Crown also isolated itself from the influence and demands of the great nobles, who had for the most part remained in Portugal during the French invasions.[32] Nor did the economic exhaustion of Portugal, compared to the prosperity of the New World provinces, encourage a return to Lisbon, especially since Rio de Janeiro was by 1814 equipped with the basic amenities of a tolerably civilized existence—a theater, an orchestra, periodicals, and an active social life with a strong Gallic flavor.[33] The prince regent's personal preference was for Rio de Janeiro over Lisbon, and in a man "whose very Character is Irresolution and Uncertainty," a habitual inertia worked against departure.[34]

Also influential in keeping the Crown in the New World was the ever-growing administrative and commercial community in Rio de Janeiro. By 1812 this community, composed of bureaucrats, merchants, professionals, and the purveyors of goods and services demanded by the presence of the court, had achieved both permanence and a sense of identity. In social and cultural terms its component elements were diverse and by no means provincial. Among the *letrados* and bureaucrats, some had served in Rio prior to 1808, others had arrived with the court, and yet others were *brasileiros* who had graduated from Coimbra after it reopened in 1811. Of the leading merchants, a few had made their fortunes in Rio before 1808, but most—both Portuguese and British—had moved their firms from Lisbon when the Crown itself left. Others had been attracted to Rio de Janeiro by the opening of the ports. The city was nevertheless small, its population some 70,000 of whom almost half were slaves, and its facilities limited.[35] Social linkages between the different groups were quickly formed and the resulting networks cemented by ties of marriage, *compadrio,* obligations of friendship, and mutual interest.[36]

As the years passed, the members of this community increasingly shared a common interest in the continuance of the Crown in the New World. Their careers, their wealth, and their prospects came to depend upon the tacit refusal of the Crown to honor its promise to return to Lisbon. There were not lacking those to give intellectual justification, and so legitimacy, to this viewpoint. Shortly after the Crown's arrival in the New World, a young *letrado* from Bahia wrote the first part of what was intended to be a long treatise entitled "Memoirs on the Establishment of the Empire of Brazil or New Lusitanian Empire." A passage in the introduction expresses concisely the outlook proclaimed in the work's title:

The epoch has finally arrived when the Sovereign of Portugal should take the title of Emperor, which rightfully expresses the Majesty of His Person, the Heroism of His August Ancestors, and the vastness of his States. Brazil, proud now that it contains within it the Immortal Prince, Who has deigned to establish there his Seat, . . . is no longer to be a maritime Colony barred to the trade of the Nations, as until now, but rather a powerful Empire, which will come to be the moderator of Europe, the arbiter of Asia, and the dominator of Africa.[37]

Although the treatise was never finished, much less published, the ideas it expressed were widely shared. They were given broad and effective publicity in a monthly journal, written in Portuguese and produced by Hipólito José da Costa, whom we last encountered in 1805 as a fugitive from the dungeons of the Inquisition finding sanctuary in Great Britain. As soon as news of the Crown's arrival in the New World reached London, in May 1808, Hipólito José began to publish *O Correio Braziliense*, a monthly which would last from June 1808 to December 1822.[38] This periodical was in effect the first uncensored journal of news and opinion ever to circulate in the Portuguese world. The novelty of its views and the clarity and pungency with which they were expressed gained for the *Correio* a wide and devoted readership on both sides of the Atlantic.[39] Hipólito José's periodical played a major role in transforming the meaning of "o Brasil" from a vague spatial term into a distinct and viable political concept and in promoting a feeling of loyalty to that new concept among the literate minority in Portuguese America.[40]

The ideas and views constantly reiterated in the *Correio Braziliense* were inspired chiefly by Hipólito José's personal experience and psychology. When the *Correio* first appeared in June 1808, Hipólito José had been absent from Portuguese America for at least sixteen years, that is, for half of his life.[41] Before leaving the New World, at the age of eighteen, he had grown up in the frontier captaincy of Rio Grande do Sul, very different in climate, ecology, and population from the other regions of Portuguese America.[42] After graduating from Coimbra Hipólito José spent nearly two years in the United States, particularly in New England and the Mid-Atlantic states, a region quite similar in climate and environment to Rio Grande do Sul.[43] The *Correio Braziliense* was from its very first issue fascinated by what it called "the new Empire of Brazil," in other words, Portuguese America as a single entity, a natural unit.[44] Hipólito José's vision of "Brazil" was drawn in part from an amplification of his memories of Rio Grande do Sul (as recalled through the prism of his experiences in the United States), but far more, it was a construct of his intellect, concocted from abstract ideals, reflecting not reality but what he believed Brazil could and should be.[45]

Hipólito José's perception of Portuguese America as a natural entity was not original, probably being fairly common among the New World–born *letrados* during the last part of the eighteenth century. The focus of identity and loyalty for many of these men was neither Brazil nor their original *pátria* but the imperial system they served. Hipólito José was in this respect different. His brush with the Inquisition and his flight to England barred him from the royal service and made him an outsider, excluded from the status quo. He created for himself a new focus of loyalty and identity, "Brazil," and gave to it the emotional commitment that others gave to their *pátria* or to the Crown.[46] With unflagging zeal Hipólito José sought to forward the transformation of Portuguese America into Brazil, and his *Correio* tirelessly urged the Crown not just to permit but to assist this metamorphosis.

It would be incorrect, however, to characterize Hipólito José as a Brazilian nationalist. In the first place, he used the word "a Nação" (the Nation) in its popular sense: it referred to all the subjects of the King of Portugal wherever they lived, within or without the royal dominions, and so its extent was not coterminous with a fixed geographic area.[47] Embedded within "a Nação" was "a Pátria," which to Hipólito José was Brazil. For him, Brazil was inherently the center of the royal dominions and the glory of the nation, but on the other hand, he could not envision Brazil existing outside of "a Nação," as attested by the fact that only in 1822, the year of independence, did he reluctantly convert to the cause of nation-statehood for Brazil.[48] As his sympathy and support for the Spanish American movements for national independence shows, Hipólito accepted the nation-state as being the ideal type of polity, but that acceptance did not override his personal commitment to what may be termed "Brazil within the Nation."[49]

The second psychological imperative governing Hipólito José in writing the *Correio Braziliense* was the traumatic period between his arrest in 1803 and his escape to England in 1805. He had been seized and held prisoner, without due process or means of defense, on the charge of belonging to an organization he regarded as not only legal but useful to society. Absolute power in general and the petty tyrannies and corruption of royal officials in particular the *Correio* never ceased to expose and denounce. "Absolute power destroys the *Public* and where there exists neither public nor constitution, there can in reality be neither *Homeland* nor Nation."[50] Harmony and prosperity would not return to Portugal, the *Correio* argued, until the Crown restored the old medieval constitution, the excellence of which lay in its close resemblance to the British constitution.[51]

In his political goals, Hipólito José was no more and no less than an English Whig, believing in a balanced constitution, a strong legislature, freedom of religion and the press, and liberty—respect for the rights of the individual.[52] This creed demanded no sweeping changes in the structure of society and challenged no vested interests beyond those of the Crown.[53]

Even in that respect, the *Correio* was wisely cautious. It always treated
D. João with the utmost respect, never questioning his beneficence. Any
failings in policy or administration were always attributed to underlings
who abused the ruler's confidence and the authority entrusted to them.[54]

The magnitude of the influence wielded by the *Correio Braziliense* can
be gauged from the comments on its articles in contemporary correspondence and from the escalating counter-measures taken by the Crown. In
1810 several pamphlets were published in Lisbon refuting articles in the
Correio.[55] In 1811 there was founded at London *O Investigador Portuguez*, a competing periodical subsidized by the Crown.[56] Finally, in 1812
the Crown decided to authorize through intermediaries an annual payment to Hipólito José, a pension intended to prevent any radicalization of
the views he expressed in the *Correio Braziliense*. The public never learnt
of the arrangement.[57]

One unintended consequence of these counter-measures was to accelerate the emergence of a periodical press, so that by 1814 three journals were
being published at London, three at Lisbon, and two at Rio de Janeiro
itself, not to mention the topical pamphlets and books also being printed
in those cities. "I have every opportunity to read all the periodicals that
arrive here for the Palace from diverse sources, and in which I am always
interested," the minor bureaucrat, previously quoted, wrote in 1813, "and
plenty come from England."[58]

The guiding assumption upon which the *Correio Braziliense* worked
was that both the journalist and his readers possessed the innate right to
be informed of, to discuss, and even to criticize their government's policies and actions. The success of the *Correio* and its rivals such as the
Investigador showed how readily the literate minority in the Portuguese
dominions responded to this assumption. There was thus formed an active reading public which not only desired to be informed on state affairs
but made their own opinions known on controversial matters. "In the *Investigador Portuguez* I have read many articles both for and against the
Porto and Algarve Companies, issues that have now become conspicuous,"
our bureaucrat wrote in 1816, "but fortunately not the two you sent me
(masterpieces), although I already knew of their existence."[60] Opinions
held on such subjects were not voiced solely within the family circle or in
private letters. They were expressed at social meetings and in the course of
business. Rash men even spoke their mind to strangers at places of public
encounter such as pharmacies and eating houses (*casas de pasto*). There
thus took shape a public opinion, which if generated by a small part of
the population, did express the views of almost everyone of consequence
among the dominant minority in Portuguese America.

As the original and longest-lived of the London journals, the *Correio*'s
most important achievement was inculcating its readers with a common
vocabulary, shared symbols, and familiar ideas which the public in turn
incorporated into its thought and speech. Such a common outlook and

vocabulary was an indispensable step toward the creation of an independent political community. What enhanced the influence of the *Correio* was that the measures adopted by the Crown, particularly in the years 1814 and 1815, could be interpreted as a coherent program of action coinciding with the political ideas long advocated in the *Correio Braziliense*.

In 1814 several appeals begging the Crown to return to Lisbon were submitted by the authorities in Portugal.[61] The British government backed this appeal and, on the strength of a half-promise extracted from D. João, dispatched a squadron to carry the court back. In December 1814, upon the arrival of the British ships, D. João denied making any such promise and accused the British envoy of insolence, forcing his recall to England.[62] To refuse to budge from Rio de Janeiro and to undercut British influence was not a sufficient response to the existing situation; the status quo which made the American dominions the residence of the Crown had to be legitimized. D. João sought to achieve this end by issuing on December 12, 1815, a Carta de Lei (Charter) which both raised the Estado do Brasil to the status of a kingdom and created "the United Kingdom of Portugal, Brazil, and Algarves."[63] Despite the restoration of peace in Europe, Brazil—as Portuguese America can henceforth with historical accuracy be termed—was to continue to be, as Hipólito José advocated, the center of the Portuguese dominions. The creation of the new kingdom stimulated the growth of identification with Brazil. "Addresses of exultation and gratitude to the Sovereign poured in, by one simultaneous movement from every part of the country," and every "township felt proud of the privilege which admitted it to address its own Sovereign under a Brazilian title, on Brazilian ground; it perceived itself to be, however humble, an integral part of the extended whole."[64]

III

Appearances can be deceiving, and such was the case for both the Portuguese Crown and Hipólito José da Costa in 1815. Their respective positions were not nearly so assured as they may have seemed. In the case of the Crown, a conjunction of factors began to work against the new political order created by the formation of the United Kingdom. The United Kingdom was a paper measure, not accompanied by the administrative restructuring necessary to make it a reality. A unification of jurisdictions and institutions in Brazil did not follow the creation of the new polity. As early as May 1809, the jurisdiction over the entirety of Brazil granted to the Rio de Janeiro Casa da Suplicação on its creation in 1808 was partially abrogated by the restoration of appellate jurisdiction over Maranhão and Pará to the Lisbon Casa da Suplicação, now freed from French rule. This restoration of the colonial status quo was confirmed and reinforced in 1812 by the creation of a new *relação* at São Luis de Maranhão. Not only were appeals from its decisions to be taken to Lisbon rather than to

Rio, but the new *relação* was given authority over Piauí and Ceará, previously under the jurisdiction of the Supreme Court at Rio de Janeiro.[65] After 1815 the Crown not only failed to remold the system: it did not even undertake any considerable expansion of the judiciary.[66]

Even more shortsighted than this failure to consolidate the new kingdom of Brazil was the Crown's treatment of Portugal in the aftermath of the Napoleonic wars. Three French invasions had devastated much of the country and had disrupted its social and economic structures.[67] For agriculture and manufacturing to revive and the social infrastructure to be restored, a long-term program of capital investment, lower taxation, and imaginative and active administration was indispensable. Despite its good intentions the Crown showed little understanding of either the magnitude or the urgency of Portugal's needs; the measures it authorized were both tardy and slight. No autonomy or initiative was allowed to the authorities in Lisbon, who had to refer even the most trivial matters to Rio de Janeiro. A double crossing of the Atlantic and processing by two bureaucracies were required before any decision could be taken.[68] In these conditions, the regents in Lisbon, even if they had proven themselves to be energetic and altruistic, could not have provided an effective administration, and the regents were not notable for either of these virtues.[69]

Compounding the Crown's errors was its policy toward the army in Portugal. Although British financing of the armed forces ceased in 1814, fears of a Spanish invasion caused the Crown to maintain the army at its wartime size. This decision denied to the economy urgently needed revenues and manpower. The retention of the British officers, and in particular of Lord Beresford as commander in chief with quasi-independent powers, offended national pride and by generating rivalries within the government at Lisbon further reduced its effectiveness.

The Crown did find one use for the swollen army of Portugal. Late in 1815 nearly 5,000 troops, having "volunteered" for service in the New World, were transported to Brazil.[70] In May 1816, the force was dispatched to the far south where it spearheaded an invasion of the Banda Oriental (modern Uruguay), then ruled by José Artigas. The motives behind this forward policy were a determination to remove a potential threat on the undemarcated borders of the far south and a desire to reverse the Portuguese expulsion from the east bank of the Río de la Plata, achieved by Spain in 1777.[71]

The venture proved far more difficult than the Crown had anticipated. Four years of warfare were required before all resistance in the Banda Oriental was crushed and control achieved. Although the expeditionary force, known as the Voluntários d'El Rei, was throughout these years paid by the Lisbon treasury, the remaining substantial costs of the war fell upon the revenues of Brazil itself. The Crown's seizure of territory still claimed by Spain threatened for a time to involve Portugal in a direct confrontation with other powers of Europe.[72] The most detrimental consequence of this policy of pushing Brazil's frontiers to the banks of the Río de la Plata was, however, the appearance of privateers, licensed by Artigas and flying his flag, which attacked Portuguese shipping, disrupting commerce along the coasts of Brazil and on the sea routes to Portugal.[73]

The mishandling of the situation in Portugal after 1815 and the continuance of the forward policy in the Río de la Plata might not have occurred if the Crown had been better advised. In June 1817 death removed the last of the senior councillors who had arrived in 1808. D. João, who became king on his mother's decease in March 1816, now turned for counsel to the second rank of those who had accompanied him from Lisbon. The king relied mainly on Tomás António de Vilanova Portugal who, the British envoy in 1820 reported, "with an unbounded complaisance for the wishes and sentiments of the King, is timid, yet worse than if he were daring; for ignorant from his Habits and Pursuits, of the Character of the Age, he is fearful of proposing any decided or any new Measure." Vilanova Portugal was, to use a modern term, the very embodiment of the Peter Principle— excellent as a high level bureaucrat and disastrous as a minister.[74]

While the king and his principal adviser, who from June 1817 to December 1820 sometimes held all and never less than two of the four ministerial portfolios, brought the invasion of the Banda Oriental to a successful conclusion, they possessed neither the knowledge nor the imagination nor the boldness necessary to confront the problems facing the royal dominions, above all the economic crisis that after 1817 affected all parts of the Portuguese world. Even after the return of peace in 1814, the economy of Portugal had achieved no more than a weak recovery. Its agriculture found it difficult to compete against the flood of cheap foreign grain entering the country. Trade with Brazil never exceeded two-thirds of its value in 1806, with manufactured goods not even recovering to that level. To the inhabitants of Portugal it appeared that the Crown was using their remaining resources in order to maintain a lavish court at Rio and advance its transatlantic ambitions.[75]

The position of the Brazilian economy—or more precisely the interlinked economies that made up Brazil—was more complex. Brazilian raw materials such as cotton and sugar profited from the short-lived boom in post-war Europe, but the ecological and economic devastation wrought in 1816 by the "year without a summer" produced a slump that deepened through 1817 and 1818.[76] Not only did European demand for all Brazilian products decline, but the two key exports were challenged on price and quality by cotton from the American South and sugar from Cuba. As both sales and prices dropped, so did the revenues received by the Crown, which tried to offset the decline through more rigorous collection. The burden of taxation thus grew as disposable income shrank.[77]

Government expenditures consistently outran revenues. The Crown covered the accumulating deficit with expedients. It borrowed constantly and heavily from the Banco do Brasil, which in turn issued paper money

to meet its obligations. Between 1814 and 1820 bank notes in circulation increased eightfold.[78] The Crown delayed the payment of debts and
salaries. As one merchant explained to another in 1819, "The minister
acknowledges [the debt] and orders payment. Targini [head of the royal
treasury] replies that he will pay out of the first monies available, but such
monies never materialize because the deficit is constant, and this flaw viti-
ates everything."[79] The policies pursued on both sides of the Atlantic after
1815 by the Crown served, in sum, to delay but not to prevent the onset
of major problems.

The challenge to Hipólito José da Costa and his *Correio Braziliense*
from 1815 was more subtle. The final defeat of Napoleon at Waterloo and
the reestablishment of peace changed the intellectual complexion of the
Atlantic world. The Holy Alliance in Europe equated monarchism with
reaction, and in the New World the United States, having fought Great
Britain to a draw in the War of 1812, began an era of prosperity and expansion. The passage of time dimmed memories of the Terror in France and
the slave revolution in Saint Domingue, so that republicanism no longer
signified social radicalism. In Brazil the coming of peace brought a decline
in government vigilance and allowed an influx of migrants from continental Europe. Brazilians now experienced the full impact of the intellectual
culture of Europe and North America.[80]

A key element in this new situation was the inflow into the port cities
of foreigners of every calling and social rank. If some came to seek their
fortunes, many from France and Italy were political radicals who had
left their native land to escape retribution from the restored monarchies.
Interacting with their Brazilian counterparts at every level of urban society,
from that of the small folk to that of the high functionaries, the foreign
immigrants acted as both agents for new ideas and as suppliers of the
latest literature, both cultural and political. As a bureaucrat then working
in Rio later recalled, these printed works "were as much coveted and as
easily procured as they were prohibited by Authority. They all circulated
in profusion and reached the hands of anyone who wanted them."[81]

In the early years of the *Correio Braziliense* Hipólito José had alone
expressed and so embodied opposition to the status quo. By 1815 many
readers had advanced beyond his Whiggish doctrines and deference to the
Crown, seeking stronger fare. The doctrines of the French Revolution,
with their denunciation of absolutism, advocacy of the rights of man, and
exaltation of *la patrie* (equated with *a pátria*), appealed strongly to the
less-privileged elements among the literate. The influx of foreign artisans
into the port cities gave the small folk a greater coherence and strength as
a distinctive socioeconomic group and intensified their sense of deprivation. The new intellectual climate also created disaffection among those
who lived on the fringes of the official world, such as petty functionaries,
notaries, unbeneficed clergy, and pharmacists. They believed their existing
position in society did not sufficiently recognize their capacities as men of

talent and culture. For them the North American republic, with its lack of inherited privilege and its open political community, offered not only the perfect but the most rewarding polity.

What acted as a vehicle for the spread of political dissent and provided the institutional structure knitting the different groups into a coherent movement was the Masonic Order. Freemasonry had certainly existed in the port cities of Portuguese America before 1808 but it was only thereafter that Masons began "to organize various lodges, each [doing so] in the city where he lived, and they set up a Grand Orient, or Supreme Government of the Society, in Bahia, where lived the largest number of those who had been initiated and advanced to senior grades in Europe."[82] Although the secrecy intrinsic to the Masonic Order prevents certainty, the full apparatus of Masonry was probably introduced by military officers and merchants coming from Portugal.[83]

The appeal of Freemasonry to Brazilians was enhanced by the resemblance of its organization and rituals to the religious and charitable brotherhoods they already knew, by the security that its rituals and oaths offered, and by the interplay of lodge meetings with the events of regular social life, which provided a convenient cover for those very meetings.[84] While Freemasonry probably drew the bulk of its members from the small folk and the groups on the fringes of the official world, the movement did attract both local notables and *letrados*. After 1815 some lodges in Brazil and Portugal had moved beyond heterodox, disloyal talk to become centers for treasonable action.[85] The presence in these lodges of people belonging to the status quo resulted, as it had done in the Inconfidência Mineira of 1788–89, in information reaching the authorities. In Portugal the leaders of a Masonic network composed of army officers resentful of British dominance were betrayed and arrested in May 1817.[86]

In Brazil, or more precisely, in Pernambuco, events took a different course. The governor of the captaincy, informed of the lodges' activities and fearing the worst, held a secret council meeting early on the morning of March 6, 1817, at which it was decided to arrest all those denounced. Betrayal can, however, be turned against itself: information about the decision was leaked to the suspects, so that when the arrest of one bold and popular officer was attempted in front of his men, he killed his would-be captors and led his troops into open revolt.[87] "The Revolution of Pernambuco," wrote the *ouvidor* of Olinda to his brother in Portugal on April 16, "was an astounding event: 5 or 6 men destroyed in an instant an established government, and all the authorities conformed to the event without hesitation."[88] On the day following the revolt, a republic was proclaimed and a provisional government installed. The new regime gathered considerable support from all ranks of society, including royal officials, *letrados*, merchants, small folk, and slaves.[89] The rebellion spread rapidly, triumphing in the provinces of Paraíba do Norte and Rio Grande do Norte and penetrating briefly into the south of Ceará. This success was short-lived. By late May the rebellion had been snuffed out through a combination of counter risings, military defeat, and a loss of the will to fight.[90]

The ideals of the revolt and its goals can be deduced from the slogans used on March 6, 1817, and thereafter: "Religião, Pátria, e Liberdade" —"Viva a Pátria, Viva a Liberdade, e Viva a Religião!" These phrases —"Religion, Homeland, and Liberty" and "Hurrah for the Homeland, Hurrah for Liberty, and Hurrah for Religion!"—reveal the outlook and aims of the rising to have been essentially traditional.[91] "Liberty" served as a code word for the rights of the individual citizen. It was a word surcharged with emotion, connoting personal liberation. "Inspiring liberty which today this land enjoys fills me with gladness and with it I celebrate the happiness of its inhabitants," wrote one partisan of the rising; "I, born in slavery and ever stifled by tyranny, today I breathe free."[92] As its linkage to "Religion" indicates, the concept of "Liberty" was far older than 1789. When in 1645 the planters of Pernambuco rose against the occupying Dutch, they had fought under the banner Religion and Liberty. It was to the battles and the heroes of that "War of Divine Liberty" that the manifestos of the 1817 uprising directly appealed:

Therefore, sons of the Pátria, be true heirs of the bravery and the glory of the Vieiras and the Vidals, the Diases and the Camarãos, waste no time in enlisting under the banner of our liberty. Parents, take this opportunity to display the worth of your sons, send them to the field of honor, and you will soon see them crowned with the same laurels won by the heroes of [the victories of] Tabocas, of Guararapes.[93]

The role played by religion in the rising was crucial. The governors of the diocese of Olinda gave the sanction of the Church to the new regime by issuing pastoral letters in its favor. Over 40 priests were eventually indicted for their participation in the revolt. An interim constitution, submitted to the municipal councils of Pernambuco captaincy, retained Catholicism as the official religion of the new republic, which would pay priests out of the state revenues.[94]

Among the three ideals, the *pátria* probably took pride of place. While the word *patriota* (patriot), adopted as the formal mode of address in the republic of 1817, revealed the influence of the French Revolution, the word *pátria* retained its traditional meaning and usage: the land and community in which a person was born, grew up, married, and pursued a living. Thus on the very evening that the revolt triumphed, its chiefs wrote in a private letter that "the Capital is in our power, the *pátria* is saved."[95] The manifesto issued by the new regime on March 8 was addressed to the "Pernambucans" alone. Its final sentence is most revealing: "The Pátria is our common mother, you are her children, you are descendants of the valorous Lusitanians, you are Portuguese, you are Americans, you are Brazilians, you are Pernambucans."[96]

The rebel government in Recife sent agents to spread the revolt to the other provinces of the northeast and named envoys to secure diplomatic recognition and support from Great Britain and the United States. No agents were sent and no attention was paid to the provinces of central and southern Brazil.[97] Each of the three provinces joining the revolt created its own provisional government, totally independent of the others. This independence, despite the giving of mutual aid, was maintained even in small matters. When the government of Paraíba decided to copy that of Pernambuco in adopting a flag, the design chosen was slightly but unmistakably different from that of the Pernambucan flag. No formal union or federation of the new republics was envisaged.[98]

In sum the evidence makes clear that despite the creation of the Kingdom of Brazil in 1815, the uprising in the northeast did not aim at the independence of Brazil as a nation-state. The leaders of the revolt, such as Domingos José Martins, a merchant who had lived in England, were conversant with the ideology of nationalism, but they employed nationalistic rhetoric only in documents addressed to the outside world, which expected such usage. It was mainly in such documents that the word "Brazil" was used.[99] That the leaders of the revolt favored the overthrow of the Crown's authority throughout the Portuguese New World did not imply that they envisaged creating a single republic and nation out of the territories now known as Brazil.[100]

One motive for the revolt was resentment against the loss of control over their own affairs suffered by the *pátrias* since 1808. The creation of the Kingdom of Brazil was equated with the increasing centralization of power in the city of Rio de Janeiro. Not only was taxation heavier, but the swelling bureaucracy in the capital demanded an ever larger share of the provinces' revenues. All the regions of Brazil had profited from the ending of economic colonialism in 1808, but it was Rio which had secured the lion's share of the benefits. A desire to end this domination by the upstart capital—what would nowadays be termed internal colonialism—was one cause for the rising.[101] The enthusiasm with which the inhabitants of Rio de Janeiro rallied to the support of the Crown and cooperated in suppressing the revolt both suggests an awareness of this motive for the rising and confirms that the 1817 revolt was not a nationalist uprising.[102]

Related to discontent over the *pátrias'* loss of autonomy as a cause for the revolt was the widespread popular resentment directed against the *europeus,* those born in Portugal. So powerful was this sentiment that the new regimes took active steps to defuse it, thus avoiding any physical outbreaks against the Portuguese-born.[103] The available evidence suggests that resentment was particularly directed against the *europeus* who had settled in Pernambuco since 1808, men who competed with the American-born for wealth and position.[104] Although embodying an elementary form of group consciousness, sometimes preliminary to nationalism, this shared resentment of intruding outsiders probably did the revolt more harm than good, by alienating many *europeus* who might otherwise have supported the cause.[105]

The 1817 rebellion was far from being totally traditional in outlook and goals. Many of the changes made since 1808 it did welcome, particularly the opening of direct trade and intellectual contact with the outside world. Popular sovereignty in the form of a republic, freedom of worship, and equality before the law were all proclaimed by the new regimes. This espousing of liberal doctrine, sincere as it was, contributed greatly to the rising's ultimate defeat. The ostentatious republicanism, with its new forms of address, offended traditionalists. Equality before the law aroused fears among the rural notables that slavery was about to be abolished. The Pernambuco regime hastened to deny the rumor, declaring that it desired to end "the cancer of slavery" but only through emancipation that "was slow, systematic, and legal."[106] This disavowal of any intention to make radical changes in the social structure prevented the mobilization of mass support.[107] A cool, perhaps cynical remark made by an inhabitant of Paraíba do Norte—"He was in the circumstance of being neither for the Homeland nor the King"—cannot have been unusual. In Recife itself, initial enthusiasm for the rising had owed much to the new regime's abolishing taxes on meat and on artisans' shops and to its increasing the military's daily pay.[108] Yet this redress of grievances was counterproductive, for it deprived the new regime, at a critical moment, of desperately needed funds for the defense of the *pátria* against the royal forces.

That the rising was made in the name of the *pátria* did not necessarily ensure support, as demonstrated by events in the *comarca* of Alagoas, then part of Pernambuco captaincy. To Alagoas's local notables Pernambuco, far from arousing their loyalty, was the oppressor of their own *pátria*. The initial rising in Alagoas was speedily crushed by a counterrevolution in the king's name. For their loyalty to the Crown the notables were to be rewarded in 1820, when the *comarca* was separated from Pernambuco and became the province of Alagoas.[109]

These factors explain what has puzzled some historians: Hipólito José's attitude towards the revolt in the columns of the *Correio Braziliense*. He had supported the risings in Spanish America from their start. "Certain that you will welcome a new era so in accord with your principles," the provisional government of Pernambuco wrote to Hipólito José, asking him to serve as their agent with the British government.[110] Instead of support, the leaders received unqualified denunciation: "Everything demonstrates not just the hastiness, errors, and partiality of the leaders but their ignorance in matters of government, administration, and the conduct of public affairs."[111]

In part Hipólito José disliked the republicanism of the Pernambuco revolt and the resort to force. However, the passage in which he sought to rebut the accusations of inconsistency leveled against him for condemning the rising in Pernambuco while supporting those in Spanish America reveals the causes for his anger:

If the reader will, then, examine the principles we have expounded concerning the fundamental difference between a mutiny by a handful of men and a revolution of a nation—for example, between the action of the entire Portuguese nation in 1640 and the riot in Pernambuco—he will perceive that we did not intend to equate the revolution in the entirety of Spanish America nor its causes with the paltry commotion in Pernambuco.[112]

Hipólito José believed, in other words, that the Portuguese in 1640 and the Spanish Americans in 1810 had revolted as *nations,* maintaining their political and territorial unity. In his eyes the Pernambucans had committed the unforgivable sin of shattering by their revolt the unity of his idol— Brazil.[113]

I V

With the suppression of the Pernambucan revolt the affairs of the United Kingdom resumed their accustomed course. In November 1817 a notable diplomatic coup was achieved by the marriage of the king's heir to Princess Leopoldina, daughter of the emperor of Austria. In an era when dynastic alliances exerted a perceptible influence on the policies of the European monarchies, this linking of the house of Bragança to that of Hapsburg-Lorraine both affirmed the importance of the United Kingdom of Portugal and Brazil in international affairs and implied that the emperor of Austria would, in his foreign policy, view favorably the interests and needs of the Portuguese dominions.[114] The alliance helped to inhibit any interference by the European monarchs on behalf of Spain while Portuguese forces struggled to complete the conquest of the Banda Oriental, a goal finally achieved in 1820 when José Artigas was forced to seek refuge in Paraguay. The humiliation suffered by Portugal in 1777 was finally wiped out and the royal standard planted once more on the east bank of the Río de la Plata.[115]

Although the crisis of 1817 produced no immediate visible consequences in Brazil or Portugal, it had in reality shaken the existing system to its foundations. Neither the Inconfidência Mineira nor the "Conspiracy of the Tailors" had given the Crown reason to believe that these seditions were any more than aberrations, involving only a handful of malcontents. The 1817 rising destroyed that comforting assumption. The structure of authority had collapsed under assault, and the elements in society most identified with the Crown had actively collaborated with the rebel regime. The Crown could no longer rest assured that its subjects were immune from infection by what Vilanova Portugal, the king's principal adviser, termed the "funereal contagion, the result of the fermentation of the spirit that has been at work, to a greater or lesser degree, in almost all of Europe, bringing ideas truly subversive of all Order." [116]

Independent evidence by which to gauge the impact of the 1817 uprising upon what constituted public opinion in Brazil is extremely sparse.[117] Two points are, however, clear: first, the revolt constituted a crucial precedent by showing that an alternative political system could function in Portu-

guese America, and second, the revolt stripped from the Crown its aura
of invincibility and inevitability. Automatic acceptance and so dependence
on the status quo *mentalité*—what Gramsci characterized as hegemony—
was after 1817 no longer certain. These influences were for a time offset
by the revulsion aroused in the minds of moderate men such as Hipólito
José by the deliberate destruction during the revolt of such sacred symbols
of authority as the king's portrait, the royal coat of arms, and the officials'
staves of authority. The public was, it is safe to conclude, disoriented, desirous of reassurance, and consequently malleable in the aftermath of the
rising.[118]

The Crown's reaction to the revolt was instinctive and unflinching. Such
a "horrible attempt upon My Royal Sovereignty and Supreme Authority"
could result only in a decision to "punish with the severity of the laws
crimes so monstrous and unprecedented."[119] In Portugal those accused of
participating in the officers' conspiracy of 1817 led by General Gomes
Freire de Andrada were tried in secret, and 12 men were sent to the gal-
lows. In Brazil the scale of repression was far broader. Not counting those
who died on the battlefield, were killed without trial, committed suicide,
or died in prison, between 150 and 200 people were arrested, and of these
some 20 were executed.[120]

Hipólito José, whose customary moderation and sense of justice overrode his anger against the revolt, was not alone in pointing out the ill-
advisedness of such a policy. The very general sent to subdue Pernambuco
expressed the same opinion to the king himself. "The more arrests made
because of the rebellion," the *Correio* commented in September 1817, "the
more its importance is impressed on the public, something totally contrary
to the interests of the government."[121] The indiscriminate and unrelenting prosecution of all those implicated in the revolt caused widespread
consternation and despair, as General Luís do Rêgo Barreto wrote to
D. João VI in April 1818. His recommendation that retribution be selective
and joined to a general amnesty was not accepted.[122]

After March 1817 the Crown acted as though it were constantly threatened by treason and disloyalty. The secrecy of the Masonic Order and its
evident attraction for the educated intensified the Crown's suspicion of
those on whom it most depended in governing. The proscription of all
secret societies by a decree of March 18, 1818, both revealed that mistrust
and provoked a wave of denunciations which the Crown was only too
willing to credit. Informers found evidence in the past behavior of many
functionaries that gave color to their accusations.[123] In respect to Portugal
these fears of resurgent subversion were not always illusory: in April 1818
a group of magistrates and merchants at Porto founded "the Sanhedrin,"
a secret society devoted to the "regeneration" of Portugal.[124]

The effect of the 1817 conspiracies was, as Hipólito José foresaw at
the time, to render the Crown more unwilling than ever to contemplate
reform policies. For Vilanova Portugal, the best was to "rectify wrong,"

and not to "embark on novelties which always generate trouble and grave inconveniences."[125] The Crown's response to the economic and social crisis which engulfed Portugal after 1817 was limited to a number of palliatives, such as small reductions in tariffs and the grant of bounties to products and manufactured goods exported to Brazil.[126] Through its own inertia, lack of self-confidence, and encouragement of spying and delation the Crown did much to undermine its credibility as a government. It was now, far more than previously, upheld by naked force, both in reality and in the public's perception.[127] Late in 1817 the Crown brought over to Brazil a second contingent from the army of Portugal, stationing two regiments at Rio de Janeiro and one each at Salvador and Recife.[128]

Dependence on force as the basis of authority had one weakness. It required the cooperation of the military, and in particular the loyalty of the officer corps. In Brazil, the dangers of this dependence were minimized since the troops were paid regularly and the units brought over from Portugal were not attracted to the cause of independence. They could be expected to cooperate in suppressing local risings against royal rule. Nor, after the fiasco of the Pernambuco revolt, was a new conspiracy probable unless the political climate altered drastically. So long as the Crown continued firmly based in Rio de Janeiro and Brazil remained the center of the royal dominions the status quo seemed reasonably secure. Despite the commercial depression in the Atlantic world, the economic regions of Brazil continued to enjoy a fair degree of prosperity, if the rising number of Brazilian-born entering Coimbra University is any guide: between 1816 and 1820 no less than 140 enrolled as students.[129]

The situation in Portugal was quite the reverse. By the end of 1819 the pay of both officers and men was eight months in arrears, and discontent among the military was visibly mounting. Economic conditions in Portugal were extremely bad. Exports of wine, a key staple, had dropped to a secular low, with the adverse balance of external trade reaching crisis proportions.[130]

On January 1, 1820, an expeditionary force gathered by the Spanish Crown at Cadiz mutinied for back pay and redress of grievances. The rising rapidly assumed political ends, and the troops marched on Madrid, demanding a return to the Constitution of 1812. In April the king of Spain capitulated, surrendering control of the government to the constitutionalists. The developments in Spain and discontents in Portugal so alarmed General Beresford, still commanding the army in Portugal, that in April 1820 he sailed for Rio de Janeiro "with the express view of representing to His Majesty the deplorable State of the Kingdom of Portugal, and the necessity of taking some Measures to ameliorate the Condition and to amend and modify its Government."[131]

Despite events in Spain and the urgings of Lord Beresford, the government at Rio de Janeiro could not easily be moved from what the British envoy in 1820 termed its "absolute inaction." In July some further fiscal

and administrative favors were granted to Portugal. The units of the Portuguese army stationed in Brazil were no longer to be paid by the Lisbon
treasury, and when Beresford left Rio on August 15 he took with him
money to meet at least part of the arrears in pay. His main goals he had
not, however, been able to achieve.[132]

On October 17, the packet *Providência* dropped anchor in Rio harbor.
The news it brought was at once embargoed.[133] On August 25 the garrison
of Porto had risen in revolt, demanding that the Cortes be summoned and
that the king return to Lisbon. Subsequent ships brought further ill news.
On September 15, the regents at Lisbon, who had by then summoned the
Cortes to meet, were overthrown by the Lisbon garrison and replaced by a
provisional government. When General Beresford sailed into Lisbon har-
bor on October 10, he was politely relieved of his cash and, with the other
British officers, sent packing home. On November 11, a mutiny by the Lis-
bon garrison forced the provisional government to proclaim the Spanish
Constitution of 1812 in force for the interim, until the Cortes, called for
January 25, could draw up a new constitution for the Portuguese nation.[134]
The system of government and the balance of power within the Portuguese
dominions initiated in 1808 and confirmed in 1815 by the creation of the
United Kingdom of Portugal and Brazil were now put in question.

3

Stumbling into Independence, 1820-1822

The revolution which began at Porto on August 24, 1820, resembled an exploding volcano or a hurricane striking land. It swept away the existing political system and disrupted the structures of power across the Portuguese world. Deprived of the familiar and disoriented by innovations on every side, the Portuguese both in Europe and in Brazil were thrown off balance, forced to function in a world as strange as space was to the first astronauts. Ensuing events had a theatrical, unreal air. During the two years following the revolt, politics were largely motivated by ideological imperatives, so that reforms were adopted and policies pursued with little thought for their practical effect or for the opposition they might arouse. The disputes generated by such measures similarly lacked rationality and restraint, the opposing sides often attributing to each other desires and intentions of a macabre malevolence. The huge distances separating the constituent parts of the Portuguese world contributed powerfully to a breakdown in communication, thwarting attempts at compromise and preventing reconciliation.

By the second half of 1822 battle lines were firmly drawn and a clear choice presented. In Rio de Janeiro a newly independent state headed by the heir to the Portuguese throne claimed sovereignty over the provinces of Brazil, while in Lisbon the Cortes, ruling through the king, sought to retain the obedience of those same provinces. Not until September 1823 was the authority of the new emperor established in all the regions of Portuguese America. A further two years elapsed before Brazil's independence was recognized by Portugal.

This period, and the years 1820 to 1822 in particular, was crucial to the forging of Brazil as a nation-state. Paradoxically, the period has never received the close research and analysis that it merits. A considerable body of literature has, it is true, been written, but when it is compared in extent and scholarship to that undertaken on the equivalent period in the United States, Mexico, or Argentina, the relative sparsity of the literature becomes apparent.[1] This paucity is in no way surprising. The Independence era encompassed a number of parallel conflicts evolving simultaneously over a vast area. Causation of events was always intricate and sometimes random, with the motivation of the contending parties often aberrant or fluctuating. Materials for research are voluminous and yet not easy of access, being scattered across two continents. Certain key episodes are poorly documented, and others have yet to be investigated. In such conditions constructing a coherent narrative of the Independence era is difficult enough: to provide a convincing interpretation of the conjunction of events that gave birth to the Brazilian nation-state is exceptionally challenging.

It is therefore no wonder that an approach predominates in the historiography of the Independence period which may fairly be called "nationalist." The strength of this interpretation is in part due to its utility in authenticating Brazil's existence as a nation, but much of its appeal springs from its imposition of clarity and coherence on a sequence of events that almost defy rational explanation. The nationalist interpretation rests upon four premises. First, by 1820 Brazil had achieved the preconditions for nationhood. According to the second premise, after the Porto rising Portugal began a deliberate campaign to "recolonize" Brazil. Third, this policy then awoke in Brazilians a full consciousness of and desire for nationhood. Finally, the government in Rio de Janeiro, headed by the prince regent, D. Pedro, and his first minister and mentor, José Bonifácio de Andrada e Silva, served as the instrument whereby Brazilians threw off the Portuguese yoke and secured national independence. Underlying this scenario is the assumption that the territories of Portuguese America were predestined by history to achieve independence as a single, united state.

What may be granted is that the overthrow of the political status quo by the August 1820 revolution rendered inevitable some type of movement for independence in the territories of Portuguese America. It does not follow that the inexorable, inevitable outcome of events was the creation of the nation-state Brazil. The harsh reality overlooked by the nationalist interpretation is that by June 1821 the Kingdom of Brazil had dissolved into its constituent parts, not because of the machinations of the Lisbon Cortes but because of the desire of the local notables to recover provincial autonomy and to escape dominance by both Rio de Janeiro and Lisbon. Had this trend persisted, movements for total independence would probably have followed the precedent of 1817 rather than that of 1815, resulting in the creation of regional republics rather than a single state. In such circumstances it may be doubted whether the ultimate result would have differed much from that in North America, where not all the colonies achieved independence.

Three factors may be identified as decisive in preventing this outcome: (1) the presence in the New World of the heir to the throne; (2) the determination of the ruling elite in Rio de Janeiro to retain its position of privilege and dominance within Portuguese America; and (3) the high-handedness of the Lisbon Cortes. From January 1822 open conflict existed between Rio de Janeiro and Lisbon. The most significant element in this struggle was not, as the nationalist interpretation would have it, the direct confrontation of the two centers of authority but rather the competition between them to secure the backing of the still-autonomous provinces. Because of this polarization the local *pátrias* were deprived of any third option—they had to choose between Lisbon and Rio de Janeiro.

The latter's eventual triumph was not due to the allure of Brazil as a nation-state. On the contrary, what decided the issue in many of the provinces was that in contrast to the Lisbon Cortes which demanded from them the total, unquestioning obedience typical of a nation-state, the claims to authority advanced by the new Empire of Brazil appeared far less absolute. By convoking in June 1822 a constituent assembly, the government in Rio de Janeiro seemed to be offering to the *pátrias* a decisive voice in the formation of the new state and so pledging that they would retain a large measure of autonomy.

The adherence of the provinces was, further, not achieved solely by peaceful persuasion. Brute force played a considerable role in bringing outlying regions, particularly those of the far north, into the new Empire of Brazil. A historian as fervently nationalist as Arthur Cézar Ferreira Reis has been forced to acknowledge that "the incorporation of Maranhão into the Empire was achieved through a bitter political experience."[2] The formation of a single nation-state was not desired by every part of Brazil, nor did its creation necessarily confer benefits on the constituent territories. These two realities were to exert a profound influence on the future development of Brazil.

I

The revolution for constitutional rule begun at Porto in 1820 enjoyed unchecked success in the Portuguese world for well over a year. This success depended less upon the use of force than on the response the revolution aroused on both sides of the Atlantic. The calling of an elected assembly and the promise of a constitution contented those of liberal views. Conservatives were placated by the revolution's ostentatious loyalty to the king and avoidance of any hint of social radicalism.[3] The pledge of "renewal" (*regeneração*), which promised the remedy of abuses and grievances without requiring fundamental reforms, appealed to everyone who desired a restoration of the nation's honor and prosperity. Difficult as it is to assess the state of public opinion during this period, there is no evidence that the Porto revolution appealed less strongly in Brazil than it did in Portugal itself. In January 1821 a leading Bahian notable commented that "the people of Brazil, accustomed to respect Portugal, regard what is done there as the best that is possible."[4]

That the promises made by the revolution raised public expectations excessively high and that existing abuses could not be remedied without offending entrenched interests is, in retrospect, abundantly clear. Further, after November 1820 the new regime in Lisbon was controlled by a group of radicals, mostly lawyers, who in outlook and policy desired far more than the rising's announced aims.[5] These realities took a great while to penetrate the public consciousness, however, and even then popular enthusiasm for the ideals of the Porto revolution, if no longer for the Lisbon regime itself, persisted unabated. The self-confidence and decisiveness displayed by the radicals at Lisbon enabled them for a long period to hold the political initiative, while the organization of resistance or countermovements was inhibited by the vast distances and difficulties of communication within the Portuguese world.

What at the start certainly aided the cause of the Porto revolution was the passivity of the government at Rio de Janeiro. The Crown was disoriented by the total collapse of its authority in Portugal and by the audacity of the Lisbon regime in ordering that the Cortes, which met on January 25, 1821, should be elected not in the traditional form but according to the Spanish constitution of 1812. "This is the first time," one of D. João VI's advisers lamented, "that the Portuguese Nation is meeting separately from its King."[6] As soon as the news of the Porto rising reached Rio there began an unending round of consultation, schemes, and counterproposals that stretched on without resolution for weeks and then for months.[7]

Behind the government's inertia lay the king's intense dislike for all the courses of action proposed and his characteristic hope that through procrastination a favorable turn of events might intervene. While no adviser recommended that the king return to Lisbon, a number did urge that his elder son and heir, D. Pedro, be dispatched immediately as regent with powers to negotiate a moderate settlement. Upon first learning of the Porto uprising, D. João VI was induced to send a message containing a grudging sanction of the regents' summoning the Cortes and a vague promise that one of his sons would eventually return to Portugal.[8] This achievement proved an illusory success for those favoring counteraction.

The king at once began to fear that D. Pedro, upon his arrival at Lisbon, would be acclaimed monarch by the people, owing to D. João's having broken his public pledge to return to Europe "upon the signing of a General Peace."[9] The king's unwillingness to let his elder son depart was strongly supported by his most-trusted advisers, headed by Tomás António de Vilanova Portugal. They objected in principle to the making of concessions, and they opposed placating men they regarded as rebels. The loyalty of anyone advocating such a course was for them suspect. Like D. João VI, they hoped for a favorable turn of events in Europe, in particular, military intervention by the Holy Alliance monarchies.[10]

The de facto division of the Portuguese dominions into two parts, one obeying Lisbon and one Rio, was viewed by these advisers with a certain complacence. They did not believe that the rebel kingdom, once isolated

and treated as an outcast, could survive on its own: "If it [Brazil] sepa-
rates and cuts off communication, Portugal will fall into decay," Vilanova
Portugal wrote to the king on January 7, 1821; "it [Portugal] should be
regarded as Hanover is in relation to Great Britain."[11] Although shorn of
the original kingdom and royal capital, the empire could continue to exist,
ruled from Rio de Janeiro. In an attempt to sway public opinion to this
view, there appeared at Rio late in January 1821 "a short pamphlet, written in French and distributed by the Police."[12] The work, entitled *Should
the King and the Royal Family in the Present Circumstances Return to
Portugal or Instead Stay in Brazil?*, was certainly authorized and probably directly inspired by Vilanova Portugal. Analyzing the issue in terms of
cold material advantage, the pamphlet asserted that Brazil could survive
without Portugal but not vice versa, that the departure of the royal family
from Brazil would inevitably cause its independence, that the king could
found a flourishing empire in Brazil, and that the wisest course was for
him to stay in the New World.[13]

In view of subsequent events, the point must be emphasized that this
original suggestion that the status quo created in 1808 and legitimized in
1815 should be abandoned—thus splitting the Portuguese nation in two
and making Brazil independent—came not from the radicals at Lisbon but
from the Crown itself. How small the appeal of independence as a nation-
state was for most Brazilians can be measured by the outrage the pamphlet
provoked. The intense public reaction forced the authorities to call in the
entire edition, which had, in the view of the British envoy, "produced the
Effect, the most contrary to the Tenour of the Work and the most to be
apprehended, of increasing the desire here, which is sufficiently strong, of
acting entirely in Unison with the Constitutionalists" in Portugal.[14]

A policy of delay and disunion in response to events in Portugal could
have succeeded only if the Crown had been firmly entrenched in its New
World possessions. Such was far from the case. The garrisons in the key
cities of Rio de Janeiro, Salvador, and Recife were dominated by the battalions brought over from Portugal after the 1817 uprising. Unrest among
these units was reported as early as November 1820. The achievements
of the Lisbon regime also appealed to recent immigrants from Portugal,
many of whom were employed as clerks and servants in these three port
cities. As the weeks passed, public opinion in Brazil, first irritated and
then alienated by the lack of government response to the demands stated
in the Porto rising, visibly abandoned the status quo.[15]

Early in December 1820 the governor of Bahia had prevented an uprising by the Salvador garrison only by giving private assurances of prompt
reforms.[16] On February 10, 1821, the threatened revolt finally broke out,
triumphing in a few hours against minimal resistance. To replace the governor the military and city notables named ten individuals to form a committee responsible for governing the province. This *junta de govêrno*, as it
was known, at once informed Lisbon of its support for the constitution-

alist cause and requested the immediate dispatch of reinforcements from Portugal for the garrison.[17]

News of the rising, which reached Rio de Janeiro on February 17, forced Vilanova Portugal and finally the king to accept that they could no longer stand pat. On February 23 a decree was published promising the immediate departure of D. Pedro for Portugal, where he would remedy grievances and send back the completed constitution, which, if acceptable, the king would then sanction. A second decree, issued on the same day, convoked a consultative assembly to be elected by the municipal councils of Brazil and the Atlantic islands, which would both recommend immediate reforms and discuss the applicability to Brazilian conditions of the articles of the new constitution. To prepare the agenda for this new assembly a preparatory committee of eighteen members was appointed and ordered to start work immediately.[18]

Despite the ostensible acceptance of constitutional rule by the Crown, the real intent of the two decrees—the outcome of a last-minute maneuver by Vilanova Portugal to keep concessions to a minimum—was so evident and the Crown's insincerity so transparent as to precipitate the military revolt the decrees were meant to avert.[19] Calling a separate consultative assembly for Brazil violated the legislative unity of the Portuguese nation. Appointing the preparatory commission, which was composed mainly of Brazilian-born, suggested that the Crown saw the new assembly only as a means of perpetuating the breach that split the Portuguese world.

At dawn on February 26, 1821, the three Portuguese army units in the Rio de Janeiro garrison mobilized in favor of the Porto revolution. In the tumultuous events that followed, a central role was played by D. Pedro, the heir to the throne. The rising was welcomed and indeed had probably been fostered by the prince, then 22 years of age. In the opinion of the British envoy, "the principal agent is no less a Person than the second in this country, I mean the Prince Royal acting under the Impulsion of others."[20] It was certainly D. Pedro who placated the rebellious troops. He induced the king both to sign a decree accepting without restriction the constitution to be written by the Cortes and to replace all his ministers and senior administrators with men drawn from a list provided by the military. In his father's name, the prince signed a formal oath to obey the forthcoming constitution. By noon, the crisis was over and the troops returned to their barracks. The city then gave itself over to several days' festivities.

On the surface the rising of February 26 changed little in the structure of authority. After initial hesitation, D. João VI accepted his new ministers, none of them strangers to him, and dispatched business with them. All five of the king's former advisers who had been arrested on February 26 were released after some days. On March 13 a decree was published announcing the king's decision to return to Lisbon, leaving D. Pedro to serve as regent in Rio until the constitution was enacted. The decree also ordered the election of deputies to the Cortes by the Brazilian provinces.[21] However, given the king's exceptional ability to procrastinate, there was no certainty that he would ever embark. Almost a month later, on April 3, the British envoy advised his government that "the Fact itself [of embarkation] is entirely problematical."[22]

These weeks of apparent calm and normality in Rio de Janeiro were misleading. The rising on February 26 had in reality disrupted the customary channels of power. It had also, for the first time, legitimized open, participatory politics. Social groups previously marginal or excluded now entered the political arena. The minor bureaucrats, petty professionals, artisans, and other small folk sought both the adoption of the political ideas they favored and access to government largesse. The military, having proved its strength on February 26, had also acquired a taste for politics.[23] Meanwhile, the established factions at court and in the high bureaucracy had been neither deprived of influence nor deterred from their intrigues.

What made this clash of rival elements so perilous was that no one was experienced in the new form of politics, at a moment when the stakes were alarmingly high. Whatever was decided—the king's departure or continuance, the appointment of D. Pedro as regent, or the creation of a governing junta—would decisively affect the political fortunes, careers, and individual prosperity of people across the social scale. Different groups favored identical outcomes for quite incompatible reasons.[24] One point is certain: the conflicts were not nationalist, for they were not based on place of birth. A common feeling—of fear for some and hope for others—that the achievements of February 26 might somehow be reversed contributed to the general state of insecurity.

In this atmosphere of anxiety and intrigue, conspiracies pullulated and finally burst into the open as the abortive coup of April 21–22. Plotting clearly occurred at two levels, among the factions surrounding the Crown and among the politicized free population. Petitions against the king's departure have "long been circulating in this Town," the British envoy reported late in March, "but they are not supported by Names of great authority among the Brazilians and the Portuguese, and are, it is said, confined to the inferior class of Artisans and Tradesmen." After D. João VI had rejected these petitions at the start of April, his departure could be prevented only by direct coercion.[25]

The scope and motives of the coup attempted on the night of April 21 were obscure at the time and remain difficult to ascertain.[26] It would appear that a faction at court made common cause with popular elements, each seeking to use the other for its own ends. Both desired to retain the king in Rio, the first to establish its own supremacy and the other to set up a more democratic polity, which they could dominate. The occasion for the conspiracy was the meeting of the parish electors of Rio de Janeiro province, who assembled at the Merchants' Exchange for the choice of the Cortes deputies.[27] The immediate cause was the Crown's decision to consult the electors on the proposed powers of the future regency and on the ministers selected for D. Pedro.

Shortly after the meeting convened in the late afternoon, the spectators admitted to the hall seized control of the proceedings. In the midst of fierce debate, two motions were successively passed. The first demanded that the king order the Spanish constitution be put in force until the arrival of the Cortes's constitution. The demand was taken by a deputation to D. João VI for his immediate approval. The second ordered the harbor forts to allow no ships to sail. On learning that, even though it was by then the middle of the night, the king had met the deputation and signed a decree declaring the Spanish constitution in force, the meeting passed a third and final resolution presenting a list of new ministers and naming an elected *junta de govêrno*. Taken together, these resolutions constituted an overt although clumsy bid for power.

The response was swift and brutal, for the conspirators had failed to secure the goodwill of the military. Someone at court—and most witnesses agreed that it was D. Pedro—ordered the garrison units called to arms and marched into the city. At first light on April 22, the troops cleared the Merchants' Exchange, leaving at least one dead and several wounded.[28] The conspiracy was thus snuffed out, at the cost of much bitterness, but for the present, resolving the situation. The decree establishing the Spanish constitution was instantly revoked, and D. Pedro was named regent of Brazil with full powers. Three days later the king, his family, and court circle boarded ship; on the morning of April 26, 1821, they set sail for Lisbon. D. João VI left behind him two legacies. The first was his appointment of his heir as prince regent of the Kingdom of Brazil. The second was his private instructions, best conveyed in D. Pedro's own words: "I still remember and I will always remember what Your Majesty said to me, two days before leaving, in your room—'Pedro, if Brazil breaks away, let it rather do so for you who will respect me than for one of those adventurers.'"[29]

II

So the king departed from Rio de Janeiro. From the end of April 1821, the Portuguese world contained four principal political actors: the Lisbon regime (or the Cortes regime, as it can also be termed); the king himself; the prince regent in Rio de Janeiro (or the Rio regime); and the autonomous governments, or *juntas de govêrno*, which increasingly assumed control of the Brazilian provinces outside of Rio. It is important to understand the interplay between these different elements in the subsequent months of 1821.

The Cortes at Lisbon had been elected to "renew" the nation, and understandably it gave its attention to remedying the most urgent ills and to drafting a constitution. Although the Spanish constitution, provisionally adopted in November 1820, included in the legislature deputies from the overseas possessions, the instructions issued for the Cortes elections did not mention those provinces. For this omission the Lisbon regime has been much blamed, both at the time and in retrospect, but given the circumstances, it was politic not to claim jurisdiction over areas which the new regime did not control. The Cortes was, from the start, conscious that it did not contain representatives from Brazil. Among the 36 articles adopted by the Cortes on March 9, 1821, establishing the principles, or "Bases," which the constitution was to embody, was one declaring that until the overseas provinces "through their legitimate representatives declare it to be their will," the constitution would not apply to them.[30]

Apart from this declaration, during its first seven months of existence the Cortes showed little or no interest in Brazil, either favorable or hostile.[31] The deputies' time and energies were given to other matters seen by them as of more urgency and merit.[32] The course of events in the different parts of Brazil did nothing to dissuade the deputies from this course. On March 27, 1821, the Cortes learned that the province of Pará had rallied to the new order, and on April 16 that Bahia had done the same. In communicating their creation to the Cortes, the new governing juntas were lavish in praising the constitutional order and in promising loyalty to Lisbon. A policy of benign passivity appeared, in sum, to be securing the support of the provinces of Brazil. Events in Rio de Janeiro from February 26 to April 26 did no more than confirm the wisdom of the Cortes's approach to Brazil. On July 13, 1821, shortly after the arrival of the king in Lisbon, the Cortes issued a proclamation to the inhabitants of Brazil, praising them for completing "the magnificent edifice of liberty and national independence," and outlining the benefits of the new constitution. "Brazilians!" the proclamation ended, "Our destinies are linked: your brothers will not deem themselves to be free unless you are as well."[33]

The actions of the Lisbon Cortes are certainly not easy to analyze without prejudice or hindsight, but the weight of evidence does not support the frequently voiced contention that the deputies were from the moment the Cortes convened in January 1821 determined to reduce Brazil to its former status of a colony.[34] At the worst, the deputies can be accused of setting the wrong priorities, of being blind to the realities of the situation, and so of taking for granted the unity of the Portuguese world. The Cortes's attitude toward Brazil was certainly motivated in part by an understandable determination to secure for Portugal the priority in attention and advantage it had been denied since 1808. The speed and spontaneity with which the New World provinces repudiated the royal government in Rio de Janeiro and rallied to the Lisbon regime reinforced the existing almost instinctive feeling among the deputies that the Kingdom of Brazil, an innovation not yet six years old, was valued highly only in Rio de Janeiro itself.

It is important to emphasize that only by omission did the Cortes intervene in the affairs of Brazil in the middle months of 1821.[35] The problems

facing the government at Rio under D. Pedro during this period were generated not by any action of the Cortes but by developments indigenous
to Brazil. Although D. João VI had delegated the plenitude of his regal
powers in the Kingdom of Brazil to D. Pedro as regent, the authority of
the prince regent was from the start far from effective or secure either in
the Brazilian provinces or in Rio. Since the king had taken with him to
Lisbon all the ready money and treasure he could secure, the prince regent started with an empty treasury. This lack of funds intensified as the
governing juntas of the provinces ceased to remit their monthly tax payments to Rio de Janeiro. The prince regent did not, therefore, possess the
financial means to bring the provinces into obedience.

Nor did D. Pedro command the political resources to do so. His reputation had been tarnished by his alleged complicity in the "massacre" of
April 22, and by character and training he was ill equipped for the task
of establishing his authority. Only four months before, the British envoy
had written that "he *is* young, utterly non-instructed and inexperienced
in Business, impetuous and warm in his Character, seeking ardently for
Employment more from Curiousity than Knowledge and occupying the
Vacancy, to which he is condemned, in the most violent and boisterous
Amusements."[36] The ministers, chosen for the prince regent by the king,
did not compensate by their own talents and standing for D. Pedro's defects. Any hopes for autonomy and effective rule that the new government
may have cherished were crushed at the start of June by a new rising of
the Portuguese army units forming the Rio garrison.

The causes for this rising were diverse and its outcome crucial in shaping events in Rio de Janeiro during the remainder of 1821.[37] In essence the
rising of June 5 completed that of February 26. By forcing D. Pedro to
dismiss the ministers his father had nominated, the troops removed the
last vestige (beyond the prince himself) of the old political order and made
certain the docility of the Rio government. By insisting that an oath be
taken by all accepting the Bases of the constitution issued by the Cortes
on March 9, the troops secured an unequivocal recognition of the Lisbon
Cortes as the supreme, omnipotent embodiment of the nation, to whom
total obedience and loyalty were due. Finally, by forcing the election of a
nine-man junta to supervise the activities of the prince regent's ministers,
the troops asserted that despite D. Pedro's presence Rio de Janeiro was a
province in no way superior to the others in Brazil.[38]

During the rising the prince regent displayed an admirable coolness and
resource, bargaining down the more extreme demands and by his personal
bearing imposing respect and obedience. D. Pedro's handling of the crisis
restored the public esteem he had lost over his role in the events of April
22. The prince regent thus established himself as the dominant figure in
the Rio regime, which had, however, lost all power of independent action.
Its survival now depended, as D. Pedro appreciated, on the goodwill of
the Portuguese army units. Realizing that both officers and men were sus-

ceptible to his influence, the prince regent at once set about charming
the units into loyalty, in which he succeeded. This sedulous cultivation of
popularity necessitated, however, a constant display of effusive obedience
to the Cortes.[39]

While the Rio regime was thus reduced to impotence, quite the opposite
was occurring in the other provinces. Upon receiving news of the constitutionalist coup at Salvador, the Cortes recognized on April 16, 1821, the
governing junta elected for Bahia and authorized the formation of such
juntas in all other provinces rallying to its cause. The Cortes also ordered
the election of deputies by the Brazilian provinces.[40] By the end of 1821
juntas de govêrno had been installed, by force or consent, in three-quarters
of the provinces.[41]

The new juntas, drawn from the local notables, enjoyed from the start
an untrammeled autonomy in internal affairs. Self-government and the
participatory politics introduced by the province-wide elections of Cortes
deputies intensified the existing identification with the local *pátrias*. Without repudiating their allegiance to king and Cortes, the notables were
confident that the *pátrias* could manage their own affairs exempt from
external direction. The new situation preserved to the provinces all the
benefits gained since 1808, particularly direct trade and contact with the
Atlantic world, and restored the local influence on administrative and fiscal affairs largely lost since that date. If the local notables can be said to
have shared a common ambition, it was to perpetuate this new independence for the *pátrias*.

Autonomy in the provinces was compatible neither with a powerful
central government in Rio de Janeiro nor the continued existence of the
Kingdom of Brazil created in 1815. Few of the juntas went as far as that
of Bahia, which in June 1821 formally repudiated the prince regent's authority.[42] However, in the far north geography had always linked Pará and
Maranhão to Lisbon and not at all to Rio de Janeiro. The most distant
and isolated provinces—Goiás, Mato Grosso, and Piauí—were in effect
marginal to the course of events. In the remaining provinces, the juntas
did not renounce loyalty to the prince regent but ceased to give his government active support. Even in São Paulo, which directly bordered on
Rio de Janeiro, the newly elected junta, as D. Pedro reported to his father
in July, promised him obedience "except in respect to sending money."[43]

Greatly as autonomy might suit the provinces, their new status would
necessarily deprive Rio de Janeiro city of the dominant position in government and commerce it had held since 1808. The city was now threatened
with the prospect of being little more than the capital of an important
province in the Portuguese nation. As July turned to August the realities
of its new existence began to press in on the city. The revenues of the
prince regent's government, by now limited to the taxes of the city and
province, were further cut by a fall in the customhouse returns. The departure of the court for Lisbon and the general political crisis depressed trade

and blighted business confidence. The British merchant houses, fearing the worst, began to remit capital home.[44] In July D. Pedro complained to his father that "instead of being regent, I am merely captain general, because I am only governing the province [of Rio de Janeiro], a position that any junta can hold." While the prince regent maintained an air of confidence in public, the accumulating difficulties of government made him wish to be anywhere but in Rio de Janeiro. By September he was imploring his father: "I beg Your Majesty by all that is sacred to be pleased to relieve me of this post which will surely kill me with the unending and horrible prospects, some now upon me and others, much worse, imminent and ever before my eyes."[45]

Because D. Pedro was, first and foremost, heir to the Portuguese throne, he could contemplate with equanimity the prospect of his return to Lisbon. The abolition of the regency government would, however, irredeemably mar the lives and careers of those tied to the capital of Brazil. Two groups were especially threatened by the likely departure of the prince. For the senior judges, bureaucrats, and other officials (such as the clergy of the Chapel Royal) who staffed the institutions of government created since 1808, the end of D. Pedro's regency would mean at best atrophy of their careers and at worst unemployment. An even bleaker future faced the second group—writers, artists, educators, and petty professionals who had since 1808 flourished on the edges of court life and benefited in different ways from government patronage. The prince's departure would not only put in jeopardy the positions they held but deprive them of their very livelihood. Without the presence of a court and central government, Rio de Janeiro would revert to being a provincial capital incapable of sustaining a large intellectual community.

Between these two groups, which together constituted the governing cadres of the kingdom created in 1815, a considerable overlap in membership and interests existed. Nonetheless, the two did differ markedly in their social background and their outlook. The dominant element in the first group were graduates from Coimbra, most born in Brazil but a sizable minority natives of Portugal. Attendance at Coimbra and subsequent service to the Crown had forged a privileged group, accustomed to rule and possessing great cohesion. In temperament they were generally cautious and conservative, their customary reaction to innovation being to thwart it by inaction. Imbued at Coimbra with Enlightenment ideas, they were familiar with liberal doctrines but rarely enthusiastic for them. Prime loyalty and obedience went to the monarch and to the empire he ruled, no matter where he resided within it. In view of their training and outlook, these men can best be termed "Luso-Brazilians."

The political structure that the Luso-Brazilians envisaged for the Portuguese nation was admirably expressed in the *Lembranças e Apontamentos* (Reminders and Suggestions) issued on October 6, 1821, by the governing junta of São Paulo. Written by an eminent Luso-Brazilian, José Bonifácio de Andrada e Silva, the document was drawn up for the guidance of the province's deputies newly elected to the Cortes.[46] It contained three chapters dealing respectively with the affairs of the United Kingdom, the Kingdom of Brazil, and the province itself.

In respect to the United Kingdom, the *Lembranças e Apontamentos* advocated the "integrity and indivisibility" of the Portuguese dominions, with "equality of political and civil rights" between them. It proposed that the king alternate his residence between the two kingdoms, each of which was to possess its own treasury, with a third treasury (to be funded by the first two) for the payment of common expenditures. In the future, regardless of population, the Cortes should be composed of an equal number of deputies from Portugal and from the overseas territories. Brazil was to possess its own executive, "to which central government the provincial governments should be subordinated," and when the monarch was not resident in the New World it would be headed by the heir to the throne.[47] In essence, the *Lembranças e Apontamentos* envisaged a renovation of the political settlement created in 1815: a confederation of the two kingdoms, with Brazil enjoying a status resembling the dominion status granted by Great Britain to Canada in 1867.

In contrast to the Luso-Brazilians, the members of the second group were far more nonconformist in political outlook. Almost all born and raised in Brazil, they possessed no personal acquaintance with the outside world, which they knew through the printed word. The lack of a university in Brazil had denied them an advanced education, and since ordination as a cleric provided the best substitute for such schooling, priests figured prominently in this group. Its members did not, as a rule, owe their success to privileged birth and family connections but had instead risen in life because of industry, ability, and mastery of the official culture. Accordingly, they were by temperament activist, adventurous, and responsive to new ideas. In their search for education, the group had acquired a deep familiarity with the ideology of the American and French revolutions. Their first loyalty was to the land of their birth, and the doctrines of nationalism offered them a sense of identity and worth.

This second group expressed its political views mainly through the columns of the periodicals newly established in Rio de Janeiro. Liberty of the press, decreed by article 8 of the Bases of the constitution, was on August 28, 1821, declared by a circular of the prince regent operative in Brazil. Three weeks later there appeared in Rio the first uncensored journal of opinion, the *Revérbero Constitucional Fluminense*. Its joint editors exemplified the second group, Joaquim Gonçalves Ledo being an official in the Military Arsenal and Padre Januário da Cunha Barbosa both a "preacher to the King" and a "royal instructor" in philosophy for the city.[48]

An article in the first issue of this periodical stated a political belief generally held by members of this group: "Let America belong to America and Europe to Europe and all will be well. . . . This European system to which they want to tie Brazil against the law of nature will always involve it in their habitual wars."[49] Brazil's future lay, in other words, with the emerging nations of the New World, and the existing link with Portugal was doomed to extinction. Political authority must derive from the people and should ideally be republican in form. Save on one essential point, these views much resembled those held by the rebels of 1817. However, whereas the 1817 rising had sought political independence for the local *pátrias*, the members of the second group equated the *pátria* with Brazil itself, or more precisely, with the kingdom created in 1815. Granted that a republic was the ultimate goal, its immediate introduction would, it was feared, splinter Brazil into several states. The continued existence of a single polity ruled from Rio de Janeiro was best assured by maintaining the monarchy. If self-interest thus made the members of the second group monarchists, they believed that the ruler's authority should derive from the people and that he should be subordinate to their elected representatives. Judged by the political standards of the time, the members of the second group were "Radicals" and will be so termed.

Neither Luso-Brazilians nor Radicals could stomach the political developments following the departure of the king from Rio de Janeiro. Identified as the two groups were with the kingdom created in 1815, they could not accept that the ending of absolutist rule might, as a natural and spontaneous consequence, result in the provinces' assumption of autonomy and thereby the Rio regime's decline into impotence. The disintegration of the Kingdom of Brazil must, in their view, spring from hostile machinations. It was not necessary to look far for the villains of the piece. The rising of February 26, 1821, had secured wide support in Rio de Janeiro, regardless of place of birth, but the main backers of the coup had certainly been the Portuguese army units and the recent immigrants from Portugal working as clerks and servants. The British envoy had been quick to report that this successful rising was viewed by the Portuguese-born as a victory over the previously dominant Brazilian-born.[50] If the evidence presented in support of this observation appears far from convincing, it is nonetheless clear that by the middle of 1821 overt distrust was growing between the Portuguese- and Brazilian-born.[51]

The critical moment was probably the Rio rising of June 5, during which the three Portuguese army units failed to receive, as they had in February, support from the Brazilian troops stationed in Rio. The popular backing so evident in the events of February was markedly lacking for the June coup. The demeaning if necessary subservience shown thereafter by the prince regent to the Portuguese troops was widely resented. Once established, open mistrust between the Portuguese- and Brazilian-born tended to intensify and feed on itself. Antagonism made the former heedless of the latter's anxieties and more insufferable in their assumption of superiority, while the latter, susceptible and aggrieved, took offense at anything resembling a slight to their New World origins.[52]

The retroactive approval given by the Cortes to the February risings at Salvador and Rio de Janeiro and to the June coup and its decree authorizing the provinces to form their own juntas made it easy, and perhaps inevitable, that the distrust felt at Rio toward the Portuguese-born should be extended to the Lisbon regime. The Luso-Brazilians disliked a government founded upon popular sovereignty, whereas for the Radicals the absence of Brazilian deputies deprived the Cortes of any right to legislate on matters affecting the New World. The trend of public opinion was evident at a ball held on August 24 to celebrate the first anniversary of the Porto rising. When cheers were offered to the king, the Pátria, and the constitution, the first two were frenetically applauded but the last received in virtual silence.[53]

Given the differences in temperament and outlook between the Luso-Brazilians and the Radicals, it was almost inevitable that the latter would be first to express their discontent in organized form. The abolition of pre-publication censorship made possible the emergence of a periodical press. Of almost equal significance was the ending of the proscription of the Masonic Order, the decree of March 1818 against secret societies being no longer enforced. In June 1821 a lodge was founded—revived might be a better word—in the city and served as a secure forum for the frank expression of views by its members, predominantly Radicals.[54] Freemasonry and the press together provided the vehicle for the formation of the first openly political movement in Brazil.

The initial activities of this new movement proved, not surprisingly, halting and ill directed. By the end of September 1821, placards were being posted in the streets calling on D. Pedro to declare himself monarch of an independent Brazil. A shadowy and abortive conspiracy did try to foster a coup to that end, to be carried out on October 12, the prince's twenty-third birthday. "It seems certain," the Austrian agent reported, "that there was a plot desiring in effect the independence of Brazil by declaring the Prince Regent Emperor."[55] The conspirators made the fundamental mistake of failing to ascertain D. Pedro's attitude to such a coup, much less to secure his acquiescence. The prince regent's reaction was explosive. "Independence was sought under the cover of myself and the troops; they have not succeeded and will not succeed with either, because my honor and that of the troops is greater than all of Brazil."[56] Virulent in his denunciations, D. Pedro was also implacable in hunting down and arresting the plotters. For the Radicals the whole episode demonstrated that their goals must be pursued with greater caution, realism, and preparation.

The Luso-Brazilians did not directly participate in these plottings. Neither by outlook nor training were they easily aroused to action. They secured their goals by more circumspect means, as demonstrated by the fate of the supervisory junta elected on June 5 at the insistence of the military. The Luso-Brazilians elected to the junta sabotaged its work so effectively that by the end of August the Austrian agent commented that "the junta is as inefficacious as if it did not exist."[57] They similarly used procrastination in the courts to shield those arrested for their part in the October conspiracy. Contact between the two groups was discreetly arranged through common participation in a committee for the founding at Rio of an academy of letters—a project which itself asserted the city's claims to primacy.[58]

As the year 1821 approached its end, public opinion in Rio de Janeiro was thoroughly aroused, with rising anger against the fragmentation of Brazil and the inefficacy of the Rio regime. A dispatch written by the French consul in mid-November caught the prevailing mood, at once anxious and defiant: "The inhabitants of this capital state everywhere and at every opportunity that if the seat of government and the national congress are not established in Brazil, separation from Portugal will follow, since Portugal is nothing more than a paltry province of the Lusitanian Empire."[59]

III

The six to eight weeks' delay in receiving news from across the Atlantic meant that the deputies in the Lisbon Cortes were unaware of the mood of intransigence that was developing in Rio de Janeiro after the middle of 1821. What the news from across the ocean did make clear to the Cortes was that even though no Brazilian deputies had yet taken their seats, benevolent passivity would no longer suffice. Pressing demands for action were coming from Brazil on two issues: the future of the Portuguese army units stationed in the New World, and the form of government of the overseas provinces.[60]

The troops, some of whom had served for six years in a tropical climate, were clamoring to be posted home. The choices before the deputies were to withdraw the garrisons entirely, to relieve them with fresh units, or to offer them benefits if they would agree to remain in the New World. The first did not appear a practical course, since the governing junta of Bahia had requested in March and again in May the sending of fresh troops for the defense of the province, on both occasions in response to news of unrest at Rio de Janeiro.[61] Given their fear of a counterrevolution and their belief in the unity of the Portuguese nation, the deputies were not likely to adopt the first course. The dispatch of reinforcements to Bahia was easily agreed upon.[62] At the end of July, a motion that 2,000 fresh troops should be sent to relieve the garrison at Rio was approved without debate. When the proposal came up for final approval at the end of August, the relevant committee recommended that instead of replacing the garrison, the units at Rio be offered inducements to re-enlist for further service there. After a fierce debate the deputies finally accepted by a margin of three votes (40 to 37) a compromise by which 1,200 rather than 2,000 troops would be sent out.[63]

Also at the end of August, a bill was presented to the Cortes establishing the form of government in the overseas provinces in the interim until the constitution could be enacted. At the moment when the project came up for debate, the first Brazilian representatives, the deputies from Pernambuco, took their seats. Under the bill each province would be ruled by a *junta provisória de govêrno* (interim governing junta), made up of seven elected members in the larger and five in the smaller provinces. In eleven major provinces the troops would be commanded by a military officer—the governor of arms—named by and responsible to Lisbon.[64]

The project was debated in detail during September. At no time did the deputies from Pernambuco express opposition to its general principles, which at the start of September were enacted as a special law applying only to their province, then in a state of virtual civil war. The sole concern voiced by the Pernambuco deputies was their objection to any further payment of taxes to Rio de Janeiro. In failing to express any anxiety about the bill's effects on the unity of Brazil, the Pernambucans were behaving consistently with their past beliefs, since most were veterans of the 1817 revolt. The bill's provisions corresponded to a significant degree with the goals of that movement. The only part of the law to arouse any controversy was the proposed governor of arms, against which post two Pernambucan deputies spoke, as did one of the newly arrived deputies from Rio de Janeiro province.[65] For the vast majority of the deputies, still overwhelmingly from Portugal, the lack of opposition by the Brazilian representatives to the new law simply confirmed their belief that it met Brazilian desires in matters of governance. This assumption was shared by others: the British chargé in Lisbon characterized the law as containing "very liberal and conciliatory regulations."[66] Given this mood, it is not surprising that protests made by two of the newly seated deputies from Rio de Janeiro against the sending of fresh troops there failed to arouse any concern.[67] On September 29 the bill was passed into law.

On the same day, a second bill was enacted complementing the action of the first. With the new *juntas provisórias de govêrno* to be installed in the overseas provinces, the prince regent's government became—or so it seemed to the deputies—an unnecessary duplication, a costly superfluity. The regency of D. Pedro at Rio had been, in any case, neither created nor authorized by the Cortes itself. The deputies, increasingly vigilant in defense of the Cortes's prerogatives and jealous of any competition, felt that the prince might become the tool of reactionary influences. These perceptions had been reinforced by a dispatch from the Bahia *junta de govêrno* read to the Cortes on August 7. "It was a monstrous anomaly in Politics to create in one Empire two centers of government," the junta asserted, perceiving behind the Rio regency "an ill-concealed desire of scattering the seeds of discord and of producing divisions between the Portuguese of both hemispheres."[68] The terms of the decree voted were simple: "The heir apparent shall return immediately to Portugal."[69] To ensure compliance the Cortes instructed the king to write to D. Pedro ordering him in the name of filial obedience to leave Rio. In fact, such concerns were hardly necessary, since the Prince was writing at that very time to implore his father to order him back to Lisbon and promising obedience to the orders of the Cortes.[70]

At the same time that these two decrees were enacted, a bill was introduced abolishing all the superior courts and administrative bodies created in Rio de Janeiro since 1808. Here again the rationality of the measure according to liberal doctrine was indisputable. Once the prince regent left Rio de Janeiro, no further justification existed for the city issuing orders to the other provinces of the Kingdom of Brazil. "There is nothing more just," a deputy from Bahia later informed the Cortes, "than . . . leveling the former Court, in Rio, down to equality with the other provinces. Let it descend from the high standing of Court to that of province."[71] A deputy from Rio de Janeiro objected to the bill being discussed before the majority of the deputies from Brazil had arrived, and the Cortes immediately agreed to postponement of the measure. The proceedings of the Cortes were patently not motivated by animosity toward Brazil.[72]

The text of the two laws creating the provisional juntas and recalling the prince regent, and that of the bill to abolish the organs of central government at Rio de Janeiro, reached that city on December 9, 1821.[73] The effect of these measures on public opinion is best expressed in the prince regent's own words:

The publication of the decree has caused a very great shock to *brasileiros* and to many *europeus* domiciled here, to the point of their remarking in the streets: "If the constitution is going to cause us harm, the devil take it; we must make a representation in favor of the Prince not leaving, to avoid his being responsible for the separation of Brazil from Portugal, and we will assume responsibility for his not complying with the two decrees just published."[74]

The Cortes's decrees provided the ideal issue on which to organize open resistance. Virtually all shades of opinion could unite in opposing, for very different reasons, the prince regent's departure from Rio de Janeiro. The first group to spring into action were the Radicals, for whom the decrees signified the negation of Brazilian nationhood and the return of colonial subordination. Working through the Masonic movement and an action committee (appropriately named the "resistance club"), the Radicals sought to bring the weight of public opinion to bear on D. Pedro, by obtaining a massive number of signatures on a formal petition to the city council begging it to intercede with the prince regent.[75]

By itself, this campaign would probably have achieved as little as did the petitions circulated in March requesting D. João VI to remain in Rio. The crucial difference was the powerful backing now given to the scheme by the Luso-Brazilians. The change was in part a question of self-interest. The bill to abolish the high courts and administrative bodies would, the Austrian agent reported, "throw into misery and despair eight hundred families."[76] Much more than self-preservation, however, motivated the change. Already alarmed by the Cortes's wholesale attack on the traditional order in the Portuguese world, the Luso-Brazilians were distressed by the Cortes's cavalier treatment of the king and his established rights, not to mention the almost open disdain expressed for the prince regent.[77] In an age when deference to the monarch was axiomatic in public affairs and loyalty to the sovereign was an important bond of union, the Cortes's presumption in instructing the king to order his son home shocked and alienated public opinion on both sides of the Atlantic.

To the Luso-Brazilians, the traditional order in the Portuguese world could survive only if the prince regent disobeyed the Cortes's decree and remained in Rio de Janeiro, where he could protect the largest and wealthiest part of the royal possessions from the depredations of the Cortes. Such a course was urged by Vilanova Portugal, the king's longtime adviser, in a letter written to a friend in Rio de Janeiro and widely circulated there.[78] Indicative of the Luso-Brazilians' change in behavior was the assistance given to the Radicals' campaign by the *juiz de fora* who presided over the Rio city council. It was this judge, José Clemente Pereira, who on December 15 suggested the urgent need to obtain supporting petitions from São Paulo and Minas Gerais and to sound out D. Pedro about his intentions.[79] The prince regent's immediate response had been to comply, but as the letter quoted above shows, the ferocity of the public reaction impressed him. Even more effective was persuasion in private by José Clemente and other Luso-Brazilians, who argued that since only the prince regent's continued presence in Rio could prevent Brazilian independence, disobedience to the decree would serve the best interest of the Portuguese Crown and nation. Equally effective were the tears of D. Pedro's spouse, then six months pregnant, who pleaded against departure.[80]

In the meantime, the Radicals pushed ahead with their campaign. The public petition to the *câmara muncipal* eventually gained some 8,000 signatures.[81] José Clemente organized the city council for action. Emissaries were sent by the Radicals to both Minas Gerais and São Paulo. In the latter province the reaction to the recall of the prince regent was all that could be desired—a formal protest against his departure signed on December 24 by the members of the governing junta, a copy of which reached the Prince on the first day of 1822. Denouncing the Cortes as "a small group of incompetents," the protest warned D. Pedro that by returning to Portugal he would have "to answer to heaven for the river of blood which will flow in Brazil because of your departure."[82]

The letters written by the prince to his father during these crucial days show him slowly yielding to these public and private pressures. Whatever his personal preference, D. Pedro decided to compromise: offering formal compliance to the recall but suspending his departure so that the Cortes could reconsider its decision in view of conditions in Rio de Janeiro.[83] At midday on January 9, 1822, the *câmara municipal*, led by José Clemente

Pereira, came in procession to the city palace, where they presented a formal petition requesting the prince regent not to depart. D. Pedro gave a brief but definitive reply: "Since it is for the good of all and the general happiness of the Nation, I am willing. Tell the people that I am staying."[84]

IV

There are some acts which, however moderate in intent they may be, take on through surrounding circumstances and immediate consequences an extremist tone. So it was with the prince regent's declaration of January 9. "It is my intention," he had told the French consul some days before, "to accede to the request, as long as it is worded with respect and on the condition that responsibility for the delay falls on the signers of the petition." Responsibility was not, however, so lightly shifted onto other shoulders. Circumspection and avoidance of the limelight were never to characterize D. Pedro's actions. His response to the city council was far more peremptory and decisive than he had intended.[85] When read in conjunction with the strongly worded protest from the governing junta of São Paulo, published in the Rio press on January 8, the prince regent's reply took on the appearance of a direct challenge to the authority of the Cortes.

It was certainly perceived as a challenge by the commanders of the Portuguese army troops. On the evening of January 11, while the prince was at the theater, soldiers from the Portuguese units began smashing windows illuminated in celebration of the prince's recent decision. A military rising similar to those of February 26 and June 5, 1821, was evidently imminent. It was a challenge that D. Pedro had to meet if he were not to suffer the humiliation of being hustled on board a ship bound for Lisbon, and it was just the type of crisis that brought out his best qualities.

The confrontation lasted for a tense 24 hours. In response to the mobilization of the garrison, the units of Brazilian troops and the local militia regiments, aided by a mass of hastily armed civilians, rallied to the prince regent's cause.[86] D. Pedro succeeded first in convincing one of the three Portuguese units to stay neutral. He then met with the commanding officers of the garrison and by the force of his personality and inherent authority so intimidated them with accusations of disloyalty, disobedience, and ingratitude as to leave them cowed and irresolute. Faced for the first time with a resolute resistance and aghast at the prospect of a bloody civil war in the streets of the city, the officers lost their nerve. In the dawn hours of January 12, they offered to withdraw their troops across Guanabara Bay to the east shore opposite the city—a withdrawal completed that day. The encampment of the Portuguese units was quickly isolated. Despite its peaceful outcome, the crisis had been a time of intense danger. The prince regent had not only sent his wife and children posthaste to a palace far outside the city but had arranged, as a last resort, his own refuge on a British frigate in Rio harbor.[87]

This double event—the decision to stay at Rio and the ousting of the Portuguese troops from the city—was of critical significance. It sharply altered the relationship between the four elements in the Portuguese world. For the first time since February 1821, the Rio regime stood free of military coercion, able to pursue an independent policy. The Cortes ceased to hold the political initiative. No longer were all the members of the royal family under the control of the Lisbon regime. Moreover, once Lisbon and Rio de Janeiro came into open conflict, the Brazilian provinces would no longer be free to pursue a separate course.

The principal problem facing the Rio regime, now that it had secured its freedom of action, was noted by the secretary of the French mission: "It is unfortunate that, at so critical a moment, there is no one in evidence who could by his firm character and suitable knowledge take control of affairs."[88] The crisis had given the Radicals a functioning organization and considerable self-confidence, but they did not possess a leader of sufficient stature and ability to take command of events. In temperament and training the Luso-Brazilians were administrators not politicians. The prince regent lacked not only maturity but the qualities required for the unremitting direction of affairs.

The necessary man was at that moment on his way to Rio de Janeiro. José Bonifácio had been chosen by the governing junta of São Paulo, of which he was vice president, to make a formal presentation to the prince regent of its protest requesting D. Pedro not to leave Brazil. A native of São Paulo province and a graduate from Coimbra in 1790, José Bonifácio in his career epitomized the success possible for men born in the New World and trained at Coimbra. He had risen to be inspector of mines in Portugal and a professor at Coimbra. Not only was his career made in Portugal but he had married there, so that when the Crown withdrew to Rio de Janeiro in 1807 José Bonifácio and several other Luso-Brazilians stayed on in Portugal. The incompetence of the regency government after 1808 and its failure to grant him further advancement had so discontented José Bonifácio that he requested retirement, returning at the end of 1819 to his native province.[89]

An experienced administrator and a veteran in bureaucratic politics, José Bonifácio possessed the tenacity of purpose, energy, and unabashed self-confidence indispensable for the task awaiting him. "Everyone agrees in recognizing his ability," the French consul reported, "but equally acknowledges that he is rather strong tempered and intransigent."[90] The prince regent, at least, had no doubts. Dismissing all save one of his ministers, he named José Bonifácio to the portfolios of the interior (Reino) and of foreign affairs on January 16, the day before his arrival in the capital.

What the French consul foresaw on January 17 was soon justified: "There is no doubt, however, that Sr. Andrada will be the influential director of his colleagues and will hold ascendancy over the mind of the Prince."[91] The new minister came with his ideas clear and his goals defined. A confirmed monarchist and believer in government by the best men, among whom he naturally placed himself, José Bonifácio did not favor government by the people. In social questions he was no conservative, openly favoring such reforms as the early abolition of slavery, a measure that many liberals deemed a violation of property rights. José Bonifácio scorned the pretensions of the Lisbon Cortes, nor did he intend to be again caught, as he had been in Portugal after 1808, on the wrong side of the Atlantic from the seat of power. He envisaged Brazil existing as a self-governing kingdom within the larger Portuguese nation and as being ruled by a young prince guided by a wise and preeminent minister. In José Bonifácio individual interest and the public weal naturally and inextricably mixed.[92]

In the looming confrontation with the Cortes the prince regent and his first minister enjoyed certain advantages, both psychological and material. D. Pedro was the very reverse of a usurper. He had been named regent of Brazil with unrestricted power by the express act of his father. While D. João VI remained the servant of the Cortes, D. Pedro could claim to act as his surrogate in defending the inherent rights of the Crown both within the Portuguese nation and in international affairs. Since dynastic connections influenced the conduct of foreign affairs, D. Pedro's marriage to the emperor of Austria's daughter ensured that his claims to independent standing would at least receive a sympathetic hearing from the great powers. D. Pedro thus enjoyed an authority and a legitimacy that rallied conservative opinion to his cause and set him apart from such self-appointed liberators of Spanish America as José de San Martín and Simón Bolívar.

What strengthened the position of the prince regent and his first minister was the enthusiastic support they commanded in Rio de Janeiro. Public opposition to the hated decrees and the Cortes which promulgated them had been expressed in and crystallized by an anonymous pamphlet published at the height of the crisis. The Cortes was embarked, so the pamphlet argued, on a systematic, unrelenting conspiracy to destroy the unity of Brazil, to submit its provinces once again to exploitation and subservience as colonies.[93] The news arriving from Lisbon served only to confirm fears of a Machiavellian plot. On December 9 the names of the eleven governors of arms, the commanding officers in the major Brazilian provinces created by the decree of September 29, 1821, had been published. Not one of the officers appointed was Brazilian-born. The bill to abolish the higher courts and administrative bodies in Rio since 1808 was taken up at the end of December and enacted on January 11, 1822.[94]

In the Cortes the question of commercial relations between Portugal and Brazil was referred in January to a special committee, which on March 15 submitted a report with a draft bill granting fiscal advantages to goods shipped from Brazil via Lisbon on Portuguese-owned vessels.[95] Given the attitudes prevailing in the Brazilian capital, any proposal that tampered with the commercial order created in 1808 was bound to alarm the merchant community of Rio de Janeiro, which by 1822 was the busiest and wealthiest port in the Portuguese world. Its customhouse provided the principal source of revenue in Brazil. Its commercial community, and especially the foreign merchants, cherished the freedom of trade decreed in 1808.

The prince regent's government could depend on the merchants to make loans and to procure it essential war supplies, from small arms to warships. In the approaching struggle, command of the sea would be the key to strategic success. Two corvettes and a frigate belonging to the Portuguese navy, anchored in Rio harbor, were secured for D. Pedro's cause. They were the start of an independent navy which the government labored hard to expand.[96]

The task facing the prince regent and his chief minister was to employ these political and economic advantages to outmaneuver the Cortes and to establish D. Pedro as the effective ruler of the Kingdom of Brazil, while still acknowledging the sovereignty of D. João VI. José Bonifácio's moves were shrewd. He planned to eliminate the threat of a military countercoup by forcing the Portuguese units, encamped on the far side of the bay, to embark at once for Portugal before the 1,200 troops sent by the Cortes could arrive to relieve them. He also sought by executive decree to end the Cortes's ability to control the internal affairs of the Kingdom of Brazil. Last, he proposed to give the provinces a voice in the Rio government and so a direct interest in the triumph of its cause, by setting up a council of advisers to the prince regent, the members of which were to be elected and recallable by the provinces.[97]

The first of these three initiatives was the most successful. The Portuguese units were finally compelled to embark, sailing on February 15, 1822, less than a month before the fleet bringing troops to relieve the Rio garrison arrived from Lisbon. Only those soldiers willing to enlist in the prince's forces were allowed to land. One of the warships convoying the troops was handed over to the prince's command and incorporated into his nascent navy. On March 23, the remnants of the expedition were sent ignominiously back to Portugal. The expulsion of the original garrison and the humiliation of the relieving expedition offered a defiance to the Cortes such that it could not ignore.[98]

José Bonifácio's second move was implemented by a decree issued on January 21 ordering that henceforth laws coming from Portugal should go into effect only after they had been seen by the prince regent and approved as applicable to conditions in Brazil.[99] The final initiative was launched by José Bonifácio on January 30, with a circular sent to all the governing juntas, exhorting them "to promote . . . the important union of all the provinces of Brazil with subordination to the regency of His Royal Highness." Two weeks later, a decree of the prince regent created a Council of Delegates (Conselho dos Procuradores) composed of two members from each province, chosen and recallable at will by each, which was empowered to offer advice to the prince regent on all matters of importance.[100]

The prince regent's cause was not, it soon became apparent, much advanced by these last two initiatives. Orders on paper could not prevent provincial authorities who so desired from implementing laws and decrees issued by the Cortes. The proposed Council of Delegates proved a complete fiasco, with none of the necessary elections taking place. The lack of success was due in part to the wording of the decree which inferred— or could be taken to infer—that the prince regent possessed the authority to settle the constitutional future of Brazil. Such a doctrine offended all those of liberal views.[101]

A more significant reason for the failure of the Council of Delegates was that in the provinces outside of Rio the prince regent still commanded far less active support than did the Cortes. The law of September 29 creating the new form of provincial government was generally obeyed; no less than thirteen of the seventeen provinces elected the new *juntas provisórias de govêrno* as the Cortes had decreed.[102] Not all these new juntas were necessarily hostile to D. Pedro. In Bahia, for example, none of the members of the original pro-Cortes junta secured election to the new *junta provisória*, which was quick to reopen relations with the prince.[103] The governing junta of the key province of Pernambuco maneuvered to avoid giving offense to either side. While lauding the prince regent's decision to stay in Rio, it refused to accept his decree creating a Council of Delegates. The governing juntas of Maranhão and Pará did not equivocate, informing the prince regent in May and June 1822 respectively that they obeyed orders from the Cortes alone.[104] At the end of January 1822, the prince regent commanded support outside of Rio de Janeiro itself from the provinces of São Paulo, Minas Gerais, Santa Catarina, and Rio Grande do Sul.[105] In the recently conquered Banda Oriental (modern Uruguay), the military governor, although Portuguese-born, feared that the Cortes would disallow its annexation to the Crown's dominions, which he had engineered in 1821, and so came out in favor of the Rio regime, which had no such scruples.[106]

The prince regent's cause suffered two serious setbacks in February 1822. The governing junta in Minas Gerais had sent its president to congratulate D. Pedro on his decision to stay in Rio. The president's absence tilted the balance of opinion in the junta, which now refused to recognize any external authority save that of the king.[107] In Bahia a military confrontation on February 19–20 ended in total defeat for the prince's supporters. When the new governor of arms named by Lisbon attempted to assume command of the troops at Salvador, the newly elected *junta provisória* attempted to exclude him in favor of a Brazilian-born officer. As the crisis escalated, the local regular troops and the city militia faced off against the Portuguese units in the garrison. In contrast to the outcome at Rio, the latter force did not flinch from bloodshed and civil war. In the ensuing conflict, fighting in the city got out of hand, with shops sacked and civilians killed. Although the Cortes thus gained complete control of the second city in Brazil, its victory was achieved at great cost, since the episode confirmed the image of the Lisbon regime as a tyranny bent on reducing Brazil to submission by any means and at any cost.[108]

José Bonifácio's personal dominance and his program for Brazilian self-government were seriously weakened by these two setbacks and the controversy surrounding the abortive Council of Delegates. Although the Radicals had applauded his appointment as minister, they had neither disbanded as a group nor renounced their political goals. The disdain for the doctrine of popular sovereignty apparent in the decree creating the Council of Delegates offended the Radicals, who were further alienated by José Bonifácio's high-handedness and use of his official position for the exclusive benefit of his kin and henchmen. The Radicals were emboldened by the February events in Salvador, which intensified public hatred of the Cortes and swung opinion behind the idea of total independence. Agents were dispatched to the northeastern provinces to arouse support for D. Pedro's cause and the "resistance club" soon became the "independence club." Although the prince regent had not lost confidence in his minister, D. Pedro's growing impatience with and antipathy toward the Cortes made him susceptible to other influences, and the Radicals now began to build up their contacts with the prince.[109]

It was at this time, on the opposite side of the Atlantic, that the Cortes first learned of the dangers it faced. The prince regent's letters describing the popular response at Rio to the September decrees were read to the Cortes in the second week of March. Appreciating the gravity of the situation, the Cortes at once named a special committee, composed equally of deputies from Portugal and Brazil, to take evidence and submit recommendations. The committee's report, presented on March 18, proposed that D. Pedro's recall be postponed until the promulgation of the constitution, that the governors of arms be placed under the juntas, and that a law regulating commercial relations between Portugal and Brazil be given priority. On the other hand, the report upheld both the Cortes's right to legislate for Brazil and the recent abolition of the courts and administrative bodies at Rio.[110]

Limited as these concessions were, they did constitute an indispensable first step if the Cortes were to pull back from disaster. Ideological obduracy and a sense of corporate dignity made it extremely difficult for the deputies to reverse their course of action. They regarded themselves as the sole legitimate embodiment of the indivisible Portuguese nation, and as much the representatives of Brazil as were the deputies elected by those provinces. The Cortes had, moreover, ruled triumphant and undisputed for over a year; nothing had transpired to make the deputies question their own righteousness and infallibility. For the Cortes to accept that it must recognize the legitimacy of another entity and share power with it would require the exercise of exceptional tact and unusual powers of persuasion.

It is doubtful whether, under these circumstances, the dispute with the

Rio regime could have been successfully resolved, but the Cortes now received a copy of the protest signed on December 24, 1822, by the São Paulo governing junta. The vituperative language of the protest and the open contempt it showed for the Cortes cut to the quick and could not be forgiven. The best that the special committee, to which the protest was referred, could do was to avoid any mention of the document in its report. This omission was hotly denounced in the debates held on March 22 and 23, and the committee members were obliged to promise that as soon as further information on the protest was received they would incorporate a recommendation on it into the report. This promise was approved, but with the result that no immediate action was taken on the report itself.[111]

What compounded resentment over the São Paulo protest was the presence in the Cortes—as a deputy from that province—of Antônio Carlos de Andrada Machado e Silva, younger brother of José Bonifácio. Not only did Antônio Carlos display to excess his brother's least amiable traits, being vain, domineering, and sharp-tongued, but he was a figure of suspect political loyalty. He had just spent three years in prison for his part in the separatist rising of 1817 in northeast Brazil. Since Antônio Carlos took the lead in proclaiming Brazil's rights and in demanding redress of grievances, debates on the subject became hopelessly personalized. On both sides deputies were free with personal abuse and yet, when opponents responded in kind, resented the insults as affronts to their honor and pride.[112]

On April 15 the Cortes received dispatches from the commander of the troops stationed at Rio, describing their expulsion from the city on January 11–12. A savage debate ensued, during which Antônio Carlos was interrupted by booing from the public galleries. In protest several Brazilian deputies announced their intention of boycotting the Cortes, and they were in fact absent for several sessions. On the day of the incident Antônio Carlos was summarily replaced, over his protests, as a member of the special committee on Brazilian affairs, on the grounds that he had brothers in the governments of both Rio de Janeiro and São Paulo. In such an atmosphere no rational discussion of Brazilian affairs could be expected, nor could either side be brought to concessions and compromise. The majority's behavior during the incident precisely conformed to Brazilian preconceptions—an assembly of haughty and intransigent men, bent on recolonization.[113]

While these events were occurring in Lisbon, and thus long before information about them could reach the Brazilian capital, the situation there was changing rapidly. Immediately after the relief expedition had been sent back to Lisbon on March 23, D. Pedro with a handful of attendants left Rio for Minas Gerais, intent on restoring his authority. His mere appearance in the province and his ability to mobilize support in the southern parts of Minas Gerais, always resentful of the prepotence of Ouro Prêto, the province's capital, enabled the prince regent to fulfill his mission in twelve days. On the evening of April 9, 1822, he entered the capital of Minas Gerais in triumph.

Important as this success was in reinforcing the power and authority of the Rio regime, it possessed no less significance because of its impact on the prince regent himself. D. Pedro had for the first time moved beyond the narrow world of the court and become acquainted with the realities of Brazil outside of Rio de Janeiro. His psychological horizons were thus broadened at a crucial moment. The rapturous reception given D. Pedro on his return to Rio on April 25 further encouraged him to perceive himself as the ruler of a New World nation rather than as the heir to the throne of Portugal.

To the Radicals, the moment seemed ripe for a decisive move toward Brazil's complete independence. During the prince regent's absence they had used placards and popular opinion to force José Bonifácio into postponing the election, set for April 18, of two delegates from Rio de Janeiro province to the Council of Delegates.[114] Now they made a direct approach to the prince regent, proposing that he establish his authority on the will of the people.[115] On April 30 the *Revérbero Constitucional Fluminense* published a personal appeal to D. Pedro:

Do not disdain the glory of founding a new Empire. On its knees Brazil bares its breast to you and on it, in diamond letters, is your name. . . . Prince, all nations receive a single chance to establish their own government which, once missed, does not return. The Rubicon is crossed; hell is behind and in front the temple of immortality. *Redire sit nefas* [to draw back would be ill omened].[116]

V

The months of May and June 1822 marked the crucial moment—in both Lisbon and Rio de Janeiro—when the contending sides arrived at the point of rupture. Each moved from viewing the other as an errant partner to regarding it as an avowed, irreconcilable foe. In Lisbon, this stage was reached on May 23 when the Cortes voted, over the strenuous protests of the Brazilian deputies, to confirm the sending of troop reinforcements to Salvador. The vote was probably motivated by a sense of affronted pride and a refusal to admit fallibility by reversing a settled decision. The aggressive language used during the debate, however, justified Brazilians in perceiving the vote as an implicit sanction of the conduct of the Portuguese troops at Salvador on February 19–20 and as a decision by the Cortes to adopt a policy of subduing Brazil by force.[117]

Some two weeks later, on June 10, the special committee on Brazilian affairs presented its long delayed recommendations on the São Paulo protest of December 24. The report, dissented to by all but one of the Brazilian deputies on the committee, proposed the criminal prosecution of the members of the São Paulo junta, of the individuals who had presented the São Paulo protest to the prince regent, and of the ministers at Rio who had signed the decree summoning the Council of Delegates.[118] Only the Cortes's obsession with its own dignity and preeminence can account for proposals so manifestly unenforceable and so destructive of political unity.

A week later, on June 17, there was presented a report diametrically opposed in content. It had been drafted by a special commission, appointed on May 24, charged with drawing up articles governing the status of Brazil which would be added to the new constitution, by then virtually complete. The members of the commission, all Brazilians, proposed that Brazil be granted its own Cortes and complete autonomy in its internal affairs. A special assembly composed equally of deputies from Brazil and Portugal would resolve matters of common concern. These proposals differed little from those suggested in the *Lembranças e Apontamentos* drawn up in October 1821 for the São Paulo deputies.[119]

The debate on the two reports, which took place during the last days of June 1822, showed the direction that the majority in the Cortes was determined to take. All the concessions to Brazil suggested in the second report were defeated, whereas the Cortes authorized virtually all the prosecutions proposed in the first report.[120] The decision meant that the leaders of the Rio de Janeiro government and José Bonifácio in particular, who faced prosecution on three separate counts, were left with no choice but personal disgrace or open defiance. The Cortes had alienated the very men who still favored the continued unity, however tenuous, of the Portuguese world.

In Rio de Janeiro during the months of May and June 1822 the regime abandoned any pretense of obedience to the Cortes. The report of the special committee on Brazilian affairs, which reached Rio on May 3, was scorned as insufficient in its concessions to Brazil.[121] The next day, the prince regent forbade implementation in Brazil of *any* decree of the Cortes not receiving his previous sanction. On May 13 D. Pedro was offered by the city council of Rio de Janeiro the title of Permanent Protector and Defender of Brazil (Protetor e Defensor Perpétuo do Brasil). The petition was the outcome of a campaign organized by José Clemente and the Radicals who wished to establish that D. Pedro's authority derived not just from hereditary right but from the popular will. Refusing to become "Protector" (a word with strong republican connotations), the prince regent accepted only the title of Defensor Perpétuo. Since Brazil required a defender solely against the Lisbon regime, the new title was an emphatic repudiation of the Cortes's authority, and the word "perpetual" constituted an implicit pledge by the prince regent not to leave Brazil.[122] If the testimony of the Austrian agent is to be trusted, José Bonifácio played some role in the offer of the new title, but his attitude was more one of acquiescence. While neither he nor his fellow Luso-Brazilians could welcome an act which asserted the sovereignty of the people, the title did not alter the realities of the situation and served as a sop both to popular opinion and to the prince's self-esteem.

In the Radicals' next maneuver, José Bonifácio almost certainly did not participate. On May 24 D. Pedro received a new petition from the Rio city council begging him to summon a separate constituent assembly for Brazil. To this request the prince regent agreed, subject to the proposal's receiving the consent of the provinces. Such a scheme could command support neither from the first minister nor from the Luso-Brazilians as a whole. It would create in Brazil a political body emanating directly from the people and possessing, so the Radicals argued, an authority superior to that of the prince regent. Yet open resistance was impossible. The prince himself favored the idea, and overt opposition seemed to smack of giving aid and comfort to the enemies of Brazil.[123] As José Bonifácio complained to the Austrian agent, "What can be done, minds are trending that way, the current of opinion cannot be resisted, we are at fever pitch, the prince will do it only if all the provinces agree."[124]

Calculating that universal consent could not be speedily secured, José Bonifácio hoped to circumvent the prince's promise. Procrastination had, however, little hope of success given the existing state of public opinion and the regime's own actions in asserting Brazil's independent rights. On the very day that the petition was presented, José Bonifácio issued credentials to the first Brazilian diplomatic agent: a consul named to Buenos Aires and instructed "to show to them [the states of the Río de la Plata] the impossibility of Brazil's being recolonized."[125] The struggle for supremacy in the provinces was at this moment intensifying. A vital element in the growing success of the prince regent's cause was the strong backing it received from the small folk who identified freedom from Lisbon with their own political emancipation. In Pernambuco on June 1, 1822, a popular and military movement, in which an agent from the Rio "independence club" played a role, forced the governing junta to acknowledge the executive authority of the prince regent.[126]

In such conditions the Rio government could not long maintain even a covert resistance, and in fact it yielded almost at once to the pressures exerted by the Radicals, confident and well organized, for the fulfillment of D. Pedro's promise.[127] To provide a semblance of popular sanction for the measure, the government hurriedly convened the long-delayed Council of Delegates, which on the very day it first met advised the prince regent to summon a constituent assembly.[128] The necessary decree was issued on June 3. While proclaiming the purpose of the new assembly to be "the maintenance of the integrity of the Portuguese monarchy," the decree also stated that the assembly would define the "bases on which its [Brazil's] independence should be established," and it would insist on a "just equality of rights between it and Portugal."[129]

The decree of June 3 marked the admission of the Radicals into the chambers of power. On the new Council of Delegates, which now met regularly, sat Joaquim Gonçalves Ledo, the editor of the *Revérbero Constitucional Fluminense*, who had been selected by Rio de Janeiro province.

Late in June the minister of war, a native of Portugal, was replaced by Luís Pereira de Nóbrega, a military officer who as a leading Freemason was closely allied with the Radicals. At the end of May there was founded at Rio a supreme governing body (Grand Orient) for all the Masonic lodges in Brazil. Although José Bonifácio was elected grand master, the new body was in fact controlled by the Radicals, who henceforth employed it as the vehicle for their schemes.[130]

The summoning of a constituent assembly signified far more than the success of a political faction. By the decree of June 3, the Rio regime recognized that political authority in Brazil must derive from popular sovereignty—an indispensable step toward the formation of a nation-state. The summoning of the assembly also contributed decisively in the provinces to the triumph of the prince regent's cause over that of the Lisbon Cortes. Until then, the local notables had tended to identify D. Pedro's government with the old, absolutist regime and with continued exploitation by Rio de Janeiro. The calling of the new assembly was taken as a pledge by the prince regent that in an autonomous or independent Brazil the popular will—that is, the desires of the notables—would predominate. With the constitution to be written by an elected assembly, the new political order would, further, respect existing rights and liberties. In short, whereas the Cortes exacted absolute obedience and total submission, the prince regent, now that a constituent assembly was summoned, seemed to offer all things to all men.

On June 25, 1822, the notables of the town of Cachoeira in the rich agricultural zone that formed the hinterland of Salvador rose in support of the prince regent, acknowledging him as Defensor Perpétuo, an action swiftly copied by the other towns in the region. Also at the end of June, a military coup forced the governing junta of the neighboring province of Alagoas to proclaim the prince regent and to dismiss its Portuguese-born members. Similar manifestations occurred in July in the northeastern provinces of Paraíba do Norte and Rio Grande do Norte and in the far south in Rio Grande do Sul.[131]

This rallying to the cause of D. Pedro should not, however, be perceived as the triumph of Brazilian nationalism. As shown by a memorandum drawn up by the town council of Maragogipe in Bahia on June 26, three days before it joined the prince's cause, the goals of the local notables were twofold: an end to rule by the Lisbon Cortes, and under the sovereignty of D. Pedro, an almost complete autonomy for the local *pátria*. The town council demanded the withdrawal of all Portuguese troops, with the province to be defended only by local units. It wanted the prince to hold the executive power in Brazil, and it demanded entire freedom of trade. It further called for "the abolition of all the taxes imposed since the king's arrival in Brazil," with the province having "its own exclusive treasury." Tax moneys were to leave the province only to meet the expenses of the king, the royal family, and the diplomatic service, all other payments "being only in the form of loans." The province should possess its own navy, the officers of which were to be drawn equally from *brasileiros* and *europeus*. Its armed forces were not to serve outside its boundaries save on loan when the dignity or security of the *nação portuguesa* was threatened.[132]

Such demands were utterly incompatible with the creation of a nation-state in Brazil. What the town really wanted was all the advantages Bahia had enjoyed before 1808 and all those it had received since the royal arrival at Rio. The list may have represented the local notables' optimum goals, but it does suggest that in the middle of 1822 the local *pátria* and not Brazil as a nation remained the focus of loyalty for many or most notables outside of Rio de Janeiro. The appeal of the prince regent and the Constituent Assembly he had just summoned lay in the fact that they seemed to impinge less upon the *pátrias* than did the Lisbon Cortes. It was for this reason that Maragogipe and other towns followed Cachoeira in its appeal made on July 5: "Aid us, Prince, we who are your devoted subjects."[133]

To these appeals the prince regent and José Bonifácio now responded. On July 14 the ships of the prince's navy, carrying what troops could be assembled, sailed from Rio to assist the Bahian forces, which were already closing in on the Portuguese garrison at Salvador. Financing of the open conflict with Portugal was assured by the raising of a public loan from the Rio merchants, secured on the credit of the prince regent's government.[134] On August 12 D. Pedro appointed agents to the courts of England and France, with instructions to each envoy to "procure from that government the recognition of the Political Independence of this Kingdom of Brazil and of the unrestricted Regency of His Royal Highness while His Majesty remains in the humiliating state of captivity to which the factious party of the Lisbon Cortes has reduced him."[135]

Justification of the prince regent's conduct, including his repudiation of the Cortes's authority, was presented in two government proclamations. The first, issued on August 1 and addressed to the inhabitants of Brazil, used the rhetoric of the French and the arguments of the American revolutions to denounce the conduct of the Cortes and to arouse enthusiasm for the cause of national independence under the leadership of D. Pedro.[136] The second proclamation, published six days later and composed by José Bonifácio, was directed at the outside world and was, as might be expected, far more moderate in language and content. Denunciations of the Cortes were balanced by assurances that the Prince did not "desire to cut the ties of union and fraternity which ought to make the Portuguese Nation a single well-organized polity."[137] This contradiction as to the future status of Brazil after the rupture with Portugal was not accidental. It represented the tension in ideology and competition for power existing between the Luso-Brazilians and the Radicals, the two principal groups in Rio supporting the break with Portugal.

For the prince regent and his minister in these weeks of tension, it was alarming that the province of São Paulo, José Bonifácio's *pátria* and crucial to the drive for independence, now erupted in revolt. A military rising had in May prevented the president of the governing junta from leaving as ordered for Rio and instead forced two other members, one of them brother to José Bonifácio, to withdraw to the national capital. To the prince regent the situation in São Paulo appeared a repetition of the disobedience he had earlier subdued in Minas Gerais. On August 14 D. Pedro left the capital for the city of São Paulo, intent on restoring his authority.[138] The supposed rebellion proved to be a fantasy, nothing more than the refusal of the local notables to tolerate the pretensions and high-handedness of José Bonifácio and his family.

While the prince regent was thus absent from Rio, the ship *Três Cora-ções* entered harbor, bringing news of the Cortes's proceedings up to the first days of July—most notably the deputies' authorization to prosecute all those involved in the São Paulo protest and of their total rejection of the proposals to grant full self-government to Brazil.[139] To public reasons there was now added personal cause for José Bonifácio to support a total breach with Portugal and the conversion of Brazil into a nation-state. "Sire, the die is cast," ran his letter to D. Pedro. "From Portugal we have nothing to hope but enslavement and horrors. Your Royal Highness should come at once and decide, since in facing a foe who will not spare us, speeches and half measures will serve for nothing, and every moment lost is a disgrace. I have many things to tell Your Royal Highness but I have neither time nor thought to spare."[140]

To the messenger carrying the dispatches to D. Pedro, José Bonifácio ordered all speed: "If you don't founder a dozen horses on the road, don't expect to be a messenger again."[141] Finding the prince absent on his arrival at São Paulo, the messenger rode south and met him in the fields by the Ipiranga stream. Never one to eschew the most dramatic action on the immediate impulse, D. Pedro required no more time for decision than the reading of the letters demanded. Mounting his horse and unsheathing his sword, he proclaimed the words familiar to every Brazilian schoolchild: "Friends, the Portuguese Cortes wished to enslave and persecute us. As from today our bonds are ended. No ties join us anymore. . . . Brazilians, let our watchword from this day forth be 'Independência ou Morte!' "[142]

4

A New Monarch for a New Nation, 1822-1825

The Grito de Ipiranga—D. Pedro's cry of "Independence or Death"—is now celebrated as the declaration of Brazil's national independence, and the Sete de Setembro as its national day. For contemporaries, September 7, 1822, held no such significance.[1] To them it was clear only that the government at Rio was now willing to repudiate the last remaining bond to Portugal: fealty to D. João VI. The ending of this personal link did command general acceptance, but no agreement existed on the precise form and character of the new independent polity. Repudiation of its previous status did not instantaneously transform Brazil into a functioning nation. Establishing the institutions of a nation-state would require a further three years of contention and crisis. Ultimately it was international recognition of Brazil's national independence, obtained through a treaty of reconciliation and recognition with Portugal in August 1825, rather than the achievement of internal consensus that determined the acquisition of legitimacy and the consolidation of political order.

The disagreement during these years over the nature of the new polity was in essence a conflict over the distribution, and so the control, of power and authority. Since independent Brazil was to be a nation-state, it followed that those holding authority would wield almost untrammeled power. Disputes over the control of authority were accordingly the more fervent and unyielding. Ideologically, the conflict was fought out not so much in terms of Brazil's needs and conditions, as in accord with pre-existing theories of the nation-state. Believers in the contract theory of political organization (basically liberals) clashed with those who regarded authority as inherited and providential (traditionalists and conservatives). Paradoxically, the disagreements themselves served to propagate a sense of Brazilian nationhood and to heighten national identity, since the controversy assumed Brazil's existence as a nation.

The crux of the conflict involved the nature of the ruler's authority. A desire for unity and a dependence on D. Pedro as the necessary leader of the independence movement made all save a few concur that the new nation should be a monarchy. The point at issue was whether D. Pedro was the direct embodiment of the nation and so at least coequal with the elected representatives of the nation, or whether he was no more than its delegate and so inferior and subject to its representatives. A further cause for controversy was whether the provinces, and thereby the *pátrias*, should be granted (by the forthcoming constitution) a separate basis of authority and, if so, to what degree. If federalism itself was taboo, being generally equated with republicanism, some form of self-government, such as provincial legislatures with limited powers, was strongly advocated. The question of political participation caused less contention, it being generally agreed that only those with a material stake in society, and so possessed of independent standing, should take an active part in politics.

Linked to these controversies were problems involving the external world. Obedience to the national authority had to be secured throughout the constituent territories of the nation, but the precise extent of those territories was not clearly established, particularly in respect to the Banda Oriental. Foreign recognition of the new nation had to be obtained, a task both complicated and made the more necessary by Brazil's being a monarchy in a continent of republics. Acceptance by the sovereigns of Europe was, moreover, entwined with the problem of the nation's future relationship to Portugal, since D. João VI never ceased to regard D. Pedro as heir to the Portuguese throne.

During its first three years of existence, the new nation was dominated by the struggle to resolve these problems. By September 1825 most of them had been settled, even though the specific outcome had been more often imposed than agreed upon. The character and structures of the nation were thus defined. The establishment of this new political order, even if not based on consensus, consolidated Brazil as a nation-state and prepared the way for functioning nationhood.

I

Late on September 14, 1822, D. Pedro returned to Rio de Janeiro. The prince and his attendants wore armbands bearing the motto "Independence or Death."[2] The moment of separation had come. In the ensuing weeks the political initiative lay not with the prince's first minister but with the Radical faction, acting through the Grand Orient and the Rio city council. A general meeting of the three Masonic lodges held on September 9 enthusiastically endorsed a proposal by Joaquim Gonçalves Ledo, by now the main spokesman for the Radicals, for "the proclamation of our independence and of a constitutional monarchy in the person of the August Prince, Perpetual Defender of the Kingdom of Brazil."[3] The immediate questions to be resolved were the new title to be taken by D. Pedro and the terms on which he would be "acclaimed" (that is, popularly recognized) as ruler of the Brazilian nation.

In contrast to earlier movements for independence, opinion in 1822 was solidly in favor of a monarchy, even among supporters of the 1817 uprising. Their change in attitude was justified in a letter sent to the *Correio Braziliense* by Antônio Carlos, José Bonifácio's brother, who had figured prominently in the northeastern revolt:

A Brazilian of liberal views could maintain in 1817 the necessity of being republican and can today be a monarchist. In 1817 the ruling house, misled by Portuguese biases, oppressed Brazil, and it was logical to adopt republicanism, which alone at that time offered us freedom. Today, thanks to Providence, His Royal Highness recognizes his true interests. . . . The republican, being able to obtain from the monarchy what he had sought from a federal republic, not surprisingly changes sides.[4]

In these circumstances, the proclamation of D. Pedro as ruler of Brazil with an indeterminate title such as "Protector" or the existing "Perpetual Defender," making him in effect life president of a quasi-republican state, was not a viable course of action.

Equally unsuitable, but for very different reasons, was the proposal that D. Pedro declare his father permanently incapacitated and himself possessed of full sovereignty as perpetual regent of Brazil.[5] Conservatives favored such a title, which would certainly conciliate the monarchs of Europe. This course of action would not, however, sever the tie with Portugal and it involved the risk that should D. João VI ever overthrow the Cortes government, he could then reassert his rights of sovereignty over Brazil.

At the Masonic meeting on September 9 it had been agreed to acclaim D. Pedro king of Brazil. Strong objections existed, however, to the adoption of this title. It was both too identified with the colonial past and too synonymous with rule by hereditary right alone. In personal terms D. Pedro could not assume a title already held by his father without offending the respect still felt by Brazilians for D. João VI—and also alienating monarchists everywhere, who would view it as an act of usurpation and filial treason.

The title of emperor avoided most of these disadvantages. Not only did it connote a total break with the past and avoid usurping any of D. João VI's titles, but in contemporary usage the word implied both the ruler of unusually extensive territories and a monarch whose accession to the throne involved an element of election. The title was therefore ideally suited for conciliating all currents of political opinion within the new Brazilian nation. Acclamation of D. Pedro as emperor was set by the city council for October 12, the day of his twenty-fourth birthday.[6]

The securing of foreign recognition, however, was in no way facilitated by the adoption of a new title. As the Brazilian agent in London reported at the end of November 1822, the British foreign secretary, otherwise sympathetic, was seriously offended. The monarchs of continental Europe regarded the act as presumptuous and foolhardy.[7] In all of Europe only the sovereigns of Austria and Russia held the title of emperor. The wording of the title assumed on October 12, 1822, made it all too overtly the expression of the popular will. The precedent of Napoleon Bonaparte, who in 1804 had his new title of emperor of France confirmed by a plebiscite, was still a vivid memory. D. Pedro was, it seemed, willing to risk his inherent rights by making alliance with radical, subversive elements.

In promoting the immediate independence of Brazil and the acclamation of D. Pedro, the Radicals sought not only the adoption of their concept of the nation but their own attainment of power through ousting José Bonifácio and the Luso-Brazilians. The Radicals attempted to flatter D. Pedro and to win him over to their goals by making him grand master of the Masonic Order, in place of José Bonifácio.[8] At the same time, they tried to ensure that as emperor D. Pedro would rule subject to the authority of the nation's elected representatives. A circular sent out by the Rio *câmara municipal* on September 17 to its fellow councils recommended that they acclaim D. Pedro emperor of Brazil upon condition that he swear acceptance of the constitution to be written by the Constituent Assembly.[9] It was the Radicals' intention that the formal offer of the imperial title to be made to D. Pedro by the Rio city council on October 12 should contain this very clause.

In the move to full independence and the selection of the title of emperor for D. Pedro, José Bonifácio played no active role.[10] The wave of public enthusiasm made any attempt to delay or to oppose not simply unwise but impossible. "The idea of conferring upon him [D. Pedro] the imperial title was no sooner made public than it caught like wildfire," José Bonifácio later remarked to the British consul-general, "and left the government no alternative but to agree to the measure." To the Austrian agent he justified his concurrence by arguing that it was preferable for the prince to assume the title on his own initiative than to be made emperor at a later date by an act of the Constituent Assembly.[11]

If he consented to the declaration of independence and to the adoption of the title of emperor, José Bonifácio did not intend that any conditions should be attached to D. Pedro's acclamation. An oath to accept the future constitution would amount to an explicit renunciation by the monarch of any claim to be an embodiment of the nation and so the source of authority within it. In recent years monarchs who had taken such oaths or had relinquished all say in constitution making had suffered humiliation, as for example Ferdinand VII of Spain, or even death, as in the case of Louis XVI of France. One cause for Brazilian independence was the Cortes's high-handed treatment of D. João VI after his return to Lisbon. The Radicals were, in other words, embarked on a course of action which only a position of overwhelming strength could justify, since it was bound to offend both moderate and traditionalist opinion. Continued successes and the excitement of the moment seem also to have blinded the Radicals to the fact that, once total independence from Portugal was achieved, they would lose their chief source of political appeal.

José Bonifácio's immediate concern was to prevent any reference to the future constitution during the acclamation ceremonies held at Rio de Janeiro on October 12. Whatever the means used—and threats of dire personal retribution may have been employed—the Radical leaders were induced to hold their hand. The official petition to D. Pedro approved by the city council on October 10 attached no conditions to its offer of the imperial title. The ceremonies themselves were conducted in harmony and with great enthusiasm. In the provinces, notably in Minas Gerais, some of the acclamation ceremonies did make their recognition of the new emperor conditional on his taking the oath.[12]

Shortly after D. Pedro had been proclaimed emperor, José Bonifácio took the offensive against the Radicals. He engineered a political crisis which would then enable him to oust the minister of war, remove José Clemente as *juiz de fora* of Rio city, close the Masonic lodges, and so smash the Radicals as an organized political movement. On October 28, José Bonifácio insisted upon the emperor's accepting his resignation as minister. The resignation set off street demonstrations (of debatable spon-.taneity) which overawed his opponents and precluded the formation of a new cabinet. Unable or unwilling to replace José Bonifácio, the emperor on October 30 recalled him to office. Having thus regained full control of affairs, the first minister showed himself implacable against his opponents. A criminal investigation was opened against what was termed the "faction of fanatical demagogues and anarchists."[13] Joaquim Gonçalves Ledo fled abroad for his life. Others, including José Clemente Pereira and Luís Pereira de Nóbrega, the former minister of war, were deported to Europe. Several more were held in preventive arrest or forced to leave Rio de Janeiro city. Freemasonry was suppressed, and newspapers hostile to the first minister ceased to publish. Although a few of their leaders, notably José Clemente Pereira, later returned to public life, the Radicals vanished as a political force.[14]

This outcome of the October crisis signified much more than a personal triumph for José Bonifácio and a victory for the Luso-Brazilians as a group. It profoundly affected the character of the monarchy and thereby the complexion of the new nation. D. Pedro I's coronation emphasized the inherent, providential nature of his authority. The ritual used followed closely the coronation service of the former Holy Roman Emperors. D. Pedro I was not only crowned but anointed: he was thus chosen and consecrated by God.[15] This public drama informed the watching world that the new monarch's right to rule transcended mere popular sanction. Continuity of authority was attested to by the presence at the coronation of the officials of the imperial court. In practice and in personnel, this privileged body functioned after Independence much the same as it had under D. João VI.

An important element in the monarch's traditional, inherent authority was his role as the fount of honors. On the day of his coronation the emperor bestowed the title of baron of Torre de Garcia d'Avila on the head of the most powerful family in Bahia.[16] By this act D. Pedro I asserted not only his innate right to grant titles but the existence of a titled nobility in the new nation. Despite the break with Portugal, D. Pedro I continued to award honors in the three ancient Portuguese orders of chivalry—Christ, São Bento, and Aviz.[17] On December 1, 1822, in honor of his coronation, D. Pedro I used his inherent authority to create the Ordem Imperial do Cruzeiro (Imperial Order of the [Southern] Cross). In its preamble, the decree made specific reference to the orders of chivalry previously set up by the "Sovereign Kings my Predecessors, . . . and especially by my August and Sovereign Father D. João VI." The decree conferred privileges, both social and legal, on recipients of the new order.[18]

D. Pedro I's acclamation and coronation did not end the dispute over the nature of the ruler's authority within the nation. That question could not be considered settled until the constitution (to be drawn up by the forthcoming Constituent Assembly) was promulgated. The terms on which the emperor was recognized and crowned did, nonetheless, profoundly affect the nature of the new monarchy in Brazil. Rather than adapting to New World conditions, the monarchy adhered to the inheritance of Europe. Such considerable pretensions, in essence asserting that authority in the new nation did emanate from above, would not easily be accommodated in a polity founded—as the summoning of the Constituent Assembly implied —on the concept of popular sovereignty.

II

At the coronation of D. Pedro I, José Bonifácio figured prominently, serving as *mordomo-mor* (lord chamberlain). His supremacy as first minister to the new emperor was now undisputed and he alone directed affairs. José Bonifácio's formidable conceit ensured that he was neither overwhelmed by the burden of responsibility he carried nor dismayed by the daunting problems facing the nation. "Everything is to be done," the Austrian agent commented in the middle of December. "There is no constitution, no [legal] codes, no system of education; nothing exists save for a sovereign recognized and crowned."[19] More immediately, the emperor's authority had to be established throughout the territories claimed by the new nation, and the nation's boundaries fixed. No less pressing were the external problems, which involved both dealing with Portugal and securing diplomatic recognition by the foreign states. An agenda of such magnitude and urgency challenged even José Bonifácio's vaulting self-confidence.

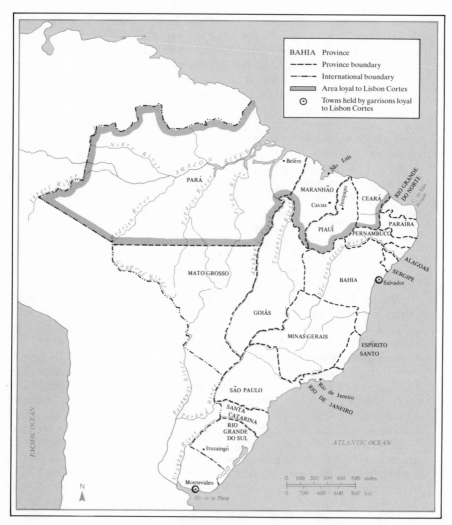

MAP 3. Brazil in September 1822: The Balance of Contending Forces. (All boundary lines are approximations only.)

Securing diplomatic recognition would be no easy task. The United States was cool toward any nation in the New World which sought independence as a monarchy. Despite its considerable commercial interests in Brazil, Great Britain did no more than offer a friendly neutrality in any conflict with Portugal. When the monarchs of continental Europe met at the Congress of Verona late in 1822, they made plain their dislike of the constitutionalist regimes at Lisbon and Rio de Janeiro.[20]

In September 1822 the four provinces of the north—a block of territory covering about one-quarter of Brazil—were firmly controlled by provisional juntas loyal to the Cortes. The key ports of Montevideo in the far south and Salvador in the northeast, although besieged by forces supporting the emperor, were held by Portuguese garrisons. The Cortes had made clear by word and deed that it would not permit its erring transatlantic brethren to depart peaceably. In October two fresh battalions reached Salvador from Portugal, bringing the number of troops in the city to almost 9,000 men. At that port a large naval squadron was also stationed. A full-scale war was clearly imminent, in which Brazilians would have to fight unaided.

By a proclamation issued at Rio de Janeiro on October 21, 1822, Portuguese-born residents in Brazil were given four months in which to choose either "the continuation of a friendship founded on the dictates of justice, of generosity, on ties of blood and mutual interests, or the most violent war."[21] In reality, a state of open war with Portugal already existed when the proclamation was issued, since fighting was taking place at Salvador. The decision of the regime on December 11 to sequester the property in Brazil of Portuguese subjects showed how little the four months' grace period actually signified.[22]

Preparations for war with Portugal had in fact begun early in August when José Bonifácio, as minister of foreign affairs, authorized the Brazilian agent nominated to serve in England to hire if need be "some regiments of Irish or any other nation, . . . under the guise of colonists."[23] If foreign mercenaries would, in the event, be little used in the struggle to defeat the Portuguese land forces, the war at sea was another matter. José Bonifácio had early grasped that victory depended upon the speedy creation of a powerful navy which could command the approaches to Brazil. On October 4 Brazil's agent in London was ordered to recruit unemployed British naval officers and to pursue an offer made by private interests in England to provide two armed frigates. Two weeks later he was instructed to procure a further four frigates.[24] Already in September José Bonifácio had written to the new Brazilian agent in Buenos Aires authorizing him to secure the services of Thomas Cochrane, a former captain in the British navy then commanding the naval forces of Chile against Spain in the Pacific. An agreement to this effect was easily made.[25] Cochrane's audacity and sharpness, amounting to trickery when victory was at stake, made the new "First Admiral" of Brazil a bonny fighter. During the next two years the successes of the Brazilian navy would owe much to Cochrane's daring and resource.[26]

Hostilities against the Portuguese forces in the four northern provinces of Brazil started long before these preparations were completed. In mid-October 1822 risings broke out in both northern Piauí and southern Ceará. The revolts were inspired as much by a desire to elect deputies to the new Constituent Assembly as by devotion to the cause of total independence. The forces supporting the risings were drawn from the local militia units, usually commanded by notables who for personal or public reasons were dissatisfied with the political status quo. Help from Rio de Janeiro was limited to some military supplies, formal recognition, and moral encouragement.[27] By the end of January 1823, the pro-Cortes *juntas provisórias* had been ousted in both Ceará and Piauí. Although in March the Portuguese forces in Piauí won a pitched battle at Jenipapo, the cost was high, the victory Pyrrhic. The Portuguese commander soon after withdrew into the province of Maranhão, where he entrenched himself in the key town of Caxias.

By the end of March both Portugal and Brazil had made ready as best they could for general war. Disregarding the needs of the northern provinces, which had urgently requested troops, the Cortes regime sent reinforcements of nearly 4,000 men to Salvador. Both sides agreed in viewing possession of that city as the key to victory. On March 29 the imperial government declared the port under close blockade, and three days later Cochrane sailed from Rio with a small squadron, assembled by the regime with some difficulty.[28] On May 4 Cochrane sighted the Portuguese fleet off Salvador and at once gave battle. Although inferior numbers and mutinous sailors soon forced him to break off action, the encounter was in fact a victory. Inhibited by Cochrane's reputation and his boldness in the fight, the Portuguese commander withdrew into Salvador and did not challenge a blockade of the port that the "First Admiral" attempted to maintain with only three ships![29]

The sea battle of May 4, 1822, effectively doomed the Portuguese offensive against the Empire. The cream of the Portuguese army and navy was locked up in the city of Salvador, isolated and impotent. They were unable to exploit a sudden crisis which at the end of May shook the besieging land forces: the commanding general, a French exile appointed by the emperor, was deposed in a mutiny organized by the heads of the local forces.[30] The land war in the north was by the month of May being fought in the province of Maranhão. Had the Cortes sent some reinforcements to that province instead of committing all of them to Salvador, it might have been possible to turn back the Brazilian offensive.

By the end of May the situation inside Salvador had deteriorated to the point that the Portuguese commanders abandoned any hope of breaking the siege and thought of little save how to extract their troops from the city before hunger and sickness immobilized them. On July 2, 1823, an evacuation was successfully carried out; the fleet set sail, with Cochrane soon in pursuit. Some of the Portuguese troop transports were sent to Maranhão to reinforce the forces there. One of these ships was captured by Cochrane, who immediately grasped the strategic opportunity offered.[31]

On July 26, 1823, a warship flying the Portuguese flag appeared off São Luís. The brig sent out to welcome it was quickly captured, a victim of Cochrane's stratagem. The governing junta was then informed by Cochrane that he was accompanied by the entire Brazilian fleet. The only

possible course open to the junta, Cochrane added, was immediate sur-
render and adhesion to the Empire. That same day the junta capitulated.
Three weeks later, on August 11, the identical trick was played by one of
Cochrane's lieutenants on the province of Pará, until then entirely loyal to
Portugal. The war in the far north was thus brought to an unexpectedly
swift end.[32]

The sudden conquest of Maranhão and Pará left under Portuguese control only the city of Montevideo. This outcome was more than a little
ironic, since that city was the most recent of the Portuguese colonies, conquered only in 1816 when the Voluntários d'El Rei had invaded the Banda
Oriental; not until 1820 had the conquest been completed. Just before his
departure from Brazil, D. João VI had ordered the calling of a congress to
decide the future of the Banda Oriental. In July 1821, the congress voted
in favor of joining the Kingdom of Brazil, a predictable decision since
the eighteen deputies were all henchmen of the military governor, who
strongly favored annexation to Brazil. No wonder that one of D. Pedro's
ministers frankly admitted to the Austrian agent in Rio that "from the
start it had been a sordid affair."[33]

Since the population of the Banda Oriental was Spanish in language
and culture and since there was, the Austrian envoy remarked, no popular
desire for union with Brazil, it would have been logical for the new Empire
to disclaim any right to the area and to evacuate its troops. Some deputies in the Lisbon Cortes, coherent with their liberal beliefs, did in April
1822 suggest renouncing all claim to the region, but the Cortes decided
to hold back and make such a renunciation part of a general settlement of
Portugal's territorial disputes with Spain.[34]

José Bonifácio's conduct and intentions had been, from the moment
of taking office in January 1822, very different. The support given by the
military governor of the Banda Oriental in February 1822 to D. Pedro's
refusal to leave Brazil was warmly welcomed by the Rio government. The
deputy elected to the Lisbon Cortes by the region did not travel farther
than Rio de Janeiro, where he worked enthusiastically both in favor of
Brazil's independence and of his *pátria*'s incorporation as the Cisplatine
province.[35] On May 30, 1822, José Bonifácio in his instructions to the first
diplomatic agent appointed by D. Pedro ordered the new consul at Buenos
Aires to dispel "any false assumptions that may exist there [concerning]
the Rio de Janeiro government's renunciation of the Estado Cisplatino,
even though in Lisbon they cede the territory either to Spain or to Buenos
Aires. . . . The real intentions of His Royal Highness' Government are to
maintain unchanged the incorporation of Montevideo."[36]

José Bonifácio's determination that Brazil should retain the Banda Oriental involved no ideological inconsistency. He had never been an orthodox nationalist and did not believe that a nation-state need be homogeneous in language and culture. More surprising, perhaps, was the strong
support for annexing the Banda Oriental evident among the Radicals.

They justified their stand on the grounds that Brazil's "natural frontiers" lay on the Río de la Plata and that incorporation represented the "spontaneous and legal" choice of the inhabitants of the region.[37]

The Portuguese garrison of Montevideo was, however, no more willing than its counterparts in Rio de Janeiro and Salvador to let the enemies of the Cortes take control. The Portuguese units held the city against the Brazilian troops in the surrounding countryside. Negotiations aimed at securing the garrison's return to Portugal on Brazilian ships broke down at the end of 1822.[38] Subsequently the *cabildo* (town council) of Montevideo declared the incorporation into Brazil null and void and asserted the right of the region's inhabitants to decide their fate freely without the presence of Brazilian troops. Not until November 1823 was the evacuation of the Portuguese garrison finally achieved, with Brazil obtaining possession of Montevideo.[39] All the territories claimed by the new nation were now, little more than a year after the proclamation of independence, controlled by the imperial government.

III

The triumphs secured on the field of battle during the year 1823 were not matched by similar achievements in establishing a new political order. Success in military affairs in fact worked against internal harmony. So long as the menace of the Lisbon Cortes persisted and D. Pedro I's rule was challenged by the presence of Portuguese troops on Brazilian soil, the necessity for unity and restraint was obvious, making men rein in their ambitions and resentments. By the second quarter of 1823, this sense of national emergency was fast diminishing. In April the Austrian agent commented on some official documents enclosed in his dispatch: "From them Your Highness will perceive better than I can tell you the immense advances that the government has made in six months."[40]

The most significant achievement was probably the formation at Rio de Janeiro of a viable (if not always efficient) central government with a sense of identity and direction. Under the parsimonious direction of Martim Francisco Ribeiro de Andrada, José Bonifácio's youngest brother, the treasury imposed some order on expenditures and punctuality in the payment of debts. Outside of Rio de Janeiro all the governing juntas not loyal to Lisbon had recognized D. Pedro as emperor. Despite their unwillingness to grant diplomatic recognition, none of the European monarchies had withdrawn their consular officials from Rio. Agents of the imperial government had succeeded in opening unofficial negotiations with the British and French governments. Both at home and abroad the new regime had, in sum, achieved an intangible but essential attribute: credibility.

That credibility was enhanced by the opening on May 3, 1823, of the new Constituent Assembly. As the emperor observed in his Fala do Trono (Speech from the Throne): "Today is the greatest day Brazil has known, a day on which it for the first time starts to show the world that it is an Empire and a free Empire."[41] The summoning of the Constituent Assembly, created by the decree of June 3, 1822, had acted as a power magnet, attracting support for the new imperial regime throughout the provinces. During the second half of 1822, elections for the 100 deputies of the assembly went forward in nearly all the provinces. The new deputies were slow to reach Rio de Janeiro, but by mid-April 1823, a sufficient number had gathered for the assembly to meet in preliminary session for the verification of powers.[42]

The members of the Constituent Assembly can fairly be said to have been as qualified and capable a group of men as could be found within the boundaries of the new nation.[43] Over half (49) of the 88 men who actually sat in the assembly were graduates from Coimbra, national bureaucrats, or both. A further 7 members were senior military officers. Of the 17 priests who sat in the assembly most were parish clergy and so may be classed among the local notables, who numbered about 30. Of the deputies, 18 had been elected to the Lisbon Cortes but only 6 had actually taken their seats in that body. In their political outlook, members ranged across the ideological spectrum, from staunch traditionalists who denounced Jean-Jacques Rousseau to veterans of the 1817 rising who at heart remained republicans. However, ideological stances were in general not rigid: the deputies were reasonable men, usually open to persuasion by debate. Whatever their political viewpoint, they shared a consciousness of the importance of the task before them, being determined to endow Brazil with a constitution worthy of the new nation.[44]

The sense of lofty mission and the correspondingly high view of their proceedings could not but contribute to the state of tension which the meeting of the Constituent Assembly inevitably engendered. In the national capital there now existed an official body possessed of an authority independent of and so rival to that of the imperial government. The new chamber further served as the forum for the venting of discontents, resentments, and rivalries, and this freedom of dissent encouraged the reappearance of the journals of opinion silenced since the end of 1822.

The emperor and his ministers seem to have fully comprehended the challenge implicit in the meeting of the new assembly.[45] José Bonifácio sought with qualified success to prevent the election of extremists. All three Andrada brothers secured seats, and it was clear from the start that Antônio Carlos, whatever his past beliefs, would put his formidable personality and parliamentary experience at the service of his brothers. A scheme for a constitution involving two legislative chambers and an absolute veto for the emperor was discussed in government circles, but the project was never presented to the new assembly. In any confrontation between the Constituent Assembly and the emperor, the Austrian agent reported, the latter would hold the decisive advantage, since he could as a last resort dissolve the chamber and was certain to be supported by public opinion.[46]

The Speech from the Throne, which surveyed past events and justified the government's conduct of affairs, left the deputies in no doubt about what the emperor perceived his position in the nation to be. D. Pedro I formally ratified the oath taken at his coronation to "defend the *pátria*, the nation, and the constitution, if it be worthy of Brazil and of me. . . . Experience has shown us that every constitution modeled upon and inspired by those of 1791 and 92 has been totally theoretical and metaphysical and so impractical, as France, Spain, and most recently Portugal have demonstrated. . . . I trust that the constitution you make will warrant my Imperial acceptance and be as wise and as just as it will be suited to the locale and the culture of the Brazilian people."[47]

These passages, in the drafting of which José Bonifácio must have had a hand, in effect asserted the emperor's claim to be—as much as the Constituent Assembly—the supreme, sovereign embodiment of the Brazilian nation. On their side, the deputies had, even before the emperor spoke, challenged any such claim by resolving that when the emperor addressed the assembly he appear not wearing his crown and so not as its sovereign.[48] The Vote of Thanks, as proposed by Antônio Carlos on May 5, declared that the assembly recognized in the Speech from the Throne "the sentiments of true constitutionalism and the principles of true liberty to which it aspires." The deputies were not, however, willing to be so conciliatory, and after a long debate in which the rival conceptions of national authority were thoroughly aired, they approved an addition to the proposed Vote of Thanks: "The Assembly believes it will produce a Constitution worthy of the Brazilian nation, of itself, and of the Emperor."[49] Thus worded, the amendment, although offering no direct challenge to D. Pedro I's statements, did by implication uphold the deputies' sole right to produce the constitution.

The drafting of that constitution was on May 5 entrusted to a special committee of seven deputies, to which three members of the Andrada family were elected.[50] While this committee was at work, a task which was to consume four months, the deputies occupied themselves with the other obligation prescribed by their oath of office: the enactment of "urgent and necessary reforms." The debates on these projects showed that on all questions of importance José Bonifácio and his fellow ministers commanded a healthy majority. On May 22 a bill granting a general amnesty, a measure which would have particularly benefited those arrested or deported at the end of October 1822, was rejected by 35 votes to 17.[51]

The political position of José Bonifácio and his brothers was, however, far less secure than these figures might suggest. The first minister's success in establishing the authority of the imperial government and in defeating the nation's foes worked against his own interest. The end of the emergency meant that he was no longer indispensable, and his achievements did not arouse a sense of gratitude. His high-handedness had made him as many foes as his engrossing of power and patronage had created malcontents. Hopes of revenge stimulated the former, and the prospect of

office emboldened the latter. What encouraged both foes and rivals was
the evident change in the attitude at the imperial court towards the first
minister.

The passage of time and the continued successes of the imperial regime
gave D. Pedro I a greater confidence in his own capacities and made
him resent anything that smacked of dependence. The filial relationship
hitherto enjoyed with José Bonifácio he now came to regard as a form
of demeaning tutelage. This incipient estrangement was fostered by the
emperor's immediate entourage, mostly of Portuguese birth, who encouraged their master's pretensions, in the hope of increasing their own
influence and standing. Of itself this court camarilla might have achieved
little had it not given José Bonifácio's enemies a secure channel of access to
the emperor. Given his prestige and tenacity, the first minister would not
easily be dislodged from power, but his uncertain health made it difficult
for him to counteract these intrigues while directing the entire business of
government.[52]

It was for these several reasons that by the middle of May 1823 there
had emerged in the Constituent Assembly rival political blocs. The Austrian envoy reported to his government:

Up to the present, the Assembly would appear to be divided into three parties,
that of the Ministry, and more decidedly that of the Andradas, which wants a
constitution on the English model . . . ; a middle party which looks more to France
and opposes the Ministerial party in the hopes of replacing the Andradas if they
are forced to quit the Ministry; . . . and last, the Democratic party, composed of
10 to 11 members, who make a great deal of noise . . . but who, up to the present,
remain in a minority on all significant questions.[53]

During its first weeks the assembly devoted its debates to the consideration of urgent reforms. Among the projects introduced were three
bills directly relating to the distribution of power and authority within
the nation. The first was a bill regulating the form of government in the
provinces. The inspiration for the reform was explained in a speech by a
deputy from Alagoas who introduced the measure:

The governments of the provinces of Brazil are still organized according to the
Decree of the Lisbon Cortes of September 29, 1821, and I consider it unworthy
of you, illustrious Representatives of Brazilian Sovereignty, to consent that these
governments be regulated as dictated by the Congress of Portugal, whose only
thought was how to subjugate us. The present organization of these governments
impedes the happiness of the peoples, and their general clamor attests to this. I
have already served on two provisional juntas and so I know and understand them
well; they only serve to sow discord.[54]

A more detailed bill regulating provincial governance was presented on
May 9 by Antônio Carlos, and it was this project which was taken up
for debate.[55] The provisional junta in each province was to be replaced
by "a president and a council." The former would be "the executor and

administrator of the province and as such strictly accountable; he will be nominated by the Emperor and removable when he judges convenient." The council, composed of six elected members, was to be consulted on all matters demanding "administrative examination and judgment," but "the president will act by himself and decide all [other] matters." The troops in each province were, by the bill, to be commanded by a military officer independent of the president and council, known as the *comandante das armas*.[56]

The new system of president and council was (under article 2 of the bill) no more than provisional, in force only until the promulgation of the new constitution. Nonetheless, the effect of the law, if enacted, would be to overturn the balance of power existing since early in 1821 between the provinces and the center and so to reinstate the colonial status quo. A governing committee chosen by and accountable to the province's electors was to be replaced by a single executive named by and answerable to the monarch alone. Despite the creation of the presidential council and despite the title of president, this nominee of the emperor would be, as one deputy was quick to point out, "perceived as a former Governor and Captain General; the impositions and despotisms of the past will be recalled."[57]

Depriving the provinces of their locally elected and virtually autonomous governments was opposed eloquently and systematically by a minority of deputies. This opposition, composed of deputies from the provinces of the northeast and from Minas Gerais and São Paulo, constituted what the Austrian agent termed the "Democratic Party," which filled the void left since the destruction of the Radicals in October 1822. In their social composition and political outlook the two groups had much in common. They were both firmly based on the petty professionals, minor officials, unbeneficed clergy, artisans, and other small folk. Ideologically, they shared a sympathy for republicanism, belief in the people as the source of authority, and support of individual rights and liberties.

The two groups also differed in important respects, so that the new movement cannot be deemed a resuscitation of Radicalism. Whereas the Radicals had supported the Brazilian nation because its existence alone made viable their *pátria*, the members of the new movement gave their prime loyalty to their local *pátrias*, which they saw as essentially self-sufficient. The nation was for them a magnification of that *pátria*, and they valued it as the *pátria*'s guardian against external aggression and internal disorder. They did not equate the Brazilian nation with Rio de Janeiro. The existing central government they distrusted as being corrupted by despotism and extravagance, qualities they identified with the Portuguese heritage. In sum, the new faction can best be characterized as nativist rather than nationalist. In contrast to the Radicals, who had been concentrated in Rio de Janeiro, the Nativist movement commanded a broad and devoted following in the provinces.

The bill for the reform of the system of government in the provinces clashed with the Nativists' basic beliefs and confirmed their worst fears and suspicions. As a leading Nativist deputy, a veteran of 1817 who had sat in the Lisbon Cortes, remarked:

How can we assure our constituents that we are incorruptible in the defense of their interests? Is it perchance by sending them, at the very start of our labors, those same abuses that formerly caused their hurt and anger: a governor with his name changed to president, an independent *comandante das armas*, a secretary who is identical to that of the old Captain General; and all sent from Rio de Janeiro, the presumed source of Despotism?[58]

"We acclaimed an Emperor to rule over us with his respective rights," another Nativist protested, "but the peoples in no way conceded that they could be stripped of the rights they might possess."[59]

The Nativists' battle was in vain. The vast majority of deputies were determined to replace the existing system. They mistrusted the *juntas provisórias de govêrno* for being the creation of the Lisbon Cortes, a mistrust confirmed by the juntas' record of factionalism, incompetence, and abuse of power. Local government based on popular election smacked, for many deputies, of federalism, which was perceived as virtually synonymous with republicanism and so incompatible with a monarchical regime: "In representative monarchies it is essential that administration be entrusted to a single being, who is the Monarch, Head of the Executive Power, deliberation being entrusted to many; and the same applies, in the provinces, to their governments."[60] At the close of the first debate on May 27 the Nativists mustered 19 votes against 32, and on the final division sanctioning the law on October 11, only 8 against 53.[61] The Nativists' worst fears were fulfilled, since it was the provisional scheme that endured: the system enacted by the law—the absolute control by the national government of the executive power in the provinces—was to continue for almost 70 years.

On May 22, 1823, when the bill regulating the government of the provinces was first debated, a Nativist deputy from Pernambuco introduced the second measure concerned with the distribution of power and authority in the nation. The bill dealt with the issue of who was to participate in the political process and so have a voice in the governance of the nation. Arguing that "in all nations the grant of citizenship is always made with the utmost care, since it is the highest honor to which a foreigner can aspire," the deputy proposed that of the Portuguese-born then resident in the nation only those who could offer "indisputable proof of adhesion to the sacred cause of independence" should receive citizenship. The rest could, under the bill's provisions, be deported by the imperial government, and in the future the Portuguese-born were to be equated with all other foreigners. Naturalization would require seven years' residence and the ownership of property in Brazil.[62]

Despite the fighting then raging at Salvador and in the far north, the project dismayed deputies of liberal outlook, including several Nativists.

The bill offended their reverence for the rights and liberties of the individual citizen: "Where has such a thing been seen? Not even in Algiers," an opponent protested. The project also contravened their conception of the nation. Believers in the "contract" theory of government, they did not equate citizenship with birthplace. As this same leading Nativist remarked:

We formed a society known as the Portuguese Nation; we were all members of that family, we all enjoyed the rights of Portuguese citizens. What happened then? The members of that same family, who inhabited the part of the Nation called Brazil, using their inalienable and inherent rights . . . broke the social ties which bound them to Portugal, proclaimed their Independence, and formed a new Pact, a new society, and a new family which they called the Brazilian Nation. But who did this? Only the inhabitants of Brazil born there? Certainly not; it was also the inhabitants of Brazil born in Portugal; therefore they became Brazilian citizens as much as did the Brazilian-born. All enjoyed in the new society the same rights as they enjoyed in the old; finally, all are members of the new family just as they were members of the old.[63]

Little support was given to the project, but what little it did receive came from a significant source: two of the Andrada brothers. Although José Bonifácio, then president of the assembly, remained silent, both Antônio Carlos and Martim Francisco backed the bill. For Antônio Carlos, place of birth was crucial:

Mr. President, let us be frank, it is almost impossible that a Portuguese can as a rule love from his heart a situation which entails the ruin of his original *pátria* and debases its dignity. . . . Love of our homes, preference for the first place where we spent the years of our youth, affection for the *pátria* which witnessed our birth are natural sentiments which can be overridden by the prospect of other advantages but which in well-formed souls continue to exist submerged. . . . Who will assert that we ought to grant immediately posts of confidence to the Portuguese resident here?[64]

When the bill was rejected by a voice vote on June 25, 1823, the two Andrada brothers and their nephew joined the author of the bill in a formal declaration that they had voted for its further consideration.[65] This vote was significant for two reasons. It showed that, even before the vote, the Andrada brothers were fully aware of who their principal opponents were. Given the brothers' habitual inability to separate their personal interests from the public cause, it was inevitable that the Andradas would perceive the Portuguese-born not just as their own foes but as enemies of the nation itself.

The last bill of the three relating to the distribution of power and authority was concerned with the very heart of the dispute over authority in the nation. On June 12 the committee on the constitution, acting on a motion submitted by a Nativist deputy, presented a bill regulating the enactment and promulgation of laws passed by the assembly. Article 3 of this bill read bluntly: "The decrees of the present Assembly will be promulgated without previous sanction."[66] The emperor was thus to be denied the right to veto laws made by the assembly. If the project were passed, it logically followed that the emperor would have no role at all in the making of the new constitution.

Some of the committee members sought to justify the bill to the emperor, so the Austrian agent reported, on tactical grounds. A concession on this issue, by conciliating liberal opinion and reassuring the provinces, would prepare the way for a constitution that preserved the emperor's supreme authority. The Austrian agent regarded the project, which he suspected would pass, as the product of a league between what he called "the middle party" and the Nativists, an alliance which in his view could only profit the latter.[67]

The bill came up for discussion in the assembly on the very day that the project on citizenship was defeated. The debate on article 3 was notable for the first articulate expression of a particular conception of the nation and authority within it, derived from Napoleonic France and which under different guises was to have enduring influence on the development of Brazil as a nation. The speaker was a Luso-Brazilian, educated at Coimbra, who had risen to be the senior official in the ministry of the interior. The article contravened, he asserted, the will of the nation, which "has delegated to us only the legislative power, enabling us to write a Constitution for a government already chosen and determined by it. . . . The essence of the constitutional, representative, and monarchical government," the speaker maintained, is "that the Supreme Chief of the Nation, the monarch, have such a role in the Legislative Power that laws which it decrees cannot be promulgated and executed without the Monarch's sanction." Further, the speaker stated, coming to the crux of this conception of the authority in the nation:

The Constitutional Monarch, besides being head of the Executive Power, . . . is the first supervising Authority, guardian of our rights and of the Constitution. This supreme Authority which makes his person sacred and inviolable and which has been considered by the wisest theorists of our time a Sovereign Power distinct from the Executive Power by reason of its nature, purpose, and character, this Authority, called by some the *Neutral* or *Regulating Power*, . . . is essential in representative governments."[68]

The theory which postulated the existence of a "guardian power"— able in emergencies to override even the people's representatives—did not on its first appearance in Brazilian history make many converts among the deputies.[69] The bill, with its controversial article 3 unchanged, passed its second reading on June 27. However, since the emperor was induced early in July to make his displeasure with the bill known to the deputies, the project was for the moment not given a third reading but consigned to limbo.[70]

July 1823 saw the intrigues against the Andrada brothers reach a climax. At the start of the month, José Bonifácio was defeated for reelection as president of the assembly. Five days later those who had been arrested on October 30, 1822, were declared innocent and released.[71] On July 15, the very day that news reached Rio de Janeiro of the evacuation of Salvador by the Portuguese garrison, the emperor dismissed José Bonifácio and Martim Francisco from office. The new cabinet named by D. Pedro I retained all the former ministers save for the two Andrada brothers—a direct and intolerable affront to their pride. The circumstances of their dismissal were such "as to make any reunion, any reconciliation with H.R.H. almost impossible, at least for the present," the Austrian agent lamented. "I can foresee only disasters and misfortunes, and I am the more distressed since they are to be attributed not to chance but to H.R.H.'s changeability and blindness."[72]

José Bonifácio's dismissal not only removed an able and self-confident man from the supreme direction of the nation's affairs but, even more important, disturbed the existing balance of political forces, particularly within the Constituent Assembly, by then in its tenth week. The new cabinet made no attempt to direct the business of the assembly, seeking only to conciliate and appease the deputies.[73] The attitude adopted by the Andrada brothers in the assembly would be of critical importance, and two political developments following hard on their dismissal from office strongly influenced the course they did pursue. On July 21 the deputies learned that the troops garrisoning Pôrto Alegre, capital of Rio Grande do Sul province, had forced the public authorities to join them in taking an oath of loyalty to the emperor and to the forthcoming constitution, "provided it be worthy of him and Brazil itself and provided that by it the said August Lord has an absolute veto."[74] The empassioned debates in the assembly showed the deputies to be at once outraged and apprehensive at the military's conduct, meddling in political affairs and rejecting the assembly's claims to supreme authority. The deputies' immediate response was to resuscitate the bill which denied the emperor the right to sanction laws, and the project narrowly passed its third reading on July 29.[75]

The second political development became known that same day. News arrived from Portugal that at the end of May 1823 troops outside Lisbon had risen in favor of the king and the traditional order. The Vilafrancada, as the coup was known, overthrew the Cortes and the constitution it had promulgated, and D. João VI was restored as absolute monarch.[76] In Brazil, the news set off immediate speculation that the same means might be employed against the Constituent Assembly.[77] It also aroused acute fears that with the Lisbon Cortes removed D. João VI would seek reconciliation with his son and restoration of his sovereignty over Brazil. The Portuguese-born who abounded in high places, particularly at court and in the military, would be incapable of resisting such an appeal from their original *pátria*—or so it was alleged by those who shared Antônio Carlos's arguments on the citizenship bill.

Even before their fall from power the Andrada brothers had been, as the debate on the citizenship bill attested, deeply suspicious of the Portuguese-born. José Bonifácio regarded them as a principal element in the conspiracy which brought about his downfall.[78] For the Andrada brothers the train of subsequent events had shown that their achievements in giving Brazil freedom from absolutism and colonial bondage was about to be undone by a vast conspiracy, masterminded by the Portuguese-born on both sides of the Atlantic.[79] They were vocal in denouncing this conspiracy and they did not hesitate to take their campaign outside the assembly. In August there appeared, under the direction of Antônio Carlos and Martim Francisco, the first number of *O Tamoyo*, a newspaper named after a native tribe renowned for its bitter hostility to the Portuguese colonizers.[80] With great skill and power, but with increasing vehemence and recklessness, the paper attacked the loyalty and the trustworthiness of the *pés de chumbo* (leaden feet), a common term of abuse for those born in Portugal. The campaign not only cast suspicion on the courtiers surrounding the emperor but ultimately raised doubts about D. Pedro I's own commitment to Brazil, born as he was in Portugal.[81]

Most of the Nativist deputies did not fear the Portuguese-born as such. They did, however, suspect the Portuguese-born in high places of holding "aristocratic ideas," and so favoring the traditionalist conception of authority. The Nativist deputies suspected that the Pôrto Alegre incident, in which the local garrison had demanded an absolute veto power for the emperor, had been inspired by this group.[82] The Vilafrancada coup in Portugal and a similar overthrow of the Cortes regime in Spain suggested that an international alliance existed against liberal, constitutional government. By harping constantly on such fears, the Andrada brothers persuaded the Nativists to forget existing enmities and to support their campaign.

The success of the Andradas in creating an atmosphere of alarm and suspicion in the assembly was revealed when the envoys sent by D. João VI to offer peace and reconciliation arrived at Rio in September 1823. So constrained was the government by the campaign and so apprehensive of the deputies' possible reaction that the letters sent by D. João VI to his son were not even accepted. Immediate and unconditional recognition of Brazilian independence by Portugal was made the precondition for any negotiations. The king's envoys were treated as little better than common prisoners of war.[83] Despite these actions, rumors abounded that schemes for reunion were favored in government circles and were being given covert assistance. Even the Austrian agent came to credit these rumors. Whereas at the end of August he did not believe what he called "the Portuguese party" (the Portuguese-born) to be "either in favor of Portugal or even of any sort of union," he reported several weeks later "the existence of a plan and a course of action, pursued in everything that has happened during the past four months, to restore this country to Portugal."[84]

In these circumstances, the relationship between the emperor and the deputies was bound to deteriorate. Nor did the assembly's proceedings improve matters. Late in August the deputies had refused, in the face of the emperor's objections, to reconsider the bill denying him the right of sanction over the assembly's bills.[85] At the start of September the long-awaited draft of the constitution was finally presented. Although article 38 did state that "the representatives of the Brazilian nation are the Emperor and the General Assembly," the balance of power clearly lay with the elected General Assembly. If ministers were to be appointed and dismissed by the emperor, they were also made responsible to the assembly, which the emperor could not dissolve. The emperor's veto power could be overriden by the assembly, and certain types of law were to be enacted without his sanction.[86]

Interminable debate and copious amendments on every clause in the draft constitution promised no swift promulgation: after one month the deputies had completed discussion of only 9 of the 272 articles. Far too much time was consumed in resolving peripheral matters, and in many cases the assembly peremptorily required information and explanation from the government. D. Pedro I seems to have alternated between a desire to prove the reality of his liberal beliefs and an exasperation at the pretensions of the assembly and the behavior of the deputies. Although the emperor did consent on October 20 to sign six bills passed by the Assembly, his air of cheerful acceptance on this occasion was misleading.[87] His resentment against the increasingly intemperate attacks on the loyalty and reliability of the Portuguese-born, and by implication of himself, mounted steadily. If in 1822 he had as prince regent refused to submit to what he termed "the pestiferous Cortes," he was no more likely as emperor to endure domination by the Constituent Assembly or vituperation from the press.[88]

Among those particularly subject to abuse in the press were the Portuguese-born officers in the Rio garrison. On November 4, 1823, two of these officers beat up a pharmacist whom they believed, incorrectly, to be the author of a particularly virulent attack. Instead of taking his case to the courts, the victim appealed to the Constituent Assembly, protesting his innocence and demanding redress. Overriding the report of the justice committee recommending that the affair was best left to the courts, the majority of the deputies, led by the Andrada brothers, made patent in a tumultuous session their determination to take up the victim's complaint. The assembly thus offered a direct challenge to the military units then in Rio de Janeiro, drawing them into the unfolding crisis.[89]

The officers' discontent persuaded the emperor to take decisive action against his and their tormentors. On November 10, 1823, he dismissed the ministers who objected to violent measures. The garrison units he personally mobilized and marched to his country palace. Meeting the next day, the deputies were suddenly faced with a full-blown crisis, which their carelessness and lack of foresight had done much to create. The atmosphere

of confrontation and the momentum of events doomed all efforts to placate the emperor and resolve the dispute. At mid-morning on November
12 the troops marched into the city and surrounded the assembly building. The deputies were read the emperor's decree denouncing the conduct
of the assembly as "perjured," dissolving it, and promising to summon a
new assembly which would enact a constitution "twice as liberal" as the
unfinished draft.[90] Threatened with expulsion at bayonet point, they had
no choice but to disperse. Six of them, including the Andrada brothers,
were that day arrested. Opposition journals were silenced. So ended the
experiment in constitutional government that had begun with such high
expectations six months before.[91]

IV

What had started as a minor dispute involving personal rivalries and
manageable disagreements over the distribution of authority had escalated, because of the lack of patience and coolheadedness on all sides, into
a full-blown crisis that seemed to threaten the very existence of the new
nation-state. Even at the time, the dissolution of the Constituent Assembly
was seen as a failure in what would now be termed "crisis management,"
the art of keeping conflicts within resolvable limits.[92] That failure was all
the more serious because the action chosen and the justification offered
were patently disproportionate to the dispute itself. D. Pedro I failed to appreciate what the consequences of using violence would be. His intention
had been to turn back the clock, to restore the political situation to what
it had been before the meeting of the Constituent Assembly. By arresting the Andrada brothers and the offending journalists and by preparing
a draft constitution "doubly more Liberal than that which the dissolved
Assembly has just made," the emperor believed he would silence his ca-
lumniators and assure the election of a new body at once cooperative and
respectful.

These happy illusions were immediately dispelled. Public opinion was
alienated or at least affronted by the crassness of the coup and by the ab-
surdity of the justification offered, that "the Assembly had perjured the
solemn oath taken to the nation to defend the integrity of the Empire, its
Independence, and My Dynasty." The foolishness of the whole affair left
some observers so aghast that they anticipated the worst: "In all proba-
bility Brazil is lost for H.R.H., the cause of monarchy, and the house of
Bragança," the Austrian agent lamented two days after the coup.[93]

The emperor found it extremely difficult to construct a durable ministry. Any hope of securing the cooperation of moderates who had sat
in the former assembly was foreclosed by the emperor's treatment of the
Andrada brothers and two of their principal allies. Since no crimes could
be charged against them, the arrested men were deported to Europe, with
pensions from the government.[94] A few ex-deputies, fearing a similar fate,

thought it best to travel abroad, and many others withdrew from Rio to their own provinces. By his use of force the emperor lost any freedom of choice and disrupted his contacts with the political community as a whole.

In these circumstances, D. Pedro I had to fall back on the traditional advisers of the Portuguese Crown. Both the ministers who consented to serve and the members of the new council of advisers (Conselho de Estado) created by decree on November 13 were almost all Luso-Brazilians—men born in Brazil, educated at Coimbra, and grown grey in the monarch's service. Since D. Pedro I named all the ministers to be members of the new Council of State, the political community of Brazil late in 1823 consisted in effect of the emperor and thirteen advisers.[95] Appreciating the perils of so narrow a base, the new government sought to broaden its support. The Council of State worked quickly to produce a draft Constitution, and elections to the promised assembly were at once put in motion. The ministry also sought to establish its presence in the provinces by nominating on November 25 the first presidents authorized by the Constituent Assembly's law reforming the governance of the provinces.

By early December it was clear that the immediate emergency was over. The crucial regions of the center and south had at least acquiesced in the course of events. "We are enjoying the greatest tranquillity," the Austrian agent reported, "and it would seem that all danger on this score has disappeared for the moment." Two weeks later he added that "it would seem that all the provinces of the South have continued firm in their loyalty to H.R.H."[96] In the northeastern provinces, which had elected the bulk of the Nativist deputies in the dissolved assembly, events were taking a very different course. The violent end to the Constituent Assembly, the embodiment of the nation, filled the Nativist deputies with horror and disbelief. To them it was inconceivable that D. Pedro I would contemplate such an act: "For his own glory, for his own self-interest, he cannot desire such a thing." More bitter than the shock of discovering that the emperor both could and would was the Nativists' disillusionment in finding that the insult to the nation's representatives did not outrage Brazilians, much less arouse them to immediate retribution. The Nativists' prognostications of woe—"if such a disgrace happened, the provinces would split apart; the Empire would no longer be Empire; the Emperor would not be Emperor" —were singularly unfulfilled.[97] Distraught and disoriented, the Nativist deputies went home to their *pátrias*. There, they witnessed with growing fury the formation of the new cabinet, the creation of the Council of State, and the nomination of the new provincial presidents.

The dissolution of the Constituent Assembly revived and confirmed the Nativists' dislike of monarchy as inherently absolutist and traditionalist and their mistrust of the Bragança dynasty as being "European" rather than "American." The creation of the Council of State proved, in their eyes, that the old regime was to be restored. As the *Typhis Pernambucano*, a Nativist periodical published in Pernambuco, accurately pointed out, the new Council of State was dominated by men who had been advisers to the Portuguese Crown prior to the establishment of constitutional rule in February 1821. Since the new assembly promised by the emperor would do no more than rubber-stamp the constitution drafted by the Council of State, its deputies would not possess constituent powers, would not represent the true will of the nation.[98] Popular fears, long-standing in the provinces, that "the chains of the former and most justly detested despotism are being readied for [the people]; and that gilded shackles under the alluring name of Independence are about to be put on them" now seemed to the Nativists to be horribly fulfilled.[99]

Compounding these fears that absolutism was about to be restored were the suspicions widely held in the northeastern provinces that the dissolution of the assembly was part of a larger plot to undo independence and secure reunion with Portugal. "It should not, therefore, be thought absurd or contradictory," asserted the *Typhis Pernambucano*, "that the Portuguese faction has in view the union of Brazil with Portugal and the establishment of the absolutist system in that same Brazil."[100] Even if a formal reunion did not occur, Brazil would be controlled by the Portuguese-born, and the nation would be nothing but a perpetuation of the old Portuguese monarchy, shorn of its non-American possessions but not of its despotic character.

Given these fears and suspicions, it is doubtful whether the Nativists in the northeast would have submitted without a struggle to the new political order being prepared in Rio de Janeiro. What made armed conflict inevitable was the imperial regime's decision to name provincial presidents. The seventeen men were selected with some care: over half those named were natives of or domiciled in the province to which appointed. In general they possessed standing, talent, and experience.[101] Although some of the choices did cause controversy, it was the simple fact of their nomination that triggered the ensuing confrontation: accepting the new presidents entailed not only recognition of the emperor's authority in the *pátrias* but loss of local autonomy.

Ever since the formation of the governing junta at Bahia on February 10, 1821, the provinces of Brazil had been in essence self-governing, controlled by their local notables. As José Bonifácio himself admitted in May 1823, the imperial government's authority was little more than nominal in most of the provinces acknowledging D. Pedro I. Power remained in the hands of the *juntas provisórias*, and little or no revenue was sent by the provinces to Rio de Janeiro.[102] Among the issues to have been resolved by the Constituent Assembly was the question of the distribution of power between the national government at Rio and the provinces. The deputies had decided, over the strenuous objections of the Nativist minority, to replace the locally elected juntas with presidents nominated and removable at will by the emperor. This solution to the question had commended itself to the deputies in part because of the juntas' bad reputation and in part because they anticipated that under the forthcoming constitution the emperor would be accountable to an elected legislature for the presidents nominated and the policies they pursued. With the dissolution of the Constituent Assembly that assurance had vanished, and the *pátrias* possessed no control, not even indirect, over the actions of the national government in the provinces.

Not surprisingly, it was the provinces participating in the 1817 revolt which now refused to recognize the new presidents and to cooperate with the new constitutional order. The lead in defying the emperor's authority was taken by Pernambuco.[103] On January 8, 1824, the province's electors formally refused to choose deputies to a new constituent assembly, arguing that it would be "contrary to the dignity and decorum of this province to name new ones, and even contrary to law. . . . The fact of the dissolution of the Congress [Constituent Assembly] had not dissolved the rights of the people to retain their existing representatives." Even though the nomination of a president for the province was already known, the electors contended that "in view of the public disfavor into which the person elected by Your Majesty has fallen," they were justified in "electing" another as president.[104] They proceeded to choose not only the province's president but its secretary and military *comandante das armas*, all of which positions were, under the new law on provincial government, appointive. The electors' formal refusal to install the emperor's nominee as president followed on February 21. The local notables simply could not grasp, much less accept, that they had lost all control over the province's government, not possessing even the right to scrutinize individuals named by the emperor as president.[105]

The conflict became overt on March 20, with an abortive attempt to depose the "elected" president by force. A blockade of Recife by the imperial navy followed. Attempts at compromise and a peaceful settlement came to nothing, leaving the opposing parties more intransigent than ever. Other provinces had by now joined Pernambuco in openly defying the emperor's authority. In April the president appointed to Ceará was deposed and replaced by an "elected" government. As confrontation grew, so the identification with Brazil as an orthodox nation-state weakened. In June, the *Typhis Pernambucano* justified the province's refusal to accept the new constitution recently promulgated by the emperor, in the following terms:

Brazil, simply by the fact of its separation from Portugal and the proclamation of its independence, became in fact independent, not only in the whole but in every one of its parts or provinces and these independent one of the other.

Brazil became sovereign, not only in the whole, but in every one of its parts or provinces.

One province does not have the right to force any other province to do anything, small as it may be, nor does any province, tiny and weak as it may be, have the obligation to obey any other that is larger and more powerful. Each therefore may follow the path it pleases, choose the form of government it judges most suitable, and establish itself in the form most conducive to its happiness.[106]

"The union of the provinces with Rio de Janeiro" after the acclamation in October 1822 had rested on two conditions, a constitutional empire and D. Pedro as emperor. "If Rio de Janeiro desires anything beyond or against either of these two conditions, the union is dissolved." The dissolution of the Constituent Assembly contravened the first condition, as did the terms of the imposed constitution. "Accordingly, the promised but not completed union of the provinces is dissolved, and for this reason, each one resumes its independence and sovereignty." In sum, what Rio de Janeiro desired and decided could not bind the other provinces.[107]

On July 2, 1824, the "elected" president of Pernambuco issued a proclamation creating "the Confederation of the Equator" and inviting other provinces to join this new and republican union.[108] Contrary to the precedent of 1817, the provinces were not perceived as entities independent of each other. Existence within a union was deemed necessary, but the existence of that union would depend on the consent of the constituent parts. Ultimate authority was thus to be retained by the individual states. The new union was not presented as a replacement or rival for Brazil. Rather, it represented the polity which Brazilians were held to desire: a loose confederation, not a centralized nation-state, was Brazil's true destiny. Accordingly, the proclamation of July 2 did not name a capital of the new union or delineate its boundaries. The Confederation of the Equator, if at the start encompassing the provinces of the northeast, might eventually be coterminous with Brazil. In its penultimate number, the *Typhis Pernambucano* equated "the cause of the liberty of Brazil" with "the Confederation of the Equator."[109]

Notwithstanding these differences, the 1824 rebellion suffered from the same ambiguity in aims and rashness in action that had doomed its predecessor in 1817. The new rising followed essentially the same course, if on a larger and bloodier scale. Although the Pernambucans gained support in Paraíba do Norte, Rio Grande do Norte, and southern Ceará, the government at Rio retained control of the sea, as it had in 1817. It instituted a close blockade of Recife while simultaneously mobilizing land forces to suppress the rising. In the middle of September 1824 the imperial troops fought their way into Recife, and in November the last rebels surrendered in southern Ceará. What marred the victory of the imperial regime was the trial by court-martial and subsequent execution of sixteen of the rebel leaders. Notable among the victims were Frei Caneca, editor of the *Typhis Pernambucano* and ideologist of the rising, who was shot at Recife, and João Ratcliffe, who was executed at Rio de Janeiro. The Nativist cause had acquired its martyrs.[110]

If the Empire easily survived the rising, the revolt did prevent the fulfillment of the emperor's promise that a new assembly would be elected to approve the new constitution. Preparation of that document by the Council of State was completed on December 11, 1823. The council's draft, while in many respects a succinct and elegant reworking of the document produced by the Constituent Assembly, departed from it on several essential points, particularly in regard to the emperor's powers.[111] Because of the incipient unrest in the northeast, D. Pedro I decided not to call a new assembly but to submit the document to the *câmaras municipais* of Brazil for their approval. Not surprisingly, only a handful of the town councils consulted were bold enough to raise objections to the draft, and none withheld consent. The Constitution was promulgated and sworn by the emperor on March 25, 1824.[112]

V

The promulgation of the Constitution and the suppression of the Confederation of the Equator resolved the basic conflicts over the distribution and control of power and authority in the new nation. Since the solutions had been imposed rather than agreed upon, leaving a legacy of distrust and bitterness, their durability was suspect, but the very fact that they had rested upon force minimized the likelihood of their immediate or early reversal. The role assigned to the emperor and the distribution of power and authority within the nation, both between the center and the localities and among the groups making up Brazilian society, were all determined by the provisions of the new constitution. The formal acceptance of the Constitution by the *câmaras municipais* and the suppression of the rebellion in the northeast had, in effect, already secured recognition of the emperor's paramount authority within the nation.[113]

Under article 1 of the 1824 Constitution the Empire was defined as "a political association of all Brazilian citizens," who "form a free and independent nation." The nation was thus conceived of as people rather than as a territorial entity; indeed, the Constitution avoided any definition of the nation's boundaries. Citizenship was not defined in territorial terms. In certain circumstances offspring born abroad to Brazilians received citizenship. On the other hand, those born into slavery in Brazil were not citizens unless and until they received their freedom, and then they acquired only limited political rights. Those Portuguese subjects born outside of Brazil who were resident in its provinces at the time of independence were declared citizens if they continued to be domiciled in the Empire.[114]

Under the Constitution, citizenship did not automatically convey political rights. As was universal at the time, women possessed no political rights, the only exception being that a female could occupy the supreme position in the nation: if no son were born to D. Pedro I, his elder daughter, D. Maria da Glória, would succeed him on the imperial throne.[115] For males political participation was regulated according to their civil condition and degree of prosperity. Those underage, the cloistered clergy, servants, and sons living in their father's homes could not vote in the elections at the parish level.[116] Nor was the vote given to those with an annual income of less than 100 milreis (U.S. $98.00). As a commentator on the Constitution remarked 30 years later: "Well, not to possess such an income in Brazil you virtually have to be a beggar or at least a wholly idle and useless man." [117] In short, the basic franchise compared favorably with those then existing in the nation-states of the Atlantic world.

Political participation was limited for most individuals, however, because of a two-tier franchise system. As article 90 stated, elections to the national and provincial legislatures "will be made by indirect elections, the mass of the active citizens electing in parish assemblies the provincial electors and these the representatives of the nation and province." [118] Such a two-tier system was not unique to Brazil but was then used in France to select the Chamber of Deputies and, as it legally still is, in the United States to choose the president. To be an elector required the same qualifications as to be a voter, save for double the income. Further, freedmen (former slaves) and those accused of crimes could not serve as electors.[119] The drafters of the 1824 Constitution clearly equated the electors with the parish notables. The qualifications for election to the national legislature and provincial councils were even more restrictive than those for parish elector.[120] Elections for these positions were provincewide, with the câmara municipal of the provincial capital tabulating the electors' votes and making the returns.[121]

The Constitution defined the internal nature of the nation as a centralized, unitary state. If the existence of the provinces was recognized under article 2, it also decreed that they could be subdivided "as the good of the State demands." The presidents created by the law of October 20 were continued, and the provinces were in addition granted elective Conselhos Gerais (General Councils), which received, however, minimal powers.[122] Resolutions they passed did not come into permanent effect until also enacted as laws by the Assembleia Geral (General Assembly), the national legislature composed of a senate with life tenure and a chamber of deputies elected for four years.[123] Articles 11 and 12 declared the emperor and the General Assembly to be "the representatives of the Brazilian nation" and all "political powers" to be delegated from the nation.[124]

"The division and harmony of the political powers," article 9 proclaimed, "is the principle preserving the rights of the citizens and the surest way to make effective the guarantees that the Constitution affords." [125] These guarantees, specified in the 35 sections of article 179, were more complete and more liberal than those contained at that time in the American Constitution or in the few European constitutions then in existence.[126]

According to article 10, "the political powers recognized by the constitution of Brazil are four: the legislative power, the regulating power [o poder moderador], the executive power, and the judicial power." The regulating power as a necessary element in the national polity had first been advocated in the Constituent Assembly where it had been described as being "considered by the wisest theorists of our time [to be] a sovereign power distinct from the executive power."[127] Defined by article 98 as "the key to the entire political organization," the regulating power was by that article "delegated to the Emperor, as supreme chief of the nation and its first representative, so that he may constantly oversee the independence, equilibrium, and harmony of the other political powers." Article 99 added that "the person of the Emperor is inviolable and sacred; he is not subject to any accountability."[128] Despite the linking by article 11 of the emperor and the General Assembly as representatives of the nation, the existence of the regulating power gave the emperor preeminence over the assembly as the embodiment of the national will. As head of the regulating power, the emperor was able at his discretion to dissolve the Chamber of Deputies, nominate members to the life Senate, name and dismiss his ministers "freely," suspend judges and magistrates, and grant pardons.[129]

The emperor was in addition "head of the executive power and exercises it through his ministers of state."[130] Since the ministers were "freely" named and removed by him and since all laws and decrees were signed by him not as head of the executive but as holder of the regulating power, the emperor's role in the executive branch of the government was predominant. The ministers, being accountable to the General Assembly for their actions, were caught between a rock and a hard place.

In respect to the legislative power, article 13 declared it to be "delegated to the General Assembly with the sanction of the Emperor." Since the imperial veto was virtually impossible to override and since the emperor named new senators (choosing one of the three candidates given the most votes by the electors in the province with the vacancy), he had, if not the dominant, surely a considerable voice in the passage of legislation.[131] In moments of contention, the emperor could through his use of the regulating power summon and adjourn the General Assembly, and "in the cases where the safety of the state requires it," he could dissolve the sitting Chamber of Deputies and summon a new one.

Although the judiciary was recognized by article 11 as the fourth "political power" and although its independence was guaranteed by article 151, the judiciary had in reality a subordinate role. Under article 163 a new Supreme Tribunal of Justice was to be created in the capital, but the powers granted to it by article 164 were narrowly defined.[132] The power to "watch over compliance of the Constitution and to promote the general good of the nation" was, under section 9 of article 13, specifically attributed to the General Assembly.[133] It was not the intention of the authors of the Constitution that the acts of either the legislature or the executive, and certainly not those of the regulating power, should be subject to judicial review.

The only restraint imposed by the Constitution on the emperor's regulating power was contained in article 142, which required that "in all serious matters and general points of public administration, . . . as on all occasions when the Emperor intends to exercise any of the functions given to the regulating power" (save for the appointment and dismissal of ministers), he had to consult with his Council of State. This body, created on November 13, 1823, was now enshrined in the Constitution, which stated by article 143 that its members were "accountable for the counsels they give which are opposed to the laws and patently harmful to the interest of the State." Derelictions of duty were to be judged by the Senate, not by the Supreme Tribunal of Justice.[134]

What made the Council of State important at this time was the absence of any other restraint upon the emperor's authority. Many of the new Constitution's provisions could not be implemented without enabling legislation, which would not be passed until the first legislature was elected and in session. Neither the necessary regulations for elections nor the elections themselves were expedited. The new legislature would not meet until May 1826, more than two years after the proclamation of the Constitution. In the interim, the emperor and his advisers were free to shape the nation as he and they considered best and as the realities of government permitted.

V I

Within Brazil the years 1824 and 1825 were notable for the consolidation of imperial authority and the restoration of effective administration in the provinces, particularly those of the north. The most enduring achievement was the creation of a viable colony of some 2,000 German immigrants in the province of Rio Grande do Sul. The São Leopoldo colony, by establishing the credibility of the far south as a home for European emigrants, had a lasting influence on the culture and demography of that region.[135]

The dominant concern of the emperor and his advisers in this period of unlimited power was, however, not internal but external affairs. Two major problems that the new nation had faced since 1822 were still unresolved: recognition by foreign states of D. Pedro I as emperor of Brazil, and agreement on the boundaries of the nation.[136] The two questions were linked but, as events showed, by no means identical. The presence of D. Pedro as prince regent and the declaration of independence as a monarchy had been indispensable in bringing all the territories of Portuguese America into the single nation-state Brazil. Yet Brazil was the single monarchy in a continent of republics. Its anomalous position combined with the absence of internal consensus to make diplomatic recognition a more immediate priority than was the case for the other states of South America. Diplomatic recognition would at once endow the new state with the legitimacy which internal conditions denied it.

The key to international recognition of the new nation lay in formal acceptance by Portugal of Brazilian independence. Such acceptance would not easily be obtained. After D. João VI had been restored as absolute ruler of Portugal in June 1823 by the Vilafrancada rising, he sought the end of hostilities and a reconciliation with his son, and therefore proffered self-government for Brazil under his nominal sovereignty. The immediate and total rebuff of these overtures and the harsh treatment of the king's envoys, while attributable to the exigencies of the situation in the Constituent Assembly, affronted D. João VI and his advisers. D. Pedro appeared an ingrate and Brazil governed by extremists. The dissolution of the Constituent Assembly by the emperor did not cause the Lisbon government to reconsider its position—to Brazil's cost, since Portugal had everything to lose and little to gain by renouncing its claims to sovereignty over Brazil.[137]

This mutual antagonism prepared the way for intervention into the conflict by Great Britain. A swift settlement was for the British an immediate necessity. On the one hand England was bound by treaty to maintain the territorial integrity of Portugal, while on the other Brazil constituted one of the best markets for British exports. Since the 1810 treaty with Portugal that gave British goods a tied market in Brazil came open for revision in 1825, the British interest in a settlement—preferably by Portugal's recognition of the new Empire—was intense.[138]

British involvement in the dispute was in fact invited by Portugal as early as September 1823, in the hope that pressure by her ally would achieve for Portugal what force of arms could not.[139] The request was renewed in December when news of the rebuff to D. João's envoys at Rio reached Lisbon. Brushing aside the preconditions for talks set by the Portuguese, the British foreign secretary had no difficulty in persuading Brazil to participate. Begun in July 1824, the London negotiations finally broke down in February 1825 over what had from the start been the sticking point: the unwillingness of the Portuguese to concede total independence and of the Brazilians to accept anything less. The actual collapse of the talks resulted from a Portuguese ultimatum requiring that "the two parts, European and American, of the Portuguese Monarchy will henceforth possess under the sovereignty of Snr. D. João VI and his legitimate descendants a reciprocally independent administration with, however, perpetual union between them." The Portuguese envoy was instructed to break off the talks unless he received full and immediate acceptance by the Brazilian agents (which the Portuguese government deemed "quite improbable") to the terms of the counter-project contained in the ultimatum.[140]

Portuguese intransigence had been encouraged by the absolute monarchs of Europe, who deplored any yielding by the king of his legitimate rights. Some of D. João VI's advisers continued to urge him to uphold those rights by organizing a fresh expedition against Brazil and thus forcing recognition of Portuguese sovereignty. These views were offset by others who, understanding the impracticality of such a course, sought to persuade the king to sacrifice his rights and recognize "what Senhor D. Pedro has done under the most difficult circumstances."[141]

News of the breakdown of the talks reached Rio de Janeiro just as a major revolt was suddenly erupting in the Cisplatine province. The Brazilian hold on the former Banda Oriental had been seriously shaken late in 1822 when the Portuguese troops garrisoning Montevideo refused to acknowledge D. Pedro's acclamation as emperor of Brazil and the *cabildo* had thereafter formally annulled the union with Brazil engineered in July 1821. Although the ensuing uprising failed and the Portuguese troops eventually evacuated Montevideo at the end of 1823, many of the rebels had taken refuge in Buenos Aires, where they found ready support. The upcoming elections to the first legislature of the Empire made clear that the region, despite its separate language, culture, and history, was to be fully integrated into Brazil and treated no differently from any other province. News of Simón Bolívar's triumph at Ayacucho over the last Spanish army in South America triggered the rising against Brazilian rule.[142] On April 19, 1825, a small band—famous as "the Thirty-Three" in Uruguayan history—crossed into the Banda Oriental and raised the flag of revolt, seeking to drive out the Brazilians and to unite with the United Provinces of the Río de la Plata. Key elements in the local militia rallied to the rebels. In September and October the Brazilian forces suffered major defeats and lost control of the countryside. The rebels were able to form a provisional government and then elect a constituent assembly. These successes encouraged the United Provinces to issue a law incorporating the Banda Oriental and threatening to expel by force anyone violating the national territory.

Such a provocation the imperial government could not overlook, and it declared formal war on the United Provinces on December 10, 1825.[143] This decision by the emperor and his advisers to go to war and to risk arousing the united enmity of the Spanish American republics was caused in part by a refusal to admit any alteration to the Empire's existing frontiers and in part by the ending in August 1825 of the confrontation with Portugal. The resolution of the conflict between father and son had been secured through the British government's use of brute power politics. Exasperated by Portuguese intransigence and determined to maintain British commercial advantages in both countries, the British foreign secretary decided to use British diplomacy to force a settlement on the two nations.[144]

Shortly after the breakdown of the London mediation talks, a senior British diplomat was sent to Lisbon. There, by warning that Great Britain would otherwise grant immediate diplomatic recognition to the Empire, he forced D. João VI into naming him to be special envoy from Portugal to Brazil, with sufficient authority to recognize (if no other choice remained) the complete independence of Brazil. Arriving at Rio in July 1825, the envoy opened negotiations. Without great difficulty he secured from the three Brazilian negotiators sufficient concessions—the right of D. João VI to use the title of emperor, retroactive nullification of the state of war between Portugal and Brazil, and a financial settlement amounting to £2,000,000 (U.S. $10,000,000)—to justify the recognition of full independence. On August 29, 1825, a treaty of recognition and amity between Portugal and Brazil was concluded and signed.[145]

Once ratified by D. João in November 1825, the treaty secured within weeks diplomatic recognition from England and the other monarchies of Europe.[146] For the emperor and his advisers, the treaty resolved the remaining major problems facing the new nation. The great powers recognized the emperor and the Brazilian nation as legitimate entities, and this acceptance in turn legitimized the existing boundaries of the nation. The recent rising in the Cisplatine province, troublesome as it was, constituted no serious threat to the integrity of Brazil. It is no wonder that on October 12, 1825, the monarch's birthday, D. Pedro I bestowed titles of nobility on 25 of his advisers and associates, including all the councillors of state. A few weeks later, on December 5, Empress D. Leopoldina gave birth to a healthy son, the long-desired male heir and the living assurance of the continued independence of the Empire. The last four months of 1825 marked the apogee of D. Pedro I's reign, a brief interlude of security and prestige before the renewal of troubles within and without.

5

Competing Conceptions of Nationhood, 1825-1831

Establishment of a political order and acceptance by the international community did not resolve the fundamental question of the nature of Brazil's nationhood. D. Pedro I's recognition as legitimate sovereign and the promise of permanence given by the birth of a son and heir appeared to cast Brazil in the mold of the constitutional monarchies of Europe. A profuse bestowal of titles of nobility in October 1825 on the nation's governing circle—cabinet ministers, councillors of state, and military commanders—was a visible affirmation that to the emperor belonged the principal source of authority in Brazil.[1]

Political structures had been created at breakneck speed, and force rather than consent used to resolve contentious issues. The form of Brazilian nationhood was, therefore, decided but not resolved. The euphoria generated by the treaty with Portugal of August 29, 1825, and the birth of a prince imperial on December 2 proved short-lived. Fundamental conflicts swiftly reemerged. Rival conceptions of nationhood once more dominated Brazilian politics. Earlier feuds and grievances inhibited settlement of disputed issues and so prevented the political community from devoting its energy and attention to new tasks.

The acquisition of independence and the creation of a political order represented a marriage in haste between the ruler and his subjects. From 1825 to 1831 the emperor and the Brazilians would attempt to exist within the relationship, mainly on the terms each wanted. If D. Pedro I came off worse in the ensuing quarrels, his past conduct would be mainly to blame. According to his own conception of the nation, he had to be the supreme embodiment of Brazil and the final arbiter of its political system. In pursuit of this goal D. Pedro I did not balk at using any means or paying any price.

The emperor's insistence on preserving the frontiers established by his father and his desire for military prowess was to draw Brazil into a long, inglorious, and ultimately futile war in the far south. Dependence on British mediation to secure international diplomatic recognition led to the perpetuation of the commercial bondage imposed in 1810 by the Anglo-Portuguese agreement and made it impossible to remedy the economic weaknesses of the nation. Retention by D. Pedro I of his rights to the Portuguese throne by the treaty of August 1825 was to impose upon him an exhausting and thankless role in Portuguese affairs. The Constitution, promulgated by D. Pedro I in March 1824, virtually assured friction by juxtaposing a powerful ruler and an unbridled political community. On each of these issues D. Pedro I had staked out an extreme position very much exposed to attack. Since his personal vanity and conception of his role in the nation would not allow him to retreat or to compromise, the remainder of his reign was to be dominated by a struggle to retain the ground he had earlier occupied with such bravado.

The history of D. Pedro I's reign has long been presented in personal terms: as a direct combat between the emperor and his myriad opponents. What makes this interpretation understandable is that the 1824 Constitution did place the emperor at the very heart of the political process and that D. Pedro I had the knack of personalizing every political issue in which he was involved. The interplay of the public and the personal was exemplified by the controversy over cabinet appointments. Under the Constitution the emperor had the right "freely to appoint and dismiss ministers." Although not denying this right, the majority in the Chamber of Deputies did demand as a condition for its cooperation that the cabinet command the legislators' confidence. D. Pedro I, however, eschewed the unfamiliar. His choice of ministers was heavily influenced by his dislike for constant contact with outsiders. By 1830 an impasse was reached. Everyone with whom the emperor felt comfortable had by then forfeited the confidence of the opposition deputies. D. Pedro I refused to give way, because of his hatred of acting under compulsion and his conviction that his honor as emperor was at stake.

The highly personalized character of this and other political disputes did not make them any less the product of a fundamental disagreement about Brazil's future as a nation. A clash between two conflicting ideologies underlay all the battles that raged from 1826 to 1831 over the organization of governance, the functioning of the political process, and the goals to be pursued in international affairs. A conception of the nation as polity based on traditional forms of inherited authority and directed by a ruler of heroic stature was increasingly challenged by a conception that equated the nation with the people and derived all authority from the popular will. Even if no personal element had been involved, compromise solutions to the outstanding problems would not, therefore, have easily been found.

I

On May 6, 1826, D. Pedro I opened the first General Assembly, to which he read his Speech from the Throne. The ceremonies at the opening served—intentionally or no—to emphasize the emperor's supreme authority. The regalia worn by D. Pedro I included the crown; three years before, at the opening of the Constituent Assembly, it had been carried before him. The Speech from the Throne, largely composed by the emperor himself, was minatory in tone, offering no olive branches to the assembled legislators.[2] After stating, "I dissolved the Constituent Assembly to my regret and for reasons not unknown to you," the emperor commented: "Revolutions do not arise from the system, but rather from those who, in its shadow, seek to gain their private ends. . . . The greater part of the senators and deputies ought to be very conscious that the ills suffered by some nations are caused by the lack of respect due to the established authorities when they, instead of being prosecuted and tried in accord with the law and universal justice, are attacked and belittled."[3] These words of menace and reproof could only emphasize the gulf separating the emperor seated on his throne in full regalia from the 50 senators and the 102 deputies who composed the two chambers of the General Assembly.[4]

The convening of the new legislature marked, far more than the promulgation of the 1824 charter, the real beginning of D. Pedro I's reign as constitutional monarch. In contrast to the ill-fated Constituent Assembly, the legislature could not claim an authority rival or superior to that of the monarch, but since both emperor and General Assembly were recognized by article 11 of the Constitution as representative of the nation, it could lay claim to considerable authority. According to the Constitution, the four political powers (legislative, regulating, executive, and judicial) were all "delegations of the nation," with the "division" of those powers being described as "the surest means of effecting the guarantees offered by the constitution."[5]

The emperor held ultimate authority because of his possession of the regulating power, "the key to the whole political system," and his control of the national government, as head of the executive. Nonetheless, the powers the General Assembly wielded under the Constitution gave it the means of exerting a considerable, even decisive, influence on the conduct of government. By article 13 of the Constitution, the legislature possessed the exclusive right to make, interpret, suspend, and revoke laws. The General Assembly was each year to authorize expenditures and impose taxes. All government loans had to be approved by it, and it regulated payment of the national debt. The right to create and abolish government positions belonged to the legislature, which was annually to fix the size of the land and sea forces. The General Assembly was further empowered "to watch over compliance with the Constitution and to promote the general good of the nation."[6] The legislators could, under this provision, force debate on all aspects of the imperial government's conduct of internal affairs. Since article 102 of the Constitution required the government to "bring to the knowledge of the General Assembly" all treaties made by the executive and to lay before it documents relating to any declaration of war and conclusion of peace, the conduct of foreign affairs was also subject to review by the legislature.[7] If the legislators were sufficiently skilled and determined, they could employ these powers to circumscribe the government's freedom of action, to restrain and even block unwelcome policies, and to influence the emperor's choice of ministers.

The General Assembly, accordingly, constituted the element in the political process through which public opinion, such as it was, would be voiced and where dissenting conceptions of nationhood could be expressed. Under the Constitution the General Assembly had to meet annually for a session of four months. Its debates were conducted in public. The legislators were "inviolable for the opinions expressed during the exercise of their functions." Nor could they be arrested during their mandate save by order of their own chamber.[8] All of these factors made the General Assembly the natural forum for venting discontents and grievances and for voicing opposition to government policies. With no responsibility for the actual conduct of affairs, the legislators were free to propose sweeping reforms, advocate ideal solutions, and denounce compromising and opportunistic conduct by the government.

Although the Constitution extolled harmony between the political powers and made the regulating power responsible for the "maintenance of the independence, equilibrium, and harmony of the other political powers," the emperor possessed (under article 101) only limited means of controlling the legislature once disharmony arose. He could adjourn the General Assembly and prolong its sessions, but he could not force it to take any specific course of action. The monarch did nominate the members of the Senate, but, since they held life tenure, once selected they became immune to government coercion. The emperor could dissolve the Chamber of Deputies; a new chamber had, however, to be elected and called into session immediately. This power was effective when held in reserve as a threat. It could not be employed repeatedly, nor would its use necessarily work to the emperor's advantage.[9]

Under the Constitution the emperor and the General Assembly therefore enjoyed in practice coequal authority. The legislature could not be coerced, it had to be persuaded. The monarch had to coexist and cooperate with the General Assembly if the political system were to function effectively. Past events did not offer much hope that either side would display the requisite goodwill, flexibility in outlook, and moderation in behavior. In 1823 the intemperate speeches of the deputies had contributed to the violent end of the Constituent Assembly. Two years' delay between the promulgation of the 1824 charter and the convening of the

General Assembly did not portend much enthusiasm on the part of the emperor and his advisers for constitutional government. Not until January 26, 1826, had the members of the Senate been chosen by the emperor from lists of candidates selected by the electors in each province.[10]

The personality of D. Pedro I, then in his mid-twenties, was as critical an element in the future development of the Empire as were the powers bestowed on him by the Constitution. In September 1825 a British diplomat observed: "The personal character of the individual who is at the head of the Government of this country will have so great an influence upon their affairs, that it may be agreeable to His Majesty's Government to learn the result of the observations which my position at this Court has enabled me to make."[11] The key to D. Pedro I's psychological makeup was abounding physical energy, which kept him in perpetual motion. His personal life was a frenetic search for action and stimulation, his favored pursuits being horses, hunting, and women. Hyperactivity gave him a fiery temper, an urge to dominate, and a brief attention span. Owing to his neglected upbringing he had never learned to bridle his words and conduct, and his innate intelligence had for want of formal schooling not been developed. As shown by such comments as "the fruit is fine even though the pod is gross," D. Pedro I understood his own strengths and limitations. He was, however, never able to turn this self-knowledge to advantage.[12] Behavior which would have excited no comment from an ancien régime aristocrat was not conduct suitable for the ruler of a constitutional monarchy in the age of progress.

In his dispatch of September 25, 1825, the British diplomat identified D. Pedro I's fundamental flaws as ruler: "The improvident measures adopted by the Government are the result of the fits of passion to which he gives way, but no man can regret more than himself the [resulting] quarrels . . . when the fit is over." The emperor's uncontrolled temper affected not just policy making but his whole relationship with his subjects. Only occasionally did his outbursts involve physical aggression, but the emperor's language when aroused was coarse and offensive. His behavior did not display the dignity and decorum expected in a monarch. Nor did D. Pedro I's character exude that basic goodwill and sympathy which had gained D. João VI the affection of his Brazilian subjects despite his manifest faults.[13]

D. Pedro I's second flaw as monarch was his inability to take advice, to accept that others' opinions and talents might be superior to his own. He told the British diplomat that "notwithstanding the bad education which he has received, he considers himself the member of the Cabinet who is most equal to the task imposed upon him." The emperor's high estimation of his own capacities stemmed in part from his desire to dominate but also from his acceptance of what may be termed the Napoleonic vision of the nation: the tenet that the ruler was a superior being, chosen by Providence and alone capable of directing the affairs of state.

The British diplomat praised D. Pedro I's "quick perception," believing that "affairs treated directly with him are settled more rapidly and more satisfactorily than when referred to all or any of his official advisers." The comment reveals, however, more about the caliber of the ministers and other councillors than the emperor's actual ability. Almost two years earlier the Austrian agent had remarked about these same advisers that they were limited "by being equally petty-minded to a high degree and by seeking in all questions the course which will advance their own personal interests." Their basic weakness was, nonetheless, not so much a want of capacity as a lack of initiative and independence in relation to the emperor. If the improvident measures of the government resulted from D. Pedro's fits of passion, it was because, as the British envoy acknowledged, "no one among his own people dares contradict him." [14]

As the wording of his dispatch also indicates, the British envoy's preference for dealing directly with the emperor was not due solely to D. Pedro I's "quick perception" but to the greater ease with which concession could be obtained from the monarch. It was D. Pedro I who yielded to the diplomat's insistence that in the ratification of the treaty with Portugal the words "by the unanimous acclamation of the peoples" in the imperial title be replaced with the innocuous phrase "by the Constitution," so that D. João VI's susceptibilities might not be offended. [15] Making concessions such as this did the emperor's reputation little good, especially since suspicions about the sincerity of his attachment to constitutional government and to Brazil's independence were already widespread.

"The defects of his character compel his Council, his family, and all around him to submit blindly to his will." The relationship was, however, less one-sided than the British envoy's remark would suggest. Despite his impulsiveness and temper, D. Pedro I was essentially a creature of habit, his behavior following set patterns, and these traits made him vulnerable to manipulation by the members of his court circle. The British diplomat rightly feared that "the numerous flatterers who surround his Royal Highness would lead him into the most dangerous excesses." [16] The emperor's personal servants and household officers knew precisely how to play on their master's weaknesses to their own profit. These men, *fardas verdes* (green uniforms) as they were called from the color of the imperial livery, were nearly all Portuguese-born who had come with the Court to Brazil in 1808 and thus had known D. Pedro I since boyhood. Closest to the emperor was Francisco Gomes da Silva, nicknamed "the Buffoon" (o Chalaça), whom the emperor had appointed his private secretary in December 1823. [17] What made this camarilla increasingly unpopular, in addition to place of birth and political views, was both its subservience to D. Pedro and its superior influence on him.

Far exceeding any member of the court circle as an influence on the emperor was D. Domitila de Castro Canto e Melo, whom D. Pedro I had met in August 1822 during his visit to São Paulo province. A year older than the emperor, D. Domitila was married but separated from her husband. Her captivating appearance did not long conceal a formidable character. The emperor, if he had never been faithful to his wife, had not previously maintained a *maîtresse en titre*. He not only brought D. Domitila and her family to Rio but in the course of 1825 named her first lady-in-waiting to the empress and created her viscountess of Santos. Shrewd and sensual, D. Domitila held D. Pedro I in an emotional and physical thrall that she exploited to the advantage of herself, her family, and those she chose to favor.[18] She acted as the ideal conduit for everyone who wished to obtain from the imperial government favors which could not be achieved by regular, legitimate means. Her influence on D. Pedro I as emperor was uniformly harmful, inflating his self-esteem, increasing his lack of balance, and warping his political judgment.

If D. Pedro's faults as ruler of Brazil are more apparent than his merits it is because he was, as a prominent Portuguese politician commented, "at his best during a revolution and at his worst when governing a state."[19] "Half measures do not," D. Pedro I conceded, "suit my nature."[20] In an emergency the emperor's abilities shone forth—he became cool in nerve, resourceful and steadfast in action. Life as a constitutional monarch, full of tedium, caution, and conciliation, ran against the essence of his character. D. Pedro I's weaknesses as ruler of Brazil were evident in his mishandling of the first General Assembly. His Speech from the Throne was not designed to woo the legislators. He failed to make best use of the opportunity given by his right to nominate the entire Senate and also to shape the membership of the Chamber of Deputies.

That the emperor could significantly influence the composition of the General Assembly was due in large measure to the narrowness of the political community and its dominance by men of official experience. The lists of candidates selected by the provincial electors, from which the emperor was to choose the original 50 senators, perforce contained 150 names. Because of the limited number of men with talent, knowledge, and experience and because the provincial electors were concerned to choose representatives whose connections would most benefit the interests of the local *pátria* when dealing with the national government, the same individuals tended to be chosen by the electors in different provinces. Thus the Senate base lists, although composed of 150 names, in fact included only 112 men, of whom no less than 42 had also been elected to the lower house.[21] The total number of potential legislators making up the two houses with a combined full membership of 152 therefore numbered only 172.

Of this number nearly two-fifths were Luso-Brazilians, men born in Brazil who had graduated from Coimbra before 1816 and then entered the royal service, mostly as judges and bureaucrats. That it was the Luso-Brazilians who most often enjoyed national standing is attested to by the fact that of the 23 men who were selected as senatorial candidates by more than one province all but two were Luso-Brazilians.[22] The Luso-Brazilians were less dominant in the Chamber of Deputies than in the upper house, being 33 out of 102. Of these 33 men, 22 had also been elected to the Senate base lists. Since the Luso-Brazilians overwhelmingly supported the political settlement imposed by the emperor in March 1824, D. Pedro I —if he used his powers of nomination carefully—could assure himself of strong support in both houses of the legislature.

In selecting the new Senate, the emperor was, however, guided solely by a desire to fill the upper house with his closest advisers. Of the 112 individuals on the base lists, he chose two-thirds of the Luso-Brazilians and one-half of the military officers but only one-third of the clergy and one-twentieth of the local notables.[23] The emperor's Senate nominations were unwise for other reasons.[24] They intensified the overlap in membership among the organs of national government. In the Senate sat all thirteen members of the Council of State created in November 1823, as well as four of his recent ministers.[25] Close to half of the men nominated to the Senate held titles of nobility. A closed circle of rule, a political aristocracy, had been created both in reality and in appearance. When in October 1826 the emperor advanced all the titled senators two steps in the peerage, he merely confirmed his political philosophy.[26]

The emperor's Senate nominations also altered the balance of forces in the Chamber of Deputies, which alone could initiate legislation on taxation and to which all government measures had to be first proposed.[27] Among the new senators were fifteen deputies, all but two being Luso-Brazilians. Not only was the number of Luso-Brazilians in the chamber thereby reduced numerically by over a third, but the emperor's nominations removed from the lower house a number of experienced men of national reputation who could have spoken on behalf of the government and managed its business.

The seats thus vacated in the chamber were filled not by fresh elections but by seating the individuals, termed *suplentes* (alternates), who had received the next highest number of votes in the relevant province. They were, in most cases, men of purely local standing, born and raised in Brazil and neither educated at Coimbra nor trained in the royal service.[28] The number of deputies with this background, many of whom were Nativist in outlook, increased by one-third, to some 28 in total. Of this group 8 had sat in the Constituent Assembly.[29]

By their presence alone, these Nativists would constantly remind the deputies of the controversial origins of the 1824 Constitution. No matter how much the use of force against that earlier assembly might be explained and excused as a regrettable necessity, the emperor's act had prevented the establishment of a new political order based upon general consent and had deprived the national government of uncontested legitimacy. The imperial regime was further compromised in the minds of Nativists and liberals in general by its identification with repression and injustice.[30] The sixteen martyrs court-martialed and executed for their role in the 1824 rebellion,

were a perpetual reminder that the new Constitution had been established
at the cost of innocent lives. That Brazil was to be a monarchy had been
resolved—but resolved in "the blood of the Canecas and the Ratcliffes,"
to quote from a work written 25 years later.[31]

Another group prominent in the lower house, some 27 deputies strong
and so outnumbering the Nativists, belonged to a distinctive new generation of Brazilians. Between 1816 and 1826 no less than 102 Brazilian-born
students had graduated from Coimbra.[32] A different attitude toward Brazil and its colonial heritage sharply distinguished these graduates, dubbed
here the "Coimbra bloc," from their predecessors, the Luso-Brazilians.
Whereas the Luso-Brazilians cherished the colonial heritage, for most
members of the Coimbra bloc it represented a legacy to be rejected. As
Bernardo Pereira de Vasconcelos, an 1819 graduate who proved himself
the ablest and certainly the most vocal of the Coimbra bloc deputies, stated
on August 7, 1826: "I studied public law at that university and I left it an
ignoramus; I was even forced to unlearn."[33]

By 1820 the Brazilian-born constituted about 5 or 6 percent of the
student body at Coimbra, a minority sufficiently large to catch the public
eye during the events unfolding from the Porto rising in August 1820 to the
recognition of Brazil's independence in August 1825. During these years
Brazilian students continued to attend Coimbra, shielded from internment
and official reprisals by the power of custom and the influence of relatives
in Portugal. However, the Brazilians, especially those vocal in support of
the independence movement, suffered discrimination and harassment from
their fellow students, while the university authorities looked on. Some
Brazilians left to finish their studies in France or Germany, but the majority
perservered.[34]

The ostracism and rancor experienced at Coimbra made the young students conscious of a shared identity and proud of what was being attacked
—their common Brazilianness. As they closed ranks to face adversity,
love of *pátria* became transmuted into love of Brazil itself.[35] A true sense
of nationality was created. The students at Coimbra during these years,
although coming from the different regions of Brazil, became the first generation to accept the nation as the supreme object of identity and affection.

An acute shortage of personnel in the judicial system assured Coimbra
bloc members of immediate employment as *ouvidores* or *juizes de fora* on
their return home to Brazil. The coming of independence did not deprive
such judicial positions of their influence, so that members of the Coimbra
bloc were well placed to achieve election as deputies. Their mistrust of
the colonial heritage and abhorrence of absolutist government gave them
a good deal in common with the Nativist deputies, and a working alliance
between the two groups, who together numbered close to half the lower
house, came into being as soon as the Chamber met in preliminary session
in April 1826.

The first manifestation of this alliance was a quarrel that had erupted

between the lower house and the Senate even before the opening ceremonies. The point at issue was whether the officials of the imperial court,
ranged behind the emperor as he read his speech, should or should not
be seated. Meeting in preliminary session, the deputies demanded that the
officials stand—and thereby both rejected any role for hereditary privilege in the national polity and protested against the influence which the
court officials, many of them Portuguese-born and of aristocratic origin,
exerted on the emperor. The intransigence the deputies displayed in this
quarrel, which delayed the legislature's inauguration for three days, revealed the tension already existing, even before the emperor had delivered
his speech, between the monarch and the deputies. This tension was in no
way diminished by the solution of the impasse: the question was referred
to the emperor, who predictably decided against the deputies' preference.
By removing his most capable supporters from the Chamber, D. Pedro I
had in effect sacrificed his best hope of managing the deputies during the
ensuing four years and so developing an effective relationship with the
General Assembly.

II

The Speech from the Throne, delivered on May 6, 1826, did more than
admonish the legislators. It surveyed the topics of immediate concern to
the emperor and his advisers and on which D. Pedro I believed the legislators were in duty bound to offer the government their full support.
All focused on foreign affairs. Priority of place was given to the war then
raging in the far south. "The entire Empire is tranquil, except for the Cisplatine province," the emperor declared. "Ungrateful men who owe much
to Brazil have risen against her and are now supported by the government
of Buenos Aires, currently at war with us. The national honor requires
that the Cisplatine province be retained, since we have sworn to maintain
the integrity of the Empire."[36] This plea for support reflected the unfavorable turn that hostilities had taken during the previous six months. On
October 12, 1825, the very day the emperor bestowed his titles of nobility,
the rebels in the Banda Oriental had won a decisive victory at Sarandí,
leaving the Brazilians in control of only three port towns. The rebels' success had stampeded the Argentine Congress first into agreeing to union
with the Banda Oriental and then into guaranteeing the integrity of its
territory. On December 10, the imperial regime responded to these acts
by declaring war against Argentina.[37]

The Brazilian cabinet had originally welcomed the war, seeing in it not
only the most effective way of stamping out the revolt but the means of
showing the superiority of monarchical over republican government. Victory for the imperial forces would once and for all validate the Napoleonic
vision of the nation. The ability of the ruler by his superior talents and by
the favor of Providence to bring strength and glory to the nation would

be confirmed. The ensuing struggle sadly disappointed these expectations. Despite their large numbers and superior resources, the Brazilian forces could not win any decisive success, either on land or at sea.

The mounting expenditures on men and munitions required to maintain the conflict in the Río de la Plata region compounded another problem noted only in passing in the Speech from the Throne: the state of "the public treasury."[38] The unfavorable fiscal and economic situation facing Brazil stemmed in part from the adverse impact on the nation's regional economies of the independence struggle and the 1824 civil war. The port of Salvador had been closed for almost a year in 1822 and 1823, and the northeast as a whole had suffered from the revolt of 1824. The embargo on trade with Portugal decreed late in 1822 disrupted a major branch of the nation's foreign commerce. Brazilian trade with the former mother country, exports and imports alike, fell in value by one-half.[39] By the end of 1825 the declining worth of Brazil's currency, the milreis, against the pound sterling signaled that all was far from well with its export sector. The fall in the milreis also reflected the swelling deficit in the government budget and the unchecked expansion of paper money.

The outbreak of hostilities in the far south simply compounded existing problems. The imperial government financed the war by borrowing from the Banco do Brasil, which made the loans in the form of fresh bank notes, thus fueling inflation. The magnitude of the decline in the milreis, which lost half its value before stabilizing in 1830, suggests causes more profound than government deficits and excessive note issue. Prices for the plantation crops on which Brazil's export economies depended appear to have declined after 1825, as a result of new areas of production in North America and Asia bringing increased competition in the markets of Europe.[40] The deteriorating fiscal situation and the soaring expenditures caused by the war left the imperial government with no choice but to seek assistance from the new General Assembly, which controlled taxation. D. Pedro I and his ministers were thus placed from the very beginning at a considerable disadvantage in their dealings with the legislature.

Diplomatic recognition of the empire was another topic of the Speech from the Throne: "The independence of Brazil was recognized by my august father D. João VI, of glorious memory, on November 15 of last year; it was subsequently recognized by Austria, England, Sweden, and France."[41] The legislators did not need reminding that as advantageous as recognition by Portugal undoubtedly was, it had been achieved at considerable cost to national pride. The article in the treaty recognizing Brazil's independence was so phrased as to suggest that nationhood had not been won by the Brazilians' own prowess but had been conferred by favor of the king of Portugal who was authorized by article 2 to take the title of emperor during his own life. The state of war existing between Brazil and Portugal was retroactively annulled, with Portuguese citizens to be compensated for all losses and their rights restored. In trade Portugal was to regain her previous status as a most-favored nation.[42] It was as though all the blood shed and all the sacrifices made since 1822 had been to no purpose, their value denied.

The resentments aroused by the treaty were intensified by the manner in which it had been ratified. The instrument of ratification had referred to D. Pedro I as emperor "by the Constitution" and not "by the unanimous acclamation of the peoples," and it also failed to state that ratification was carried out under article 102 of the Constitution. Yet more alarming were the actions of D. João VI. When publishing his ratification, the instrument appeared after—and thereby subordinate to—a decree originally issued on May 15, 1825, which had created the title of emperor of Brazil for the king and then ceded it to his son.[43] Taken in conjunction, these acts suggested a concerted plot between father and son to undo the achievements of the past three years and—despite the express wording of article 1 of the Constitution forbidding "any bond of union or federation with any other [state] contrary to its independence"—to restore the old colonial union between Brazil and Portugal.[44]

In the Speech from the Throne the emperor did not refer to the secret convention annexed to the treaty of August 29, 1825. This document was not communicated to the General Assembly until June 1826. By it Brazil was bound to pay a large indemnity to Portugal, as compensation for losses arising out of the independence struggle. Brazil assumed responsibility for the loan of £1,400,000 (U.S. $7,000,000), which Portugal had raised in 1823 on the London market to finance its war of reconquest against Brazil. The remaining £600,000 of the indemnity was to be paid in cash within one year of ratification.[45] By signing an agreement so offensive to the national honor and deleterious to the public credit the emperor and his ministers made even moderate men doubt their honor and wisdom.

Had the securing of diplomatic recognition involved no costs other than the treaty and secret convention of August 29, 1825, the damage done to the imperial regime would have been substantial but manageable. Such was not the case. What the emperor also failed to mention in his Speech from the Throne was that the signing of the treaty having been the work of British diplomacy, that nation expected a substantial recompense from Brazil. The British envoy who acted on behalf of Portugal in the treaty negotiations had been quick to present his own country's demands: a new commercial agreement in place of the expired 1810 treaty and a convention committing Brazil to a swift abolition of the slave trade with Africa. By the end of September 1825 the two treaties had been not only signed but ratified by D. Pedro I. The British government then refused ratification, deeming the terms insufficiently favorable. The account to be paid was still outstanding. None of these facts, all of them public knowledge by May 1825, were even touched on by the emperor in his speech.[46]

The only topic which the emperor did discuss in some detail and on which he offered justification for his conduct was the current state of affairs in Portugal. "On April 24, the anniversary of the embarkation for Portugal of my father D. João VI, I received the unhappy and unexpected news of his death."[47] His father's decease presented D. Pedro with a major dilemma. The treaty of August 1825 had deliberately avoided specifying what effect, if any, recognition of D. Pedro I as emperor of Brazil had on his position as heir to the Portuguese crown. D. João VI was determined that D. Pedro should succeed, believing that the Portuguese world might thus be reunited. On the king's death, his wish was followed and his elder son proclaimed Pedro IV of Portugal.[48] News of his recognition, received at Rio de Janeiro on April 24, 1826, involved D. Pedro in a major constitutional crisis in which, he informed the General Assembly, he had found "the means of making the Portuguese nation happy without offending the Brazilian nation, and of separating them both (although they were already separated) so that they could never be united."[49]

Under article 1 of the Brazilian Constitution D. Pedro could not legally be both emperor of Brazil and king of Portugal, nor would public opinion in Brazil have consented to such a personal union of the two crowns. It was necessary to find at once a successor to the Portuguese throne, who, under the rules of inheritance, had to be an offspring or sibling of the existing monarch. D. Pedro's son, being the indispensable heir to the Brazilian throne, could not be spared. In resolving the dilemma the emperor consulted twice with the Council of State, but the solution published on April 29 was devised by him alone.[50] Acting as king of Portugal, D. Pedro granted a constitution modeled on that of Brazil. He then abdicated the Portuguese throne in favor of his eldest daughter, D. Maria da Glória, aged seven, subject to two conditions: the swearing of the new constitution by the Portuguese authorities, and the marriage of D. Maria to his brother, Infante D. Miguel. Given the constraints of time and the limited options available, D. Pedro's scheme was audacious but not impracticable. It sought to offer reconciliation and to establish a middle way between the two factions, liberal and traditionalist, in conflict in Portugal since 1820. To the former D. Pedro offered a constitution and to the latter the assurance that much of the old political order would survive.[51]

For all its merits, this settlement remained a bold gamble. Upon the throne D. Pedro placed a girl of seven who could not for at least a decade serve as a real ruler. Even as an adult she would, in the opinion of many, always be subject to male control. While the queen was still young, it was likely that her father would act as puppet master, controlling the affairs of Portugal from Rio de Janeiro. Such a possibility revived painful memories of the execrable years from 1808 to 1820 when Portugal had been no better than a satellite of Brazil. Further, D. Miguel, exiled from Portugal in 1824 because of his devotion to absolutism and his ambition to rule, did not bode well as a husband for his niece or as a willing collaborator in his brother's plans.[52] The accession of D. Maria as queen and the new constitution were imposed on Portugal by a monarch who having spurned his native land and deprived it of its richest territories now preferred his new fangled title to the crown of his ancestors.

In his Speech from the Throne D. Pedro I boasted to the legislators that "those few Brazilians who still doubted now know (as they should already have known) that my interest in Brazil and love of its independence is so strong that I abdicated the crown of the Portuguese monarchy, which was mine by indisputable right."[53] What the emperor failed to appreciate was that in terms of his position in Brazil his settlement involved one fundamental flaw: it ensured that D. Pedro, as father of the young queen, would for the foreseeable future be deeply involved in the affairs of Portugal.

Only in the final paragraph of his speech did the emperor mention the nation's internal condition and its most urgent needs: "You should pay particular care to the education of the young of both the sexes, the public treasury, all the other public institutions, and above all, to both the passage of regulatory laws and the repeal of those patently contrary to the constitution."[54] If the Speech from the Throne dealt almost exclusively with foreign affairs, it was because these questions held most significance for D. Pedro I as monarch. The war over the Banda Oriental involved maintaining the territories received from his father. Diplomatic recognition signified acceptance by D. Pedro's fellow monarchs. The settlement of affairs in Portugal meant the protection of his family's right to rule that country. The thrust of the speech did not accord with the emperor's assertion that his concern for Brazil and regard for its independence took priority over all other interests.

The Speech from the Throne failed to sway opinion in the Chamber of Deputies. In the election held on May 8 of a committee to draw up the Vote of Thanks to the emperor the controlling alliance of Coimbra bloc and Nativist deputies carried all three places. While profuse in its protestations of loyalty and regard, the draft Vote of Thanks eschewed specifics and avoided any pledge which would commit the deputies. The original draft did not even mention the war in the Rio de la Plata. A belated amendment did no more than state that "in matters affecting the national honor, the Chamber of Deputies will make every effort, within its own sphere, to ensure that it suffers no slight or breach."[55] The Vote of Thanks avoided any open disagreement with D. Pedro I but indicated that the deputies would be guided by their own priorities for the nation, not by the agenda laid down by the emperor.

The course to be followed by the alliance was made clear on May 27 when the chamber addressed a formal request to each of the six cabinet ministers for "a precise account of all the affairs of the public administration, so that it may be fully cognizant during its debates of the legislative remedies needed by each branch."[56] This request seemed to the emperor and his advisers little less than interference by the legislature into the conduct of government. The ministers saw themselves as accountable to the monarch, and their reports were written with an unctuous deference which implied that he alone carried out the actual business of government and that his judgment was impeccable.[57] The chamber's request was treated by the ministers, all but one of whom were senators, with a hauteur that did not disguise their disdain. Information they eventually supplied was at best general.[58] The ministers' response, by deepening the gulf between the executive and the deputies and so lessening the chances of cooperation, did no benefit to the emperor's cause.

What clogged the work of the chamber was not just the executive's reluctance to cooperate but the lack of government leaders in the lower house who could establish a legislative program, draft the necessary bills, and oversee their passage into law. The fate of the Constituent Assembly made the deputies conscious of the need for caution in speech and moderation in policy. Direct criticism of the emperor was eschewed and open confrontation with the government avoided. The controlling alliance used discretion in stating its views and pursuing its goals. As the chamber debates reveal, the deputies were overwhelmed by the mass of business facing them and daunted by the magnitude of the ills troubling the nation, all demanding urgent remedy. The deputies were conscious that the future structure of the nation would in part depend on the order in which they sought to apply remedies. Further, the Chamber's procedures facilitated endless debate, allowing the postponement of hard decision making until a consensus had emerged, often the result of simple fatigue.[59]

During the legislature's first year a wide range of bills and motions were introduced and debated. The frequency with which certain themes surfaced during the debates indicates the deputies' predominant concerns. They viewed themselves primarily as guardians of constitutional government, protecting the 1824 charter from abuse.[60] The deputies saw themselves as a small advance guard in the fight against absolutism and oppression. One of their tasks was to arouse Brazilians out of their colonial torpor and make them conscious of their rights and duties. Only when the nation's citizens were mobilized, the deputies believed, would the cause of constitutional government triumph.

The desire to make good citizens and to form a consciousness of nationhood was apparent in the attention given during the 1826 session to the issue of education, a motive of equal importance being the urgent, even desperate need for trained men to staff the apparatus of government. While the deputies concurred in deploring the neglect of education during the colonial era, they disagreed on which aspect should receive priority. What the nation needed most, some deputies argued, was an effective system of universal schooling. The most incisive case was made not by a Nativist deputy but by a Coimbra graduate: "Youth should have the means of studying at all ages and of gaining advanced knowledge without depending on a university. With the establishment of a university, we will be committed to a conspicuous expenditure, and I must state that this institution will only be for the rich; the poor will receive no benefit."[61] The small folk would have been the main beneficiaries of mass education, and it may seem surprising that the Nativist deputies did not support that idea more strongly. Since many, perhaps most, were largely self-taught they did not necessarily see the need for formal structures of education. The debates showed that a majority of deputies viewed higher education as the more urgent necessity: "Owing to our lack of a law school, we shall shortly be forced to choose between either not having men to staff the judiciary and the courts or being dependent on foreign countries to which our youth must go to beg for training and to which they must pay fat fees." [62] The outcome was a compromise, with the passage of two laws, the first creating law schools at São Paulo and Olinda, and the second setting up a system of primary education. [63]

Other objects of major concern for the deputies were the arbitrary powers possessed by the executive and the oppression and venality that characterized the judiciary. Two laws enacted in 1827 addressed these concerns. [64] The first measure defined the crimes of abuse of power and dereliction of duty for which cabinet ministers and councillors of state could be convicted. The intention was, by rendering the emperor's advisers accountable for their actions, to limit the powers of the executive and so protect the rights and liberties of the citizen.

The second law defined the powers and duties of the *juiz de paz* (justice of the peace), a post within the judiciary created by article 162 of the Constitution. Elected by the parish electors for three-year terms, the new officials were given a broad if vague jurisdiction in both civil and criminal matters. By this means the framers of the law hoped to diminish the role of the existing appointed judiciary, which the deputies correctly perceived as serving the imperial regime as its principal instrument of rule in the *pátrias*. The deputies also desired that administration of justice be removed from a privileged caste and entrusted to ordinary citizens who would be responsive to the popular will. The new measure would thus, it was argued, render justice less tardy and corrupt. [65] In political terms, the new law succeeded—against the evident intent of the 1824 Constitution— in creating an elected authority in the localities independent of the agents of the imperial government.

The law regulating the *juizes de paz* was the first of several measures reforming the judiciary. When the second session of the General Assembly adjourned in November 1827 the legislators were debating bills setting up a Supreme Tribunal of Justice and enacting two legal codes, those of criminal law and criminal procedure. At the midpoint of their legislative term the deputies were displaying considerable self-confidence and competence. They moved with growing vigor to create an effective system of justice which would treat all Brazilian citizens as equals. The deputies' constant goals were to limit the ability of the executive, that is, of the emperor and his ministers, to abuse the rights of the citizen, and to make the executive accountable to the legislature. This record of achievement contrasted strongly with the government's failure during the same period to master the objects of major concern discussed by the emperor in his Speech from the Throne on May 6, 1826.

III

In August 1826 the British chargé sent home a long report on current conditions in Brazil, which ended, with a certain gloomy satisfaction: "Such is the lamentable point of view in which I regard the present state of this Country, upon the very edge of a precipice from which it can only be saved by a change in the Sovereign's sentiments, by His disengaging himself from His present entanglement [with D. Domitila], and perhaps more than all by the friendly and steady interference of Great Britain."[66] Despite the overweening conceit of the final phrase, the report was accurate in its assessment of conditions in Brazil and almost prophetic in its evaluation of D. Pedro I's position in the country. During 1826 and 1827 the emperor's political standing deteriorated steadily, as a result of adverse developments in the areas of concern mentioned in the Speech from the Throne: the war in the Río de la Plata, relations with Great Britain, the fiscal crisis, and affairs in Portugal. D. Pedro I's conception of the nation required him to be both undefeated warrior and exemplary ruler whose exceptional qualities justified his preeminence and supreme authority. As the emperor now discovered, the concept possessed one fatal flaw: too wide a gap between theory and reality deprived the monarch of credibility and so legitimacy.

Throughout this period the military situation in the Río de la Plata went from bad to worse, despite the commitment of the army's crack units and the use of the most trusted generals. On February 20, 1827, the imperial army suffered a major defeat at Itazuingó in Rio Grande do Sul. In the Banda Oriental only Montevideo and Colônia do Sacramento, both closely besieged, remained in Brazilian hands. During the rest of 1827 and into 1828 the opposing sides exhausted their reserves of men and money as they strove in vain to gain a decisive victory.[67]

The armies of a Napoleonic ruler should not only crush their enemies but do so under his leadership. During a brief visit to Rio Grande do Sul in December 1826, the emperor never reached the war front, much less commanded his troops in person. Shortly after his arrival in the province, he was forced to return to Rio due to a domestic tragedy for which he bore a heavy responsibility. His infatuation for D. Domitila de Castro had become both blatant and limitless. In May 1826 he recognized their daughter as his offspring, ennobling the child as duchess of Goiás with the title of Highness.[68] In October he created her mother marchioness of Santos. The Empress was subject to public snubs and private disdain, forced to suffer the constant presence of her triumphant rival.[69]

Shortly after the emperor left for the south, D. Leopoldina fell ill, probably from complications of a new pregnancy. In popular report physical abuse by the emperor had brought on her fatal sickness. Her last hours revealed the misery of spirit and lack of will to live caused by her husband's behavior. Detailed information on the whole affair was sent home by the foreign envoys.[70] Outraged by his daughter's treatment, the emperor of Austria in effect ostracized his son-in-law, ceasing to regard him as worthy of support and sabotaging his settlement of affairs in Portugal. The effect of D. Leopoldina's death was to strip from D. Pedro any remaining aura of sanctity, either at home or abroad.[71]

Thus weakened by military defeat and international disfavor the imperial regime was in no condition to withstand the "friendly and steady interference of Great Britain," demanding payment in full for the assistance given in 1825 in forcing Portugal to recognize independence. The first installment on the debt was settled on November 23, 1826, two days before D. Pedro I left Rio for the far south, when the emperor ratified a treaty with Great Britain which declared the slave trade with Africa to be piracy and bound Brazil to make the trade illegal within three years. Given the trade's importance to both mercantile and agricultural interests, any agreement on the subject was bound to cause offense, but the limited grace period and the system of joint prize courts set up by the treaty to try suspected slavers emphasized Brazil's impotence and its dependent relationship with Great Britain.[72] It may be questioned whether any government of Brazil, no matter what its form, could have at that moment resisted British pressure to end the trade, but the more general failings of the imperial regime made it the ideal scapegoat for doing what so many disliked.

The humiliation suffered in 1826 was repeated with double severity the following year. For Brazilians, British exploitation was epitomized by the Anglo-Portuguese treaty of 1810, from which it sprang. Under international law, it was debatable whether the new Empire was bound by the provisions of the treaty once its political independence was recognized, and even if Brazil were subject to the agreement, the treaty's provisions became open to revision in June 1825, at which date the signatories could suspend any article until the agreement was renegotiated. In September 1825, a new commercial treaty had been negotiated which the British government refused to ratify. Accordingly, from June 1825 the imperial government was legally entitled to raise customs duties not only on all British but—thanks to the most-favored-nation proviso—on all foreign goods entering Brazil. That the emperor and his ministers did not enforce that right, despite occasional outbursts of Anglophobia, was due to their unwillingness to risk alienating the British government and so losing its protection. When a new British envoy arrived at Rio de Janeiro in October 1826 with powers to conclude a new commercial agreement, the imperial regime at once opened negotiations.

The new trade treaty signed on August 17, 1827, perpetuated all the most exploitative and humiliating clauses of its predecessor. British goods were still to enter Brazil at a maximum duty of 15 percent, a debilitating concession because the bulk of government revenues was drawn from duties on imports, which were mostly of British origin. British merchants further received the right to set the monthly *pauta*, the valuation of goods for customs duties. Clause 6 overrode the Brazilian Constitution by perpetuating the right of British subjects to be tried by special courts whose judges were paid by the British community. The agreement was to last fifteen years, at the end of which either side could terminate upon two years' notice. Brazil was in effect to be held in bondage until 1844 by a treaty offensive in countless ways to the independence and honor of the nation.[73] The failure of the imperial government to make public the treaty until after the adjournment of the General Assembly on November 16, 1827, served to confirm existing suspicions and deepen the sense of outraged nationalism among the regime's opponents within and outside the assembly.

The emperor's willingness to concede in the treaty all that Great Britain demanded showed how crucial British support was for maintaining the settlement D. Pedro had imposed on Portugal as its king in April 1826. A constitution had been sworn and a Cortes convened. However, the new order received support in Portugal only from a group of liberal politicians hungry for office. Traditionalist elements, openly backed by Spain, launched several revolts. Only the intervention of Great Britain, which sent troops to Lisbon in December 1826, maintained the authority of the regency which ruled in the name of D. Pedro and the young queen.[74]

To Brazilians D. Pedro I's conduct since April 1826 suggested that he was willing to sacrifice their nation's interests to those of Portugal and that article 1 of the Constitution was not being observed. The emperor had not hesitated, despite his abdication in favor of his daughter and the regency government in Lisbon, to act as king of Portugal, granting offices and titles and intervening in the conduct of foreign affairs. At the very least D. Pedro had difficulty in keeping his role as guardian of his own and his daughter's rights distinct from his duties as constitutional monarch of Brazil.

If his concern for Portugal led D. Pedro I to disregard Brazil's interests in the negotiation of the commercial treaty with Great Britain, the emperor gained no advantage from the sacrifice. On August 8, 1827, nine days before the treaty was signed at Rio, death carried off George Canning, the architect since 1822 of British policy toward Brazil and Portugal. Canning's successors decided to withdraw British troops from Lisbon and adopt a neutral role in Portuguese affairs. The way lay open to the ambitions of D. Miguel, who was entitled under the constitution authored by his brother to act as regent for the young queen on his becoming 25 in October 1827. To assure his rights, D. Miguel, then living in exile at Vienna, both swore allegiance to the new constitution and married by proxy his niece, still in her father's company at Rio de Janeiro. With the change in British policy nothing prevented D. Miguel's return. Amid popular rejoicing he entered Lisbon on February 22, 1828, and four days later took the oath as regent under the new constitution. His oaths alone stood between him and the throne.[75]

On March 13 the Cortes was dissolved. At the end of April, on the petition of the Lisbon municipal council, D. Miguel was acclaimed king with absolute powers. Only in Porto and Coimbra, where liberalism attracted the support of merchants and students respectively, did risings occur in favor of the deposed queen and constitution. The revolts were swiftly crushed, and all parts of society acknowledged D. Miguel as their legitimate and absolute monarch.[76] In Rio de Janeiro D. Pedro I, who had on March 3, 1828, made absolute his abdication in favor of his daughter, observed powerless the destruction of the settlement he had so boldly conferred on Portugal two years before. In July 1828, in a final and belated attempt to reverse the tide of events, he sent his daughter to Europe in the hope that her grandfather, the emperor of Austria, might be persuaded by her presence to uphold her rights.[77]

If the affairs of Portugal probably took first place in the emperor's mind in these years, for the ministers the most urgent matter was the catastrophic financial situation faced by the regime. Prodigal government expenditure and the plethora of copper coins and paper money issued to cover that expenditure, along with the devastation caused by drought in the northeast during 1826, exacerbated inflation and further depressed the value of the milreis.[78] The imperial regime was, it could be said, bankrupt in more ways than one.

In November 1827 the emperor was forced to make a concession which went against his most cherished principles. He appointed a new cabinet, which for the first time included ministers who were deputies. Two of the three deputies belonged to the Coimbra bloc.[79] By these appointments the emperor implicitly acknowledged that his right under the Constitution "freely to select and dismiss ministers" was not absolute and unfettered but subject to the need to secure the confidence of the Chamber of Deputies. In May 1828 he made a further concession by nominating as senator from Minas Gerais a leading Nativist deputy. The alliance that controlled the chamber thus began to make its voice heard in the upper house.[80]

This experiment in what may be termed parliamentary government did not flourish. On the one hand the concessions were too slight to dispel the suspicions of the deputies who feared that the new ministers were selling out on principle for the sake of office. On the other side, the new ministers found that they did not possess the emperor's confidence; D. Pedro I could not bring himself to submit to their advice, to subject his acts to their veto. Instead, he increasingly turned to his camarilla for advice, especially to Gomes da Silva, o Chalaça.[81] His dependence on this "secret cabinet" provided the opposition with further proof of the emperor's untrustworthiness as a constitutional monarch.[82]

IV

The middle months of 1828 marked the turning point in D. Pedro I's reign, when the political balance tilted over against the emperor, who thenceforth lost command of events. The following three years witnessed an intensifying struggle for mastery between the contending conceptions of what the Brazilian nation should be: the traditionalist, providential vision, in which the ruler personified the nation, and the liberal vision, in which representatives elected by the people embodied the nation. The escalating level of conflict precluded any compromise. Channels of understanding and communication collapsed. The struggle continued to revolve around the same problems which had dogged the imperial regime since the end of 1825.

The conduct of the Chamber of Deputies showed how decisively events turned against D. Pedro I. In their reply to the Speech from the Throne, which the deputies approved on May 14, 1828, the opening paragraph included the phrase: "The Brazilian nation . . . , trusting rather in the virtues of Your Imperial Majesty than swayed by the splendor of your birth, placed you on the throne it created."[83] By thus inferring that D. Pedro had been *chosen* by the nation to be emperor, the deputies were for the first time since the dissolution of the Constituent Assembly in November 1823 openly challenging the imperial claim that the monarch embodied the nation. Their avowed aim was to establish the full accountability of the executive to the legislature in all matters of government. Brushing aside such placatory gestures as the selection of deputies to be ministers and a moderately worded Speech from the Throne, the deputies in May 1828 went over to the political offensive against the emperor. During this session and in that of 1829 they grew ever bolder in denouncing abuses and harassing unpopular ministers. Of the laws passed in 1828, nine sought either to demolish administrative bodies inherited from the colonial era or to reduce the powers of the government over the citizen.[84]

In June 1828 an army mutiny in Rio de Janeiro city dealt a fatal blow to the military power on which the emperor's authority largely depended. Since 1822 the imperial regime had recruited mercenaries abroad, both to strengthen the army and to encourage immigration. By 1825 there existed in Rio de Janeiro two "foreign" regiments, composed mostly of Germans. Control of the capital depended on the Germans, the British envoy reported in August 1826, but any use of them would cause an explosion.[85] If the officers in these two regiments fared well enough, the treatment of the soldiers was by all accounts pitiful. Lured to Brazil by specious promises, they were subjected to demeaning treatment and brutal discipline, which in June 1828 provoked a mutiny. For some days the mutineers held virtual control of the capital, and only with the greatest difficulty were they finally subdued. This military debacle not only led to the immediate dissolution of the two foreign regiments but destroyed what remained of the army's prestige. The incident forced the minister of war to resign, and one of the two cabinet members belonging to the Coimbra bloc also judged it politic to withdraw from the ministry.[86]

The June mutiny had a decisive impact on the external affairs of Brazil, by destroying any possibility of persisting with the struggle to retain the Banda Oriental. Since March 1826 the British government had been pressing for an end to the war, and it favored a mutual renunciation of the Banda Oriental by Brazil and Argentina. The emperor, hitherto adamant in refusing to settle for less than full sovereignty, now swung round with his usual impetuosity to favoring a rapid settlement of the question through the good offices of the British. A preliminary peace treaty was signed at Rio on August 27, 1828. The contested region became the sovereign republic of Uruguay, its independence to be guaranteed by Brazil and Argentina, both of which had to approve the new state's constitution before it took effect.[87]

With the publication of the peace treaty on October 27, 1828, the emperor's conception of his role in the Brazilian nation was utterly discredited. He no longer possessed prestige either as a soldier or as the head of a strong and trustworthy military, both indispensable to a Napoleonic ruler. The regime had failed to secure the integrity of the nation's territory, at the cost of huge losses in men, materials, and money. The emperor was blamed both for prolonging an unnecessary conflict and for yielding national soil and demeaning the nation's honor.[88] To the controlling alliance in the lower house, the circumstances of the treaty's negotiation constituted yet one more instance of the regime's pusillanimous dependence on and deference to Great Britain. By the treaty of August 27, 1828, it was alleged, Great Britain alone had profited, enhancing its trade and prestige in the Río de la Plata at Brazil's expense. The controlling alliance thus became increasingly open in its opposition to the emperor and his policies.

Intensifying the emperor's humiliation in the middle months of 1828 was the disastrous news from Portugal: D. Miguel's usurpation of the throne from his niece and the abortive risings at Porto and Coimbra. In these upheavals Brazilians studying and living in Portugal were inevitably implicated. Retribution by the regime followed swiftly; some 50 Brazilian students were summarily expelled from Coimbra and others were arrested.[89] To D. Miguel's regime Brazilian nationality was synonymous not just with liberalism but with rebellion in general. Students, merchants, even diplomats, "far from enjoying the protection and security enjoined by the treaties, have been and are subject to violence, arbitrary treatment, and great losses, due to the hatred which this government has developed against all that is Brazil." [90] In other words, contrary to the treaty of August 29, 1825, the Miguelite regime refused to accept that the former colony now possessed total independence. Horrifying tales of humiliation and oppression, including arbitrary imprisonment and sudden deportation, were carried to Brazil both by Brazilian refugees and by Portuguese liberals seeking asylum. These stories lost nothing in the retelling and served not only to discredit the Portuguese heritage but to consolidate popular support for the political opposition.

By his own conduct D. Pedro concentrated on himself much of the anger aroused by his brother's perfidy. D. Pedro persisted, despite his abdication of the Portuguese throne in May 1826, in acting as though he were still king. [91] Brazilian envoys were ordered to handle diplomatic questions relating solely to Portugal. In July 1828 the emperor replaced the court uniform adopted after independence with the traditional court dress used during his father's reign. The change symbolized the apparent willingness of D. Pedro to identify himself with the heritage of despotism and colonialism and to subordinate the Brazilian nation and its interests to the prosperity of the house of Bragança. To the opposition, Brazil seemed in late 1828 to be in imminent danger of becoming an appendage of Portugal. [92]

As a result of the May mutiny, the loss of the Banda Oriental and the state of oppression in Portugal, public opinion in Brazil became increasingly polarized. If the Chamber of Deputies provided the focus and was the prime mover for the growing opposition, the process of politicization was also dependent upon the reemergence of a national press. Of the newspapers published at Rio the most significant were the *Astreia*, founded in June 1826, and the *Aurora Fluminense*, which first appeared in November 1827. [93] The latter, edited by a young bookseller, Evaristo Ferreira da Veiga, was notable for the incisiveness of its arguments and the moderation of its language. Presenting a compelling vision of what Brazil might be, the *Aurora* became the inspiration and model for opposition newspapers in the provinces. The regime proved incapable of countering the influence of this political press, the newspapers it subsidized (often under the editorship of foreigners) being as ineffective in argument as they were intemperate in language. [94]

The changing balance of power and the evolving structure of politics were revealed late in 1828 in the elections for the new Chamber of Deputies, which would begin its four year term in May 1830. The press provided the means of marshaling the electors behind candidates opposed to the emperor and his conception of the nation. In Minas Gerais a list of 21 names, men recommended as "very liberal" and "devoted to constitutionalism," was printed to aid the electorate. Thirteen of those recommended were elected for Minas Gerais, and a further four became deputies from Rio de Janeiro province. [95]

These electoral successes consolidated and emboldened the opposition coalition of the Coimbra bloc and the Nativists. As an observer at Rio noted at the end of 1828: "The elections have returned the most fervent radicals; those attached to the court are atremble and seek means to escape the storm, which they expect in 1830, when the new reformers of Brazil will begin to play a role and have influence."[96] Within the legislature itself, the sitting deputies now moved from insisting that the ministers be accountable to asserting that only those holding the full confidence of the legislature be named ministers, a demand to which the emperor was resolved never to accede.

The 1828 elections also provided the catalyst for a new phenomenon: political activity which was neither focused on the national legislature nor directed from above. This activity was ideologically radical, on the extreme fringe of Nativism, and openly advocated republicanism and federalism. The fervor of those involved soon gained them the name of *exaltados*, or zealots. They functioned through local clubs meeting in private and through small, ephemeral periodicals purveying opinion rather than news. In social terms this political activity appealed strongly to the small folk in the coastal cities. In the national capital it received support from the young cadets at the two military academies and from the Brazilian-born among the city's clerks, cashiers, and minor bureaucrats.[97] Given the particular conditions of Brazilian society at the time, the Exaltados may be termed a popular, if not a mass, movement.

The upsurge of those whom D. Pedro I characterized as "agitators and revolutionaries" and the increasing polarization of opinion brought over to the imperial cause the most moderate members of the opposition alliance, who now found themselves shouldered aside by more active and intolerant men.[98] The ablest of these converts was certainly José Clemente Pereira, who as *juiz de fora* of Rio city in 1821 and 1822 had played an indispensable role in the struggle for national independence. José Clemente's Portuguese birth and upbringing and his increasing political moderation combined to detach him from the opposition. In June 1828 when the army mutiny caused one of the two Coimbra bloc ministers to resign, he stepped into the breach. For a year and a half he served the emperor effectively, thus intensifying his former allies' rage against a turncoat to their cause.[99]

The emperor profited little from this accretion of support, since his general position continued to weaken as 1828 drew to a close. Abroad the European monarchies refused to give any active backing to the cause of his daughter, D. Maria da Glória.[100] Attempts to find a princess who would wed D. Pedro I ended in failure, owing to his unsavory reputation and to the covert opposition of the emperor of Austria. Worst of all, the threat of the British government to expel the Portuguese troops who took refuge in England after the failure of the risings against D. Miguel raised the unwelcome prospect that the General Assembly would have to be convened in special session, since under the Constitution foreign troops could enter Brazil only with the prior consent of the legislature.[101] Additional grounds for calling the legislature into special session were provided by the financial situation, which was nothing short of calamitous: a loan for £400,000 (U.S. $2,000,000) raised on the London market vanished without any discernable benefit into the maw of the accumulated deficit.[102]

These circumstances explain why early in 1829 the emperor set down on paper a scheme which, had it been made public, would have confirmed the very worst suspicions of the opposition. The emperor's justification for his plan is worth quoting in some detail, for it reveals much about D. Pedro's current mood and basic character:

It is necessary, looking to the future and in view of the deplorable condition in which Brazil finds itself (a condition which, if it continue, will *in less than two years* make the Empire vanish, to be replaced not by a Republic but rather by anarchy), to take steps, and gigantic steps, suited to the greatness of the Empire and to its *totally deplorable circumstances.* . . .

I see no means better and, I can boldly say, no means other than an appeal to the sovereigns of Europe, the sole and true defenders of thrones. . . . This business is very sensitive, and it can and should, for this reason, be handled only at the level of sovereign to sovereign. . . .

The Empire is surrounded by Republics, full of republicans, the government without physical and moral force, the treasury without credit or money, the people without respect for authority: how then can it [the Empire] continue to exist? . . . This plan of mine cannot be carried out unless the Assembly gives me leave to go to Europe, but being convinced of its advantages for my descendants, for whom I am working, should leave not be granted *I will not fail to abdicate.*[103]

The actual plan, communicated to only three chosen advisers—the emperor's chaplain, his personal physician, and the most trusted of the councillors of state—proposed that D. Pedro should, "having effected a reconciliation with the influential monarchs of Europe now unfriendly to me, ascertain their willingness to supply troops in support of the new Constitution, which would be truly monarchical."[104] With greater or lesser circumspection and flattery, all three replies advised against such an extreme course. It would, the chaplain stressed, violate the emperor's oath to the Constitution, and it was, as the councillor of state remarked, not viable owing to "the appalling and hopeless state of the Public Treasury."[105] Their opposition might not of itself have sufficed to deter the emperor from his course had not the situation in respect to Portugal shown some improvement. Forces favorable to D. Maria da Glória succeeded in maintaining a firm foothold in the Azores, to which went the troops no longer welcome in England.[106] Rebuffed by his advisers, the emperor took no overt step to carry out his plan.[107] Its basic concepts remained planted in his mind, however, and were to influence his handling of events.

The emperor returned to the ongoing business of government. To deal with the financial emergency he summoned the General Assembly to meet in special session during the month of April 1829. The deputies were scathing in their denunciations of incompetence and maladministration, which were attributed to the current ministers. Since the minister of finance in his report to the legislature estimated that revenues in 1828–29 were little more than half the amount of expenditures and proposed that the deficit be covered mainly by borrowing, the deputies' anger was legitimate.[108]

Despite the real urgency of the financial crisis, the legislature failed in 1829, as in previous years, to pass a law establishing a budget. Nor was any remedy for the financial situation enacted, beyond a law dissolving the Banco do Brasil. Bankrupt as this institution had become, its dissolution deprived Brazil of even the rudiments of a national banking system. While the deputies' inertia might appear inconsistent with their avowed zeal for remedying abuses, their inaction was entirely explicable, even deliberate. The complexity and dangers of the financial and monetary situation were so great that caution was imperative, a caution reinforced by the deputies' habit of discussing divisive issues to the point of exhaustion and beyond. The remedies available were not great, since the only obvious source for new revenue—increasing the customs duties—was in practice unavailable because of the flat 15 percent duty levied on British imports under the 1827 treaty and extended to other countries by the most-favored-nation clause. The alternative was to reduce the deficit by a drastic pruning of expenditures, but such a remedy would offend vested interests and so meet with strong opposition from the Senate and the emperor.

An element of policy must also have influenced the deputies, since what Mirabeau had remarked of France in 1789 was true for Brazil in 1829: "The deficit is the nation's greatest asset." While the financial crisis continued the imperial regime would remain dependent on the General Assembly. To render the government solvent was to surrender the deputies' decisive advantage in the political struggle.[109] The fourth and final session of the first legislature, which ran from April to September 1829, proved largely abortive. Few laws were passed and the deputies spent most of their time denouncing the ministers for being the cause of the nation's woes. The emperor's exasperation with his situation as constitutional monarch burst out at the ceremonies closing the session on September 3. Choosing against established practice the Chamber of Deputies for the ceremony, the emperor offered not the customary thanks and compliments but a single blunt sentence: "The session is closed."[110]

A rebuke so direct and so public delivered to the deputies in their own chamber showed how completely communication and trust had broken down between the contending parties. On the one side stood the emperor who, viewing the opposition as disobedient radicals, was weary of his role as constitutional monarch. On the other side was arrayed the opposition, no longer believing in D. Pedro I's good faith as a constitutional ruler and unwilling to accept anything less than the legislature's unquestioned supremacy in the political system. The situation of 1823 was being repeated, with the contending parties so committed to their respective positions that only a violent confrontation could resolve the conflict.[111]

The threatened crisis was postponed and it seemed for a time even averted by a change in the emperor's personal life. The envoy who had taken D. Maria da Glória to Europe in July 1828 had not succeeded in persuading the European monarchs to support her as queen of Portugal. He had, however, been able to find for D. Pedro a bride of acceptable rank and ravishing beauty: Amelia, daughter of Napoleon's stepson, Eugène de Beauharnais, and niece to the king of Bavaria. The banishment from court of D. Domitila de Castro and her offspring had been a precondition for the marriage negotiations. When Princess Amelia and D. Maria da Glória arrived at Rio in October 1829 the emperor immediately fell captive to the princess's beauty and her good sense. The influence of "the Rose Princess" (*princesa côr de rosa*) on D. Pedro in both personal and political terms was wholly good, and she restored the harmony of his family life, giving the children of his first marriage much-needed love and attention.[112]

In the personal and political honeymoon which followed his marriage to D. Amelia, the emperor became more tolerant of compromise. He was induced to dismiss José Clemente Pereira and the most discredited ministers, replacing them with a new cabinet organized by the envoy who had negotiated his marriage.[113] The cabinet pressured the emperor into agreeing that o Chalaça and another leading member of his "secret cabinet" be dispatched on personal "missions" to Europe, a polite form of exile.[114] As 1829 drew to a close, a fresh start in government and a revival of political trust seemed possible.

Such hopes proved deceptive, because the factors which had produced the new cabinet were transitory. The basic elements in the political equation were in truth unchanged, so that the momentum toward a confrontation was not reversed but only checked. Composed of heterogeneous elements, the cabinet of December 4, 1829, did not and could not command full confidence and support from either of the opposing sides; to achieve backing from one would automatically alienate the other. The dilemma became acute when the new legislature elected at the end of 1828 convened in May 1830. The opposition alliance, composed of the Coimbra bloc and the Nativists, had grown in number and become more radical and aggressive in mood. Attempts were even made to annul the election of the notable supporters of the regime, such as José Clemente Pereira. The defeat of these motions showed that no decisive shift in the composition of the new chamber had occurred.[115]

The continuing intransigence of the opposition alliance and the growing ferocity of their attacks quickened the emperor's reversion to the mood of frustration and defiance which had dominated him early in 1829. The virtual banishment to Europe of D. Pedro I's personal advisers served in the long term not only to undermine his confidence in the cabinet but to switch his attention to the affairs of Portugal. The emperor corresponded with his absent advisers, who in turn were in close contact with the exiled supporters of D. Maria da Glória. These exiles, believing that the young queen's cause would never prosper until her father took command, begged him through his banished advisers to leave Brazil and take personal control of the constitutionalist forces.[116] Disgusted by his exposed and demeaning position in Brazil, D. Pedro found in his daughter's cause everything that appealed most to his character. By going to Portugal he could champion the oppressed, display his chivalry and self-denial, uphold constitutional rule, and enjoy the freedom of action he so craved. His brother's usurpation revived in him an identification with his original *pátria* and made him ready to go to the aid of his native land.

The emperor's growing indifference, if not repudiation, of the nation he had brought into being in 1822 was reinforced by the conduct of the new Chamber of Deputies which convened in 1830. Holding the political initiative, the deputies passed a series of bills highly objectionable to both the Senate and the emperor but which neither dared to reject.[117] In the new criminal law code, treason, which carried the death penalty, was so defined as to be virtually impossible to prove. The new press law gave political writers almost total impunity. The budget for 1831–32 reduced total government spending by a third and military expenditure by a quarter.[118] A law regulating the size and the personnel of the armed forces ordered the immediate discharge of all officers born outside of Brazil, save for those who had served in the wars of independence or had been wounded or disabled in the nation's service.[119] The weakness of the emperor's position was patent in his failure to veto what was, given his Portuguese birth, a personal affront to his honor.

The confrontation between the deputies and the emperor was matched by the deepening polarization of political opinion. The laws enacted late in 1830 by the legislature threatened the livelihood of many government employees, and those of Portuguese birth faced the loss of citizenship guaranteed to them by article 6 of the Constitution.[120] Traditionalist elements in the bureaucracy and the military had in 1829 formed a secret society, the "Columns of the Throne," pledged to uphold the prerogatives of the monarchy. On the opposite extreme the Exaltados became more open and aggressive, their frenetic activity compensating for their fairly small numbers.[121]

The final crisis of the reign was set off by the arrival on September 14, 1830, of news of the July Revolution in France. An attempt by King Charles X to dissolve the Chambers, restrict the franchise, and limit freedom of the press had been met by *les trois glorieuses*, the three-day uprising in Paris that had overthrown the despot and replaced him with Louis Philippe, "the Citizen King." The parallels with the existing situation in Brazil seemed, to the opposition at least, very close. The emperor, himself outraged by the opposition's presumption in comparing him to Charles X, gave credibility to the comparison by, on September 30, 1830, dismissing the minister who had organized the compromise cabinet of December 4, 1829. The decree of dismissal implied that the fallen minister had while head of the special mission in Europe in 1828 and 1829 personally prof- ited from the funds expended. To the allegation, the dismissed minister, a senator, replied in a printed pamphlet which not only gave a detailed rebuttal but referred to the existence of "secret councillors." [122] The whole affair not only confirmed the opposition's suspicions but alienated from the emperor an influential section of moderate opinion.

Events now moved with gathering speed. The emperor succeeded in reforming the cabinet and persuaded no less than two deputies to accept portfolios, but the new cabinet like its predecessor lacked both homo- geneity and authority. It could do nothing to prevent the final enactment in special session of the objectionable laws. The atmosphere of suspicion and hatred was intensified by the murder at São Paulo city on November 20, 1830, of Libero Badaró, a young immigrant from Italy who had made his mark as a liberal journalist. To the opposition he was nothing less than a martyr: what passed for his dying words—"a liberal dies but liberty is not dead"—became its watchword. [123]

If the opposition suspected that the emperor was about to repeat the brutal coup of November 1823, D. Pedro I saw himself as facing a repe- tition of the situation in early 1822 when by his personal conduct he had rallied the people to his cause. He now determined to repeat the visit made in March 1822 to the province of Minas Gerais. One of the newly appointed ministers sat as deputy for that province and was required by the Constitution to seek reelection upon accepting office. The emperor hoped that his own presence in Minas Gerais during the contest would aid his minister. The past could not, as D. Pedro I learned during his visit in January and February 1831, be so repeated. The minister went down to crushing defeat and the tour proved far from successful. [124]

During the emperor's absence the Exaltados began to organize their supporters in the capital into street gangs. They also started to tamper with the loyalty of the units composing the garrison. In response, the supporters of the emperor in Rio de Janeiro, particularly strong among business elements, also organized. As a direct challenge to the opposition they held three nights of celebrations in honor of the emperor's return to Rio on March 15, 1831. When the Exaltados' gangs tried to disrupt the celebrations, the monarch's supporters not only routed them but forced householders to illuminate their windows in honor of the emperor. [125] The humiliating defeat of the radicals in the *noite de garrafadas* (night of the broken bottles) inaugurated the final phase of the growing crisis.

What alarmed all elements in the opposition was the arrest of army officers who had intervened in the street clashes in order to protect the Exaltados under attack. A manifesto was issued by the members of the parliamentary opposition then in Rio, demanding the instant release of these officers and "the restoration of public safety and quiet." [126] On March 19, 1831, the emperor responded with a major concession: he replaced the existing ministers with a cabinet drawn from known supporters of the opposition. However, since any politician agreeing to accept a portfolio immediately became suspect, the new cabinet failed to establish its authority or to restore tranquillity.

As the emperor later admitted, he was by then "tired of being subjected to demands which it demeaned him to grant." [127] D. Pedro decided to rule Brazil on his own terms or not at all. On the night of April 5, 1831, he dismissed the ministers and replaced them with a cabinet composed of his most trusted advisers—five marquesses, a count, and a viscount.[128] Opposition leaders saw this act as the first move toward a coup d'état. Contact was at once made with officers in the army units garrisoning the capital.[129] Popular reaction to this calculated defiance of public opinion was immediate. Late in the afternoon of April 6 large crowds gathered in the Campo de Santa Ana near the center of the city, demanding the immediate return of the dismissed ministers. When this demand was formally presented to the emperor at his country palace, he replied, "I will do everything for the people and nothing by the people." [130] In that retort was encapsulated the emperor's political philosophy, the history of his reign, and the causes of his fall.

The very suddenness of the emergency, the emperor's intransigence, and his alienation of moderate elements doomed all efforts to resolve the crisis. As darkness gathered, the crowds in the Campo de Santa Ana grew in size and strength. Troops of the garrison began to join them. In contrast to November 1823, the emperor was not backed by the military. By midnight D. Pedro knew that the garrison commander had abandoned his cause and that his personal guard had gone over to the revolt.[131] His position as monarch could be maintained only by embarking on a civil war, with no certainty of victory. Far better to preserve his honor by becoming champion of his daughter's cause in Portugal. At three o'clock in the morning of April 7, 1831, D. Pedro wrote out a single sentence that cut short the constitutional crisis, ended his career in Brazil, and passed to his foes the government of the nation: "Using the right conferred on me by the Constitution, I hereby totally and unreservedly abdicate the throne of Brazil in favor of my beloved son, D. Pedro de Alcántara." [132]

6

The Liberal Experiment, 1831-1837

The sudden abdication of D. Pedro I left the leaders of the political community literally holding the baby. As April 7, 1831, dawned, the nominal ruler of Brazil—symbol of national authority and head of the government—was a boy aged five years and five months. Not until December 2, 1843, would D. Pedro II come of age under the Constitution and personally exercise the powers given by it to the emperor. D. Pedro I's renunciation of the throne marked the elimination of the monarch as the center of power in the political order. With abdication of the emperor it became possible for the leaders of the parliamentary opposition to make real that ideal nation they had extolled in the press and the assembly.

For ten years, from 1831 to 1840, following D. Pedro I's abdication, the Brazilians held responsibility for the fortunes of their nation without the support of an inherited and external source of authority, the monarchy. Political legitimacy now derived from the popular will alone. Brazil's new leaders were free to experiment, to refashion Brazil into what they believed a nation-state could be: a homogeneous and harmonious society which worked efficiently because it functioned by consent. Brazil could not become such a nation without extensive changes in the existing political structure. Accordingly, these ten years witnessed a major redistribution of power within the nation. However, in part because of the innovations and in part because of conditions then prevailing, these years were also a time of disappointment and crisis which put in jeopardy Brazil's identity and its very existence as a nation. The struggle to preserve Brazil as a nation-state forced men to abandon their principles and to sacrifice their dreams. The prolonged crisis bred disillusionment and undercut national self-confidence. "Burnt child fire dreadeth." The functioning of Brazil as a nation was permanently affected.

The years of D. Pedro II's minority fall into two periods. In the six years to September 1837, Brazil's rulers sought to equate the nation with the *pátrias*. Thereafter they sought, no matter what the cost, to reestablish the primacy of nation over *pátria*. It is with the first six years—the time of failed ideals and frustrated innovations—that the present chapter is concerned.

I

As daylight broke on April 7, 1831, the exhilaration of the night's triumph yielded to a consciousness among the victors of the unprecedented situation facing them. The emperor had abdicated, bringing down his abortive cabinet with him. The government was in limbo, with no one in authority.[1] Only to the Exaltados was the way plain: the immediate proclamation of a republic. To the leaders of what had been until that moment the parliamentary opposition, the course to be taken by the nation was not so clear. Much as they had denounced D. Pedro I as a ruler, they had not seriously envisioned what would follow him if his reign did end. To proclaim a republic, for which support was fervent but limited, meant assuming entire and naked responsibility for the nation and its governance. So long as the former emperor physically remained in Rio, a countercoup was not impossible, and proclaiming a republic would increase the dangers of such a reaction. Being pragmatists at heart, the new leaders of the nation preferred not to meddle with the status quo. When a group of Exaltado stalwarts inquired of Senator Nicolau Vergueiro, the most eminent of the Nativist leaders, how or what the people should now acclaim, he finally replied, "Long live the Constitutional Emperor, D. Pedro II in his minority!"[2]

Vergueiro's response symbolized the collective decision by the leaders of the former opposition that government should be in the name and under the nominal authority of the infant prince. This step did not resolve the constitutional problem. A regency was necessary until D. Pedro came of age in 1843. However, no member of the imperial family met the necessary constitutional conditions to be regent.[3] The Constitution stated that in such a contingency a three-man regency was to be elected by the General Assembly, and if that body were not in session (as it was not on April 7), then an interim regency was to be formed by the ministers of the interior (Império) and of justice along with the two senior councillors of state.[4] On April 7, there were no accepted occupiers of these two ministries. By his determination not to compromise, D. Pedro I achieved revenge on his foes: no legal means existed by which they could assume control of the government.

Paradoxically, it was this very hiatus in legal authority that facilitated and accelerated the transfer of government to D. Pedro I's opponents. Fears that the vacuum in legal authority might cause a breakdown in social and political order made even the Exaltado leaders cautious.[5] The same fears persuaded the vast majority of those loyal to the former emperor to cooperate in finding a way to resolve the constitutional conundrum.[6] Sixty-two members of the General Assembly then in Rio de Janeiro responded to a summons issued by the bishop of Rio de Janeiro, the president of the Senate. Meeting in the Senate house, these men agreed to elect what they termed a "provisional" regency (*regência provisória*), which would govern Brazil until the legislature, scheduled to convene in May, could elect a permanent regency.[7]

The meeting then proceeded to elect three temporary regents, and the balloting made clear that moderation and unity were the predominant concerns. The first chosen was José Joaquim Carneiro de Campos, who despite his title of marquess of Caravelas, his role as councillor of state, and his service as minister under D. Pedro I retained the respect of the former emperor's opponents. The second regent was Senator Vergueiro, the Nativist leader. Third was Francisco de Lima e Silva, whose refusal as military commander (*comandante das armas*) of the capital to support D. Pedro I had been a critical factor in forcing the abdication. It was less Lima e Silva's character and talents than the hope that he could through his numerous relatives among the officer corps secure the loyalty of the army that prompted his selection.[8]

The meeting also issued a proclamation, largely drafted by Evaristo Ferreira da Veiga, the foremost opposition journalist, which equated nationalism with moderation:

As of the Seventh of April, 1831, our political existence began. Brazil will henceforth belong to Brazilians and will be free. . . .

Brazilians! No longer must we blush to own this name. Henceforth the independence of our country and its laws will be a reality. . . .

Everything now depends on us—on our prudence, our moderation, and our energy. Let us continue as we have begun, and we shall be viewed with admiration among the most advanced nations. Long live the Brazilian Nation! Long live the Constitution! Long live the Constitutional Emperor, Dom Pedro II![9]

The intensity with which the proclamation stated the case for moderation and almost begged for restraint sprang in large part from concern about how the Exaltados of Rio city, having been denied their republic, might react. The proclamation was also designed to reassure the nation at large. For the first—but by no means the last—time, the fate of Brazil had been decided by a crisis confined to the national capital, without participation and consent by the rest of the nation. Having seized control of the national government, the former parliamentary opposition might hope but could not be certain that the rest of Brazil would accept them as its new rulers.

For a few brief weeks it seemed as if the new regime would receive universal support and avoid serious troubles. In Rio de Janeiro something resembling a political honeymoon ensued, so that the provisional regency and the cabinet it named—basically the same ministry dismissed by D. Pedro I on April 4—met with no difficulties in taking charge of the administration. In this atmosphere of goodwill the General Assembly opened its session on May 3.[10]

The legislators' first task was to define the structure of the national government during the minority of D. Pedro II, since the Constitution gave the assembly the right not just to choose the permanent regency but also to determine its powers.[11] The assembly was also faced with a controversy over the office of guardian (*tutor*) to the new emperor. D. Pedro I had purported, by a decree he dated April 6, to appoint José Bonifácio, who had recently returned from exile in France. Not only was the emperor's right to make the appointment contestable, but he had in fact done so after his abdication. José Bonifácio seems to have been chosen due more to his past services and to D. Pedro I's memories of events in 1822 than to suitability for the post. His age, nearly 68, partisan record, and lack of tact counted heavily against him. In the end the assembly compromised: it rejected the former emperor's claim to name a guardian, but it did choose José Bonifácio over Vergueiro for the post.[12]

By then the assembly had also defined the powers of the permanent regency and elected the three regents. A law passed on June 12, 1831, suppressed for the duration of D. Pedro II's minority the monarchical element in the government, by withholding from the new regents major attributes of both the regulating and executive powers: the regents could not declare war, grant titles and honors, veto laws, or dissolve the Chamber of Deputies. They retained the right to appoint and dismiss ministers, name senators, name government employees, and call the General Assembly into special session or prolong its ordinary sessions.[13] Since the regents were chosen by the General Assembly and since they lacked any source of power independent of it, they were in truth subordinate to it. Until the emperor came of age, Brazil would have a parliamentary system of rule, one in which the Chamber of Deputies would predominate. By indirect yet entirely legal means, the former opposition to D. Pedro I thus achieved what had been one of its major political goals.

The member of the permanent regency receiving the highest number of votes was Francisco de Lima e Silva, the representative of the armed forces, who was continued over from the provisional regency. Next came José da Costa Carvalho, a native of Bahia who after graduating from Coimbra in 1819 had married and made his career in São Paulo province. The third regent was João Bráulio Moniz, an 1819 graduate of Coimbra and member of a prominent Maranhão clan, who was selected mainly as a representative of the political interests of the far north.[14] The collective leadership adopted by the former opposition before April 7 had been maintained since then; accordingly, the new regents would not be in a position to rule. The actual business of government would be carried on by the ministers acting in cooperation with the Chamber of Deputies. On the other hand, the regents appointed the ministers, signed all decrees and important orders, and oversaw the functioning of government. They held a central if not a commanding role in the new regime.

The regency elections marked the accession to power of a new political generation: both of the civilian Regents belonged to the Coimbra bloc. Although comparatively young, each only 35 years of age, they were already political veterans, Costa Carvalho having even sat in the Constituent Assembly. By 1831 the Coimbra bloc, then numbering some hundred men, had successfully "rerooted" itself in Brazil and gained fresh recruits by replicating there the system of training its membership had until the early 1820's received in Portugal. The revolt following D. Miguel's usurpation of the Portuguese throne had closed Coimbra university for a year. Nearly all the Brazilian students, whether or not implicated in the risings, had returned home, where most of them had completed their degrees at the newly founded law schools of Olinda and São Paulo.[15] Since they constituted the first graduating class and since most of the faculty were Coimbra trained, the Coimbra bloc both shaped the traditions and ethos of the new schools and absorbed into their own ranks the first students. The ascendancy of the Coimbra bloc in national affairs was thus reinforced and prolonged.[16]

Control of the regency by representatives of the Coimbra bloc necessarily excluded rival groups—in particular the Luso-Brazilians, many still in the prime of life, who found themselves stripped of their accustomed status. They were no longer appointed ministers. The Council of State ceased to play any significant role in government decision making. Only through the Senate, which retained its importance, did the Luso-Brazilians continue to exert influence. So sudden and brusque an exclusion was scarcely politic: entrenched in the upper house and experienced in the arts of government, this group of men was capable of so sabotaging the conduct of affairs as to threaten the stability of the regime. In José Bonifácio and his two brothers, all resolute and unscrupulous, the Luso-Brazilians soon found formidable leaders.[17]

The Coimbra bloc's success in the regency elections also produced considerable tension with the Nativists, senior in years of experience and similarly aspiring to the control of power. To the confirmed Nativists, those who had in the years before 1808 attended a seminary or educated themselves in Brazil rather than abroad, the events of April 1831 both sanctioned and made feasible a devolution of power from Rio de Janeiro to the *pátrias*. They now faced a new government controlled by those who shared neither their background nor their views. For all that Lima e Silva, the first regent, was of Brazilian birth and upbringing, he was suspect to the Nativists, since he had commanded the forces which had so bloodily repressed the 1824 uprising in the northeast.[18]

Formidable for their numbers, dedication, and command of broad support in the provinces, the Nativists were not to be trifled with. Common opposition to D. Pedro I and his system of rule had brought the Nativists and the Coimbra bloc into alliance during his reign. However, in upbringing, outlook, and socioeconomic status the members of the Coimbra bloc had far more in common with their opponents, the Luso-Brazilians, than with the Nativists. These flaws in the basic structure of power within the national political community meant that the honeymoon which followed D. Pedro I's abdication could not long endure.

Political instability after April 1831 had causes far deeper and more complex than rivalries between the ruling groups. Mounting strife on the national scene had mobilized geographic areas and social groups which, in the early 1820's, had been little involved in the political process. A periodical press and political activity were by 1831 common even in such isolated areas as Mato Grosso. The small folk were now taking an active role in politics, particularly in the towns and cities. Not only did they possess the qualifications to be voters and even electors, but their literacy, which distinguished them from the general population, gave them access to the medium through which politics were mainly conducted.[19] Due to the administrative and judicial reforms being enacted at this time, the role of the small folk expanded beyond the simple reading of tracts and casting of ballots, so that although they were no more than a minority of Brazilians who were adult, male, and free, during the 1830's the small folk constituted the majority of the active political community.

Accommodating so considerable an expansion in the political community and incorporating so large a number of political novices would have taxed the resources and stability of a nation more cohesive and longer established than Brazil was in 1831. Certainly the new regime's collective leadership—formed of legislators, administrators, and journalists—did their best to respond to the challenge by issuing a stream of directives and exhortations through the progovernment press and by creating Sociedades Defensoras da Liberdade e da Independência Nacional (Societies for the Defense of Liberty and National Independence), a network of clubs in the national capital and the provinces that brought together the regime's supporters and coordinated their activities.[20] A parallel and indeed overlapping function was played by the lodges of Freemasonry, which now revived, having been banned since 1823. The advantages that the new regime initially gained from this strategy were, however, soon lost, since the government's foes adopted the same techniques for political organization.[21]

The problems caused by strife within the ruling circles and by increasing political mobilization among the ordinary population were compounded by Brazil's continued lack of many of the attributes of nationhood, such as a coherent educational system, which might have made Brazilians at the local level identify with the nation. The formation of what may be termed the infrastructure of nationhood had been blocked by parliamentary conflicts with D. Pedro I, but even if they had been created before 1831 their existence would not necessarily have averted the crisis then approaching. The problems Brazil confronted in the early 1830's stemmed, at bottom, from its organization as a nation-state in the liberal mold, with authority being derived from the people. As a consequence, a number of

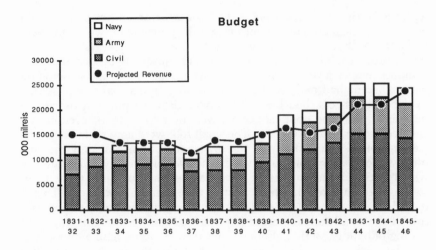

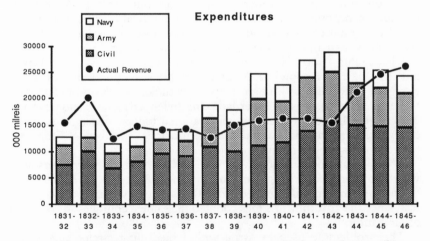

FIG. 1. Brazilian National Government Finances, Budget and Expenditures, 1831–32 Through 1845–46. Data from Liberato de Castro Carreira, *Historia financeira e orçamentaria do Imperio do Brazil desde a sua fundação*, pp. 183–260. Rio, 1889.

social groups hitherto excluded from the political order and discontented with their socioeconomic position now used the political process to seek a share in the fruits of governance. These demands for material reward were advanced at the very time when the ruling politicians were wracked by disputes over the control of power.

Political unrest did not spring directly from economic distress, since most of the regional economies prospered in the first half of the 1830's. Increasing consumption of coffee in Europe and North America boosted its price and caused a boom in the production of what was becoming the staple product of Rio de Janeiro province.[22] Demand for Brazil's other exports also increased. From its low in 1830 the milreis made a rapid recovery, by 1835 reaching three-quarters of its value a decade before. Much of this recovery was due to action by the national government. Cuts in expenditures, particularly on the armed forces, kept the national budget in surplus until 1836, as Figure 1 shows. The money supply was finally brought under control and began to shrink. On the other hand, by cutting expenditures and inducing deflation the new regime prejudiced the interests of key social groups, which not surprisingly were to figure prominently in the political unrest of the period.[23]

The abdication crisis might be described in retrospect as the opening of Pandora's box, releasing all the evils which were thenceforth to plague the Brazilian nation. A more precise image, given the troubled development of the nation under D. Pedro I, might come from the tale of the genie in the bottle. April 7, 1831, had released from confinement the genie of power, to be used for either good or ill. Brazil's new rulers expected good to follow. One point only was certain: the nature of both government and politics had decisively changed.

II

The troubles that beset the new regime were of two types. Within the political community, still largely synonymous with the ruling minority, there now emerged rival factions competing for the control of power. Among the general population there also emerged political movements basically impelled by social and economic discontents. The first difficulties to vex the government after April 7, 1831, were factional disputes in the provinces outside of Rio de Janeiro. In many of those provinces the elements supporting the opposition alliance which had at the national level fought against D. Pedro I now tried to seize power locally by purging the provincial administration of current officeholders, on the grounds that they were untrustworthy and compromised. Although willing to accept a limited number of dismissals, the new regime at Rio was not ready to sanction such wholesale purges, which would have weakened its authority and disrupted the machinery of government in the provinces as well as alienating key political elements there. As a result, several provinces became embroiled in a three-sided strife involving competing local factions and the president, representing the national government.[24] These conflicts —essentially struggles within Brazil's ruling circles—both fostered unrest and facilitated its outbreak among the small folk and the general population.

The root cause for these popular movements was resentment against social and economic conditions. Lacking any strong ideological motivation, the movements tended to support whichever political faction seemed most likely to overturn the existing order. Factions hostile to the new regime were quick to court these popular movements, whose leaders proved remarkably willing to switch their allegiance from one cause to another at a moment's notice.[25] It did not take long for the two types of unrest to converge and coalesce.

That a regime claiming to govern in the name and interests of the people should almost from the start of its rule have aroused deeply rooted hostility from the ordinary population is not as paradoxical as it might appear. To the supporters of the regime created on April 7, 1831, government was accountable to the people, its principal duty being the protection of their rights. However, "people" was taken to mean "citizens," men who were civilized—that is, literate and rational—and possessed of a material stake in society. Ranking high among the rights to be protected was the sanctity of property.[26] This ideology was confirmed by practical considerations: if it were to survive, the new regime had to retain support from the local notables, among whom landowners and merchants figured prominently. In these conditions the regime had to oppose any political program that threatened the social and economic status quo, such as the Exaltados' persistent demand for the dismissal of all Portuguese-born officials and the deportation of certain prosperous and powerful Portuguese nationals.[27]

The extent to which liberalism in politics was in the early 1830's synonymous with conservatism in social and economic questions can be measured by the new regime's attitude toward slavery and the slave trade. Slaves still constituted the largest section of the population, and among free Brazilians a considerable number were descendants of slaves. Fear that they might lose their freedom caused very real concern for many black and mulatto poor. Despite their declared belief in the rights of the individual, the politicians who controlled the regime made no effort to ameliorate the slaves' position and treatment. Abolition of servitude was not even mentioned, much less advocated. Slaves were property and property was a sacred right, interfering with which the government had no business. If "resistance to oppression" was an inalienable right of the citizen, the slave could not claim it. In 1834 the legislature passed a new law prescribing immediate execution for all slaves convicted of attempted rebellion. The same contradiction between declared belief and actual behavior characterized the new regime's handling of the slave trade with Africa. As required by the 1826 slave trade treaty with Great Britain, the General Assembly rather grudgingly passed a law on November 7, 1831, banning the trade with Africa. The provisions of the new law, making participation in the trade a crime and declaring all Africans thenceforth imported free on arrival in Brazil, were enforced little and soon not at all. The slaving merchants, well endowed with money and influence, pursued their activities quite openly, without any hindrance from the government.[28]

Identified as the new regime was in the common mind with the land-owners and merchants who exploited the poor and the slaves, it is not surprising that the government failed to achieve much popular backing. Mistrust of the new regime accounts for the widespread support secured by two major rural revolts, the Pinto Madeira rising in southern Ceará in late 1831 and the Guerra dos Cabanos in southern Pernambuco in early 1832. In the latter, communities of fugitive slave and free Indians provided the backbone of the rising.[29]

That unrest broke out so quickly and proved so difficult to control was the result less of the new government's lack of popularity among the general population than of its inept handling of the institution on which the maintenance of law and order primarily rested. Already in 1830 the law enacting a budget for 1831–32 had reduced expenditures on the army by one-quarter. The budget for 1832–33, approved on November 15, 1831, cut them by a further third (see Figure 1, p. 166).[30] Loss of pay, perquisites, and promotion made both officers and men resentful, the perfect target for the propaganda spread by the Exaltados, who believed that they too had been deprived of their rights in the aftermath of April 7.

In Rio de Janeiro approaching trouble was evident by the end of May 1831, and as a precaution the General Assembly passed on June 6 a law granting the national government sweeping powers over the judiciary and police and also authorizing it to ban public meetings.[31] These measures did not dispel the atmosphere of crisis and confrontation in the national capital. Agitation by the Exaltados for immediate political reforms and the expulsion of Portuguese-born notables continued unchecked. Discontent among the troops exploded on July 12 and rapidly developed into a mass mutiny both by the army units garrisoning the capital and by the military police. After three days of near anarchy, order was restored only by the government's making specious promises and concessions and by the arming of an ad hoc police force. The crisis revealed simultaneously the nakedness of the regime and the formidable forces that could be mobilized against it.[32]

The July crisis in the national capital dispelled any lingering hopes for political accord and national prosperity. The exposed position of the new regime caused the majority of the Nativists and of the Coimbra bloc to form a political alliance, known as the *moderado,* or "Moderate," party. Their parliamentary leaders took office in the midst of the July crisis, when the regents replaced the existing cabinet. The new ministers included established politicians such as Bernardo Pereira de Vasconcelos, but the dominant figure was the minister of justice, Diogo Antônio Feijó.

The new minister was, in his own phrase, *rustico*—a hick, a hayseed. His surviving letters reveal the man: the handwriting is ill formed, frequently illegible, and the Portuguese rough, often ungrammatical. In Feijó a want of tact, imagination, and social grace was complemented by a grinding persistence, forthrightness, and zeal for his chosen cause. An in-

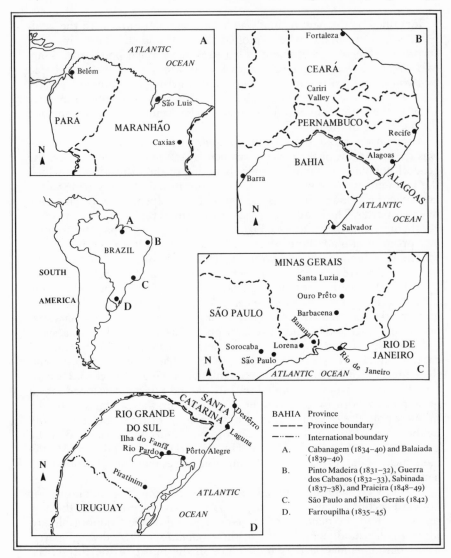

MAP 4. Regional Revolts During the 1830's and 1840's. (All boundary lines are approximations only.)

nate pessimism led him to expect and so to prepare for the worst. These qualities alone kept him in office during twelve months of accumulating crises and disasters, perhaps the most dangerous period in Brazil's entire existence as a nation. As minister of justice from July 1831 to July 1832, Feijó had to handle five risings in the national capital, two major revolts in Ceará and Pernambuco, as well as lesser conflicts in other provinces.

Feijó epitomized, so far as any one man could, the Nativist group. Born in São Paulo province, ostensibly a foundling but probably the son of a priest, Feijó was largely self-educated. An ordained priest, he was unorthodox in behavior and belief. He had a mistress and five children, and he denounced both clerical celibacy and the pretensions of the pope. Despite considerable abilities, which had gained him election to the Lisbon Cortes and to the 1826 chamber, Feijó never felt at ease in the larger world outside his native *pátria* of São Paulo, to which he retreated whenever possible.[33]

The survival of the Moderado government in power after July 1831 depended, as friend and foe alike appreciated, on the minister of justice, who responded with an iron hand to the mounting challenge from the opposition forces. Attacking the Moderados from the left were the Exaltados who from the end of 1831 began to coordinate their activities through the founding of Sociedades Federais (Federalist Societies).[34] With little representation in the chamber and none at all in the Senate, the Exaltados were more a sect than a party. What made them dangerous as a political movement was the energy and persistence of their leaders, mostly editors of small newspapers, and the fierce commitment of their supporters, mainly drawn from the small folk in the coastal cities.[35] The Exaltados' program consisted of federalism, republicanism, and an implacable hostility toward the Portuguese-born, including the *adotivos,* those who, resident in Brazil in 1822, had been granted citizenship by the 1824 Constitution. Underlying this hatred was a form of class conflict, since the Portuguese-born were denounced as wealthy, mean, and exploitative. Anti-Portuguese feeling played a large role in an Exaltado revolt at Salvador in April 1833 and in the Nativist risings in Mato Grosso in 1834.[36]

Troublesome as were the Exaltados, they did not match the challenge to the Moderado regime presented by the formidable coalition which emerged early in 1832. The new movement was organized around the Sociedade Conservadora da Constituição Jurada do Império (Society for Conserving the Constitution as Sworn) but was identified by the name of its principal newspaper, O *Caramurú.*[37] The Caramurú party secured support both from the ruling circles—the Luso-Brazilians in the Senate and Council of State, the imperial household, the officer corps of the army —and from small folk in the towns and the free rural population. If the ostensible goal of the Caramurús was the return of D. Pedro I, either as restored emperor or as regent for his son, their real purpose was to restore the traditional form of order and authority to the polity, a cause identified with the figure of the monarch. The coalition proved both willing and able to use Freemasonry and the press to advance its cause. The very simplicity of the Caramurús' program—the emperor's return—increased its attractiveness. The basic weakness of the coalition—lack of certainty that D. Pedro I would consent to return—was not immediately apparent, and indeed the ruling Moderados reacted as though nothing were more likely.[38]

To defeat the menace from both left and right, the Moderado cabinet adopted a two-part strategy. The first was to arm their supporters and entrust them with the defense of the political order created by the events of April 7. In August 1831 the General Assembly passed a law replacing the old militias and *ordenanças* by an unpaid national guard modeled on that of France. The law encharged the National Guard units with maintaining law and order in their own districts. Units could also be "detached" to deal with more general emergencies. Service was made attractive by, among other inducements, allowing the guardsmen to elect their own officers. As organized by Feijó, the National Guard was recruited from the social groups supporting the political status quo, with local notables as officers and small folk the rank and file. At a moment when the army could not be relied on, the loyalty and steadfastness of the National Guard units throughout the nation was a principal factor in the new regime's survival.[39]

The second part of the Moderado strategy was to deprive the Exaltados of at least part of their ideological appeal by granting a substantial devolution of political power to the provinces. The criminal procedure code enacted in 1832 entrusted the initial organization of the new judicial system in each province to the president and his council, with the town councils being given a role in the selection of the lower ranks of the judiciary.[40] Under the 1832 code the small folk could actively participate in local governance. To fill the major positions in the province of Ceará alone (without including such minor jobs as ward inspector) would require, it was reported, a minimum of 3,000 citizens, that is, men qualified to be voters.[41]

Much more important was the action begun by the Chamber of Deputies to amend the Constitution. Under the 1824 Constitution the provinces possessed no rights or powers of initiative. The provincial councils (Conselhos Gerais) enjoyed a very narrow jurisdiction, with their "resolutions" needing approval by the General Assembly before taking effect. Enlarging the political role of the provinces was an urgent priority. The process of constitutional amendment was, however, extremely slow, cumbersome, and by no means certain of success. A law had first to be passed authorizing the electors who chose the deputies for the new Chamber to empower the new deputies to reform specified articles of the Constitution. So authorized, the General Assembly could enact a law reforming the articles in question. On October 11, 1831, the Chamber of Deputies passed on third reading the necessary bill, empowering the electors to start the process of constitutional reform. The project authorized the abolition of the regulating power and the wholesale devolution of power to the provinces.

So radical a measure inevitably created tensions and excited opposition. Debate on the bill in the Senate was so protracted as to suggest deliberate sabotage. To the majority of senators the proposed reforms were anathema, strengthening their sympathy for the Caramurú party. Much more seriously, the debates in the lower house had revealed a deep ideological split within the Moderado ranks over the nature of Brazil as a nation, a split pitting the Nativists against the members of the Coimbra bloc. The Nativists' perception of the ideal national polity had not changed significantly since the revolt of 1824. The nation existed for them in terms of the local *pátrias,* which they equated with the provinces and which they wished to be essentially autonomous. The role of the national government at Rio de Janeiro was to protect the *pátrias* from external aggression and to maintain order among them. Loyalty to both *pátria* and nation was thus reconciled.

In contrast, the members of the Coimbra bloc viewed the nation as the font of all authority. The people, that is, individual citizens, should directly elect the national government, which in turn should directly rule the nation. Endowed with limited powers and dedicated to the preservation of individual rights, the national government was despite its restricted role the prime mover in the national polity. In the opinion of some in the Coimbra bloc, the proposed constitutional reform was compatible with these beliefs. For others the reform bill was the bitter bit, a necessary sacrifice of principle in order to prevent what was far worse—anarchy or a restoration of the former Emperor. For a minority of the Coimbra bloc the reforms were unacceptable on any grounds, and these men withdrew from the Moderado party.[42]

The Senate's failure to act on the reform bill during the 1831 session meant that the government had to face unaided the onslaughts from right and left. The climax came in April 1832 when two successive risings, the first inspired by the Exaltados and the second by the Caramurús, attempted to seize the national capital. Behind the Caramurú conspiracy Feijó saw the hand of José Bonifácio, the young emperor's guardian, since among its participants were members of the imperial household.

Although both revolts were suppressed with little trouble, the protection given to the insurgents by men entrenched in the very heart of the polity so infuriated Feijó that he turned to drastic remedies. Complaining to the General Assembly when it convened in May 1832 that "everything I have to report is sad, and darker still is the future I foresee," Feijó demanded the instant removal of José Bonifácio as guardian. "If he was not implicated [in the rising of April 14], he was so obtuse as to ignore what the capital had long foreseen."[43] The deputies authorized the dismissal by a fair margin, but the Senate rejected it by a single vote. Since the senators had been busy passing amendments which gutted the proposed constitutional reform, the Senate was perceived by Feijó as an accomplice in the war against the regime. On the day of the Senate vote, July 26, Feijó resigned as minister, declaring inadequate "the means available to the government to repress the factions and to make Brazil prosper."[44]

The resignation did not imply that Feijó had given up the struggle. He had simply resolved to gain by direct action what he could not achieve by parliamentary means. What followed was "the coup d'état of July 30."[45]

After the entire cabinet joined Feijó in resigning, the regents informed the legislature of their inability to continue in office. The National Guard units in the capital went on full alert. With an atmosphere of threatening crisis thus nicely created, Feijó's Nativist allies in the Chamber of Deputies proposed that the speaker name a special committee to recommend remedies for the emergency. The plan was that the committee should immediately advise the chamber to constitute itself a national convention and proceed at once to adopt a new constitution in which the regulating power had no place and the provinces were granted a considerable autonomy.

The deputies voted the creation of the commission, but at that point the plot began to falter. Instead of immediately submitting a report, the committee delayed, and delayed so long that the deputies finally voted for a two-hour adjournment. When they reconvened, the psychological moment had passed. The committee did finally recommend that "the Chamber convert itself into a Constituent Assembly so that it can adopt the measures required in the present crisis," but the report, instead of being put as planned to an immediate vote, was thrown open to debate.[46]

The first deputy to speak delivered the deathblow. With commanding presence and total conviction, he pointed out that the project was rash, illegal, and incapable of receiving sufficient support from the nation. With this speech, against which the Nativists' oratory proved vain, Honório Hermeto Carneiro Leão established himself as a dominant figure in the Coimbra bloc. Graduating from university in 1825, he had entered the judiciary the next year and in 1828 had been elected a deputy from his native Minas Gerais. Honório Hermeto's speech, delivered by candlelight in the gathering dusk, displayed the self-confidence, energy, and command which were soon to earn him the name El Rei Honório (Boss Honório) and to keep him at the center of politics for the next 25 years.[47] None of his subsequent achievements quite equaled the panache and efficacy of his debut. Despite the Nativists' cajolings the special committee withdrew its report, and the deputies then sent a message to the regents, declining their proffered resignation and requesting them to name a new cabinet. Feijó and the Nativist faction in the Moderado party had gambled all on a single throw, hoping to gain supreme power and to reshape the nation to their ideals. They had singularly failed.

III

The long-term consequences of the abortive coup of July 1832 were considerable. Even though the coup had failed, the precedent was set for the disregard of legal procedures in order to gain political advantage—the subordination of means to ends. The internal cohesion, the sense of mutual respect and trust which had bound the Moderado alliance together, had been broken. The three years following saw a growth of factional strife in which principles took second place within the Moderados' ranks, and the alliance slowly disintegrated. The abortive coup cruelly revealed the basic weaknesses of the Nativists: their lack of political finesse and their lack on the national level of a strong, capable leadership. The crisis initiated a slow movement of the Coimbra bloc to the right, toward alliance with the Luso-Brazilians, still the largest group in the Senate, with whom they shared a common training and culture.

The immediate effects of the failed coup were not so disastrous. The crisis showed how strong were the pressures for an immediate devolution of power to the provinces and how urgent was the necessity for making concessions. On August 1, 1832, the day after the coup failed, the Senate finally sent back to the chamber the reform bill authorizing the next legislature to amend the Constitution. The senators had purged the bill of all radical elements. After consenting to two of the Senate's fourteen amendments, the chamber requested a joint session, as authorized by the Constitution, to resolve by voting in common the questions in dispute. To this demand the Senate, which would have been rendered impotent if the July 30 coup had triumphed, quickly consented. After eleven days of debate and common voting, there emerged a bill much closer to the Senate's version than to the lower house's original project.[48] Having passed this bill and having promulgated the new criminal procedure code, the General Assembly finally adjourned on October 30, 1832.

The passage of these measures marked a change in the nature of the problems facing the national government. For the time being the challenge from the left in favor of federalism and republicanism subsided, while the threat from the right, in favor of the restoration of D. Pedro I, appeared to strengthen and to become urgent. The appeal of the Caramurú party was certainly increased by the passage of the constitutional reform bill and other concessions made to the left, but the obsessive fear of an imminent restoration that now gripped the politicians supporting the regime was to a large degree self-induced, caused by a consciousness of the weakness of the regime.

In July 1832 D. Pedro I, having recruited an army of exiles and mercenaries who undertook to serve wherever ordered, landed in Portugal and captured the city of Porto. One year later a second invasion force landing in the far south of Portugal took Lisbon and restored D. Maria da Glória to the throne she had lost in 1827.[49] These successes, magnified by the Moderado regime's suspicions, seemed to portend the early arrival of a military expedition on Brazil's shores. A military rising in March 1833 in the capital of Minas Gerais province, Ouro Prêto, which had deposed the provincial president, was ascribed to Caramurú plotting. In May the government presented evidence to the chamber showing the likelihood of D. Pedro I's return, and it requested the deputies to take such action as would prevent a restoration. On July 8, rejecting the report by a committee which questioned the validity of the evidence, the chamber voted by 50 to 32 to comply with the government's request. The deputies also passed a motion presented by Honório Hermeto, resolving that the former emperor be banished in perpetuity from Brazil. A bill to this effect was immediately introduced.[50]

These extreme measures, proposed by politicians obsessed by the apparent dangers facing the national government, were in essence counterproductive. They failed to deter the Caramurús, and further, they alienated a broad spectrum of opinion offended by the disrespect shown to the imperial family. Within a week of the vote José da Costa Carvalho, one of the regents, withdrew from Rio to his estates in São Paulo province. Ostensibly he had taken a temporary leave of absence because of ill health, but he never returned and in fact abandoned his post.[51]

If wrong in imputing responsibility to D. Pedro I himself, the regime was correct in fearing an organized plot to restore the former Emperor, for a conspiracy was being prepared in Brazil itself. Antônio Carlos, the former republican of 1817, now sailed for Europe, secretly carrying a formal petition begging the former emperor to return.[52] In November 1833 the regime received news from Europe about Antônio Carlos's mission and, fearing the worst, took decisive action. The Sociedade Militar (Military Society), which served as a front organization for the Caramurú party, was closed down and its premises wrecked by a mob which also smashed up the presses of two Caramurú journals. José Bonifácio was suspended by ministerial order from his post as guardian of the emperor and arrested for plotting against the state.[53]

These measures were effective but in a sense unnecessary. Already in October 1833 the former emperor had refused the petition brought to Lisbon by Antônio Carlos, a rejection D. Pedro confirmed in writing.[54] Although this rebuff was reported in the *Times* of London, the Rio government may well not have seen or credited it, especially since Antônio Carlos had the effrontery to send that paper a flat denial of the purpose of his mission.[55] Further, in view of the former Emperor's past conduct, particularly his variableness of mood and his preference for dramatic action, no great trust could be placed in the permanence of any denial he made, especially one given in private.

The abortive Caramurú petition and the persisting fears that D. Pedro I might yet decide to return to Brazil backed by a battle-hardened army served to bring the Nativists to a peak of influence. In the new Chamber of Deputies, which had been granted constituent powers by the electors and which convened in May 1834, the Nativists formed a large and experienced bloc of deputies. All six of the Senate seats which had become vacant since April 1831 had been filled by committed Nativists, of whom the most notable was Feijó himself.[56]

Fears about the imminence of a restoration were the controlling factor during the parliamentary sessions of 1834, especially after news arrived of D. Miguel's final defeat and departure from Portugal.[57] Although rejecting the bill for the perpetual banishment of D. Pedro I, the senators did consent (by 23 to 16) to the removal of José Bonifácio as guardian. In political terms the Senate consented to a major loss of power by not disputing the Chamber of Deputies' claim (asserted by a vote of 70 to 16 on June 16) that to the lower house alone belonged the right to enact the actual amendment to the Constitution.[58] The chamber spent the last half of June and the whole of July determining the various sections of the amendment. The completed articles of that amendment, subsequently known as o Ato Adicional (the Additional Act), were passed in third reading by 64 to 20 votes. On August 12, 1834, the Ato Adicional was promulgated by the regents. Supreme constituent power, which D. Pedro I had in 1823 denied to the Constituent Assembly, was now secured by its successor, the Chamber of Deputies. In a real sense the Ato Adicional canceled out the dissolution of November 1823, so that the imperial Constitution at last rested on consent, not force.

Compared with the original project for constitutional reform discussed in 1831, the Ato Adicional was a fairly moderate document. The Council of State was abolished, and instead of the General Assembly electing a three-man regency, a single regent was to be chosen by the provincial electors. Neither the Senate nor the Chamber of Deputies was touched. Devolution of power to the provinces was the major objective of the Ato Adicional, 23 of its 33 articles dealing with that subject. As the orator who presented the document to the regents stressed, it was designed to "confer on the provinces all the resources for their new existence."[59]

The heart of the Ato Adicional lay in the replacement of the Conselhos Gerais by provincial assemblies, organized according to the Nativists' conception of what the ideal legislature should be. The new assemblies were elected for a two-year term, during which they could not be dissolved. Their sessions were to last for only two months each year. The provincial president could veto the assembly's bills, but if the law concerned strictly local matters, the provincial assembly was empowered to override the veto by a two-thirds majority.[60] The new assemblies received jurisdiction over the civil, judicial, and ecclesiastical organization of the province; the siting of its capital; primary and secondary education; the affairs of the provinces' municipalities; public works, roads, and navigation in the province; the creation and abolition of posts in the provincial administration; and the levying and expending of strictly provincial revenues.[61]

Sweeping as was the devolution of power, the Ato Adicional had been worded so as to ensure that "the national interest . . . prevails over all petty local advantages: the provincial liberties are carefully delineated and circumscribed so as to prevent conflicts and enduring disputes, which can be so fatal to the people's interests, undermining their peace and security."[62] Provincial and municipal taxes were not to "prejudice" those levied by the national government, import taxes being specifically banned. No laws affecting the interests of other provinces might be passed; if the president vetoed any law on these grounds, that veto could not directly be overridden, but upon a two-thirds vote the bill would be referred to the General Assembly in Rio for decision. Almost all government officials of importance were specifically declared to be neither provincial nor municipal. In particular, the provincial president remained appointable and removable at will by the national government. Only in the incapacity or absence of the appointed president would a substitute named by the provincial assembly govern the province as vice president.[63]

Whatever its imperfections, the Ato Adicional of 1834 marked a significant change in the development of Brazil as a nation. From the first creation of a single polity in 1808, unity had always been identified with the concentration of power at the center. The brief experience with *juntas de govêrno* from 1821 to 1824 served to reinforce this equation of unity with centralization. The Ato Adicional committed Brazilians to the creation of provincial governments enjoying substantial powers that were largely independent of the national government. For this venture in federalism to work, cooperation between the two levels of government was indispensable.

Most of the Coimbra bloc had consented to the reform of the Constitution not through ideological conviction but in the hopes of saving the nation from a worse fate. The triumph of D. Pedro I in Portugal, which released the former Emperor for a new adventure in Brazil, convinced many deputies that the only means of preventing his regaining the throne was an immediate and substantial devolution of power from a single center at Rio, easily captured by a coup, to eighteen provincial centers. Only this fear, together with a recognition of the danger on the left and a sense of obligation to the Nativist wing of the party, can explain the massive vote in the lower house in favor of the Ato Adicional.[64]

Early in December 1834 news reached Rio that D. Pedro I had died. On September 24, just six weeks after the passage of the Ato Adicional, the former emperor and king had succumbed to tuberculosis. The threat to Brazil was removed. The sacrifice of principle had been unjustified, the concessions unnecessary. The sense of relief was outweighed, among the Coimbra bloc at least, by chagrin and bitterness. In death as in life, D. Pedro I dictated the course of Brazilian politics. Deprived of its reason for existence, the Caramurú party disappeared overnight. The bond that had since 1826 allied the Coimbra bloc with the Nativists snapped. The latter, or rather the more radical among them, were no longer kept in check by the threat of a restoration and could now strive for the conversion of Brazil into a true federation, with the *pátrias* enjoying absolute control of their affairs. At the moment when the single regent and the new provincial assemblies were being elected, the dominant issue which during the last three years had shaped national politics suddenly vanished.

IV

A hiatus in power inevitably occurred between the promulgation of the Ato Adicional and the installation of the new provincial assemblies and the single regent. Having been displaced, the two remaining members of the outgoing regency suffered a commensurate loss of prestige and authority. As holdovers, they did not possess, any more than did the ministers they appointed, the means to curb the rival political factions that sought to gain control of the new system by winning the separate elections at the provincial and national levels. Writing on September 20, 1834, an observer in Rio de Janeiro made this precise point: "Positions and employments are, however, so desired that for this motive there has already appeared, between province and province, a tendency towards civil war, and I greatly fear that the elections for the Provincial Assemblies and the single Regent, according to the reform just made to the Constitution of this Empire, will accelerate it." [65] At this critical moment the national government, already lacking authority, was further crippled by the virtual collapse of the outgoing regency. Not only was one regent permanently absent on his estates in São Paulo province, but by May 1835 a second regent, João Braúlio Moniz, had fallen mortally ill, incapable of transacting any business. The remaining regent, Francisco de Lima e Silva, soon showed that he lacked the ability and determination to carry on the government by himself in such desperate circumstances. [66]

If the election of the new regent had preceded and not followed that of the provincial assemblies, the crisis might have proved less formidable, since only a newly elected national government armed with prestige and authority could have overseen effectively the elections to the assemblies and guided the creation of what were in essence autonomous regimes in the provinces. Even after a decade of constitutional rule, politics at the local and provincial levels remained a struggle between individuals and clans to control the fruits of power for private advantage. The introduction of a free press and greater popular participation did not alter existing practices. Quite the opposite, the established system simply assimilated the new methods, finding in them greater scope and opportunity for the attainment of traditional goals. The new participants in politics, basically the small folk, contributed to the perpetuation of the old system, because in politics they also pursued not ideological but traditional goals—office, however, minor; patronage, however paltry; and profit, however small. What the president of Ceará deplored in February 1833 about his province could be applied to all of Brazil: "The whole province has been and still is seething with intrigues and cabals over the elections, and in consequence, the electors, deputies, and councillors will be those who, rather than serving the public cause, promote and protect dangerous factions and unjust pretensions, and favor relatives and protégés." [67]

The newly created provincial assemblies simply intensified the rivalries and magnified the rewards offered. With the passage of the Ato Adicional the center of popular politics shifted from the national to the provincial level, as a contemporary pointed out in July 1834: "Their entire national feeling as Brazilians has of a sudden withered, and there exist only party factions, with the mass of the people almost uncaring about politics in general."[68] The devolution of power contained in the Ato Adicional guaranteed that the implementation of the constitutional amendment would produce confrontation in the *pátrias*.

In each province power would go to those who could control the proceedings of the new assembly; this required electing a majority of its deputies. Since the winners would use the assembly's powers to entrench their supremacy and to damage their traditional foes, no family clan or interest group with any claim to influence could afford to abstain from politics. The result was a ferocious if confused struggle between the rival interests. Given the absence of any ideological basis for the conflict and the lack of organization, provincial politics were highly personalistic, usually dominated by the heads of the most powerful clans or by men of unusual charisma or ability.[69]

As it turned out, the elections for the new provincial assemblies took place with no more violence and fraud than was customary. The same electors who had chosen the new assemblies later cast ballots for the new regent. Just as the selection of the assemblies intensified confrontation at the local and provincial levels, so the elections for regent caused the polarization of politics at the national level—but for very different reasons. The basic cause was the candidacy of Diogo Antônio Feijó, who despite his resignation as minister in July 1832 continued to be a central figure on the national scene. To the leaders of the battered but still powerful Moderado party, he was the obvious choice for regent: "Sr. Diogo Antônio Feijó is still the man of 1831," the Moderados' newspaper, the *Aurora Fluminense*, assured its readers, "and good citizens will, by rallying around him, easily triumph over evil actions and blind fanaticism."[70]

This advocacy of Feijó was based on a false appreciation of the political situation. At the time that the Ato Adicional had created the post of a single, popularly elected regent, D. Pedro I was alive and victorious, the restorer of constitutional rule in Portugal. Had Brazil continued to be threatened by the former Emperor's return, many politicians would have set personal feelings aside in order to make Feijó regent, as the only man capable of averting a restoration. What the Moderado leaders failed to appreciate was that D. Pedro I's decease transformed Feijó from a consensus candidate into a virulently mistrusted politician. A loose coalition of Feijó's foes soon formed, and Antônio Francisco de Paula e Holanda Cavalcanti de Albuquerque eventually emerged as the candidate whose diverse qualities made him most capable of defeating Feijó. Holanda Cavalcanti came from the northeast, a member of a leading clan of Pernambuco.

A graduate of Göttingen University, he was a deputy and had served thrice as minister. That Holanda Cavalcanti's ambition was inordinate—and his scruples few—did not, for Feijó's opponents, reduce his attractiveness as a candidate.[71]

The system established by the Ato Adicional for electing the regent favored Holanda Cavalcanti. Each elector cast two ballots, one of which had to be for a candidate not resident in the elector's province. The candidate receiving the most votes would become regent.[72] Electors' second votes were actively canvassed for Holanda Cavalcanti; when the votes cast on April 7, 1835, were computed, Feijó had obtained 2,826 votes and Holanda Cavalcanti was in second place with 2,251. Over 2,000 votes were given to three members of the Coimbra bloc, and if these men had not been candidates, Feijó might well have lost. Although his foes failed to defeat him, they did succeed in depriving him of any claim to a national mandate. One-third of Feijó's votes came from a single province, Minas Gerais, and in the north and northeast he carried only Ceará and Rio Grande do Norte.[73]

The slowness with which the electoral returns were received at Rio and the closeness of the result meant that not until the middle of July was Feijó's victory certain.[74] By then Feijó was displaying extreme reluctance to become regent. Prior to the death of D. Pedro I, he had been active in promoting his own candidacy, but by June he was described as "fearful of accepting." Feijó's unwillingness, which he expressed openly, was enough to reduce the Moderado leaders to despair, given the state of the outgoing regency, described in June as being "already almost without force."[75]

Feijó's reluctance and his failure to secure a strong mandate in the elections emboldened his foes, who schemed to prevent his installation as regent. They promoted a dispute between the Senate and chamber over the legal requirements for counting the election returns, in the hopes of delaying the count until the next session opened in May 1836. The death of the regent João Braúlio Moniz on September 20, 1835, furnished them with a fresh opportunity. At their instigation the Senate voted that the vacancy should be filled. If the lower house agreed, they hoped in the ensuing vote to slip in Holanda Cavalcanti as regent. The Moderados had great difficulty in defeating this proposal, but the prospect of Holanda Cavalcanti's governing Brazil finally forced Feijó into a reluctant agreement to serve. The deadlock between Senate and chamber at last resolved, the votes were finally counted on October 5 and 6.[76]

During the months that the national polity was dominated by this struggle for supremacy, factional strife had in two provinces escalated into open and uncontrollable conflict. In the province of Pará events took a tragic and horrifying course. Pará's incorporation into the Empire in 1823 had been obtained by a military stratagem, and throughout D. Pedro I's reign the national government never established a secure hold on the province, isolated as it was geographically from the rest of the nation. Politics in Pará were characterized by an intense, ruthless factionalism in which hatred of the Portuguese-born played a major role. Twice since April 7, 1831, the local Exaltados had deposed presidents newly named by the national government. Persecuted and desperate, the Exaltado faction was ready for revolt, restrained only by the authority of its leader. His death on the final day of 1834 removed the last barrier to violence.[77]

On January 7, 1834, a rising by Exaltado supporters broke out in Belém, the province's capital. The president, the *comandante das armas*, and other ranking officers were slaughtered. Within the rebel camp a split rapidly developed between the notables and the small folk, who on January 21 revolted. The "interim" president and his staff were massacred in their turn. Despite the arrival in July of an expedition from Rio commanded by a new president, attempts to restore peace failed. In August the conflict expanded into a full-scale, devastating rising by the ordinary population, in which the exploited and the Indians (groups who largely coincided) took revenge upon the whites and the wealthy. The outbreak of a "race" war, frightening as it was, did assure the national government of eventual victory. Since it alone could restore law and order, there rallied to its cause all those possessing any stake in the existing social order.[78]

Far more dangerous to Brazil as a nation—because the rising did not openly threaten the social order—was the revolt which erupted in the far south in September 1835. The frontier province of Rio Grande do Sul was both highly militarized and heavily factionalized. The economic and fiscal policies of the national government caused many grievances. The provincial president, in office since May 1834, was not only a native of Rio Grande do Sul but linked by blood to one of the competing factions. If his own conduct was reasonably fair, he failed to control his brother, whose behavior in the new provincial assembly proved so intemperate as to embitter local politics. By September a majority of the assembly were united in opposition and the quarrel assumed larger dimensions. The gathering crisis could have been defused by replacing the president, but the weakness of the regency prevented any swift remedial action by the national government.[79]

Deepening confrontation gave influence to the more radical and impetuous elements. In a dawn raid on September 19, 1835, a band of armed horsemen, *gaúchos* (cowboys) from the cattle ranches along the border with Uruguay, seized Pôrto Alegre, the provincial capital. The leader of this rising, a military officer who had made his reputation in the Cisplatine wars, later published a proclamation that revealed his complaints and his ideals: "We have carried out, Riograndenses, a sacred duty defeating the first steps toward arbitrary government in our dear *pátria*: she will thank you, and all of Brazil will applaud your patriotism. Justice will strengthen your arm in deposing an inept and partisan regime and in reestablishing the rule of law."[80] In this revolt, which erupted just three weeks before Feijó was sworn in as regent, the basic incompatibility of *pátria* and nation became patent. For the rebels the needs of their *pátria* took precedence over all else, so that if the requirements of the nation conflicted with them the nation must give way. In this outlying section of the country, the *pátria* was challenging the nation. The moment of truth had arrived for Brazil, just as the votes for the new regent were counted and Feijó on October 12, 1835, assumed responsibility for the nation's affairs.

V

To the leaders of the Moderado party, Feijó constituted the best, if not the only, hope for the resolution of the problems plaguing Brazil. He could once more save the nation in danger. By declaring that the new regent "is still the man of 1831" the Moderado party revealed that their hopes for the future rested on two false expectations. The emergency facing Brazil in 1835 was very different from the one overcome four years before, and Feijó himself was physically no longer the man he had been in 1831. Nor were the talents he had then demonstrated what the situation now demanded.[81]

In 1831 the regency, having been elected by the General Assembly, functioned without independence, virtually as the executive arm of the legislature. Now the new regent was the choice of the people (or to be exact, of the 5,000 electors who acted for the people) and so possessed an authority distinct and independent from that of the legislature. Given the existence of what were in essence two competing centers of power the situation demanded of the new regent qualities of tact and diplomacy —almost of cunning–which Feijó conspicuously lacked. His dogged pessimism, narrowness in outlook, and refusal to compromise—all of which had made him "the man of iron" in 1831—now doomed his relationship with an assembly in which his enemies were numerous.

Upon becoming regent Feijó did attempt to attract support by offering government positions to members of the Coimbra bloc. This tactic failed and Feijó rapidly antagonized the legislators by making clear that he expected them to respect his prerogatives as the ruler of Brazil.[82] What certainly contributed to the new regent's poor judgment in handling both the General Assembly and the larger questions of government was the deterioration in his health since 1831. Then Feijó had taken up the burdens of power with a certain gloomy relish. In 1835 he accepted office only because of the overpersuasion of his political allies. The illness he suffered in early October, a minor stroke or heart attack, seems to have been the product of acute psychological stress.[83]

Even if Feijó had enjoyed good health in 1835 and displayed unsuspected talents as a conciliator and leader, his regency would probably still have developed as it did. Feijó's conception of the nation, which he had formulated as long ago as 1822 in a speech to the Lisbon Cortes, prevented him from taking effective action to resolve the problems then facing Brazil. What Feijó had argued in 1822 he still believed in 1835. To him political authority resided in the constituent *pátrias*, and a national polity derived from their collective will. Only with their joint consent could the form of government be changed, as happened in 1822 with the declaration of independence and again in 1834 with the passage of the Ato Adicional. Since the national government did not possess direct authority from the people but only that delegated by the *pátrias*, it could not in Feijó's opinion take action against any *pátria* without its consent.[84]

In 1831 Feijó had not hesitated to use strong measures against the foes of the national government, whether Caramurús or Exaltados, because in his eyes they threatened the safety of the *pátrias*, and it was the principal task of the national government to protect the *pátrias* from external attack and internal subversion. In 1835 the position of the national government had changed, in Feijó's eyes, because the provinces were now autonomous by the provisions of the Ato Adicional. Most of the difficulties now facing Brazil stemmed from that transfer of power. It was not that the new regent did not believe in Brazil as a nation or that he did not cherish it, but according to his perception of the nation, the measures necessary for its salvation could not be implemented without violating the rights and liberties of the *pátrias*. What intensified Feijó's general reluctance to act was his conviction that the election results showed that he had not secured from the *pátrias*, particularly those of northern Brazil, the acceptance necessary for him to govern effectively. As a memorandum he drew up prior to assuming the regency shows, he anticipated that the northern provinces would separate from the nation shortly after his inauguration.[85]

That Feijó's inaction as regent was the result of these inhibitions rather than of any failing in mind and health is demonstrated by his very different reactions to the revolts in Pará and Rio Grande do Sul. "By good means or bad, [Pará] will be regained from the wild beasts who control it." As for Rio Grande do Sul, "the good of the state has advised a conciliatory approach, and up to the present it has prevented the outbreak of violence," although a refusal to come to terms would, he warned, set "the full resources of the state in motion to bring [the rebels] into obedience."[86]

By the time Feijó took office in October 1835, the revolt in Pará had become a conflict which threatened the very existence of that province as a society. Against the rebels, Feijó acted with all the vigor and severity that had in 1831 made him "the man of iron." At his request the General Assembly voted a six-month suspension in Pará of the civil rights guaranteed by the Constitution. Feijó not only appointed a Portuguese-born officer to be both president and *comandante das armas* in the province but authorized him to use all means necessary to suppress the revolt. The recapture of Belém, the provincial capital, in May 1836 was rapidly followed by the reoccupation of the other major towns in the province. Although guerrilla warfare smoldered on in the countryside until an amnesty was granted in 1840, Feijó's quick and almost brutal response broke the back of the rebellion.[87]

Feijó's handling of the revolt in Rio Grande do Sul differed totally from his swift action in Pará. Even though in the weeks following the rebels' capture of Pôrto Alegre the revolt became openly separatist, Feijó perceived the rising in terms of defense by the local *pátria* of its infringed rights. The most that could be done was to seek a negotiated settlement which would remedy the province's grievances. As early as December 10, 1835, Feijó wrote: "It seems to me that the province's separation is inevitable; it should, however, eventually rejoin, provided that the respectable part of the public supports the recommendations to be presented to the General Assembly, which will no doubt reject or fail to approve them." [88] Since the General Assembly would not meet until May 1836, six months later, Feijó's response to the revolt in the far south was at best a policy of procrastination, at worst an abdication of responsibility.

To Feijó's foes, most of them members of the Coimbra bloc who had since the 1820's placed devotion to the nation and its security above all other loyalties, the regent's different response to the two revolts was simply incomprehensible. His actions aroused the gravest suspicions. If the full might of the national government could be promptly mobilized against the rebels of Pará, why did Feijó, eight months after the loss of Pôrto Alegre, still refrain from using force against the rebels in the south? To Feijó's opponents in the legislature, such conduct came perilously close to complicity with the revolt. It confirmed their belief that the regent could not be trusted with responsibility for the nation and its future. Despite Feijó's exhortations to the assembly on its duties to assist him—"finding effective remedies depends on your wisdom: the nation has the right to expect everything from your patriotism"—the opposition in the chamber, under the leadership of Bernardo Pereira de Vasconcelos, from the start demanded that the regent must follow its dictates and adopt the measures that it considered necessary.[89]

Since Vasconcelos, along with others in the Coimbra bloc, had by now well embarked on what he himself termed a "return" (Regresso) to traditionalist principles, away from the liberalism he had so ably championed during the 1820's, it was highly unlikely that Feijó could, in ideological terms, accept the measures that the opposition might propose.[90] Equally, believing as he did in his independent prerogatives as regent, Feijó would not willingly take direction from the General Assembly. For his part the regent failed to treat the legislators with tact and respect. The tone of the Speech from the Throne was minatory and on some subjects deliberately provocative.[91] From the start, the regent and the Chamber of Deputies were locked in bitter, unrelenting hostilities.

The deadlock was convenient to Feijó, since it allowed him to ascribe responsibility for the deteriorating condition of the nation to the opposition and thus to relieve himself of any sense of guilt for his own failure to act. Feijó perceived himself to be the victim of a vast conspiracy. "We are surrounded by Caramurús, who on every side plot our downfall," he

wrote to a friend in March 1836, "and they don't shrink from stealing letters, etc."[92] The confrontation was also convenient to the opposition, since
Feijó's increasingly paranoid conduct turned former friends and potential
allies against him. Common hostility to the regent knit together the disparate groups who rallied behind Bernardo Pereira de Vasconcelos in the
Chamber of Deputies.

The confrontation between regent and legislature was for the nation an
unmitigated disaster. During the four or five months the assembly sat, the
time and resources of the national government were absorbed in fending
off attacks by the legislators.[93] The quarrel weakened the national government in a second respect. Given the small number of men of national
standing among the Nativists, the regent had a limited pool of qualified
individuals from which to choose his ministers. Since the opposition in
the Chamber of Deputies was ruthless in attacking any minister of whom
it did not approve and since Feijó steadfastly refused to appoint anyone
who might win its approval, the result was that few men of reputation
and ability were willing to serve in the cabinet. The conduct of government business tended to fall on the ministers, so that the efficiency and
effectiveness of the national government declined during Feijó's regency.

This decline had serious consequences for the establishment of the new
quasi-autonomous governments set up in the provinces by the provisions
of the Ato Adicional. If the two coexisting systems of government introduced by the constitutional reforms were to operate effectively, both the
creation and the working of the parallel systems of administration had to
be guided with great care by the national government. Their respective
spheres of authority had to be precisely delineated and their activity both
in fiscal, police, and executive matters monitored to ensure cooperative,
consistent functioning. The principal difficulty to be faced was that the
existing sources of revenue hardly sufficed for the current system of government, let alone two parallel systems. Taxes were divided between the
two levels of government by a law of October 4, 1834, with the lion's share
going to the central government, so much so that most of the provincial
regimes were from October 1836 onwards granted subventions from the
national revenues.[94]

Feijó's conception of nation and *pátrias* inhibited him from intervening in the affairs of the provinces and thus prevented him from effectively
directing the establishment of the new federalist system of government.
The ensuing problems were compounded by the regent and his ministers'
lack of the time, energy, and—most vital of all—ability necessary to ensure
that the two levels of government worked harmoniously and efficiently.
The new regimes in the provinces tended to take action with little concern
for the national government. In the field of law and order, the provincial assemblies frequently passed measures which, designed to create an
effective police system at the local level, exceeded their prerogatives and
contravened the provisions of the legal codes of 1830 and 1832 and the

National Guard law of 1831. Instead of two systems interlocking to provide mutual assistance, the outcome was confrontation, with the national government seeking to thwart the provincial network of law officers, and provincial administrations acting to isolate nationally appointed officers. A serious weakening of the whole apparatus of social control ensued.[95]

For a while in 1836 it seemed as if good fortune might aid the national government in its struggle to suppress the rebellions in the far north and the far south. Not only had the city of Belém been reconquered, but in June a counter-rising in Pôrto Alegre restored the capital of Rio Grande do Sul to government control. Yet the rebels' loss of Pôrto Alegre and the major defeat they suffered in October at the island of Fanfã served only to strengthen their resolve. Rio Grande do Sul was proclaimed a republic by the town council of Piratinim. The government's forces proved unable to eliminate the rebels, mostly horsemen, who moved at will across the ranch country bordering on Uruguay. That republic provided arms, essential supplies, and when pursuit pressed too close, a place of foreign refuge from which the rebels would return to fight another day.[96] As much as the existence of this refuge complicated suppression of the revolt, the government forces displayed alarmingly little initiative and resource. Defeating the rebels was admittedly not aided by the national government's failure to "set in motion the full resources of the state" as Feijó had promised in May 1836. During his regency, as Figure 1 (p. 166) reveals, expenditures on the armed forces barely exceeded the modest sums allocated by the budget laws.

The inability of the government to conquer the *farrapos* (ragamuffins), as the rebels were known, was the decisive factor in undermining the viability of the national government. By May 1837 it was obvious that time was running out for Feijó. The death of Evaristo Ferreira da Veiga early in May, just after he had broken publicly with the regent over his conduct of affairs, symbolized the demise of the Moderado party, for which Evaristo had long served as spokesman through the columns of his *Aurora Fluminense*.[97] Discredited by its failures, particularly by the crisis in the far south, the cabinet insisted on resigning rather than facing the legislature. To replace them Feijó had no choice but to appoint a cabinet of political mavericks, because he was in his own words "forced . . . to accept anyone willing to enter, since I made but one condition—Nothing from the Opposition." The universal scorn with which this new cabinet was greeted caused Feijó to admit defeat. "I am eagerly awaiting an occasion to resign," he wrote on June 1, characteristically adding, "I cannot bear the ingratitude, injustice, and knavery; besides which my health is suffering and I was not made for public life, being by nature a rustic."[98]

No amount of pleading by his closest friends could move Feijó, as it had done in 1835, from this resolve. He was adamant and he was open only to advice on the question of who should succeed him. Under the Ato Adicional it was the current minister of the interior (Império), but every effort made by Feijó and his allies to find a viable candidate friendly to their cause and willing to accept that portfolio proved vain. As in 1835, so in 1837 the weakness of the Nativist movement's leadership at the national level was clearly demonstrated.[99]

Feijó thereupon offered the post to the speaker of the Chamber of Deputies, Pedro de Araújo Lima, whom he had characterized less than two years before as "a constant enemy of the ideas of April 7." [100] Now, given the new order of politics, Araújo Lima's manifest moderation and integrity commanded general respect and made him preferable to any other member of the Coimbra bloc. The nomination accepted, on September 18, 1837, Feijó wrote his resignation: "Being convinced that my continuation in the regency cannot remove the public ills which daily increase due to the lack of necessary laws, and not wishing to stop some more fortunate citizen from being entrusted by the nation with the handling of its destinies, I declare myself by this document removed from the office of regent of the Empire." [101] The era of liberalism, innovation, and experiment engendered by one abdication now received its deathblow through a second surrender of power. A new approach to the problems plaguing the Brazilian nation was about to be tried.

7

The Triumph of Tradition, 1837-1842

The vacating of the regency on September 18, 1837, signified much more than the transfer of office from one politician to another. It marked a moment of change in the dynamics of Brazilian politics, the close of an ideological and psychological era. Not for half a century would the political process once again display the open, spontaneous nature it had possessed during the first six years of the regency. Feijó's resignation inaugurated five years of evolution toward traditionalism in both government and politics. Although few changes were made to the formal structures of authority during these years, by the end of the period the distribution of power within the nation and the actual workings of the polity differed decisively from what they had been while Feijó held the regency. The security and prosperity of the nation-state as perceived by the Rio government had become paramount, overriding the needs and concerns of the local *pátrias*.

The five years should not, however, be seen as a direct, unwavering retrogression to past forms and practices. All the political groupings, of no matter what ideological persuasion, contributed to the eventual triumph of traditionalism in 1842. Accordingly, it is inaccurate to view the period in terms of a triumphant conservatism, even though historiographically the year 1837 is customarily described as marking the first appearance of what was to become the Conservative party.[1] The period from 1837 to 1842 would witness as thorough a deception and humiliation for those (mainly members of the Coimbra bloc) who saw themselves by reason of their talents and breeding as the natural governing elite of the nation as the previous six years had for the Nativists. These pretensions foundered on the harsh realities of Brazilian existence—the allure of national power proved superior to ideological consistency, distorting and corrupting the whole political process. To an equal degree, but in a very different fashion, the years 1837 to 1842 were as significant as the preceding six had been in shaping Brazil's formation as a nation.

I

Since he was minister of the interior, Pedro de Araújo Lima became interim regent when Feijó resigned on September 18, 1837. Although Feijó's reasons for selecting Araújo Lima are not entirely clear, he was both eminent (speaker of the Chamber of Deputies) and a man of proven moderation. The unsuitability of the leading Nativists or their unwillingness to occupy the post made Araújo Lima the least objectionable alternative. Some hope was even expressed that he might be won over to the Nativist cause.[2] Such hopes were vain. On September 19, the day after he took office, Araújo Lima appointed a new cabinet in which Bernardo Pereira de Vasconcelos was the dominant figure, holding the portfolios of both justice and the interior. For the Coimbra bloc this cabinet represented its apotheosis, the pinnacle of power. Only one member of the new ministry was not a graduate of Coimbra, and he held a doctorate from the Faculty of Medicine at Paris. In fact, all the ministers save for Vasconcelos had either studied or resided in France, England, or Germany.[3] In contrast to their predecessors under Feijó, the new ministers were men of exceptional ability, and the cabinet was soon dubbed o ministério dos capazes (the ministry of the capable).[4]

Pedro de Araújo Lima and Bernardo Pereira de Vasconcelos exemplified the two dominant influences in the political coalition which now controlled the nation. Born in 1793, the son of a landowner of Pernambuco province, Araújo Lima appeared from the start to be more mature and more cerebral than his contemporaries in the Coimbra bloc.[5] He was one of the select few to gain a doctorate at Coimbra. His native province elected him to both the Lisbon Cortes and the Constituent Assembly. He had sat continuously since 1826 in the Chamber of Deputies, and Feijó had just named him senator from Pernambuco. Araújo Lima was by nature an administrator, a man of business who believed that government must be carried on. Already at three moments of crisis—following the dissolution of the Constituent Assembly in November 1823, in November 1827 when D. Pedro I sought out deputies willing to be minister, and after the failed coup of July 1832—he had agreed to take a portfolio. The new regent was not, however, enamored of power as such and never clung to office for its own sake. A sense of self-protection and a talent for timely withdrawal had enabled him in all three cases to extricate himself without damaging his reputation. In November 1823, for instance, he had served only three days before resigning and departing into voluntary exile in Paris, where the French police noted his discretion and his application to work, key ingredients in his success as a politician. All these qualities were to be displayed throughout Araújo Lima's tenure as regent.[6]

A faintly anachronistic air hung about Araújo Lima even in his early career. He was in character and thought a belated child of the Enlightenment.[7] Endowed with sensibility but eschewing the emotions, Araújo Lima did not question the existing ordering of society but was at the same time by no means averse to undertaking "improvements," whether intellectual or material, designed to increase the well-being of the nation. Change for its own sake he did not favor. The new world of industrialization and scientific discovery lay, if not beyond his grasp, outside his intellectual interests. Yet he was no hidebound conservative: in the late 1850's he would play a crucial role in ensuring the construction of the first major railroad in Brazil.[8]

Born in Minas Gerais in 1795, only two years the junior of the new regent, Bernardo Pereira de Vasconcelos was formed in a very different psychological mold. His character harbored the extremes so typical of the Romantic era. Like Lord Byron, Vasconcelos aroused in others a fascination compounded with repulsion; "He is as much admired for his talents," the French envoy reported in 1837, "as he is despised for his vices."[9] From the moment he took his seat in the 1826 chamber there could be no question about his abilities or his self-confidence. He proved himself not only a superb parliamentarian—"the only Brazilian who has any idea of legislative tactics"—but a lawmaker of the first order.[10] From his pen had come the original drafts of both the criminal law code, enacted in 1830, and the Ato Adicional passed in 1834. Vasconcelos's capacity to govern was proved during his term as minister of finance from July 1831 to May 1832, although his foes accused him of illicit dealings with government suppliers to his own benefit—a typical example of the charges repeatedly levied against him.[11]

Notwithstanding the hatreds he aroused, Vasconcelos not only voiced the changing views and goals of the Coimbra bloc but played a central role in molding them. The offspring of two well-connected Luso-Brazilian families, Vasconcelos exemplified during the 1820's the devotion to liberalism engendered among recent Coimbra graduates, by a rejection of absolutism, a dislike of the colonial heritage, and a resentment of the closed circle of power. The events of April 1831 brought Vasconcelos both political recognition and the fruits of office—while his faith in the tenets of liberalism was being undermined by the growing social disorder and the political threats to the nation's integrity. The turning point for Vasconcelos had come in 1834 with the enactment of the Ato Adicional which he may have drafted but which he nonetheless characterized as "the Charter of Anarchy."[12]

What deeply influenced Vasconcelos and others in the Coimbra bloc was a fear graphically expressed by the minister of the interior in May 1835: "Our current revolutions contain no idealism or philanthropism; their character is one only of ferocious passions, base evils, brute stupidity, and barbarous insolence."[13] To this fear of the horrors of social revolution was added in Vasconcelos's own case personal reasons for discontent. In 1835 and again in 1836 Feijó had failed to select him as senator of

Minas Gerais. Moving into open opposition in May 1836, Vasconcelos inaugurated a movement of political opinion which by 1837 had become known as the Regresso (Return).[14] The nature of and justification for the Regresso were to be explained by Vasconcelos in May 1838 in a fervent speech to the Chamber of Deputies:

I was liberal. Liberty was new in the country then; it existed in everyone's aspirations, but not in the laws, not in concrete ideas. Power was everything; I was liberal. Today, however, society presents a different face: democratic principles have conquered everywhere and have often proved prejudicial. Society then threatened by power is now menaced by disorder and anarchy. My desire now, as it was then, is to serve society, and therefore I am reactionary. I am no turncoat. The cause I defended I do not abandon in its time of peril and weakness. I leave it when its triumph is so absolute that excess is harming it.[15]

In Vasconcelos the main motivation for political action, no matter how strong the intellectual justification, was emotional.

Although their psychological formation differed, the two elements in the government personified by Araújo Lima and Vasconcelos concurred in perceiving the nation as threatened principally by social and racial anarchy. Not only was the opening up of the political process challenging the existing control of Brazil by "civilized" groups—the educated and the local notables—but political mobilization was producing a fundamental questioning of the status quo. In 1830 and again in 1837 the province of Bahia elected as a deputy Antônio Pereira Rebouças, a dark mulatto. Respected for his ability as a self-trained lawyer, Rebouças was vocal in denouncing racial prejudice and in advocating the cause of the nation's large colored population, both black and mulatto, free and freed.[16]

By himself Rebouças was more an irritant than a threat. Much more dangerous was the extent to which the movements of political dissent, common since April 1831, deliberately appealed to the racially and socially oppressed and gave them ideal instruments for attacking the status quo. Both the Guerra dos Cabanos of 1832 in the northeast and the 1835 Cabanagem revolt in Pará had begun as factional feuds but soon expanded into mass risings, the first of fugitive blacks and the second of exploited Indians. What made such popular revolts so peculiarly dangerous, even when not overtly racial, was the damage done to the apparatus of social control and the consequent undermining of slavery, the key element in the labor system. Since the slave population contained a large number of recent arrivals from Africa, unassimilated and resentful of their lot, the slave system was under constant stress. The wave of popular risings could not but foment resistance among the slaves. In 1835, for example, the city of Salvador was convulsed by a revolt of the Malê (Muslim, Arabic-speaking) slaves. Three years later it took the combined efforts of police and troops to crush a rising by fugitive slaves in Rio de Janeiro province.[17]

The most logical response might have been a policy of fairly rapid emancipation, especially since slavery in Brazil could not maintain itself without fresh supplies of captives from Africa. That trade was illegal, forbidden by the law of November 7, 1831.[18] The response of Vasconcelos and others was quite the reverse. To them any tampering with slavery would violate the rights of property, jeopardize the prosperity promised by the current boom in coffee production, and hasten the disintegration of the social order. The social and economic health of the nation demanded the maintenance of slavery, which thus became for Vasconcelos the keystone to the existing social order.

Slavery's survival in turn demanded the continuance—despite its illegality—of the slave trade with Africa. The demand for labor created by expanding agricultural production and the great profits to be earned from trafficking in African slaves meant that by the second half of the decade the illegal trade was bringing in some 40,000 to 50,000 captives a year.[19] As early as July 1835 Vasconcelos had presented a motion to the Chamber of Deputies proposing the total repeal of the law of November 7, 1831. Vasconcelos was certainly influenced by the fact that two bulwarks of the existing political order were the large-plantation owners and the leading urban merchants, the first desirous of more slaves and the second busy supplying them. If most politicians viewed Vasconcelos's scheme to legalize the slave trade as "impolitic and redundant," they did agree that whatever their philosophical ideals might suggest the realities of the situation precluded any action against the illicit trade with Africa and any measures ameliorating the slaves' lot.[20]

Restoring peace and order to the nation was the dominant concern of the new government installed on September 18, 1837. The remedies proposed were, in appearance at least, simple and direct. The principal goal of the cabinet was to crush the rebellions in the provinces of Pará and Rio Grande do Sul and to restore local order throughout the nation. Concurrently, the cabinet intended to force the provincial regimes to acknowledge and obey the national government's authority over them. To achieve these ends, the cabinet was resolved to use all the fiscal and administrative resources at its disposal. As Figure 1 (p. 166) shows, until 1837–38 government revenues usually exceeded its expenditures. Thereafter, the Regresso ministry's determination to restore law and order meant that spending on the navy and particularly on the army far exceeded budget allotments, producing horrendous deficits.

The long-term goal of the cabinet was to recentralize power in the hands of the national government. To this end the ministers planned to secure a law "interpreting" the provisions of the 1834 Ato Adicional—as article 25 of the Ato did allow—so as to restrict the provinces' powers and autonomy. Once such a law was enacted, the criminal procedure code could be amended to remove police powers from the *juizes de paz*, the locally elected justices of the peace, and put it into the hands of officials appointed by and answerable to the national government and its representatives. The government's program rested on the assumption that by restoring political authority and respect for hierarchical order it would end social and racial conflicts and so consolidate the existing social order.

If the new cabinet's concerns were predominantly military and political, it did devote some attention to developing the nation's infrastructure, for reasons succinctly stated by a progovernment newspaper in March 1838: "Education and steam will be the most powerful centralizing forces in Brazil." [21] As minister of the interior Vasconcelos was responsible for both transportation and education. In respect to the former his main concern was to ensure that the Companhia Brasileira de Paquetes a Vapor, a steamship line authorized to run from Rio de Janeiro up the coast to the port of Belém do Pará and back, became at last a functioning reality. Inauguration of the line was of critical importance for national unity, since only steamships could sail against the currents that swept westward along the northern coast. Once working, the steam packets would ensure the government regular and comparatively swift communications with the provinces of the far north. Although the new company had signed its original contract with the government in 1836, in order to keep the project alive Vasconcelos was forced in November 1837 to grant an extension in the contractual date for the inauguration of the line. The first packet bound for Belém did not steam out of Rio harbor until March 1838, but the company's steamships had already proved their value by that date. Had it not been for the "increased facility of communication by steam, of which the Imperial Government has made prompt and efficient use for the conveyance of intelligence and troops," the British envoy later remarked, "it is probable that some of the provinces would have been utterly lost." [22]

In the field of education more decisive action could be taken. On December 2, 1837, the birthday of the young emperor, Vasconcelos issued a decree ordering the conversion of the São Joaquim seminary in Rio city into the Colégio D. Pedro II. [23] By his personal intervention in the necessary repairs, he was able to open the new secondary school on March 25, 1838, in the presence of both regent and emperor. His speech on that occasion expressed the social philosophy underlying the government's political program. The college was designed to be "an example or model for those already established in this capital by private individuals." Believing that "knowledge is power: . . . [an] indispensable component of modern society," the government desired "the good education of youth and the establishment of fruitful studies." Through the new school, "youth . . . will learn to respect the laws and institutions and to perceive the advantages of subordination and respect." Although as Vasconcelos admitted, "the Government can do no more than sow in order to reap in the future," it anticipated that the Colégio D. Pedro II would "provide the *pátria*, the nation, liberty, the Throne and the Altar with faithful servants, the honor and glory of the Brazilian name." [24]

The Colégio, itself intended to be the exemplar for Brazilian secondary education, was in turn derived directly from that model of elite secondary education, the French lycée. From the early nineteenth century the lycées had provided the training and testing ground for young men of promise, creating the future governing cadres of France.[25] As Vasconcelos's speech made patent, the Colégio D. Pedro II, along with similar institutions in other cities, was designed to play an equivalent role in preparing the future rulers of Brazil. The opening of the college signified that birth or wealth alone was no longer sufficient to gain entry into the circle of power: talent and culture were now required. It would, however, be misleading to emphasize the cabinet's interest in the nation's infrastructure, since most of its time and attention were absorbed in the suppression of disorder. By concentrating all available resources—all its energy and determination—on that task, the cabinet believed that its efforts would rapidly achieve success.

II

On November 7, 1837, seven weeks after the new government had taken office, a revolt against it broke out in the city of Salvador. "Given the public's needs [and] the notorious ill will of the central government, which always seeks to weaken the provinces of Brazil and to treat them as colonies, thus belittling their dignity and status," the rebels that same day declared "the Province of Bahia to be completely and wholly separated from the central government of Rio de Janeiro and deemed a free and independent State."[26] Four days later, with the rebels in firm control of the city, the goals of the uprising were modified at a public meeting: "The separation of this State will exist until the coming of age at eighteen of Our Sovereign Lord His Imperial Majesty D. Pedro II."[27] This change, although motivated in part by a desire to rally support for the revolt, demonstrates how strong remained the appeal, fifteen years after the creation of a nation-state, of the original link between *pátria* and El Rei Nosso Senhor. Equally obvious was the continuing inability of the nation-state to command loyalty in what had been the original capital of the Estado do Brasil and was still the second city in the country.

This rising, known as the Sabinada, was no transitory affair.[28] It commanded from the start a passionate support among the mass of the city's population. As a contemporary reported, "The revolution was not, it is true, begun by the rabble, but in the end the rabble called the tune and the Negroes with their battalions terrified everyone."[29] The interior of the province was also affected by the movement, a rising at Barra on the São Francisco River being suppressed with difficulty by the local National Guard units. Although the revolt was contained within the city of Salvador, which was blockaded as in 1822–23 by land and sea, the rebels were determined not to submit to what they perceived as "the recolonizing union with Rio de Janeiro," and they refused "obedience to the tyrants of the interregnum, the despots of the central government, until the coming of age at eighteen of our Sovereign Lord D. Pedro."[30]

What the outbreak of the Sabinada revolt made clear was the extent to which the new government had both misunderstood the political mood of the country and misjudged its own strength and popularity. The Regresso had triumphed at the national level only because Feijó had voluntarily decided to capitulate, to abdicate power—not because of its inherent strength. Despite the assertions of historians, for whom September 1837 has marked the appearance of organized party politics, the Regresso was no more than a loose coalition of like-minded politicians, brought into temporary union by their common opposition to Feijó. It was not a disciplined, cohesive, or broadly based political movement, as a newspaper supporting the new government pointed out: "September 19 was not the result of a conspiracy—who are its partisans, its leaders, where are the arms, the groups that produced it?"[31] What made the Regresso powerful was the majority it commanded among the deputies during the 1837 session. That was, however, the fourth and final session of the chamber. In May 1838 a new Chamber of Deputies would convene, one which had been elected in late 1836—before the Regresso had taken full form—and which was not controlled by supporters of the new government.[32]

The leaders of the Regresso advocated restoration of the integrity and supremacy of the nation; they perceived the national government at Rio to be "a power immune to local intrigues, strong and impartial, against which the upstart leaders of turbulent minorities can do nothing."[33] What the supporters of the Regresso did not grasp was that their vision of Brazil as a nation was very narrow and bound to give offense to the provinces. In geographic terms the nation was increasingly equated with the city of Rio de Janeiro and its hinterland. Such an identification of the nation with its capital is fairly frequent among long-ruling political elites, and by 1837 the leading members of the Coimbra bloc had been putting down roots in Rio de Janeiro for a decade or more. Other factors encouraged the correlation. The Ato Adicional of 1834, which gave autonomy to Rio province with a separate government and capital (Niterói), left only the Côrte, or *município neutro* (the city of Rio and adjacent territory), under the direct rule of the national government.[34] The inevitable consequence was the devotion of disproportionate quantities of time, energy, and resources to that area, making the wealthiest and most developed part of the nation yet richer and more privileged. Vasconcelos's creation of the Colégio D. Pedro II in Rio city not only exemplified this process but intensified it, since the school inculcated the equation of capital and nation in the minds of its students, the future rulers of Brazil.

Both personal and policy considerations encouraged the identification of the nation with the capital and its hinterland. Through the port of Rio de Janeiro flowed over half of Brazil's external trade. The economy of the Rio de Janeiro hinterland was booming with the rapid expansion of coffee planting. By the end of the decade coffee exports equaled in value all other agricultural products sold abroad.[35] Dominating the economy of the Rio de Janeiro region were the leading city merchants and the coffee planters, who in the eyes of the Regresso constituted two pillars of the social order. Equally identified with the court and capital was the corps of officers commanding the regular army, a body perceived as a bastion of society and for the new government an indispensable instrument for achieving its goals. These general considerations were reinforced by personal ties. Both the minister of marine in the new cabinet and the president of Rio de Janeiro province were married to daughters of a prominent landowner of the region.[36] Honório Hermeto Carneiro Leão, the deputy who had defeated the parliamentary coup of July 1832, bought land and started a coffee plantation in 1836. Three years later he secured as his Rio business correspondent a leading city merchant.[37]

To the Nativists the Regresso therefore represented a compound of geographic, social, and economic exclusivity and privilege. Since many of the Rio merchants, a considerable portion of the officer corps, and not a few planters were Portuguese-born, a strong ethnic element reinforced the distrust.[38] When denouncing "the recolonizing union with Rio de Janeiro," the Sabinada rebels were not using a figure of speech to refer to social and economic domination. They feared a literal return to the colonial era, with absolutist rule by Portuguese-born. These fears were fed by the actions of the new government. Shortly after replacing Feijó as regent, Araújo Lima revived the traditional ceremony of the *beija-mão*. He knelt in the open street to kiss the hand of the emperor, then eleven years old. An act so symbolic of hierarchical order and personal deference could only deepen suspicions, intensify dissension. Even supporters of the government were disturbed by it: "The monarchy ought to be sustained by means other than antiquated practices which in no way accord with the spirit of the present century."[39] What further poisoned the political atmosphere was the presence of Vasconcelos in the seat of power, as much distrusted by his enemies as Feijó had been by his foes.

It was no wonder then that the new government and its program, far from restoring authority and order, intensified political opposition, as the outbreak of the Sabinada revolt attested. In response the government employed much stronger doses of the same remedies. Although the Sabinada revolt did not expand beyond the city of Salvador, thanks in large part to support given by the planters, so fiercely did the rebels resist that it was not until the middle of March 1838, after a four-month siege by land and sea, that the revolt was bloodily repressed.[40] The Sabinada revolt, despite its failure, severely damaged the government's cause. To suppress the rising, men and materials had to be diverted from fighting the rebellions in Rio Grande do Sul and Pará. As a consequence, the government could neither seize the offensive nor secure military supremacy against the rebellion in the far south. In April 1838 the *farrapos* won a major victory over the imperial forces at Rio Pardo. In such adverse conditions the national government's public offer to the rebels of an amnesty, provided they would submit, could only be construed as an admission of weakness.[41]

In its efforts to reestablish the authority of the central government over the provincial administrations, the new cabinet met with no greater success than in its handling of outright rebels. In contrast to Feijó's willingness to give up the regency, the Nativist groups at the provincial level had not lost heart, nor were they ready to surrender control of the provinces they dominated. The provincial administrations had by late 1837 become entrenched systems which had arrogated to themselves, no matter what the distribution of authority ordained by the Ato Adicional, most of the powers of government. The provinces had created educational systems, naming the teachers. Many provincial assemblies had also set up a network of *prefeitos*, officials nominated by the president and acting as his agents in the municipalities, who were not answerable to the national government. The provinces tried to take over control of appointments to the National Guard and the judiciary.[42] What intensified the unwillingness of provincial administrations to cooperate with the new national government, much less to submit to its dictates, was the intense—and largely justified—suspicion with which the ruling groups in the provinces viewed Vasconcelos and his allies.

The cabinet possessed very limited resources by which to force these independent networks of power to recognize its authority and obey its orders. It could—and did—replace the presidents of the provinces: by the end of April 1838 ten of the eighteen were new. A president's staff was so small, however, that he had to manage single-handedly most of the administration as well as relations with the provincial assembly, which he could not dissolve.[43] To be effective a provincial president had to be more than a mere cipher of the national government. Those who accepted appointment as president had, moreover, their own careers to make and obligations to meet. The distribution of power within the provinces since 1835 meant that the presidents often identified with local interests instead of being responsive to the orders of the national government.[44] The consequences of repressive, heavy-handed conduct could be fatal, as the assassination of the president of Rio Grande do Norte in April 1838 proved.[45] More importantly, replacing so many presidents was not wholly beneficial, because to the Nativists the changes amounted to a political purge, thus justifying their resistance in the provinces to the government's policies.

The Regresso cabinet's failure to achieve either of its principal goals—the suppression of rebellion and the establishment of authority—was accompanied by a slow loss of power at the national level. Although at the start a docile ally, Araújo Lima soon established his independence from the cabinet. Accepted as the consensus candidate for regent, he triumphed in the special election held on April 22, 1838, overwhelming his main opponent Holanda Cavalcanti by 4,300 to 1,981 and carrying all but three of the provinces.[46] By obtaining this decisive vote of confidence from the electors, the regent secured both a mandate to rule and an authority distinct and independent from that of the General Assembly. Araújo Lima's cautiousness made him avoid Feijó's error as regent of resenting the legislators' parallel power and snubbing their pretensions. As elected regent, however, he had no intention of remaining subordinate to the Regresso cabinet or of being compromised by the ministry's lack of success.

The Regresso had originally been made formidable by its dominance over the Chamber of Deputies which ended its term in 1837. When the new chamber convened in May 1838, it rapidly became clear that the dominance could not be sustained. Not only were the Nativists numerous and vocal, but by June the press was commenting on the emergence of a "third party," composed of new deputies committed to neither the Regresso nor the Nativist cause.[47] During the long first session, which dragged on until October 20, the government decidedly failed to secure passage of its legislative program. Of the 64 laws enacted, only 23 concerned public business —and of these only 7 were of substance.[48] The draft law "interpreting" the Ato Adicional, which the Speech from the Throne strongly recommended, did pass through three readings in the chamber but at the end of September it had stalled before receiving final passage and dispatch to the Senate.[49] The cabinet's position in the lower house was seriously weakened in September 1838 by Vasconcelos's nomination as senator from Minas Gerais, which deprived the ministry of its most effective speaker and tactician in the chamber. Although this change and the cabinet's general lack of success were contributing factors, the basic problem remained that from the start the ministers were not able to exact unquestioning support from the deputies.[50]

If nothing succeeds like success, so nothing fails like failure. By the end of 1838 "the ministry of the capable" had lost the internal cohesion, self-confidence, and public reputation essential for its survival. The process of disintegration fed on itself, with rumors of internal dissension being encouraged by public denials.[51] The process was accelerated by the evident coolness of the regent toward the cabinet. In the opinion of the British envoy at Rio, who kept a close eye on Vasconcelos and his associates, the ministers were not at all eager to face the legislature which would reconvene in May.[52] All that remained was to find a suitable occasion for ending the ministry. In April 1839 the regent passed over both the minister of finance and José Clemente Pereira, a supporter of the Regresso, when choosing a new senator from Rio de Janeiro province. The politician selected was not hostile to the cabinet, but Vasconcelos persuaded his colleagues to treat the regent's choice as showing a want of confidence in the cabinet and therefore to resign at once.[53]

The regent soon discovered that Vasconcelos and his colleagues were easier to displace than replace. The new cabinet named to succeed them was a mere stopgap, which survived less than five months.[54] Since a second cabinet, formed on September 1, 1839, retained as ministers of war and marine the current holders of those portfolios, it not surprisingly failed to provide the strong and effective government which alone could remedy the intensifying social and military crisis.

In June 1839 the rebels in Rio Grande do Sul burst out of the province in a northwards advance. On July 22 they captured the town of Laguna in southern Santa Catarina. A week later, local sympathizers declared the province a republic. The rebels then moved towards Destêrro, the province's capital and a key port and supply base. Without it, the government would have difficulty in carrying on the war.[55] Simultaneously, in the northern province of Maranhão a new and—in social terms—extremely threatening revolt erupted. The south of the province formed a frontier of cattle ranching and subsistence farming, where both fugitive slaves and other outcasts and victims of society found refuge. In this area the fabric of authority, flimsy in the best of times, was by 1838 destroyed by factional conflicts and crass exploitation. What began as banditry and armed resistance was transformed by success into a formidable social uprising. Three different armed bands—two drawn from the free population (mostly mestizo) and one composed of fugitive slaves—combined into a force which, on May 24, 1839, laid siege to Caxias, the town controlling entry into northern Maranhão with its cotton and sugar plantations and large slave population.[56] With the fall and sack of Caxias in July, the door to the north lay open. So conspicuous a success challenged the viability of the social order: from being a local trouble, the Balaiada now became an immediate threat to the social fabric of the nation.[57]

In August and September 1839, Brazil's fortunes as a nation can be said to have reached their nadir. Its political integrity was challenged in the south and its social order menaced in the north. On September 18 the British envoy commented: "Some of my Colleagues here, and some persons for whose opinion I have much respect, think that this Empire is on the eve of Dissolution, or at least of a crisis, of which the result cannot but be most fatal, and that some great and organic changes are at hand."[58]

The emergency achieved a crucial shift in outlook among the ruling circles of Brazil. It was conceded by all save the most fervent Nativists that the control of law and order must be returned to the hands of the national government. The triumph of the philosophy of the Regresso so soon after the fall of the Regresso cabinet was not so paradoxical. Once divorced from the figure of Vasconcelos—and of Vasconcelos in power— the ideas became if not palatable at least conceivable. In June 1839 the bill interpreting the Ato Adicional received final approval from the chamber and was sent up to the Senate. There, since the upper house had no closure, the project might have been indefinitely stalled by the Nativist groups had it not been for the national crisis. The bill's progress through its two readings in the Senate was laborious but irresistible.[59] Eventual enactment into law became certain.

In anticipation of that passage Vasconcelos introduced in the Senate on June 17, 1839, a bill amending the criminal procedure code so that the central government and its agents controlled the whole apparatus of law and order.[60] Even though Vasconcelos's measure was premature and not destined for early debate, it foreshadowed what must come, since the enactment of a law interpreting the Ato Adicional would serve no purpose unless it were followed by amendments to the criminal procedure code of 1832. Once those amendments were passed, the cabinet would be responsible for organizing the new system of law and order. Integral to that process would be a mass of police and judicial appointments. Those who held or obtained office at that moment would then be able to entrench themselves in power by appointing their friends and dependents, in effect buying political support through patronage. So absolute a concentration of power offered, in anticipation, too tempting a prospect to be resisted, and among the leaders were not a few who had already shown themselves avid for power on any terms. Once the law interpreting the Ato Adicional was passed, a major struggle for the control of national power would almost inevitably follow. Too much was at stake.

III

"Here all is rejoicing and preparing celebrations," it was reported from Rio de Janeiro at the end of November 1839. "News has just arrived that General Andréa has succeeded in regaining the port of Laguna, chasing the rebels into Rio Grande, and capturing six or eight ships they had armed as privateers. All this, combined with the excitement and enthusiasm with which they are preparing the festivities for the Emperor's birthday (December 2), has generated a general ecstasy."[61] If to the modern mind the first item of news was certainly a cause for rejoicing, the fourteenth birthday of the nation's nominal ruler would not seem to warrant three days of spontaneous, intense public celebration.[62] A conjunction of factors, however, made Brazilians perceive the adolescent emperor as their potential savior. "We are patiently awaiting the moment when Your Imperial Majesty assumes the reins of government, which by so many titles belongs to you," ran the address presented by the vice-rector of the Colégio D. Pedro II, "and then we will be sure of the strength and the stability of this great Empire."[63] These words reveal what underlay the crisis engulfing the nation: a breakdown in political authority and a collapse in collective identity. The ousting of the first emperor on April 7, 1831, had signified the supersession of traditional loyalties and forms of authority by the collective identity and consensual authority which constituted the essence of nationhood. Since April 1831 the search had been for an institutional framework which would make that nationhood function.

None of the three experiments—neither the parliamentarianism of the three-man regency, the semirepublican federalism under Feijó, nor the oligarchic centralism of the Regresso—had proved viable. Although the ill success of each could be ascribed in part to specific failings, the three shared one fatal weakness: they did not constitute a source of authority and power acceptable to the inhabitants of the nation, and so could not command their loyalty. The young emperor now provided the sole element of stability, the single hope of deliverance in a political crisis inexorably destroying Brazil as a nation. By looking to a boy of fourteen for salvation, the Brazilians were not simply reverting to traditional modes of loyalty. They were acknowledging their inability to accept consensual authority, their lack of a common identity. Brazil might call itself a nation but—nationhood was not functioning. Contrary to the assumption, common even in that period, about its universal applicability, the nation-state could not be transplanted on command. The monarch thereby became, as he had been before April 7, 1831, a central, indispensable figure in the polity. He acted as a focus of loyalty and identity and as a source of authority. At the end of 1839, when D. Pedro II reached fourteen, there existed three different, if not always distinct, perceptions of the role he should assume within the nation.

To the surviving Luso-Brazilians and others of a traditional outlook, supreme political authority rightfully and naturally belonged to the monarch. What the emperor decided on any matter was not to be disputed on the grounds of popular preference; his orders once issued had to be obeyed. This conception of the emperor as the fount of authority had been since September 1837 encouraged by the gradual revival of the imperial court, with its traditional ceremonial and formal etiquette. Integral to this process was the resumption of the *beija-mão*—a public acknowledgment of subordination and obedience—and the hanging of the emperor's portrait in government buildings throughout Brazil.[64]

For those Brazilians who believed that "the monarchy should be sustained by means . . . [more in] accord with the spirit of the present century," this first conception of the emperor's role was both too simplistic and too antiquated.[65] Their preferred model was to be found in contemporary Europe, in France over which Louis Philippe, *le roi citoyen*, had been reigning since 1830. "What then is the citizen-king? The term describes Louis-Philippe," a Rio newspaper explained in June 1838. "If that be what is meant by a citizen-king, we call that a strong king. That is what we want, what all Brazilians want: a strong monarch who curbs the ambitions of the discontented and suppresses the fanaticism of the masses, an able monarch who reconciles liberty with order, with internal peace, with the development of the country, with its artistic and literary glory." The emperor was to act as the guardian and regulator of the polity, a devoted servant of the nation, as "an Emperor who knows his duties and his rights, which are, in reality, nothing less than duties in respect to the public order and to the maintenance of the social structure."[66] Most members of the Coimbra bloc shared this view of the monarch.

The third perception of the emperor's role was simple and direct: he was the only individual possessing the qualities which the salvation of Brazil as a nation required. D. Pedro II was credible in this role because he was a pristine figure, untainted by the feuds and failures of the past, his innocence and youth assuring a more honorable future. Supporters of this third view were to be found at all levels of society, but particularly among the ordinary population. The conception of the monarch as God's anointed, a special being set above ordinary mortals, had endured since the colonial period. The difficulties suffered by a regime based on popular sovereignty did nothing to discredit this perception of the boy who was, after all, the living representative of the house of Bragança.

This final image was enhanced by what little the public knew in 1839 about D. Pedro II as a person. Since the removal of José Bonifácio as guardian in December 1833, D. Pedro II and his sisters had led a quiet, ordered life. His new guardian, the elderly marquess of Itanhaém, was dull and unimaginative but also inoffensive and dutiful. His watchfulness helped the young emperor through bouts of ill health complicated by occasional attacks of epilepsy.[67] Indifferent health did not preclude long hours of study. The emperor's teachers were solid men, conservative in their learning and orthodox in belief, and they were both conscientious and kindly.[68] With little liking for physical exercise and much for books, their pupil proved a model and precocious student: "He is very talented, passionately loves study, and has a marked predilection for men of merit and knowledge; on top of which, [he is] grave, restrained, and amenable in character, with a learning far above what is usual at his age."[69]

These qualities could be seen in a very different light. In January 1838 the emperor was described by a foreign prince then visiting Rio as "a punkin . . . , taut, odd, ill formed," and as "acting like a man of forty."[70] What mattered to Brazilians, however, was not what a boy of just fourteen should be but rather what they urgently wanted the emperor to be. Traits that in less urgent times might have aroused disquiet were transformed into assets. His youth was seen not as a disqualification but as freeing him from identification with the past. His preternatural solemnity and intellectual precocity did not imply an alarming absence of the high spirits and rebelliousness normal in adolescence but indicated that he already possessed the mental and psychological capacity to rule. Given the existing crisis, all these traits were precisely what Brazilians wished their emperor to possess.

The road to this political paradise was, however, barred—or seemed to be barred—by nothing less than the Constitution itself. Under article 121 "the Emperor is underage until he reaches 18," which meant that D. Pedro II could not take over the government until December 2, 1843.[71] Four years seemed an inordinate time to wait; some doubted whether the nation would endure. Since the emperor, it was believed, already possessed the degree of maturity usual at eighteen, the constitutional requirement appeared not a protection but a self-defeating legalism, detrimental to the nation's well-being. *Salus populi suprema lex est.*

Precedents aplenty existed for overriding the Constitution if the salvation of the nation so required. In September 1834, despite an identical clause in the Portuguese constitution, the Cortes declared D. Maria II of age at fifteen, an act prompted by the imminent death of her father, the former D. Pedro I.[72] The next year in Brazil Vasconcelos, inspired by this precedent, proposed that the emperor's elder sister (D. Januaria, age thirteen) be declared of sufficient age to act as regent.[73] The scheme failed in part because of her sex and the huge discrepancy between her actual and the required age of 25 but mainly because it was patently a stratagem to oust Feijó from power.[74]

The idea of an early majority for D. Pedro II was first proposed in June 1834, when a deputy introduced a bill making the emperor of age at fourteen, that is, on December 2, 1839.[75] Offering no immediate solution to the nation's problems, the bill was not even debated. Three years later, in May 1837, one of Feijó's foes presented a project which declared the emperor of age, though subject until he reached eighteen to guidance from a revived Council of State and a first minister. The bill was strongly attacked by Araújo Lima, then speaker of the chamber, and secured only ten votes in its favor. However, among the ten were Holanda Cavalcanti and Martim Francisco, political veterans of grasping ambition, never restrained in their pursuit of power.[76]

When next revived the proposal came from a very different quarter. In December 1838 the newspaper expressing the interests of the Nativist groups in the General Assembly proposed that the emperor be declared of age at fourteen, on December 2, 1839.[77] That the journal could support a proposal so at odds with the Nativist creed indicated that the leading Nativists were now more interested in power than the politics of principle. Earlier in 1838, seeking any candidate who might defeat Araújo Lima in the elections for regent, the Nativists had first backed Antônio Carlos (brother of Martim Francisco) before switching to Holanda Cavalcanti, Feijó's opponent in 1835 and "without a single quality to recommend him."[78] After Araújo Lima's decisive victory over Holanda Cavalcanti in April 1838, the Nativists faced four more years in the political wilderness unless they could find a means of ousting the regent. Declaring the emperor of age offered the best means to that end. As the year 1839 progressed the campaign attracted increasing public support. In late July the British envoy reported: "I am almost led to believe that the Minority of the Emperor will not, under any circumstances, last beyond the year 1841, if it last so long."[79]

The public euphoria apparent during the celebration of D. Pedro's fourteenth birthday both expressed support for his immediate coming of age and intensified desire for it. If many sincerely believed that an emperor, regardless of his age, was superior to any elected regent no matter how able, others supported the proposal with ulterior motive.[80] Since the emperor's coming of age was but one aspect of the larger crisis of authority and identity engulfing the nation, of which the bill interpreting the Ato Adicional was another part, such an interweaving of motives was inevitable. As the bill came closer to enactment so the campaign to advance D. Pedro's coming of age gathered force. The two issues can be said to have proceeded in lockstep from the middle of 1839 onwards—both involved a radical change in the existing distribution of power.

The law of interpretation, once passed, would make possible a centralization of power in the hands of the national government, and the coming of age, when it occurred, would also change the distribution of power at the center.[81] Should the first occur without the second, then those currently holding office could entrench themselves in power. However, should the emperor's majority be accelerated to coincide with the bill's enactment, then those who had promoted the early coming of age could reasonably expect to be appointed to office by a grateful emperor, especially since the Constitution gave him unfettered right to name and dismiss ministers. They would thus reap the rewards that came from the recentralization of power. Achieving an early coming of age offered the fruits of power; failure to do so would condemn its advocates to a long exclusion.

It was, paradoxically, the regent himself who early in 1840 enabled his political opponents to organize a campaign for the emperor's immediate majority. Araújo Lima called the General Assembly into special session on April 9 so that the budget for 1839–40, unfinished in the previous session, might be voted.[82] A week later on April 15 a small group met behind closed doors at the house of José Martiniano de Alencar, senator from Ceará province and a leading Nativist. The four senators and three deputies who decided to set up a secret "club actively engaged in gaining from the legislature a declaration that the Emperor is of sufficient age to assume the government at once" represented the principal political elements then in opposition.[83] Named president of the new Clube de Maioridade (Club for the Majority) was Antônio Carlos, a maverick member of the Luso-Brazilian generation and a sometime Caramurú. The vice president was Holanda Cavalcanti, political leader of the Cavalcanti clan, which was powerful in Pernambuco and neighboring provinces. Named first secretary was Senator Alencar, who spoke for the Nativists of the north and northeast.[84]

Only the scent of power could make these diverse elements overlook vicious feuding and accumulated hatreds and combine for mutual benefit. While the Andradas and the Cavalcantis had already boxed the political compass in the quest for power, the presence of the Nativists confirmed their new expediency. After 30 years of advocating a democratic, egalitarian polity, they now supported restoring the emperor as the supreme authority within the nation. It was especially ironic that Alencar, a veteran of the republican risings of 1817 and 1824, should be at the center of a monarchist conspiracy.[85]

At this first meeting of the conspirators, Holanda Cavalcanti proposed a twofold strategy: each member was to recruit support among the legislators, and to seek to ascertain through contacts at court D. Pedro II's reaction to the prospect of an immediate coming of age.[86] In the following three weeks four Nativists from Minas Gerais joined the Majority Club, and a further four deputies and a senator promised support for the scheme. On May 4 Antônio Carlos reported that after several soundings he had been assured that the emperor was in favor and desired that his majority should be declared at once.[87] From this moment events began to develop rapidly.

On May 5, 1840, the regent opened the regular session of the assembly by reading the customary Speech from the Throne, and two days later a draft Vote of Thanks, prepared by a committee of three elected by the chamber, was presented for debate by the deputies. The chairman of this committee was none other than Antônio Carlos. On it also sat Aureliano de Sousa e Oliveira Coutinho, who as minister of justice in 1834 had masterminded the ouster of José Bonifácio from the guardianship of the emperor. The new guardian had been named by Aureliano, who had subsequently maintained close links with court officials. Aureliano now emerged as the parliamentary head of the court clique, which naturally supported an immediate majority.[88] The third member of the committee, a politician notorious for his opportunism, was easily won over, and so the draft reply contained the words "seeing with pleasure Your Majesty's Majority approach."[89] Seemingly innocuous, the phrase served as a catalyst, bringing the campaign into the open. That same day the club learnt that the emperor's desire for an immediate majority had been confirmed by his guardian.[90]

On May 9 the Majority Club agreed to launch the campaign in the Senate, in the form of a bill signed by the six senators who supported the idea. Whether the bill should in addition to declaring the emperor of age also provide him with a Council of State caused some dispute. Clinging to the remnants of his liberalism, Alencar proposed a council drawn from all the provinces and with a limited term. He was overridden, but as a compromise it was later agreed to present the two proposals as separate bills, to be introduced by Holanda Cavalcanti on "the 13th inst., which was a notable day, being the anniversary of el rei D. João VI, the august grandfather of His Imperial Majesty."[91] To this sentiment the Nativists appear to have consented without complaint.

Matters had now reached a point of crisis. On the very same day that these measures were approved in the club, the regent signed into law the bill interpreting the Ato Adicional. Vasconcelos's project to reform the criminal procedure code was well on its way to passage through the

Senate. On May 12 Honório Hermeto presented an amendment to the draft Vote of Thanks deleting the phrase that welcomed the emperor's approaching majority. Reassuming the role which had made him notable in July 1832, Honório Hermeto led the defense of the constitutional order against a parliamentary coup.[92]

In this first clash between the contending forces the supporters of the status quo held the advantage. The chamber voted by 42 to 37 to delete the controversial phrase in the draft Vote of Thanks, and in the Senate the bill authorizing the emperor's immediate majority was rejected by 18 to 16 on May 20.[93] A margin of victory so narrow meant that the question could not be banished from the political agenda. The amount of support gained at the very opening of the campaign indicated how strongly the concept appealed. Time was on the side of the campaign, since every day that passed brought the emperor closer to his fifteenth birthday and enhanced his learning and maturity. The seriousness of the situation was implicitly acknowledged by the regent when on May 18 he reorganized the cabinet, appointing political veterans identified with the Regresso. On that same day, Honório Hermeto introduced a bill granting constituent powers to the electors who would shortly choose a new chamber: it authorized them to empower the new deputies to amend article 121, which fixed the age of the emperor's majority at eighteen.[94] Since Honório Hermeto's motion authorized by legal means an early majority for the emperor, it conceded the main argument of the opposition. The motion did, however, serve an immediate tactical purpose, by rallying sufficient votes in the chamber to remove any reference to the majority from the draft reply.

Although the bill appeared to outflank Antônio Carlos and his colleagues, it was in strategic terms a disaster. Its passage into law required four separate readings, which guaranteed that the topic would remain the subject of intense public debate. Since the election of the new chamber was scheduled to take place in the last months of 1840, failure to enact the bill into law before that date would render it pointless—the new deputies would be elected without power to amend article 121. All that was required to sabotage the bill was for the supporters of an immediate majority to prolong debate of the project. Not only would they thus thwart the bill, but their campaign would dominate the legislature.

The standoff thus created endured for several weeks. The advocates of an immediate majority were held in check, but the government made no attempt to give priority to Honório Hermeto's bill. The appearance of an impasse was deceptive. Popular support for an immediate coming of age began to mount, giving to its advocates a fresh means of attack. The bill introduced by Vasconcelos in June 1839 to amend the criminal procedure code was now passing through its second reading in the Senate and would shortly be sent down to the lower house. On July 10, Honório Hermeto brought his bill forward for immediate discussion in the chamber, and the whole controversy once again dominated the lower house. The ensuing debate showed that the bill could not be forced through in the face of the concerted oratory of Antônio Carlos and his colleagues.

On July 17, 1840, the drama entered its final phase. On leaving a religious ceremony in the center of Rio de Janeiro, the emperor was greeted by a patently organized mass rally in favor of his majority. The political street gangs, so common at the start of the regency period, were now revived at its close. The organizers of the majority campaign were willing not only to use popular coercion to decide the issue, but to work on the officers commanding the troops and National Guard units, thereby ensuring that they would not obey orders to crush popular demonstrations.[95]

The pressure on the supporters of the status quo became overwhelming. Even Honório Hermeto became disheartened and the next day withdrew his bill in a mood of despair. Yet the deputies still resisted, although now delaying a decision only from day to day, virtually from hour to hour. As a last resort, late on the evening of July 21 the regent turned to Vasconcelos, the man he had ejected from power in April 1839. Appointed minister of the interior, Vasconcelos proposed to secure partial victory on the eve of defeat: the General Assembly was to be immediately adjourned, with the session to resume only on November 20, in time for a formal celebration of the emperor's majority on his fifteenth birthday, December 2, 1840. Although the decree justified adjourning the assembly by claiming that the forthcoming majority "ought to be handled with tranquillity and careful thought," the four months' delay and the absence of the legislators would allow the government to regain control and by punishing foes and rewarding friends ensure that it would continue in power. As ever, Araújo Lima made no attempt to cling to office but consented to withdraw for the general good.[96]

Vasconcelos's own presence in the Chamber of Deputies, where he read the decree, secured a stormy, reluctant compliance. In the Senate, however, events ran a different course. Its president, the marquess of Paranaguá, was a veteran of political crises, having served as minister of the interior in November 1823 and as minister of marine in April 1831. A member of the now-vanishing Luso-Brazilian generation, he was a fervent monarchist, seeing in the campaign for the emperor's majority a posthumous vindication of D. Pedro I. On May 20 Paranaguá had, despite being president, both spoken and voted in favor of the bill declaring D. Pedro II of age. Now, on July 22, he refused to permit the decree of adjournment to be read to the Senate, and keeping the senators in session, he summoned to the upper house the deputies favoring an immediate majority.

In open defiance of legality, this reunion addressed a petition to the emperor—signed by 18 senators and 40 deputies—imploring D. Pedro II "to assume at once exercise of your high functions."[97] These signatures did not represent a majority in either house. Nor was support nationwide. Signing were the majority of the deputies from São Paulo, Ceará, and Paraíba do Norte and half those from Minas Gerais, but only seven of the 37 deputies from the major provinces of Pernambuco, Bahia, and Rio de Janeiro.[98] Despite this failure to win over a majority of the legislators, factors were working in favor of the coup. It could count on the support of the military, notably the Rio garrison commander (*comandante das armas*) and the students of the Rio military school. Of equal importance to the conspirators was their virtual certainty that given their preparation of the ground in the previous weeks, the emperor would favor their plan.[99]

In such a moment of urgency and uncertainty, the course of action taken by the emperor would be decisive. A deputation of eight, headed by Antônio Carlos, hurried with the petition to the emperor's country palace of São Cristóvão. To the palace also came the regent who that very morning had secured—as he then supposed—D. Pedro II's consent to the adjournment and to his coming of age on December 2. Now he found the deputation awaiting the emperor's decision on the request in the petition. Displaying a characteristic self-control, Araújo Lima found a graceful formula by which to elicit the emperor's decision. The government intended to declare D. Pedro II of age on December 2, but "some deputies and senators having met in the senate and some unrest existing among the people, [the Regent] had come to know whether His Imperial Majesty wanted to be acclaimed on the 2nd or now; His Imperial Majesty replied that he wanted it now."[100]

This decisive *quero já* ("I want it now"), a phrase which was to echo down the years of D. Pedro II's reign, settled the question. The conspirators, fearful that even now the fruits of power might be snatched from them, insisted on rushing through the transfer of authority to the emperor. In a decree issued immediately the regent revoked the assembly's adjournment and called it into joint session the very next day, July 23, 1840. To the assembled houses the marquess of Paranaguá, "as agent of the national representation in general assembly," declared D. Pedro II "already of age . . . and in full exercise of his constitutional rights."[101] At half past three that afternoon, with full pomp and ceremony, the Emperor took the necessary oaths and was invested with power.

I V

By these drastic means the campaign for D. Pedro II's immediate majority triumphed. The rest of the nation accepted with greater or lesser enthusiasm what had been decided. The organizers of the coup did not have to wait long for their reward: on July 24, the emperor named his first cabinet. Antônio Carlos and his brother Martim Francisco received the portfolios of the interior and of finance, and to Holanda Cavalcanti and his brother, Paula Cavalcanti, went those of marine and of war. Justice was taken by Antônio Paulino Limpo de Abreu, who had held the post under Feijó and who represented the Nativists.[102] Aureliano Coutinho, who spoke for the court clique, became minister of foreign affairs.[103]

If the new government's position in relation to the Emperor was strong, the same could not be said in respect to the political community as a whole. Although the heterogeneous makeup of the cabinet reflected the disparate elements supporting the new government, this diversity generated internal disputes which undermined its authority.[104] Nor was the cabinet's parliamentary position strong, as Antônio Carlos admitted on July 29 when presenting the ministry to the Chamber of Deputies: "The administration . . . hopes to gain . . . a majority [in the assembly], . . . an honorable majority engendered by its actions and its convictions."[105]

In this search for support the Nativists—who enjoyed no more than junior status in the cabinet despite the central role they had played in the majority campaign—saw yet more of their strongest convictions sacrificed. Using the monarch's prerogative, the cabinet showered titles, honors, and court positions on its supporters and sympathizers. In his speech of July 29 Antônio Carlos conceded that since the legality of the law interpreting the Ato Adicional was indisputable, the government would respect and enforce its provisions until experience showed the necessity for revision. Although he opposed the bill now passed by the Senate reforming the criminal procedure code, Antônio Carlos declared that he would nonetheless abide by his cabinet colleagues' decision on the subject. In other words, the conquest of power vanquished all previous objections to both these reforms.

The new cabinet did, in its handling of the nation's affairs, inherit one advantage from the despised regency. By July 1840, the Balaiada revolt in Maranhão province had been crushed by a swift campaign directed by Brigadier Luís Alves de Lima. Appointed in December 1839, Luís Alves displayed military, organizational, and political talents essential to what is now termed "counterinsurgency."[106] In Rio Grande do Sul the new cabinet proved much less fortunate. Despite the Nativists' belief that their common ideological outlook and former comradeship with the *farrapos* would enable them to arrange an honorable end to the rising, their emissary was used by the rebels simply to gain a breathing space. Nor did the assumption of government by the boy emperor make military operations more effective than they had been under the regency.[107]

It was not the intention of the cabinet that its future should be determined by anyone but itself. References in Antônio Carlos's speech of July 29 to gaining "an honorable majority" and to "*reconciling the parties*" did not jibe with his statement that "the government . . . must change the top layers of the administration when, in its opinion, they are not performing their duties well or when they do not enjoy its confidence."[108] These words were ominous, since Antônio Carlos as minister of the interior had oversight of both the provincial presidents and the electoral system. By December 1840, less than four months after taking office, he had replaced two-thirds of the provincial presidents.[109] This virtual purge was accompanied by a vigorous reshuffling of the lower ranks of the judiciary, carried out by the minister of justice.[110] The reason for these wholesale changes became clear after the General Assembly adjourned on September 15, 1840. At every stage in the electoral process which selected the new Chamber of Deputies to convene in 1842, the government and its agents intervened to ensure through fraud, subornation, coercion, and—if necessary—physical violence that only its supporters triumphed in the first and second levels of elections held on October 25 and November 15, 1840. The intervention was particularly visible and brutal in the city and province of Rio de Janeiro, since in no other way could the government succeed in what was the heartland of the Regresso.[111]

The 1840 elections were thereafter notorious as *as eleições do cacête* (the elections of the club). Fraud and violence were not new to the electoral process, as the annulling by the Chamber of Deputies of the 1836 elections in the province of Paraíba do Norte attested.[112] Nor was the use of official positions for electoral advantage unfamiliar, as shown by the frequency with which presidents secured election as deputy from the province they governed. What was unprecedented and what contemporaries found so repulsive was the systematic, unblenching determination with which the government sought to subvert the democratic process in order to manufacture a majority in the new Chamber of Deputies. Far from achieving its purpose—since it was both belated and indiscriminate—this intervention wrecked the cabinet's relations with the wider political community, leaving the ministers dependent on the emperor's goodwill.

The risks involved in entrusting real power to an immature ruler had been foreseen as early as April 1837 by a Ceará deputy. "If they succeed in placing the Emperor on the throne, it will be a very great calamity for Brazil," owing both to "the ample powers bestowed on him by the Constitution" and to his "tender age and uncertain temperament, surrounded by courtiers and self-seekers."[113] The prophecy proved correct in every respect. D. Pedro II was on the one hand highly conscious of his rank, dignity, and powers and extremely resentful of any incursion upon them. At the same time, his youth and inexperience left him exposed to manipulation by the covert influence of his court circle, among whom Aureliano Coutinho held first place after July 1840. The evidence suggests that at this period Aureliano served as a substitute for the father D. Pedro II had hardly known and that his courteous manners and deft ways provided a model for the gawky, taciturn monarch.[114]

The Andrada brothers could not be bothered, it would appear, either to understand the emperor's psychology or to guard their position in court circles. Once ensconced in office, they seem to have regarded the emperor with the same patronizing superiority which some twenty years before had undone Martim Francisco and José Bonifácio in their relations with D. Pedro I. A remark attributed to Martim Francisco, in connection with the grant of the emperor's civil list (grant of a fixed annual income), is indicative: "It is a great deal. The Treasury is poor and the Emperor would have been content with less. He is a good lad, he has patriotism, and something can be made of him." [115]

Given their lack of popular regard following the *eleições do cacête*, the Andradas would have been wise to avoid clashing with Aureliano Coutinho as they did early in 1841. The failure of the Nativists' overtures to the *farrapos* in Rio Grande do Sul caused disagreement in the cabinet over future policy in that province, pitting the Andrada brothers directly against Aureliano. If the ministers all agreed that strong measures must follow the humiliating failure of the peace talks, they strongly disagreed as to what those measures should be.

Since 1835 the rebellion had found its sinews of war in the monies generated by the mule and cattle exports to Uruguay and within Brazil to the province of São Paulo. Although little or nothing could be done about exports to Uruguay, the internal trade could be interdicted, if at considerable economic and political cost. Such a ban Aureliano Coutinho now strongly urged in the cabinet. To the Andrada brothers and their fellow deputies from São Paulo the proposal was anathema. Not only was the trade central to the provincial economy, but the leaders of the Nativist faction in São Paulo were prominent mule and cattle merchants. [116] Unwilling to alienate the notables of their native province, the Andrada brothers tried to compel acceptance of their views in the cabinet by offering their resignation on a related issue. [117]

The stratagem failed. The resignations not only were accepted by the emperor but they brought down the cabinet with them. Under Aureliano Coutinho's guidance the emperor had no difficulty in installing a new ministry on March 23, 1841. Aureliano retained the portfolio of foreign affairs, but the other ministers were drawn from the ranks of the opposition. Two veteran Luso-Brazilians, José Clemente Pereira and the marquess of Paranaguá, took the portfolios of war and of marine. The new ministers of the interior and of justice were both members of the Coimbra bloc. The latter had even held the same portfolio in the last cabinet of the regency. [118] In background and outlook the new cabinet possessed far more homogeneity than its predecessor. The ousted cabinet had fallen by precisely the same means—intrigue and influence at court—which had gained it power in July 1840. In their alarm and chagrin at their dismissal, the ousted ministers can hardly have appreciated the appropriateness of their end.

What added to the humiliation of the ousted ministers was the ease with which the new ministry not only established itself in the good graces of the emperor but secured majority support in both chambers when the final session of the fourth General Assembly began on May 3, 1841. It was this majority which enabled the cabinet to complete the legislative program espoused by Vasconcelos and his associates in the Regresso. By the law of November 23, 1841, a new Council of State was created to advise the emperor and the government; the law of December 3 enacted Vasconcelos's amendments to the criminal procedure code. The second law did not abolish the *juizes de paz* but did strip them of all police powers; these were transferred to the newly created *delegados* and *subdelegados da polícia*. In each province, under the direction of a police chief responsible to the president, the new agents and underagents wielded large discretionary powers and held office at the government's volition. The district attorney (*promotor público*) and the lowest rank of the judiciary (*juiz municipal*) were made directly appointive posts, no longer chosen from a short list presented by the local municipal council.[119]

The law of December 3, 1841, placed in the hands of the cabinet both unprecedented control over the police system and sweeping powers of patronage. Believing as the minister of justice proclaimed in his annual report in May 1841 that "the state of the Empire . . . cries out for heroic remedies," the cabinet did not hesitate in its appointed task.[120] Most of the provincial presidents named by its predecessor were replaced, and it secured the appointment of its friends as the new police agents, chiefs of police, and judges in the key provinces of Rio de Janeiro, Minas Gerais, Pernambuco, and São Paulo.[121] The cabinet and the presidents began systematically to remodel the police system and the lower judiciary.[122] The local *pátrias* lost the large measure of autonomy that they had long enjoyed. While the friends of the cabinet received their rewards, its foes—and the Nativist factions in particular—were thrust out into the cold, their networks of power disrupted. Never before had the government succeeded in establishing its presence in the very core of the *pátrias*.

So massive a disruption of the existing structures of power was bound to cause tensions, even open disaffection. In the provinces of São Paulo and Minas Gerais, these discontents were intensified by fears that the cabinet intended to employ its fiscal powers to damage the economic interests identified with its political foes. The mule and horse trade of western São Paulo and the gold mining of Minas Gerais were controlled by interests closely linked to the Nativist cause, whereas in these two provinces the political interests allied with the cabinet were based on the burgeoning coffee zones. Since both gold mining and the mule trade were in economic decline, any change in the government's existing fiscal and administrative policies, generally favorable to them, would hit extremely hard. The cabinet's imposition in February 1842 of a temporary ban on trade in mules and horses with Rio Grande do Sul seemed to presage far more drastic measures.[123]

Determined to sway the cabinet from its course and appalled by the loss of their local bailiwicks, the politicians then in opposition—those ousted from office in March 1841—turned to desperate measures. They set up a network of secret clubs, together known as the Society of Invisible Patriarchs, which would organize a national revolt should the government persist in its policies. The opposition's expectation clearly was that the simple existence of the clubs, which resembled the familiar Masonic lodges, would be sufficient to recall the government to its senses.[124] The mixture of veiled threat and entreaty used by the conspirators to this end is evident from a letter that the emperor's personal physician, deeply involved in the conspiracy, sent to his master in January 1842: "Once the rock is dislodged from the mountaintop, no one can foresee where it will stop or the damage that it will do in its passage." [125]

The more realistic elements among the cabinet's opponents anticipated that when the new assembly convened in May 1842, deliverance would come. Since thanks to the *eleições do cacête* they controlled the Chamber of Deputies, it would be easy to pass a motion of no confidence in the existing cabinet and so compel its replacement by one more sympathetic to their cause. To ensure that such would occur, the opposition deputies used the chamber's examination of election returns to deprive their known opponents of their seats, thus increasing their own majority.[126] This purging proved to no purpose, for the opposition underestimated not only the cabinet's influence but also the total control over the political process that the regulating power gave to the emperor. On the recommendation of the cabinet and with the concurrence of the new Council of State, D. Pedro II issued on May 1, 1842, a decree which dissolved the chamber —even before it had convened—and ordered the election of a new lower house, to convene on November 1, 1842.[127]

At a blow the opposition was deprived of its anticipated victory. Already excluded from power at the provincial and even the local level, the opposition now lost all leverage on national policy. In São Paulo province many of the local notables faced not just political but economic disaster as well. On May 17, 1842, the cabinet decided that the ban on the mule and horse trade with Rio Grande do Sul imposed as a temporary measure in February should continue until the *farrapos* were defeated. On that same day a revolt broke out at Sorocaba, the town in western São Paulo which served as the terminus and distribution center for the mules and horses brought up from Rio Grande do Sul.[128] The leader of the revolt, acclaimed as "interim president" of São Paulo, was both the wealthiest merchant in the trade and the most powerful Nativist leader in the province. In July 1840 the previous cabinet had appointed him president of São Paulo province; he was as promptly removed by the existing ministry.[129]

Instead of opening a coordinated national revolt, the Sorocaba rebellion found itself supported only by risings at Lorena and Bananal in the Paraíba valley on June 1 and at Barbacena in Minas Gerais on June 10, 1842.[130] Government vigilance accounted for part of this disarray, since authorities in the national capital carried out a preemptive roundup on June 18, arresting the principal conspirators. Four of them were exiled to Europe, with the rest transferred as prisoners to the province of Espírito Santo.[131] Even in the areas which did revolt, a lack of resolution, an absence of fighting spirit was patent. This indecision and timidity contrasted strongly with the single-minded resolve of the government, which named Brigadier

Luís Alves de Lima, the pacifier of Maranhão province, to head its forces. The lack of coordination between the three revolts allowed them to be defeated in sequence. By the end of June, Luís Alves had put down the São Paulo revolt. The Paraíba valley revolt was suppressed by the middle of July. Defeating the Minas uprising tested even Luís Alves' skills—the margin of victory at the battle of Santa Luzia on August 20 was narrow but nonetheless decisive. The rebellion was over.[132]

Historians have been puzzled by the hesitation and indecision shown by the rebel leaders, failings which can in part be ascribed to reluctant cooperation or to fears about disrupting the social order.[133] Although both these factors no doubt contributed, the main cause for the lack of conviction can be deduced from the public documents issued by the rebel leaders in São Paulo and Minas Gerais: the risings were inspired by and conducted according to a political philosophy which antedated the concept of the nation. The purpose of the revolt was to defend the traditional, established rights and liberties of the *pátrias*, which the government was considered to be violating. The resort to extralegal, nonpeaceful remedies was not a shift to radicalism but rather a symbolic act, a traditional means of warning the authorities that they had transgressed the bounds of acceptable behavior and were trespassing on the rights of the *pátrias*.

The resort to rebellion and the accompanying replacement of local officials did not, according to this political tradition, imply any rejection or denial of obedience to the monarch in his proper sphere of authority. The inhabitants of São Paulo, the rebel president proclaimed, "know how to defend their rights, just as much as they are faithful to the throne." In Minas Gerais the interim president named by the rebels hastened to send the emperor a letter assuring him of undiminished loyalty.[134] That same letter revealed the orientation of the Minas Gerais rising, since it assured D. Pedro II that the only purpose of the revolt was to deliver him from his current state of coercion. This promise referred to the generally accepted convention that since the monarch would not intentionally adopt oppressive policies, he would do so only if misled or forced to do so by "wicked" advisers. By this tradition a formal act of rebellion became a proof of supreme loyalty, since it would cause the dismissal of the "bad" advisers and the abandonment of the offensive policies, thus restoring harmony between the sovereign and his loving subjects.[135] "Many of the participants," a recent study of the 1842 rebellion has concluded, "had no intention of resorting to bloodshed, and seemed to believe that the mere fact of a general uprising would lead to the ministry's downfall."[136]

The fallacy in the rebels' position derived from their vision of Brazil as a union of autonomous *pátrias*. Twenty years after independence they still could not accept Brazil as a nation-state in which the national government possessed total power, subject only to the limitations imposed by the Constitution. The cabinet had no intention of either relinquishing that position or modifying its policies. Nor was the emperor, who resented any challenges to his supreme authority, willing to dismiss the cabinet. The clash between the old and the new perceptions of Brazil was epitomized by the letters exchanged in June 1842 between Diogo Antônio Feijó who had supported the São Paulo rising, and Luís Alves de Lima, the commander of the government forces. The first sought to persuade the soldier not to cooperate in the destruction of provincial autonomy, and the latter replied that "the orders I received from the Government are the selfsame orders that I received from the minister of Justice in April 1832, and now, as then, I will suppress rebellion against authority." [137]

Accordingly, the rebels found themselves faced with a cruel dilemma: they had either to fight a bloody civil war to win total power—at long odds and at the risk of social disorder—or to surrender unconditionally to an unrelenting, vengeful government. The only means of escaping this dilemma was the dishonorable course of abandoning the cause and fleeing to safety, a course adopted by both interim presidents.[138] Those among the rebel leaders who opted for the first alternative were too few in number, too young in years, and too slight in influence to prolong the conflict.[139] Unable to resist further, they chose unconditional surrender to their enemies over safety in flight.[140]

The middle months of 1842 marked, therefore, the decisive moment when the concept of the nation-state triumphed in Brazil over the older concepts of sovereign and *pátria*. Thenceforth the interests of the nation-state would take precedence over local right and local needs, no matter how urgent or how justified. The authority of government became paramount and within the national polity the emperor's decision was final. Whatever political group received power from him possessed legitimacy and retained office until it lost the confidence of the emperor or the legislature. The one final challenge to this system, the Praieira revolt of 1848–49 in Pernambuco province, would serve only to confirm and consolidate the supremacy of the nation.

8

The Nation Forged, 1842-1852

The defeat of the 1842 uprisings following on D. Pedro II's declaration of age signified the triumph of the nation-state ideal in Brazil. Thenceforth, no rival concept of the polity could be considered a licit, much less a viable, alternative. For Brazil's rulers, warding off threats to national unity and territorial integrity remained a basic if not always overt concern, but their attention was to be concentrated on completing the structures of statehood and on achieving full nationhood.

In the decade after 1842 the consolidation of Brazil as a nation-state was completed. In 1844 the expiration of the commercial treaty with Great Britain extinguished almost all extraterritorial rights and commercial privileges held by foreign states. Brazil thus finally secured full national sovereignty. The ending of the Farroupilha revolt in 1845 eliminated the threat of separatism in the far south, with Rio Grande do Sul being reintegrated into the nation. The cycle of local revolts against domination from Rio de Janeiro which had begun with the 1817 revolt in the northeast was brought to a close by the suppression in 1849 of the Praieira rising in Pernambuco province. These ten years of national consolidation would be crowned by two notable achievements. In 1851 the national government forced merchants and planters to accept the abolition of the slave trade with Africa, which, although made illegal in 1831, had continued to flourish. By masterminding in 1852 the defeat and exile of Juan Manuel Rosas, the dictator of Argentina, the imperial government made Brazil for the first time a powerful and respected element in the affairs of South America.

As part of national consolidation during the decade, important changes occurred in the dynamic of Brazilian politics. With the creation in 1847 of the post of president of the Council of Ministers there was established a stable and effective form of governance, a compromise between the personal rule of the First Reign and the parliamentarianism of the regency. The ruling circles became homogeneous in composition and outlook, so much so that they were soon denounced by the remaining Nativists as "the oligarchy" (*a oligarquia*). The most significant political development was probably the emergence of organized political parties. The new party system served as the nexus by which local interests, thus assured of access to the fruits of power, were tied to the nation. Through the party system the ruling circles were able to direct the political process and bring the political community under control, without formal restriction on the extent of political participation. After a generation of turmoil, the nation was by the 1850's consolidated and its institutions functioning. A feeling of stability and order at last existed so that Brazilians could face the future with some confidence.

Gratifying as they were, the achievements of the decade after 1842 served to confirm and to deepen a fundamental dichotomy—social, cultural, and political—existing within Brazil. A profound gulf separated the "official" nation from the "real" nation. The inhabitants of the official Brazil, mostly literate, cultured, and prosperous, lived in accord with the latest models of nationhood. The vast majority of Brazilians, both free and slave, belonged to the real country, in which conditions differed little from those of 1822 or for that matter the late eighteenth century. Illiterate, short-lived, and exploited by the ruling minority, the inhabitants of this second world had not profited one iota from the establishment of a nation-state.

Three decades of nationhood had, moreover, done very little to change the basic structures of Brazil. The nation continued to be, as in the colonial period, an agglomeration of regional economies, each orientated to the exterior rather than to the others. Had it not been for the spread of the printing press and the introduction of steamship lines, communications would have differed not at all from what they had been in 1822. In respect to the social infrastructure, the system of schooling was almost as imperfect as and the state of personal security was little better than they had been at the time of independence. Much had been achieved in the past 30 years, but as some Brazilians realized, as much or more remained to be done.

I

The defeat of the São Paulo and Minas Gerais risings confirmed the supremacy of the nation over the *pátrias*; henceforth power would be concentrated in the national capital. Authority and so decisions flowed from Rio de Janeiro outwards into the provinces. The provincial assemblies, although they continued to act as a check on the central government's ability to dispose of the provinces' affairs as it pleased, did not provide competing sources of power and authority. The expansion of coffee production, which continued unabated during the 1840's, reinforced the supremacy of Rio de Janeiro and so of the nation-state. Dominance of Brazil by the national capital, if widely resented, met with no effective challenge. Because of the superior economic, social, and cultural opportunities it offered, Rio de Janeiro city acted as a magnet, attracting from the provinces anyone of talent, thus reinforcing its hegemony over the nation.

In political terms, the triumph of the nation over the *pátrias* consolidated control by the Coimbra bloc, the most ardent advocates of the nation's supremacy. Death and old age now removed the Luso-Brazilian generation from the scene. The Exaltados ceased to play any role in national politics, although in the provinces some stalwarts remained active. The events of the early 1840's left the Nativists in disarray and some discredit. Their support for the emperor's immediate majority in 1840, far from installing them in power, had ultimately drawn them into rebellion in 1842. From their abandonment of principle the Nativists had benefited not at all.

What characterized members of the Coimbra bloc, apart from devotion to the nation, was their possession of university degrees, generally in law. The career pattern they exemplified now served as the model and indeed the norm for ambitious young men. In order to rise in the political world it was henceforth necessary to secure a degree, preferably in law.[1] The *bacharel em direito* (bachelor of law) became the archetypal figure not just in national politics but in the official world encompassing all facets of culture and governance. From the early 1840's enrollment increased markedly at the two law and two medical schools. That three of the four schools were situated outside the national capital did not prevent them from being effective agents of the dominant system. The professors, most of whom were active (and often very successful) politicians, naturally believed in the system and propagated its values to their students.[2] The outlook of the rising generation of *bacharéis*, "discreet, intelligent, and capable," contrasted strongly with the rustic, self-educated culture typical of the Nativists.[3]

Control by the Coimbra bloc, the rise to dominance by the *bacharéis*, and the concentration of political power in the national capital were all manifestations of a fundamental change in the nature of organized politics in Brazil. The 1842 rising served as the catalyst for this change. The dissolution of the Chamber of Deputies on May 1, 1842, before it had even convened, necessitated the election of a new chamber. Because of the rebellions the government postponed the elections, and they were finally held in what can only be termed abnormal conditions. Not only had the revolts produced an atmosphere of polarization and confrontation, but the government had not hesitated to crack down on its foes—throughout Brazil, not just in the provinces involved in the risings.[4] Indictments, dismissals, and imprisonment were used with little discrimination. The law of December 3, 1841, amending the criminal procedure code gave the authorities the ability to purge the administrative and judicial systems in the provinces. In a document written in 1851 the politicians who had held power in 1842 contended that the emergency had demanded no less of them: "The rebellions offered the right moment . . . to oust their opponents in the provinces and to install their own supporters. Nor given those events could it have been otherwise. It was not possible to leave the public power in the hands of those who had just resorted to arms."[5]

The 1842 revolts became the divisive issue within the political community. The ruling politicians henceforth called their defeated opponents *luzias*, a perpetual reminder of the battle at Santa Luzia which ended the Minas rebellion. Since the cabinet and its backers regarded themselves as the natural rulers of Brazil under the emperor's supreme authority and their foes as traitors, they had no scruples in seeking victory in the chamber elections held late in 1842. Widespread use was made of the *chapa*, a list of approved candidates. This slate, usually printed, was circulated among authorities and electors in the appropriate province.[6] The cabinet mobilized all the government agencies—judiciary, National Guard, and bureaucracy—to secure victory. If electors could not be persuaded by fair means or foul to vote for the candidates on the *chapa*, then they should be deterred from voting at all.

Government interference in the elections, far more sweeping and systematic than had been the case in the *eleições do cacête* of 1840, was generally successful. When the new chamber met on January 1, 1843, the cabinet could count on the support of a disciplined majority among the deputies. The magnitude of this electoral victory aided the cabinet not at all in achieving a permanent occupation of office. Manipulating the elections and treating opponents as irredeemable traitors did not provide a secure basis for an exclusive hold on power. These measures affronted what is best termed moderate opinion within the political community. They drove Aureliano Coutinho out of the cabinet and into active opposition. Most serious of all, they offended the emperor.

Moderate opinion was alienated in two different ways. The accusations of treason which the cabinet levied against the rebels of 1842 were excessive. The revolts had been inspired by a political custom dating back to colonial times, a tradition which although henceforth unacceptable could not be retroactively deemed treasonable. The consistency with which juries acquitted those charged with complicity in the revolts in Minas Gerais and São Paulo confirmed this rejection of the cabinet's viewpoint. Further, the ferocity with which the revolts had been suppressed and the subsequent pursuit of retribution were quite contrary to Brazilian practice. Whereas deporting prominent politicians at the moment of crisis was seen as a justifiable if illegal action, the cabinet's insistence on keeping them in exile after peace had been restored late in 1842 gave deep offense. So did its insistence on pressing in the Senate charges of having participated in the rebellion against Diogo Antônio Feijó, even though he was known to be mortally ill.[7]

The cabinet's policy of political exclusivism also alienated many provincial notables whose standing in their locality had entitled them to consideration and support from the government authorities. Of these *influências legítimas* (legitimate influences), as they were termed, those who failed to rally behind the cabinet in the 1842 elections found themselves ostracized and denied government largesse. Just how dangerous such a policy of political exclusivism could be was evident from the split which now developed between Aureliano Coutinho and the rest of the cabinet. Having been named senator from Alagoas in 1842, Aureliano Coutinho did not himself need a seat in the 1843 chamber, but regarding himself as a legitimate influence in Rio de Janeiro province, he did expect the election of his brother Saturnino as deputy from that province. The leading politicians of Rio province were determined to reserve the province's seats for themselves and their followers. Aureliano Coutinho's pretensions were resented and his claims ignored; Saturnino was roundly defeated.[8]

Not content with this rebuff, the ministers proceeded to organize a public snub which drove Aureliano Coutinho from office and caused the resignation of the cabinet. The occasion for the slight was Aureliano's handling, as minister of foreign affairs, of two questions pending with Great Britain. The fifteen-year term of the 1827 commercial treaty had run out in November 1842, but with two years' notice needed to terminate the agreement. The slave trade treaty of 1817 would expire in March 1845. Determined to retain the legal and economic rights granted by the two agreements, the British government contended that notice terminating the commercial treaty could not be given before the end of the fifteen years, thus prolonging the agreement until 1844. It also pressed for the opening of negotiations for a new slave trade treaty.[9]

That Aureliano Coutinho gave in to both British demands, accepting the continuation of the commercial treaty until 1844 and agreeing to treat with the special English envoy on the slave trade question, furnished the perfect justification for his public humiliation. The draft Vote of Thanks presented in the chamber on January 5, 1843, contained a sentence on foreign affairs which could be read, the minister of justice publically hinted, as a censure of Aureliano. Two days after this slur, on January 16, Aureliano resigned his portfolio, to be followed by the other ministers. On January 23 the emperor summoned Honório Hermeto Carneiro Leão and authorized him to organize a new cabinet. Thus was the exclusion of Aureliano Coutinho from power secured.[10]

The new cabinet led by El Rei Honório—the product of intrigue, ambitions, and political exclusivism—never transcended its origins.[11] Dogged by an aura of uncertainty and insecurity, the ministry undertook no new initiatives, grimly defending the extreme policies of its predecessor. It refused to consider an amnesty for political offenses, continuing the prosecution of Feijó and objecting to the return from Europe of those deported in 1842. It ended the system of financial subsidies which most of the provinces had received annually since 1837, thereby restricting their activities

—particularly in primary and secondary education, for which the provinces had been responsible since the Ato Adicional.[12]

The cabinet was not barren of achievement, though none was substantial. British pressures for new commercial and slave trade agreements were rejected. The pacification of the province of Rio Grande do Sul went slowly forward. In May 1843 the emperor's younger sister married a son of the French king, and in September D. Pedro II wed his relative Princess Maria Teresa of Naples, both marriages being sumptuously celebrated. The emperor's marriage gave promise of an heir to the throne and emphasized that D. Pedro II was no longer a child.

It was the cabinet's intransigence and the emperor's sense of maturity that in late 1843 set monarch and ministers on a collision course. From the start of his reign D. Pedro II had resented any attempt by the ministers to impose policies upon him or to reduce his powers. By nature and training D. Pedro II disliked partisan politics, seeing himself as benevolent ruler of all his subjects and favoring policies of "justice and tolerance." The ruling politicians could continue to monopolize power only as long as they could persuade him that the rebels of 1842, the Luzias, were indeed traitors. With the ouster of Aureliano Coutinho from office, his allies at court began to present the Luzias as loyal subjects, misrepresented, oppressed, and deserving of better treatment.[13]

The moment of collision was reached when Saturnino, who held the important post of inspector of customs for the national capital, announced his candidacy for the Senate seat from Rio province vacated by Feijó's death. Having achieved Saturnino's defeat in the Senate election, Honório Hermeto brusquely demanded from the emperor Saturnino's dismissal as inspector, not on grounds of incompetence but of political hostility. "I felt that the dismissal was unjust," the emperor noted many years later, "and the *way* in which Carneiro Leão insisted on it made me feel that if I gave in they would think me weak."[14] Not only did the emperor's refusal constitute a public rebuke to the cabinet, but the interview terminated in remarks by Honório Hermeto so disrespectful as to make his continuance in office impossible. The cabinet resigned on February 2, giving as the formal cause its unwillingness to grant a general amnesty to the rebels of 1842.[15]

To form a new ministry the emperor turned not to the Luzias but to those national politicians who had not supported the 1842 revolts yet were not identified with the last two cabinets, men who advocated politics of "justice and tolerance." The principal figures in the new cabinet formed on February 2, 1844, were two Coimbra graduates: José Carlos Pereira de Almeida Torres and Manuel Alves Branco. Alves Branco had served as a minister both under Feijó and under Araújo Lima. As minister of justice in 1840 he had countersigned the law interpreting the Ato Adicional. Almeida Torres had served mainly as an administrator and judge prior to his nomination in 1843 as senator from his native Bahia, the post which gave him a leading role in politics. To him the emperor entrusted the actual organization of the new cabinet.[16]

An earnest of the new cabinet's desire for the end to exclusivism and polarization was the decree of March 14, 1844, which granted full amnesty to the rebels of 1842. Those deprived of honors and employment were restored, and those convicted were released from prison and fully pardoned.[17] In its handling of government appointments and dispensing of patronage, the cabinet attempted to be moderate and evenhanded. It did not replace provincial presidents wholesale, and it tried to respect all legitimate interests in the provinces. The intention of the ministry was to attract the support of all men of moderation and goodwill. The basic weakness in this policy was the lack of any positive political creed or concrete program which would consolidate support and tempt individuals and groups from their existing allegiances. Without solid backing the cabinet could not hope to defeat the factions entrenched on both the national and the provincial levels. Further, by the mere fact of its existence, the new cabinet incurred the systematic enmity of the ousted politicians. Hostility was confirmed when on April 12, 1844, Aureliano Coutinho was named president of Rio de Janeiro province. Despite its intentions, the cabinet and its supporters were slowly being forced into close alliance with the Luzias.[18]

When the General Assembly met on May 5, 1844, the government secured a majority in the Senate, but despite all its concessions and cajoling it was not able to attract support from more than a third of the deputies. The majority remained firm in their existing loyalties, deaf to all the blandishments the cabinet could offer. Subjected to unrelenting attacks in the debate on the Vote of Thanks, the government had no choice but to resort to the emperor's regulating power. On May 24, amidst violent protests by the deputies, the decree was read dissolving the chamber and summoning another for January 1, 1845.

In order to win the parliamentary elections of 1844, the cabinet had to construct an effective electoral machine which backed by the instruments of government could defeat the entrenched interests opposing the existing ministry. The methods developed in 1840 and 1842 were once more employed. The provincial presidents and the chiefs of police were replaced. A wholesale remodeling of the judiciary was carried out, the cabinet's supporters receiving key positions and its opponents being either moved to the most isolated posts or left without employment until the elections were past.[19] *Chapas* were drawn up for each province and every form of subornation and intimidation employed to secure majorities for the approved candidates.[20] When all else failed, outright violence might be used to keep electors from casting their votes. The election results proved eminently satisfactory. When the new chamber met on January 1, 1845, so few of the cabinet's opponents had won seats that they were derisively nicknamed *a patrulha*, the patrol.[21] The process of polarization was thus completed. From 1844 onwards two organized parties—Conservative and Liberal—dominated Brazilian politics.

Although the concept of party was not a novelty, the word having been used in the early 1830's to describe both Moderados and Caramurús, these "parties" had been no more than ephemeral coalitions of diverse political elements, possessing neither mutual loyalty nor electoral machinery.[22] The ease with which heterogeneous political interests, hitherto hostile and incompatible in outlook, could marshal under the same banner is evident from the composition of the Majority Club which in 1840 led the campaign for the emperor's immediate coming of age. The Conservative and Liberal parties which emerged by the middle of the 1840's did possess the durability that their predecessors had so markedly lacked.

The Conservative party, represented in the new chamber by *a patrulha*, dated from the elections of 1842. As attested by its very name and by the past careers of its leaders, most of whom had supported the Regresso, the Conservative party favored monarchical rule, centralized power, and a hierarchical society—not that it possessed any formal program for achieving these goals. At the same time, the Conservatives inherited from Enlightenment thought a belief in an activist and interventionist government which would advance the national over local and private interests. The Conservatives also tended to distrust the British and, in consequence, favored both manufacturing and the slave trade.

The Conservative leadership was mainly drawn from the members of the Coimbra bloc, and particularly from those—notably Honório Hermeto—who had opposed the abortive constitutional coup of July 30, 1832. The leadership was closely linked to the coffee planters of Rio de Janeiro province and the great merchants of Portuguese birth in the national capital. Similar ties existed in the other provinces with planters and merchants involved in export agriculture, such as the great sugar families of Pernambuco and Bahia.[23] These were alliances in which each side remained master in its own sphere. Conservative politicians respected the position and needs of the landowners, who on their side did not issue orders to the politicians.

The elections of 1844 had brought into being the Liberal party, a loose coalition of disparate "out" groups, united as much by their opposition to the Conservatives as by any shared outlook. The party included the different Nativist groups, principally those from Minas Gerais, São Paulo, Ceará, and Pernambuco, and once the civil war in Rio Grande do Sul was brought to a negotiated end in March 1845, the former *farrapos*. Many of the Brazilian-born merchants in the national capital and their counterparts in Minas Gerais and São Paulo rallied to the party. Also attracted in the provinces were the *influências legítimas* which had been deprived of local power when their rivals allied with the government in the elections of 1842. A key element in the new party was a small but indispensable group drawn from the Coimbra bloc. Some had been supporters of Feijó and others had participated in the majority campaign of 1840. Also influential at first was the court clique, notably Aureliano Coutinho, who would remain ensconced as president of Rio province during the next five years.

Insofar as these groups shared any common vision of society, it was a desire to protect established rights and liberties, both of individuals and of groups. The doctrines of laissez-faire, laissez-passer appealed far more to the Liberals than to the Conservatives. Also distinguishing the two parties was the Liberals' tendency to attribute the nation's ills to the maleficent presence of the Portuguese-born, a fear inherited from the past and reinforced both by the intense competition for urban employment offered by recent immigrants and by the close links of the great Portuguese merchants to the Conservative party.

The elections of 1844 completed a cycle of change that had begun with the majority campaign in early 1840. The first half of the decade saw the recentralization of power in Rio de Janeiro and the restoration of the emperor's authority over the legislature and executive. The national government's control over the provinces had been reestablished and a new political relationship between the ruling circles at Rio and the notables in the *pátrias* inaugurated. The development of party politics and the manipulation of elections by the government, although maintaining political participation by the small folk, deprived those social groups of an independent role and so prevented them from exerting decisive pressure on the political process. Taken as a whole, these changes obviated the risks of territorial fragmentation and of social revolution but did not facilitate the achievement of functioning nationhood.

A basic flaw of the new organization of politics lay in its dependence on the manipulation of the electoral process. Although the ruling cabinet, no matter what its party color, possessed the power and authority sufficient to ensure electoral success, it lacked adequate personnel to staff the mechanisms of control in the *pátrias* and was thus forced to rely on political elements in the provinces to deliver victory at the polls. Electoral manipulation, although preventing hostile or incompatible elements from intruding into the ruling system, rendered the ruling party so obligated to the local and provincial interests that the capacity of the national government to undertake bold, independent action in internal affairs was severely jeopardized.[24]

Given the nature of society in the provinces, the competing political parties found it easy to forge links with local interests. From colonial times life in the *pátrias* had been dominated by competing networks of influence based on family ties and *compadrio*. The Ato Adicional of 1834, which devolved much power to the provinces, had politicized these networks through their fight to gain control of the disbursement of revenues and patronage. The key to success in the second half of the 1830's had been for the emergent factions to elect their supporters as members of the provincial assembly, as justices of the peace, and as National Guard officers. A faction could strengthen its position in the province by persuading cabinet ministers to name its supporters to the posts in that province appointed by the national government.[25]

In the provinces the creation of electoral alliances associated with the establishment of organized political parties at the national level eventually caused the competing interests to coalesce into two loose, opposing factions. As their very names testified—such as Cabeludos (Hairies) and Lisos (Smooths) in Alagoas, and Cristãos (Christians) and Judeus (Jews) in Santa Catarina—the factions had no ideological orientation, despite their identification with Conservatism or Liberalism.[26] In Santa Catarina the "Christians" and the "Jews"—respectively Conservative and Liberal in allegiance—formed, in the words of a contemporary, "two parties which were exclusively electoral, seeking, for personal reasons, the triumph of their candidates as deputy to the General Assembly, without espousing any ideas, principles, or system of provincial administration."[27]

The relationship between the ruling cabinet and the provincial factions on which it depended for winning elections was in one important respect asymmetrical. The polarization of politics since 1840 meant that the cabinet, if it clashed with its partisans in a particular province, could not easily secure support from alternative influences; these were all arrayed on the opposing side. On the other hand, nothing stopped those same influences from switching party allegiance when doing so seemed advantageous or necessary. Changes in party allegiance by provincial interests were far from unusual. Accordingly, any cabinet which pursued policies threatening the status quo in the *pátrias* ran a very real risk of forfeiting electoral support for the political party it represented.

If provincial interests could thus constrain the national government in the policies it adopted, they could not—and in actuality never did—coerce it into following a particular course of action. The influence exerted by provincial factions on Rio de Janeiro was severely limited. Control of the principal sources of revenue and patronage gave the national government the upper hand in its dealings with provincial interests. Bonds of personal and group loyalty, such as existed between members of the Coimbra bloc, and a common devotion to the nation coexisted with party allegiance and guarded the ruling circles against external manipulation. In contrast, the vision and interests of the provincial factions were bounded by their own *pátrias*. Cooperation between them was rare, and their leaders, when they became a nuisance, could easily be neutralized by co-option into the ruling circles at Rio.

A second flaw of the new organization of politics was the change it wrought over the long term in the composition and recruitment of the ruling circles. Hitherto, a successful career in national politics had demanded not only ability and a talent for survival but a strong provincial base. Government manipulation of elections changed these criteria for success. In 1842 Justiniano José da Rocha, a leading journalist in the national capital, was elected deputy from Minas Gerais despite having no connections with that province, solely because he was included on the official *chapa*. As Rocha himself acknowledged, "My election for Minas is entirely a party election; in order for me to win [again] my party must be on top; I don't have sufficient faith in my friends or in my own prestige to believe that I can win as an opposition candidate. Should therefore my party not be in power, my exclusion is certain."[28] Personal connections and party influence rather than innate ability and proven competence could now provide the basis for a political career. The onset of what was in essence recruitment by co-option justified the Nativists' denunciations of rule by *a oligarquia*.

In the late 1830's one of the most effective arguments used in favor of recentralization had been that it alone could eliminate the factionalism then corrupting provincial politics. By the end of 1844 it was clear not only that the remedy had failed to restore purity to local and provincial politics but that recentralization had, through the formation of the Conservative and Liberal parties, promoted the factionalization of national affairs. Elections to the Chamber of Deputies no longer reflected public opinion but rather the will of the ruling cabinet. The parliamentary system of government which had emerged since 1826 would now have become an illusion were it not for the existence of the regulating power. Since elections could not oust a party from power, it fell upon the emperor to make the political system function. He alone could keep the two parties roughly in balance, by alternating them in office. The monarch stood above the fray, the supreme arbiter of power and symbol of legality. What was merely an assertion when uttered by Honório Hermeto in July 1841 had become the literal truth three years later: "The Emperor always heads a legitimate government."[29]

II

Political and economic conditions in Brazil underwent so marked an improvement in the middle of the 1840's as to give hope that the nation might now achieve its full potential. Most significant was the end of the civil wars which for a decade had wracked Brazil. In March 1845 Luís Alves de Lima brought the Farroupilha revolt in Rio Grande do Sul to an end through a skillful blend of victory in the field, political and economic concessions, and personal diplomacy.[30] In November 1844 the commercial treaty made in 1827 with Great Britain finally expired, and the nation at long last achieved control over its economic policies, being now able to set tariffs.[31] Imports could henceforth be taxed at a rate sufficient to supply the government's financial needs. After the enactment of the new customs tariff in 1844, government revenues in the fiscal year 1845–46 exceeded expenditures, the first surplus in nearly a decade.[32]

The 1844 tariff law, named after Alves Branco, the minister of finance, offered sufficient protection to local manufacturing to stimulate the first industrial ventures, notably the iron works and shipping company at Ponte d'Areia, on the shore across the bay from the national capital.[33] Similarly, the new tariff encouraged the opening of the first cotton mills in Brazil, one in Rio province and the other in Bahia.[34] By the mid-1840's the company of steam packets, authorized by the law of 1837 and in operation since 1839, had drawn the coastal regions into close, regular communication with the national capital. The swift suppression of the 1842 revolt in São Paulo province owed much to the company's steamboats.[35]

These economic changes were matched by what may be termed a shift in the political perceptions of the ruling groups. Of the 49 members of the Senate in April 1831 only 17 were still living at the end of 1845, and of the 41 senators named since 1831, 8 were already dead. The Coimbra bloc by then formed the effective majority in the upper house.[36] Their admittance to the highest circles of power made room at the middle levels for the first generation of graduates from the São Paulo and Olinda law faculties. These graduates resembled the Coimbra bloc in giving their principal loyalty to Brazil as a nation. To those born since 1822 and now reaching adulthood, Brazil's nationhood was axiomatic. This new perception was epitomized by the decision in 1840 of the fledgling Instituto Histórico e Geográfico Brasileiro to hold a prize competition on the theme, How should the history of Brazil be written?[37] These investigations, which focused on the colonial period, attested to the desire to find a "usable past" that would by showing the antiquity of national identity legitimize nation-statehood.[38]

The Liberals, during their period of rule from February 2, 1844, to September 29, 1848, failed to make best use of this conjunction of favorable developments. In four and a half years five cabinets rose and fell. These ephemeral ministries did no more than respond to events initiated by others; they failed to control the polity and society over which they presided. Save for passing in 1846 a law reforming the electoral process, in a vain attempt to prevent fraud and intimidation, no major legislation was enacted during this half-decade.[39] The Liberals held office but they did not govern.

For a party dedicated to reform and progress, failure and inertia so absolute requires explanation. The immediate cause could be found in the intense factionalism that rent the Liberal party throughout these years. Whereas the Conservatives developed a sense of identity and self-discipline, the Liberal party never outgrew its origins as a coalition of disparate opposition groups, more interested in their own needs than the party's well-being. Among the most persistent offenders were the Nativist factions, which did not hesitate to bring down a cabinet if that would help to consolidate their political dominance in their own province. The principal culprit was the Praieira faction of Pernambuco, which had not learned discretion through suffering defeat in 1842. The dozen votes the Pernambucan delegation commanded in the Chamber of Deputies could make or break any cabinet, and this power was used ruthlessly by the *praieiros* to obtain virtual autonomy in their control of Pernambuco province.[40]

Feuding within the Liberal party was intensified by the covert influence of two court cliques. Aureliano Coutinho worked against any cabinet that tried to restrict his independence as president of Rio province. Equally influential was the Clube de Joana, a palace group named after the residence of the emperor's majordomo, Paulo Barbosa da Silva, who from 1844 to 1847 played a key role in the rise and fall of cabinets.[41] The political disruption caused by intrigues at court was intensified in the later 1840's by the actions of the emperor, who as he grew older and more confident in his role, worked to extricate himself from the web of obligations in which the court cliques had involved him. In 1846 Barbosa da Silva was maneuvered into becoming Brazilian envoy to Russia, an honorable exile which both ended his influence and served as a salutary example.[42] The creation of the post of president of the Council of Ministers on July 20, 1847, signified the emperor's willingness to entrust the formation of a new cabinet to a single politician who would also act as manager of the government's affairs in the General Assembly. The innovation deprived the court circles of the influence they had since 1840 exerted on the formation of cabinets. The decree also signified D. Pedro II's maturity as a ruler.[43]

The inertia and weakness displayed by the Liberal governments from 1844 to 1848 was in part due to an ideological schizophrenia. Liberal doctrines appealed to two distinct currents of political opinion, which coexisted uneasily within the party. The first saw the party as the means of turning Brazil into the France or Britain of South America, through a series of radical social and political changes such as land reform, the abolition of slavery, and the elimination of privilege. The second interpreted the party's belief in "liberty, security, property, and resistance to oppression" as committing it to the defense of vested rights and established interests. Within the party this second group was the more influential, in part because it commanded greater electoral strength and in part because only the most dedicated Liberals were willing to countenance the risk of social and political upheaval that an activist program might provoke. Unwilling to renounce its ideals and yet unable to undertake effective reforms, the Liberal party thoroughly merited the quip made at its expense by Antônio Carlos, himself identified as a Liberal. Before his death in 1845 the last of the Andrada brothers remarked that "nothing so much resembles a Conservative as a Liberal in power."[44]

Despite the end of civil war and the growth of the economy, the years of Liberal rule saw no improvement in Brazil's position in foreign affairs. In the last years of the 1830's both Great Britain and France had advanced the frontiers of their colonies on the Guiana coast southwards towards the Amazon. The barrenness of the territories in dispute rather than Brazilian strength or diplomatic skill caused the two nations to withdraw. The situation on the southern frontier, despite the pacification of Rio Grande do Sul, gave infinitely greater cause for concern. Juan Manuel Rosas, the dictator of Argentina since 1835, manipulated the contending factions in Uruguay with great skill, reducing Brazil's prestige in the area, threatening its allies, and keeping the southern frontier with Uruguay in a state of continuing unrest. The successive Liberal cabinets proved incapable of counteracting Rosas's intrigues.[45]

An even greater affront to Brazil's national pride came in 1845 with Great Britain's passage of the Aberdeen Act. When the imperial government refused in March 1845 to renew the 1817 slave treaty with its bilateral machinery for suppressing the African slave trade, the British government, on the basis that the treaty signed in 1826 had recognized the trade to be piracy, secured a law giving its warships the right to seize and its admiralty courts the power to condemn all Brazilian ships suspected of slaving. Against this "infringement of the sovereignty and independence of Brazil" the Liberal government protested in vain. Unwilling to break off relations, Brazil could only look on in impotence as British cruisers seized nearly 400 ships in the next five years.[46]

Weakness in external questions derived in large part from the national government's lack of authority and its inability to control internal affairs. Rosas found it easy to obtain information and support from inside Brazil itself. Similarly, the Liberal cabinets' refusal to deal with the British over the slave trade stemmed only in part from anti-British feeling. The minister of foreign affairs in 1847 did not, as he admitted to the British envoy, believe that any government was able to suppress the trade, so great was the influence of the slave traders and the landowning interests allied with them.[47] The slave trade was the most obvious but not the only example of the Liberal party's subordination to vested interests.

Even if an attempt had been made by any of the five Liberal cabinets to enforce the law of November 1831 banning the slave trade, it is doubtful whether the existing apparatus of administration was then capable of suppressing the trade. The organs of governance were remarkable only for their slightness: the ministry of justice, on which responsibility for suppressing the trade would fall, contained only fourteen bureaucrats.[48] Outside of the national capital administration was inefficient, often corrupt, and always responsive to political pressure. The judiciary, the backbone of the governance of Brazil, was functioning poorly or not at all, with the most desirable posts being filled on a purely partisan basis and those in the more distant or isolated areas of the country either vacant or held by men who found reasons (personal or familial) for never actually occupying them. In 1847 only four of thirteen *juizes de direito* in Minas Gerais and one of six in Piauí province were resident in their *comarcas*.[49] Substituting for the absent judges were local officials, often with no legal training and usually belonging to local factions. In short, notwithstanding the recentralization of authority in 1841, the actual powers of the national government underwent a slow decline in these years.

By 1848 lack of success and diminished authority left the Liberals with a very uncertain hold on office. Weakened control over local affairs resulted in the election of a substantial minority of Conservative deputies to the new chamber that convened in May 1848. An attempt to attract support from the moderate wing of the Conservative party by making two of their leaders minister produced the cabinet of March 6, 1848. This ministry aroused every partisan feeling among the Liberal majority in the chamber and fell at the end of May. In what amounted to a final effort to restore credibility to government by the Liberal party, Francisco de Paula Sousa e Melo, a senator and veteran of the Nativist cause, was charged with forming a new cabinet. His integrity, genuine idealism, and long service made him widely respected. Paula e Sousa, as he was usually known, had been elected to the Lisbon Cortes and had sat in the Constituent Assembly. He now undertook the double task of restoring his party's prestige and resolving the nation's major problems by implementing the principal reforms long advocated by the Liberals.

The most immediate problem and therefore the most urgent reform was certainly the African slave trade. Since the Liberals had taken office in 1845, nearly 150,000 slaves had been imported. Liberal opinion in Europe and North America had turned decisively against slavery.[50] On September 1, 1848, the new cabinet introduced an anti-slave-trade bill which was designed to replace the ineffective law of November 7, 1831. Such an open challenge to the slave trading interests would have been bold at the best of times, but it was particularly courageous given the existing political atmosphere in the nation.

In February 1848 a street rising in Paris had overthrown the Orleans dynasty and replaced it with a radical, democratic republic. Throughout Europe there followed a series of risings, often nationalistic and egalitarian in mood, which brought down the established order. The influence of the 1848 revolutions was felt across the Atlantic. In Brazil they encouraged a mood of xenophobic social protest, particularly evident in Rio de Janeiro city and the province of Pernambuco. During the elections to the capital's municipal council anti-Portuguese riots broke out on September 7, recalling the days of July 1831 when the Exaltado street gangs had held the capital to political ransom.[51]

In these conditions the deputies debated the government's bill to suppress the slave trade. The most controversial article in the bill was the thirteenth and last, which repealed the existing law of November 1831 outright—a repeal that would retroactively legitimate the enslavement of all those imported. Debate was conducted in secret over two days, and on September 26, 1848, the deputies voted 32 to 29 to postpone further discussion of the clause until the next session, due to open in May 1849.[52] On September 28 the Paula e Sousa cabinet resigned as a result of its defeat on the bill. Making no effort to find a Liberal replacement, the emperor turned to the Conservative opposition. He summoned José da Costa Carvalho, the former regent and since 1841 ennobled as baron of

Mont'Alegre. The resulting cabinet was composed of the leading Conservatives, with Araújo Lima, now viscount of Olinda, included as nominal head to give greater prestige to the ministry.

The ouster of the Liberals from office triggered a crisis that shook the political order to its foundations. On October 4, 1848, the new cabinet prorogued the legislature and began the task of "dismounting" the Liberals' electoral machine by replacing presidents and moving *juizes de direito*. To this loss of national and local control all factions in the Liberal party save one acquiesced, due either to caution or to harsh experience learned in 1842. The single exception was the Praieira faction, which having since 1844 held unfettered mastery of Pernambuco province and being confident in its popular support, refused to submit. The faction's local leaders brushed aside the fears expressed by the Pernambucan deputies returning from the national capital. On November 7, 1848, a revolt began, spreading rapidly through the interior of the province.[53]

What made the Praieira rebellion formidable was its ability to win over the National Guard units, which were meant to act as a bulwark for the established order. By January 1849 the national government could count only on the province's capital, Recife, and even there its hold was uncertain. Yet this strong point proved sufficient. As in 1842, so in 1848 the steam packets allowed the government to rush troops to Pernambuco once it became clear that the rest of the nation was quiet. Thus reinforced, the garrison of Recife was able to repulse, if only by a narrow margin, a two-pronged assault on the city launched on the night of February 2, 1849. Having staked all on this gamble, the rebels lost any hope of victory. With the capture of their leaders in March the revolt collapsed, although guerrilla warfare continued until 1850 in the forests of southern Pernambuco.[54]

The Praieira rebellion has been interpreted by some historians as a social movement inspired by the revolutions of 1848 in Europe. Although those risings did influence the ideology of the revolt to a considerable extent, the Praieira rebellion is best understood as the last in the cycle of local revolts, nativist in inspiration, which had begun in Pernambuco in 1817. The rebellion also constituted the final assertion of the political tradition sanctioning the use of force to manifest rejection of unacceptable government policy. The very formidableness of the Praieira revolt discredited any future resort to arms. Political radicalism was discredited. Liberal doctrines lost their charm.

Buoyed up by this triumph, the Conservative government proceeded to consolidate the power and prestige of the nation-state both at home and abroad. In particular, it successfully resolved two major crises in external affairs: the first with Great Britain over the slave trade, the second with Juan Manuel Rosas over the affairs of the Río de la Plata. From the middle of 1849 British warships began to seize slaving vessels in Brazil's territorial waters. Although suppression of the trade was favored by several ministers, the Conservatives' long-standing ties with slaving and

MAP 5. Brazil in the Early 1850's. (All boundary lines are approximations only.)

landed interests, which had a redoubtable champion in Bernardo Pereira de Vasconcelos, inhibited any strong course of action.[55] Then in June 1850 the British authorized their cruisers to enter Brazilian harbors (though not Rio itself) and to seize and destroy all vessels suspected of slaving. Such intrusions could not be countenanced if Brazil were to exist as a nation. Unwilling and unable to fight Great Britain, the cabinet decided on July 12 to suppress the illicit slave trade.[56]

Several factors combined to favor this scheme. Vasconcelos's death in

May opportunely removed a chief obstacle to action, and the emperor let his support for the plan be known. The Conservatives who, if they were the allies, had never been the puppets of the slaving and landed interests now forced compliance by stressing the lack of alternatives. The cabinet skillfully turned anti-Portuguese sentiment against the slavers, many of them Portuguese nationals, by pointing to their reckless pursuit of profit as the cause for British aggression.[57]

The crisis of July 1850 was used by the Conservatives not just to suppress the slave trade but to reestablish the national government's authority over local affairs. On July 12 debate on the 1848 slave trade bill was resumed, and the controversial clause 13 repealing the 1831 law was rejected. Jurisdiction over slavers and ships was removed from the ordinary courts to the admiralty judges (*auditores da marinha*), who sat without a jury. The new law was promulgated on September 4, 1850. By then enforcement measures were already in place. The navy was rapidly built up, and on land it was made clear to all government officials that present favor and future advancement depended on energetic action. Most effective of all, the government summarily deported the most notorious slave traders of foreign nationality; others found it best to withdraw from Brazil.[58] Within eighteen months of the new law's enactment, the slave trade with Africa was, in the words of the British envoy in Rio, "utterly destroyed."[59] Given the weakness of the administrative system, the power of the interests favoring the trade, and the immemorial dependence on slave labor from Africa, the government's achievement was remarkable.[60]

This triumph was complemented in February 1852 by the defeat of Juan Manuel Rosas at the battle of Monte Caseros outside Buenos Aires and his ousting as dictator of Argentina. This victory was the product of almost three years of careful diplomacy by the Brazilian minister of foreign affairs, who worked to unite the opponents of Rosas into a war alliance.[61] So successful was the policy that the Brazilian naval and army units participating in Rosas's defeat were welcomed as liberators, not resented as invaders. For the first time in its existence as a nation, Brazil had achieved a diplomatic triumph—and one which established it as a major influence in the affairs of the Río de la Plata.[62]

While these successes were being secured in foreign affairs, the cabinet was pursuing a policy of reform and development at home. From 1849 to 1852 a plethora of new laws and decrees were promulgated. Some were designed to strengthen the nation's administrative structures both at the center and in the provinces. The department of the treasury at Rio and its agencies in the provinces were reformed. The judiciary was reorganized and career advancement made conditional on the actual occupation of posts. Positions in the National Guard became strictly appointive, and its units were brought under tight central control. The area of the Amazon basin, now beginning to prosper with the export of raw rubber, was created a province and so linked directly to the national government.[63]

Another group of laws and decrees was devoted to economic matters. A commercial law code was promulgated, and the fiduciary system was improved. A new, private Banco do Brasil, drawing heavily on the capital freed by the end of the slave trade, was authorized. A law regulating the ownership and acquisition of land was passed, a new government bureau being created to survey and register title. Steps were taken to encourage the flow of European colonists into Brazil.[64]

The third and final group of laws and decrees was concerned with developing the national infrastructure. The construction of a railroad from the national capital into its hinterland was authorized by a law of July 1852. The government took powers to reform the medical and law schools as well as schooling in the national capital (primary and secondary education elsewhere in Brazil having been under provincial jurisdiction since 1834). Steps were taken to improve sanitary conditions in the cities of Brazil, all adversely affected by the invasion in 1850 of epidemic yellow fever.[65]

September 1852 marked the thirtieth anniversary of Brazil's existence as a nation-state. Only a minority of Brazilians had experienced any form of rule save the Empire, and for most the nation was an accepted, indisputable reality. Circumstances appeared to be favoring Brazil. By its swift suppression of the slave trade the national government gained a strength and prestige in internal affairs it had not previously enjoyed. Partisan politics were out of favor and party identity largely in abeyance. Coffee exports continued their rapid expansion. Much capital was available for investment, and schemes for its employment began to multiply. An era of conciliation and improvements seemed at hand.

This new mood and the course of action to be followed were admirably expressed in the final words of the speech the emperor read to the General Assembly at its adjournment on September 4, 1852, almost 30 years to the day after D. Pedro I had proclaimed Brazil's independence:

Protected by our institutions, we have succeeded in enrolling ourselves among the independent and civilized peoples. To them [the institutions] are due the quiet and prosperity which we now enjoy. I trust therefore that you, on returning home, will endeavor to make them yet more respected, seeking to stamp out political dissensions and internal divisions, and that at the same time, you will teach your countrymen that observance of religious duties, respect for the laws, and love of work constitute the surest elements in the greatness and happiness of empires.[66]

III

The closing words of the emperor's speech constituted an oblique but frank recognition not only that Brazil was divided into two worlds but that the majority of Brazilians did not belong to the official nation. In Portuguese America in the late colonial period there had existed a fundamental duality in life and outlook, embodied on the one hand by D. Rodrigo de

Sousa Coutinho presenting at Lisbon his plans for the future of the New World dominions, and on the other by the poor, mulatto freedmen plotting at Salvador to rid their *pátria* of racial and economic exploitation. That duality remained no less sharp and profound some 50 years later, despite the gaining of political independence and the ending of all formal vestiges of economic colonialism. In the middle of the nineteenth century most of the seven or eight million people who inhabited Brazil enjoyed conditions of life no better than had been the lot of the Bahian conspirators.[67]

About a quarter of the population were slaves. A majority of the freeborn were black or mulatto, and so subject to discrimination. Most of the ordinary population lived in the countryside, serving as slaves, hired hands, or tenant labor. A minority existed as independent subsistence farmers but usually without any legal title to their holdings. The amenities of life, whether medicine or schooling, were notable by their absence. Disease, violent death, and exploitation were all too common. Conditions in the coastal cities were in some respects superior, especially for the small folk. In the early 1850's this section of the population, particularly the artisans, shared in the general prosperity created by the boom in export agriculture. The small folk had yet to face the challenge of industrialization in the Atlantic world—an increasing inflow of manufactured goods undercutting local products in price and quality.

The dichotomy between official and real nation was brought to the fore by the outcome of the imperial government's attempt in 1851 to carry out a national census and to introduce a system of civil registration of births and deaths.[68] To the ministers and indeed to all the members of the official world the two measures formed an intrinsic part of functioning nationhood, providing indispensable information for the conduct of government. Their adoption would bring Brazil into line with the practice of "independent and civilized peoples." To the inhabitants of the real nation the measures were unwelcome innovations that could only serve exploitative ends: the information provided would surely be used to levy fresh taxes, organize an efficient military draft, or impose some system of forced labor. In the provinces of Paraíba do Norte and Pernambuco late in 1851, the rural population took up arms rather than comply with the two measures. It was only thanks to mediation by Italian friars of the Capuchin order, active since 1840 in missionary work across the northeast, that bloodshed was averted and a major revolt prevented. In January 1852 the minister of the interior had no choice but to order the "suspension" of the census and of civil registration, a diplomatic way of abandoning both measures.[69]

Neither this episode, known as the "War of the Wasps," nor any other incident could, however, shake the members of the official nation in their belief that Brazil—thanks to its Portuguese heritage—was one of the Latin nations and potentially the France of South America. No opportunity was lost to demonstrate Brazil's civilized condition. When the French poet Lamartine was reported to be in need, a public subscription was at once opened in Rio and a considerable sum rapidly raised for personal presentation to him in Paris.[70] Devotion to the ways of civilization was evidenced by the willingness to wear—regardless of heat and humidity—the *casaca*. This black woolen tailcoat was a virtual uniform, distinguishing the members of the official world from the ordinary population. Indeed, *homem de casaca* became a shorthand way of describing anyone who qualified as a member of the official nation. Feijó is said to have remarked that, as Regent, he "could name as minister any man in a tailcoat."[71] A "man in a tailcoat" was presumed to be literate, cultured, and cognizant of the affairs of his country.

The official world was, in short, defined as much by a shared outlook and culture as by the possession of any common racial, social, or economic standing. Manuel Gonçalves Dias, whose sonnet beginning "Minha terra tem palmeiras, Onde canta o Sabiá" (In my land there are palm trees where the sabiá sings) first captured the essence of Brazil's separate nationhood, was neither wealthy nor white. Yet as a poet and a man of letters, Gonçalves Dias was beyond dispute an *homen de casaca*.[72] Despite the openness of the official world and the flexibility of its boundaries, it did exclude as much as it embraced. Many of the small folk now found that literacy and political participation, which had long set them apart from the ordinary population, no longer sufficed as qualifications for entry into the official world. Only notable talent or exceptional perseverance would admit individuals without wealth or connections.

If the institutional framework of the official world had been created during the decade following independence, it was the economic expansion of the 1830's and 1840's that made the official world a reality. In those years a network of newspapers, journals, book publishers, and printing houses emerged which together with the opening of theaters in the major towns brought into being what could be termed, but for the narrowness of its scope, a national culture.[73] Part of this official culture was the educational system created since 1822, which despite its manifest imperfections did serve the offspring of the *homens de casaca*. Deficiencies in education at the primary level could be remedied by resorting to private schooling, tutors, and even self-instruction. On the secondary level only a very few government-funded schools existed, all in the provincial capitals and mostly modeled on the Colégio D. Pedro II. The essential goal of these institutions, as well as of the more numerous private secondary schools, was to prepare their pupils for the entrance exams (*os preparatórios*) to the two faculties of law and the two faculties of medicine, which were the gateways to an individual's acceptance and success in the official nation. The law of December 3, 1841, which had restored the judiciary as the exclusive domain of the law graduate, combined with the growing wealth of the nation to produce an increasing demand for lawyers and doctors, keeping enrollment in all four faculties high.[74]

Money and influence (*empenhos*) could assure entry into the faculties, yet academic standards and fees were not so high as to exclude young men whose lack of wealth and connections were balanced by intelligence and determination. Some attended through the support of a patron, usually a relative or local notable; the offspring of the small folk and others literally worked their way through law or medical school.[75] Such students, if no more than a minority of those graduating, were prominent enough to stimulate the hopes of the ambitious and numerous enough to keep the official world from becoming a closed caste. In truth, the official world depended on this group of talented newcomers because Brazil was not yet plagued with an excess of educated men.[76]

The *bacharéis*, the core element of the *homens de casaca*, by 1850 formed the dominant cultural type in the official nation. Upon graduation from law school an ambitious *bacharel* would secure appointment first as a district attorney and then as a municipal judge. At the end of five years he could aspire to be named a *juiz de direito*. Once so appointed, increasing seniority and a modicum of talent and discretion would eventually gain him a post as *desembargador* on one of the four appeals courts (*relações*). Ambitious *desembargadores* maneuvered to be transferred to the Rio de Janeiro *relação*, from which judges of the Supreme Tribunal of Justice were usually drawn.[77]

Career advancement was aided by a skillful involvement in politics. A *juiz de direito* with the right connections or marked talent could hope for a seat in the provincial assembly. A *desembargador* could expect one almost by right. More crucial to a career in politics was to establish credentials as an administrator, the first step typically being service as president of a minor province, a position often awarded to dependable *juizes de direito*. This step passed, connections and good reputation could achieve appointment to a more important province. An effective president could also hope to be elected to the lower house by a grateful province. Once a national deputy, the *bacharel* could strive to penetrate the inner circle of power —cabinet, Senate, and Council of State. Although few succeeded, many aspired to scale these heights.[78]

Despite the triumph of party in the national polity, the functioning of the inner circle of power—notably the Senate and the Council of State— remained little affected by party allegiance, many of the politicians possessing only nominal links to one or the other party. The importance of the inner circle was greatly enhanced at the end of the 1840's by the eclipse of the court clique as a political factor. D. Pedro II, while retaining his affection and respect for those among whom he had been raised, ensured that they no longer enjoyed a role in politics. Thus when Paulo Barbosa da Silva returned in 1855 from virtual exile in Europe to resume his post as majordomo, he avoided the political connections which had forced him from Brazil in 1847.

By the early 1850's the emperor had perfected both his style of governance and his control over the political system. His self-control, patent desire for justice and fairness, and openness made him extremely effective and gained him much devotion. Few politicians could match D. Pedro's energy, his memory for detail, or his firmness of purpose. Inside the courteous, attentive, unassertive monarch of all the Brazilians existed an iron-willed ruler who was resolved not to surrender control of affairs. In the early 1850's this determination was neither galling nor resented. The political community shared D. Pedro II's concern for moderation and justice and was content to submit to his decisions as ruler. The emperor's dominant position was reinforced by the fact that although he had attended no faculty D. Pedro II was both in outlook and in culture the quintessence of a *bacharel*. From the start of his reign, his devotion to the arts, sciences, and education was unflagging.[79] The emperor served as a patron and a protector of all talented and aspiring *bacharéis*, a preference that encouraged ambitious men to shape their careers and personalities to that pattern.

What amounted to the monopolization of the political, administrative, and cultural life of Brazil by the *homens de casaca*, and more particularly the *bacharéis*, encouraged such men to perceive themselves and their official world as identical with the nation, an identification confirmed by the manifest failure of most Brazilians to behave as citizens of a nation should. From the emperor on down to beginning students in law and medical school, the *bacharéis* did not question that their identity with the nation gave them the right to impose their standards and their goals on the real world. Their self-confidence was revealed in a letter written by the president of Bahia province, who as a graduate of the Olinda law school, a doctor of laws from the University of Jena, and a former student at Paris, typified the *bacharéis*: "Prejudices and passing whims are the sole movitations of elections, in which the government takes no role, since it knows from the start who is most suitable [to be elected]."[80]

Politics in Brazil were therefore increasingly cut in two. At the parish level—among the voters—the influence of the notables, and to a much lesser degree of the small folk, remained significant. Among Brazil's few thousand electors government influence reigned supreme, enforcing the choice of candidates on the official *chapa*, whether for the provincial assembly, Chamber of Deputies, or the three-name list from which the emperor chose a new senator. These electoral triumphs served, as the ministers admitted to the emperor in November 1851, to make "the honors, posts, and rewards given to the government's agents so much electoral cash and the conduit for an unstable party influence."[81] The same point was more bluntly expressed in 1853 by an influential merchant and planter who deplored "the great damage wrought by political parties on our moribund institutions, which menace our country with disorganization and anarchy."[82]

Against the existing system of party politics two principal objections were increasingly leveled. The intensely partisan nature of the system barred all members of the opposition from holding any position of authority in the structures of government, and this exclusivism bred resentment and alienation. To the more radical members of the Liberal party the growing hegemony of the ruling Conservatives was simply *a oligarquia*, the oligarchy which had cornered power at the expense of the people.[83] By the early 1850's the system was under attack by those who argued that factional politics prevented both the mobilization of Brazil's resources and the employment of all men of capacity in a concerted pursuit of progress so that full nationhood might be achieved.[84]

The second objection to the system of party politics was that it made the whole system of law and order a simple tool of factional interests, thus depriving the government of control over the localities and depriving ordinary citizens of what was termed *segurança individual* (personal security).[85] In order to win elections, the ruling party had to depend upon the cooperation of local interests, which it backed with the apparatus of authority and to which it ceded the local organs of the policing power. Little or no distinction was made between private and public interests at the local level. Murder, violence, and other offenses against personal liberties were common; just how common became clear when statistics on crime in the nation were first collected in the early 1850's.[86]

The extent to which the first, official world was encircled and vitiated by the second was not limited to law and order. Even in fields where the nation seemed to have made progress since independence, the outcome was not necessarily beneficial to the official world. An example was the very rapid growth in the nation's population during the first half of the nineteenth century. Although the official world accepted that an expanding population was necessary if Brazil's vast interior were to be settled and its many natural resources opened up, the ruling circles wanted an increased population of the right type. Instead of the thousands of sturdy and industrious peasants from Europe they desired, between 1822 and 1852 three-quarters of a million slaves from Africa poured into Brazil. Although the predominance of males among the new slaves and their very high death rate reduced the demographic impact of this forced migration, it was sufficient to create fears about the effect on Brazil of "the slothful and impure civilization imported from Africa" and to foster support for the abolition of the slave trade.[87]

This influx from Africa had been offset to some extent by a continuing flow of Portuguese into Brazil since independence. Like the Africans most of the Portuguese were male, but being free, they were able to marry (often to local girls) and father large families—in sharp contrast to slaves with their pitifully low birthrate.[88] From the viewpoint of the official world the Portuguese were far from ideal settlers. A small minority were *homens de casaca*, either political refugees or professionals seeking a better living. Most, however, were poor and very young, often no more than ten or eleven years old. They crowded into the towns, seeking jobs as clerks and salesmen in the retail and wholesale trades. A minority served as mechanics and overseers on the plantations.[89] In any case, they followed traditional occupations and were often sojourners in the land, guarding profits and remitting capital home, a homeland to which only the most successful would retire in old age.[90]

The bulk of growth in population probably came, however, not from immigration but from a rising birthrate, particularly in the countryside. Numbers rose, despite wretched living conditions and endemic diseases such as smallpox. A swelling population was a main factor in pushing forward the frontiers of both cattle raising and subsistence agriculture, an advance evidenced by the multitude of new settlements which sprang up in these decades and the many new parishes and municipalities thus created.[91]

What was far more significant in the eyes of the official world was the advance of the export-agriculture frontier—above all the spread of coffee cultivation, which continued in the 1850's the rapid expansion begun in the preceding decades. As a letter of 1839 had remarked, coffee "is one of the most powerful agents of civilization we possess: coffee leaves in its wake the seeds of civilization."[92] The concept expressed more hope than truth, since life on the coffee frontier was crude and simple, offering few of the amenities of civilization. The planters were often near-illiterates, fiercely partisan, and hopelessly parochial in outlook.[93] For the official world the greatest benefit from coffee was the wealth it brought to Rio city, the indispensable bastion of civilization. Between the early 1840's and the early 1850's trade through the port of Rio de Janeiro increased in value by nearly two-thirds.[94]

The more traditional of Brazil's export crops, such as sugar and cotton, continued to prosper, although because their increase in exports did not match the boom in coffee their importance as staples diminished.[95] In the far north, the province of Pará finally began to recover from the ravages of the Independence period, enjoying a boom based on North American and European demand for the wild rubber tapped in its forests. In the far south, the end of the Farroupilha revolt in 1845 made possible the recuperation and expansion of mule and cattle breeding, the animals being indispensable to the expanding coffee regions for transportation or as foodstuffs.[96]

These developments in export agriculture, although they brought a growing prosperity to Brazil and swelled revenues for the imperial government, wrought no fundamental change in the economic structure. No single, integrated, national economy had been created. The existing regional economies remained distinct and disparate; and their internal integration was not much improved. The coffee crop was still brought down to Rio de Janeiro city over dirt roads on the backs of mules. A week of rain sufficed to make these tracks impassable and produced a shortage of coffee for the export houses.[97] Nor had the growth of the export trade produced any improvement in communications between the different regions of Brazil. At the start of the 1850's local steamship lines existed only in Rio Grande do Sul, Rio de Janeiro bay, and Bahia province.[98] The steam packet company set up with government backing in the late 1830's remained the sole means of communication. In technical terms, there was little spin-off from the export boom, which possessed very slight forward and backward linkages.

The economic expansion of the 1830's and 1840's had likewise failed to assist the growth of what may be termed a "social" infrastructure, in particular a developed system of education. The Ato Adicional of 1834 assigned to the provinces responsibility for primary and secondary education and other social services, and until 1845 the provinces had received sufficient subsidies from the national government to maintain a substantial network of primary schools.[99] The withdrawal of these subventions in 1845 left the provinces unable to provide any adequate system of education so that the number of children receiving a formal education rapidly declined. By the early 1850's no more than 61,700 pupils across Brazil were enrolled in primary schools, and only 3,713 in secondary schools. It was obvious that the educational system was not serving the national interest.[100]

To the Brazilians of the official world who in the early 1850's desired that the nation should keep up with "the independent and civilized peoples," the way ahead, though not easy, was both simple and clear. Brazil must introduce the technological innovations and the social improvements which had led to progress in other nations in the last 30 years. "The country [must] understand how advantageous it would be for it to follow the United States in its system of railroads and canals and thus favor immigration and settlement."[101] None of these benefits could be secured without the provision of basic literacy for the masses and professional training for those who would rule the nation. Factional strife had to be eliminated and the security of individual citizens assured. Only thus could the ordinary inhabitants of Brazil be made part of the nation. Not until the entire population were united in securing for Brazil the blessings of progress would full, functioning nationhood be achieved.

This vision of the future, which perceived functioning nationhood in terms of adopting external models and seeking material progress, would for the next half-century give direction to the ruling circles. The dangers of the past decades no longer threatened Brazil, which could now strive to catch up with the nations of Europe and North America. In June 1853, Eusébio de Queirós, who had graduated from the Olinda law school in 1832, served as chief of police of the national capital from 1833 to 1844, and as minister of justice been chiefly responsible for suppressing the slave trade with Africa, voiced the mood prevailing in the official world: "Brazil is decidedly developing, showing progress in every respect. If only I might sleep for a hundred years!"[102]

REFERENCE MATTER

Notes

Complete authors' names, titles, and publication data are given in the Bibliography, the opening section of which consists of a discussion of the archival and other sources consulted. While modern spelling of Portuguese words, proper names, and places is used in the text, in the Notes and Bibliography authors and titles are cited as they appear on the title page of the original works. The following abbreviations are used in the Notes:

CL   *Collecção das leis brasileiras, desde a chegada da corte ate a epoca*
          da independencia. Vol. 1: *1808–1810,* and vol. 2: *1811–1816.* Ouro
          Prêto. 1834–35.

Correio   *O Correio Braziliense.* London, 1808–22.

DH   Biblioteca Nacional. *Documentos históricos.* Vols. 101–9: *Revolução*
            de 1817. Rio, 1953–55. Vol. 110: *Devassa de 1801 em Pernambuco.*
            Rio, 1955.

FO   Foreign Office. Series 13 and series 63. Public Record Office, London.

LB   *Collecção das leis do Brasil para o anno* (1808–89). Rio.

INTRODUCTION

1. Nation and nation-state are distinct in conceptual terms, as Walker Connor has recently stressed. See "A Nation Is a Nation," p. 379. When studied as historical phenomena the two are, however, extremely difficult to keep distinct. Nor for the purposes of this study is it necessary to do so, since in the case of Brazil the emergence of self-perception as a nation and the formation of a nation-state occurred almost simultaneously.

2. That homogeneity in speech, culture, and ethnicity is frequently lacking in nation-states does not contradict the theory. Only a handful of nation-states, of which Switzerland is the exemplar, have been built from the start on a basis other than linguistic and cultural homogeneity. Recognition of, much less support for, pluralism in language and culture by nation-states is a recent and often reluctant development.

3. The topic of nationalism has attracted a devoted band of researchers, in-

cluding Karl W. Deutsch, J. H. Carlton Hayes, Elie Kedourie, Hans Kohn, Boyd C. Shafer, Antony D. Smith, and Louis L. Snyder, to name but a few. The influence of their studies on wider scholarship has been limited, not comparable to the impact of, for example, the theory of recent world development propounded by Wallerstein in *The Modern World System*. The scholarship on nationalism is surveyed and assessed in Shafer, *Nationalism*; and A. D. Smith, "Nationalism." For an overview of the rise of the nation-state, see Seton-Watson, *Nations and States*.

4. "The consensus of opinion among all disciplines is that the term nation is tantalizingly ambiguous," involving "many differences of opinion within each discipline." See Snyder, *The Meaning of Nationalism*, p. 54; and Tilly, *The Formation of National States*, p. 6.

5. See B. Anderson, *Imagined Communities*, pp. 15–16.

6. One reason for the lack of impact of the scholarly studies mentioned in n. 3 above is that they have not only focused primarily on nationalism rather than on the nation and nation-state but have overwhelmingly perceived and analyzed nationalism as though it were an intellectual phenomenon.

7. Potter, "Nationalism," p. 930.

8. Excellent testimony to this effect is provided by the doyen of scholars on nationalism, who in old age wrote: "Most of my adult life has been devoted to observation and study of nationalism. My interest in it was first aroused by the outbreak of World War I. That event took me by surprise and shocked me out of the easy optimism about a future of uninterrupted progress and international peace which I had shared with many of my generation." See Hayes, *Nationalism*, p. v.

9. Potter, "Nationalism," p. 935.

10. The problems with what might be termed the traditional approach are epitomized by Alan Smith, *The Emergence of a Nation State*. The work discusses neither the causes for the evolution of England into a nation-state, nor the effects on English society of that evolution.

11. Hobsbawm, *Workers*, p. 6.

12. If the recognition of the people, rather than the monarch, as the basis of state authority were the test for the changeover, then the dates would be 1649 and 1789 in England and France respectively. So tardy an emergence of the nation-state offends the longevity prejudice discussed above; moreover, and more important, in both instances a plausible case for an earlier date can be made.

13. For a succinct overview of the confused and contentious history of the nation-states in Central and Eastern Europe, see Seton-Watson, *Nations and States*, pp. 89–185.

14. Lipset, *The First New Nation*. Only Serbia, which first revolted in 1805 and gained partial autonomy in 1815, and Greece, which rebelled in 1822, can dispute precedence as nation-states with the countries of Latin America. Total political independence was proclaimed by Argentina in 1816, Chile in 1818, Mexico in 1821, Brazil in 1822, and the remainder of continental Latin America by 1828. Panama was not separated from Colombia until 1903.

15. Not until after the 1910 revolution did identification with its pre-Columbian culture predominate in Mexico over its Hispanic and European heritage.

16. The single English-language work of note on the subject is Burns, *Nationalism in Brazil*.

17. In Mexico too a monarchy was adopted after achieving independence, but it was ephemeral.

18. The three exceptions, as explained in Chapter 5, were the war with Argentina from 1825 to 1828 for possession of what is now Uruguay, involvement in the affairs of Portugal from 1826 to 1831, and the legal and economic privileges held by Great Britain from 1822 to 1844.

19. A classic study of this dilemma is Linz, "Early State-Building."

20. Potter, "Nationalism," p. 925.

21. The only exception to this rule in the Americas was the fragmentation in 1838 of the Central American Union, originally created in 1825, into five independent republics.

CHAPTER I

1. This honorific, Dom for men and Dona for women, was applied to those of royal and noble birth and also to members of the hierarchy of the Catholic Church, which was the state religion in Portugal.

2. On the international position of Portugal in this period, see Serrão, *História*, 6: 316–24.

3. Maxwell, *Conflicts*, p. 234; and Alden, "Late Colonial Brazil," pp. 627–41, and table 11. See also Novais, *Brasil e Portugal*, pp. 287–94.

4. As used in this work the word "Crown" means not simply the monarch alone but the immediate circle of individuals—family, favorites, and officials—who could influence the monarch or who, as the marquess of Pombal did from 1750 to 1777, wielded power in his or her name.

5. Two printed transcripts of this speech exist, the first in Carneiro de Mendonça, *O intendente Câmara*, pp. 277–98; and the second in an article by Pires de Lima, "Memória," pp. 405–22. The first is taken from a copy in the Biblioteca Nacional at Rio de Janeiro; the second from one in the Arquivo Histórico Ultramarino at Lisbon, which, unlike the first, is dated: "outr.° 1797." The differences between the two texts are minor and usually insignificant. The second is used here.

6. Pires de Lima, "Memória," pp. 420–22.

7. Ibid., pp. 406–7.

8. Ibid., p. 407.

9. See Prado Jr., *The Colonial Background*, pp. 1–2. This work remains the best account in English of the physical and social setting of Portuguese America at the close of the colonial period.

10. Pires de Lima, "Memória," p. 407.

11. Boxer, *Golden Age*, pp. 260–67.

12. Ibid., pp. 273–74.

13. See tables 2.5 and 2.18 in Lugar, "Merchant Community," pp. 78, 100; see also table 12 in Alden, "Late Colonial Brazil," p. 651. The types of products sent to Portugal by its American colonies and their value in 1798 and 1806 are given in table 11 of Alden, p. 647.

14. Alden, "Late Colonial Brazil," p. 643; and Prado Jr., *Colonial Background*, pp. 242–44.

15. Alden, "Late Colonial Brazil," pp. 635–39, 641–42.

16. Ibid., pp. 648–49.

17. Ibid., pp. 628–37; and Lugar, "Merchant Community," pp. 96–110.

18. Alden, "Late Colonial Brazil," pp. 629–31, 645–56; Prado Jr., *Colonial Background*, pp. 195–212; and Maxwell, *Conflicts*, pp. 84–90.

19. See Bauss, "Rio Grande do Sul." On the mule trade in general, see Goulart, *Tropas*.

20. Alden has estimated the population as being, at the minimum, 1,555,000 ca. 1776 and 2,000,000 ca. 1800; see tables 1 and 2 in "Late Colonial Brazil," pp. 603–4. Other authorities would set these figures higher by a third; see Merrick and Graham, *Population*, pp. 28–29.

21. See table 4, based on a population count of 1810, in Alden, "Late Colonial Brazil," p. 607.

22. Boxer, *Golden Age*, pp. 1–9, 162–203; and Rodrigues, "Influence of Africa." A classic study of the influence of African culture on that of the planters in the northeast is Freyre, *The Masters*.

23. Russell-Wood, *Black Man*; Klein, "Colonial Freedman"; and Schwartz, "Manumission."

24. Table 5 in Alden, "Late Colonial Brazil," p. 611.

25. Boxer, *Race Relations*, pp. 98–99.

26. Prado Jr., *Colonial Background*, p. 106.

27. Hemming, "Indians."

28. On internal conditions in Portugal in the second half of the eighteenth century, see Serrão, *História*, vol. 6.

29. *Reinóis* meant "those from the Kingdom [*reino*]" of Portugal. The New World–born were also termed *filhos da terra*, or "offspring of the land."

30. See the comments in the letter of Sebastião Xavier de Vasconcelos Coutinho, Rio, July 30, 1791, quoted in Maxwell, *Conflicts*, p. 192; and those in the letter of the marquess of Lavradio, Rio, July 5, 1770, quoted in Alden, *Royal Government*, p. 482. See also the remarks on the inhabitants of Salvador written in 1802 by a *europeu*, Santos Vilhena, in *Recopilação*, 1: 43–45.

31. After the governor was deposed, in Nov. 1710, proposals that Pernambuco become a republic "like that of Venice" or accept the rule of the king of France were firmly rejected; see Boxer, *Golden Age*, pp. 113–14.

32. See Merrick and Graham, *Population*, p. 29; their figure of 460,000 is contested by Dauril Alden, who, in a personal communication to the author, estimated total immigration during the century at half that.

33. Only in the captaincy of Santa Catarina in the far south, which was settled by the Crown between 1748 and 1753 with colonists from the Azores, did an area reflect the vernacular and culture of a single region of Portugal; see Boxer, *Golden Age*, pp. 250–54.

34. On Portuguese migration in general, see Prado Jr., *Colonial Background*, pp. 91–96; and on migration during the gold rush, see Russell-Wood, "Colonial Brazil," pp. 554–55, 575–76. Research into this interesting and important topic is badly needed.

35. At the end of the eighteenth century two-thirds of the merchants at Salvador whose origin can be determined were born in Portugal; see table 1.5 in Lugar, "Merchant Community," p. 55.

36. See Serrão, *História*, 6: 314–15.

37. Although simplistic in approach, F. A. Oliveira Martins' biography of Diogo Inácio Pina Manique, who served as Intendente Geral da Polícia da Côrte e Reino (Intendant of Police for the Court and Kingdom) from 1780 until his death in 1805, provides illuminating materials on the workings of government in this period; see *Pina Manique*.

38. Maxwell, *Conflicts*, p. 207.

39. See Boxer, *Golden Age*, p. 324.

40. Pires de Lima, "Memória," p. 407.

41. Ibid., p. 411.
42. Alden, "Late Colonial Brazil," p. 625; and Lugar, "Merchant Community," p. 103.
43. Pires de Lima, "Memória," p. 411.
44. Carleton Smith, "Two Copies."
45. Most notorious was the incident of the Crown's suppression in 1711, after the necessary licenses to print had been granted, of Father Andreoni's *Cultura e opulência do Brasil*, a work that gave precise information on how to reach the newly discovered gold mines. So thorough was the suppression that only six surviving copies of the 1711 edition appear to have escaped destruction. See Boxer, *Golden Age*, pp. 369–70, 419; and Antonil, pp. 15–18, 35–46.
46. Ramos de Carvalho, *Reformas*, pp. 92–109; and Santos Vilhena, *Recopilação*, 1: 283–98, 303–4.
47. See Cardozo, "Azeredo Coutinho," pp. 19, 27–34; and Homem de Mello, "Documentos," pp. 5–7.
48. Hoornaert, "The Catholic Church," p. 554; and Boxer, *Golden Age*, pp. 127, 395.
49. See Russell-Wood, "Brazilian Student." Two universities had originally existed in Portugal, the royal university at Coimbra and a Jesuit university at Évora (closed when the Jesuits were expelled).
50. On the employment by the Crown of American-born graduates for the advancement of scientific knowledge, see Simon, *Scientific Expeditions*.
51. Between Pombal's reform of Coimbra, in 1772, and 1808, 584 *brasileiros* enrolled and 347 graduated. The precise figures for enrollment are: 1772–75, 116; 1776–80, 81; 1781–85, 88; 1786–90, 88; 1791–95, 77; 1796–1800, 54; 1801–5, 61; 1806–8, 19. For graduation, 1776–80, 87; 1781–85, 59; 1786–90, 59; 1791–95, 55; 1796–1800, 39; 1801–5, 42; 1806–8, 7. See Barman and Barman, "Prosopography."
52. Hoornaert, "Catholic Church," pp. 554–55.
53. Pires de Lima, "Memória," p. 408.
54. Schwartz, *Sovereignty*, pp. 239–313; and Santos Vilhena, *Recopilação*, 2: 308.
55. There is no evidence to support Andrée Mansuy-Diniz Silva's claim that the captaincies of the dissolved Estado were after 1774 "integrated into an enlarged Estado do Brasil"; see her "Portugal and Brazil," pp. 478–79.
56. Pires de Lima, "Memória," p. 408.
57. Boxer, *Golden Age*, p. 275.
58. Alden, *Royal Government*, p. 273.
59. The nine others were subordinated (*capitanias subalternas*) with only a governor; see the excellent commentary in ibid., p. 40.
60. Ibid., pp. 30–44, 143–44, 452–58, 480–81.
61. Pires de Lima, "Memória," pp. 408–9.
62. Morton, "Military," pp. 250–55.
63. Opinion (*parecer*) of the *camara municipal* of Campos, Feb. 3, 1812, quoted in the obituary of the baron of Santa Rita, *Jornal do Commercio* (Rio de Janeiro), June 19, 1854; and Morton, "Military," pp. 264–65.
64. Pires de Lima, "Memória," pp. 408–9.
65. A list of judicial positions and their holders is given in the *Almanach do anno de 1807*; see "Almanak de Lisboa," pp. 170–71, 177.
66. Schwartz, *Sovereignty*, pp. 3–21.

67. Pires de Lima, "Memória," p. 410.
68. Ibid.
69. Alden, *Royal Government*, pp. 437–43; Santos Vilhena, *Recopilação*, 2: 457–86; and Hoornaert, "Catholic Church," pp. 549–54.
70. Pires de Lima, "Memória," p. 410.
71. Prado Jr., *Colonial Background*, pp. 356–57.
72. Alden, *Royal Government*, pp. 422–30; and see Boxer, *Portuguese Society*, pp. 72–109.
73. See Santos Vilhena, *Recopilação*, 2: 77–79.
74. Schwartz, *Sovereignty*, pp. 256–57.
75. The ban was specifically against lay bodies, because the formation of lay brotherhoods and third orders of the Catholic Church, which were voluntary associations, was permitted. They existed under the oversight of the clergy, and the Crown could and did intervene to control them.
76. The abolition of the Bahian Mesa do Bem Comum was motivated by Pombal's suppression in 1755 of the Lisbon board because of its overt opposition to his economic policies; see Lugar, "Merchant Community," p. 27.
77. See, for example, Schwartz, *Sovereignty*, pp. 326–41.
78. Alden, *Royal Government*, pp. 443–46; and Kuznesof, "Clans." An almanac for the captaincy of Rio de Janeiro in 1794 identifies almost all the *ordenanca* officers as landowners; see "Almanak histórico," pp. 237–42.
79. Morton, "Royal timber"; and Boxer, *Golden Age*, pp. 306–8.
80. Letter to Luís Pinto de Sousa Coutinho, quoted in Maxwell, *Conflicts*, pp. 46–47.
81. Manoel Cardozo's article on Bishop Azeredo Coutinho's career in Pernambuco is an excellent case study of such an official and his fate; see "Azeredo Coutinho."
82. See Boxer, *Golden Age*, pp. 144–45.
83. Whereas the Spanish monarchs lavished titles of nobility on the most prominent of their New World subjects, the Portuguese Crown steadfastly avoided granting any titles, and it was parsimonious in bestowing on its American vassals habits in the three orders of knighthood, which it liberally awarded in Portuguese Asia; see ibid., pp. 308–9.
84. Maxwell, *Conflicts*, pp. 230, 234–35. A percipient assessment of Sousa Coutinho's character and abilities is given in an obituary, translated from the German original, published in *Investigador Portuguez*, 12 (Apr. 1815): 181–82.
85. An individual's race was to a large degree determined by his or her socioeconomic status, as the following anecdote from the early nineteenth century makes clear. "A mulatto enters into holy orders or is appointed a magistrate, his paper stating him to be a white man, but his appearance plainly denoting the contrary. In conversing on one occasion with a man of colour who was in my service, I asked him if a certain *capitão-mor* was not a mulatto man; he answered: 'he was, but is not now.' I begged him to explain, when he added, 'Can a *capitão-mor* be a mulatto man?'" See Koster, *Travels in Brazil*, p. 175.
86. The word "men" is used advisedly. By law the only females to possess independent legal standing were widows. For a recent study of the life cycle among the different social levels in a rural town of eighteenth-century Portuguese America, see Metcalf, "Families."
87. See Santos Vilhena, *Recopilação*, 1: 5.
88. For an early use of the word *pátria* in this sense by a *brasileiro* student,

see the letters of Antônio Alvares Pereira, dated 1695 to 1698, quoted in Russell-Wood, "Brazilian Student." A sermon preached in 1718 to the American-born students at Coimbra used the word in precisely this sense: "The conversations, the friends, the excursions, the amusement, everything appears before our eyes, everything gives us pain! This air was more benign, the waters more pure, the winter not so severe, the trees I never saw without leaves, the fields there were never without fruit! . . . Oh, Homeland, Homeland, how distant are you? Your very stones, your very woods, what consolation could they now not give me if I could cast my eyes upon them!" See Cardozo, "Internationalism," pp. 191–92.

89. The multiple loyalties are evident from Santos Vilhena's remark already quoted in the text and his characterization of the prince regent "as the Head of the Nation, as the Father of the Homeland" (*como a Chefe da Nação, como a Pai da Pátria*); see *Recopilação*, 1: 5, 6.

90. See the stanza from *Estaquiados*, written by Frei Manuel de Santa Maria Itaparicá, quoted in Osório, *Itaparicá*, p. 113. Compare this statement with one contained in the diary of a drummer boy involved in the rising against Spanish rule in Upper Peru (modern Bolivia): "*Patria* is the soil on which we step and on which we live; *Patria* is the real cause which we must defend at all costs; for the *Patria* we must sacrifice our interests and our lives," quoted in Arnade, *Emergence*, p. 52.

91. These differing perceptions can be deduced from Santos Vilhena, *Recopilação*, 1: 5, and from the depositions given at the judicial inquiry into the "Conspiracy of the Tailors" at Salvador in 1798, transcribed in "Inconfidencia da Bahia."

92. See Manuel da Câmara de Bethencourt e Sá to D. Pedro I, undated [1822], in *Câmaras municipais*, 2: 387.

93. See the recent edition of this work, published at Belo Horizonte in 1977.

94. It is because the reader seeing "Brazil" immediately endows it with its modern meaning that the word (although extensively used in the eighteenth century) has not been employed in this chapter; it will not appear until the text reaches the period when the word took on its current meaning.

95. Martinho de Melo e Castro to the viscount of Barbacena, quoted in Maxwell, *Conflicts*, p. 107.

96. See Santos Vilhena, *Recopilação*, 1: 5. In 1797, the minister of the colonies referred to the "provinces of America, which are known under the generic name of Brazil"; see Pires de Lima, "Memória," p. 401.

97. A modern parallel, a word equally equivocal in meaning, is "America": does it refer to the Western Hemisphere, to the northern continent, or to the United States alone?

98. Speech by José Joaquim Carneiro de Campos, future marquess of Caravelas, session of June 19, 1823, in *Diario*, 1: 245.

99. An ephemeral academy founded at Salvador in 1724 was called Academia Brasílica dos Esquecidos; see Burns, "Enlightenment," pp. 269–70. Santos Vilhena called his work "uma collecção de noticias brasilicas"; see *Recopilação*, 1: 5. In 1808, at the close of our period, Hipólito José da Costa, who did perceive Brazil as his *pátria*, founded in London a monthly periodical, which he named O *Correio Braziliense*. The adjectives used could be translated as "Brazilic" and "Brazilial."

100. As Santos Vilhena, using the word *pátria* in its more general sense, noted: "What makes the citizen is property, and the fear of losing it is what unites him to the *pátria*." See *Recopilação*, 2: 931.

101. Hoornaert, "Catholic Church," pp. 551–55; and Russell-Wood, *Fidalgos*, pp. 38–41, 106–7, 116–36.

102. For the situation in the captaincies of Bahia, Pernambuco, and Minas Gerais, see Boxer, *Golden Age*, pp. 100, 134–35; Russell-Wood, *Fidalgos*, p. 368; and Maxwell, *Conflicts*, pp. 92–95.

103. See Gudeman and Schwartz, "Cleansing."

104. See, for example, Schwartz, *Sovereignty*, pp. 336–43.

105. At the start of the "War of the Mascates" in 1710, the destruction of the *pelourinho* (pillar of royal justice) in the newly created town of Recife exposed those responsible to savage retribution by the new governor of Pernambuco, sent to restore royal authority. In Minas Gerais in 1720, the count of Assumar ordered garroted and dismembered without any trial a gold miner who incited a rising and advocated the independence of the region; see Boxer, *Golden Age*, pp. 113, 120–21, 196–97.

106. It can be argued that since a number of separate, often competitive, economies existed in Portuguese America, no basis for a single ruling class existed. For a contrary interpretation of the notables' class cohesion, outlook, and political capacities, see Manchester, "Aristocracy."

107. The Albany Congress, the eleventh inter-colonial conference since 1684, had been summoned by the British government to treat with the Indians. The delegates exceeded their instructions by approving the plan of union. The unfavorable reaction of the colonial legislatures was due, in R. C. Newbold's opinion, in part to fears "that it might endanger their rights and liberties" and in part to a reluctance "to surrender to a central government the authority demanded by the Albany plan"; see *Albany Congress*, pp. 118, 170. On the Articles of Confederation, see Jensen, *Articles*.

108. Maxwell, *Conflicts*, pp. 224–25.

109. Ibid., pp. 107–14.

110. For an account of the conspiracy see ibid., pp. 115–76; and Santos, *Inconfidência*.

111. Maxwell, *Conflicts*, pp. 90–98, 199–200. The sole conspirator not to belong to either group was Joaquim José da Silva Xavier, "o Tiradentes" (the Toothpuller), who became a Brazilian national hero because he alone of those arrested was executed.

112. On the form of the intellectual responses to the American and French revolutions, see Mota, *Idéia*.

113. Only twenty of the Bahian students can be identified as sons of major landowners and "fewer still" as offspring of the leading merchants of Salvador; see Morton, "Conservative Revolution," p. 55.

114. Cardozo, "Internationalism," pp. 190–192.

115. See the speeches of José Bonifácio de Andrada e Silva, a 1787 graduate, and J. J. Carneiro de Campos, future marquess of Caravelas, a 1797 graduate, session of May 31, 1823, in *Diario*, 1: 155–56.

116. Rizzini, *Hipólito da Costa*, pp. 3–15; and Dourado, *Hipolito da Costa*, 1: 15–100.

117. See Novais, *Brasil e Portugal*, pp. 213–39, 299–302; and Galloway, "Agricultural Reform."

118. Morton, "Conservative Revolution," p. 55.

119. This statement is based on a survey of the officeholders in these institu-

tions, listed in the *Almanach do anno de 1807*; see "Almanak de Lisboa," pp. 36–45, 79–93, 99–100, 162–78, 207–33.

120. See Maxwell, "Generation," pp. 131–39.

121. Ibid., pp. 202–3; and Oliveira Martins, *Pina Manique*, pp. 271–307.

122. An anonymous subversive letter received in 1793 by the *juiz de fora* of Rio de Janeiro occasioned a full judicial inquiry into what proved to be a mare's nest; see "Autos de exame." In 1794 the viceroy closed down the Rio Literary Society (founded in 1786) and when informed that its members were continuing to meet for private conversations, often voicing—it was alleged—heterodox ideas, authorized a *devassa* (legal investigation), which resulted in the arrest of ten men. No evidence of any conspiracy was discovered, but those arrested in Dec. 1794 were not released until June 1797. See "Devassa ordenado"; and Higgs, "Unbelief and Politics." In 1801 the delation of some incidental disloyal remarks made during a private conversation between two notables threw the Crown's agents in Pernambuco into a frenzy of activity. The ensuing judicial investigation petered out as the local community closed ranks to prevent awkward inquiries into their behavior and beliefs. See *DH*, v. 110; on the cover-up, see the testimony of Francisco do Rêgo Barros and D. Jorge Eugênio de Lossio e Seibltz, *DH*, 110: 89–91, 94.

123. In one case, a young physician was kept in Lisbon from 1797 to 1800, denied a passport to return home to Minas Gerais; see the obituary of Faustino José de Azevedo reprinted in Macedo, *Rio Verde*, pp. 33–35.

124. Oliveira Martins, *Pina Manique*, pp. 291–92; and Maxwell, *Conflicts*, pp. 222–23.

125. Maxwell, *Conflicts*, pp. 204–6.

126. Maxwell, "Generation," pp. 131–39.

127. See Alden, "Late Colonial Brazil," p. 608; and Boxer, *Race Relations*, pp. 120–21.

128. See the informative discussion of the social background of the witnesses in the judicial inquiry and the Inquisition proceedings held at Rio de Janeiro in 1794 in Higgs, "Unbelief and Politics." See also a comment by Santos Vilhena: "The whites native to the country will only be soldiers, traders, notaries, clerks, officials in one of the administrative tribunals or of the fiscal or judicial courts, or some other public calling which does not contain blacks, such as surgeons, druggists, ship pilots, masters or captains of vessels, cashiers of warehouses, etc. Others, but few or rare, work as painters, sculptors, goldsmiths, etc." See *Recopilação*, 1: 140–41.

129. Santos, *Inconfidência*, p. 101. The son, José Joaquim da Maia Barbalho, gained posthumous fame through having in 1786 approached Thomas Jefferson, then American envoy in Paris, with a plea for help from the United States in securing the independence of Brazil; see Maxwell, *Conflicts*, pp. 80–81.

130. At Rio de Janeiro during the viceroyalty of the marquess of Lavradio, when militia officers came on official occasions to compliment the viceroy the white officers were admitted first and could kiss his hand, but those of the mulatto and black units were barred from the room and had to bow to him from a distance; see Alden, *Royal Government*, p. 483.

131. Ibid.; and see the comments on the mulattoes and American-born blacks living in Salvador by Santos Vilhena, a *europeu*, in *Recopilação*, 1: 46.

132. The writings on this conspiracy are now copious. The most percipient account in English is Morton, "Conservative Revolution," pp. 113–51; and see

Ramos, "Social Revolution," and the works quoted therein. The ideological motivation for the conspiracy was sharpened by the soaring prices of basic foodstuffs.
Economic pressures on the small folk probably explain why the plot emerged
when it did; see Maxwell, *Conflicts*, pp. 217–18.

133. In addition, two men who escaped arrest were tried in absentia, being
convicted. A slave who was arrested committed suicide before the trial, at which
he was acquitted. Only the 32 men were present at the trial. See "Inconfidencia da
Bahia," pp. 172–77, 345–46.

134. Of those arrested and accused, 22 were born in Salvador, 4 elsewhere
in Bahia, 4 in the northeast, 1 in Portugal, and 1 in Africa. Of the 32, 18 were
freeborn, 4 freedmen, and 10 slaves. Of the freeborn, 10 were white and 8 mulatto.
Of the freedmen and slaves all save 1 (an African-born slave) were mulatto.

135. By occupation, 10 of the accused were tailors, 7 enlisted soldiers, 2 car-
penters, 1 stonemason, 1 embroiderer, 1 gem setter, 1 shoemaker, 1 hairdresser,
1 barber-surgeon, 1 royal teacher, 1 *letrado* (licensed to practice surgery), and 2
army lieutenants. There were also 3 slaves with no declared skills and 1 drifter
without profession. Since 1 of the accused was recorded as both soldier and tailor,
the total for occupations is 33.

136. "Inconfidencia da Bahia," p. 87; and see Mattoso, *Presença francesa*, pp.
9–33.

137. Testimony of José Felix [da Costa], a *pardo* (mulatto) slave, Sept. 5, 1798;
and conversation of João de Deus do Nascimento with Joaquim José da Veiga,
a *pardo* freedman ironworker, as reported in the latter's denunciation, Aug. 27,
1798, in "Inconfidencia da Bahia," pp. 88, 111–12. Lucas Dantas de Amorim
Torres, a freedman soldier, and João de Deus do Nascimento, a freeborn tailor,
both mulattoes, were the moving spirits in the conspiracy.

138. See Sousa Coutinho to Fernando José de Portugal, Lisbon, Jan. 9, 1799,
in ibid., pp. 320–21. Of the half of those accused who were condemned 3 were
publicly hanged and quartered, with the parts displayed at their former residences;
6 were expelled forever from the royal dominions, being shipped to Africa and
dumped at the trading posts of other nations; 3 were banished to distant captaincies; and 4 received prison terms. The remaining accused were acquitted or
released on appeal. The weight of punishment fell on the mulattoes, the freedmen
among them suffering the most, followed by the freeborn and the slaves. Not surprisingly, 6 of the 10 whites were ultimately acquitted, with the other 4 receiving
prison terms.

139. R. Stein, "Free Men of Colour."

140. See Flory, "Fugitive Slaves." In the decades following independence, this
charge was to be often leveled at ambitious politicians of humble origin and mixed
ancestry.

141. Denunciation against Francisco de Paula Cavalcante by José da Fonseca
Silva e Sampaio, Recife, May 21, 1801, in *DH*, 110: 19–20. The delator was an
American-born merchant of Recife.

142. It is patent that by denouncing what were strictly private conversations
Silva e Sampaio breached the accepted code of behavior, as his own statements to
the inquiry reveal; see his deposition of May 28, 1801, in ibid., pp. 30–33.

143. As José Francisco de Paula Cavalcante wrote to his brother, Francisco
de Paula Cavalcante, after arriving in Lisbon, "Nothing here has impressed me
because I expected much more"; Lisbon, Dec. 16, 1800, in ibid., p. 165. A less-

ening sense of cultural dependence on Portugal may be reflected in the fact that despite the economic boom, the number of American-born students matriculating at Coimbra between 1796 and 1805 declined by about a third from that of the previous decade, 115 against 165. Writing at Salvador in 1802, Santos Vilhena remarked on the lack of "those who wish and can afford to send their sons to the University"; see *Recopilação*, 2: 480. On the other hand, conditions in Europe were threatening and the Atlantic passage hazardous, José Francisco de Paula Cavalcante's ship, for example, having been attacked by a French frigate; see *DH*, 110: 165.

144. Thus, when Francisco de Paula Cavalcante sought to dispel the dismay that his original remarks had caused, he stated that independence was desirable only "in the case of the ruin of Portugal and in the case of His Royal Highness [the prince regent] not coming to Brazil," so as "not to suffer a foreign yoke"; see Silva e Sampaio's deposition of May 28, 1801, and also the testimony of João Carneiro da Cunha, May 28, 1801, that "he had never heard of them talking about gazettes and public affairs." See ibid., pp. 30, 45–50.

145. See "Quadro da situação política da Europea, apresentado ao Principe por D. Rodrigo de Sousa Coutinho," Aug. 16, 1803, in Pereira, *D. João VI*, 1: 131.

146. It has been argued that the emancipation of the European colonies in the New World—from the original revolt of the Thirteen Colonies in 1776, through the revolution in Saint Domingue in 1791 and the revolt of the Spanish colonies from 1810 to 1825, and concluding with the independence of Brazil in 1822—was due not to political and ideological factors but to the disruption of the "Colonial Pact," the mercantilist system common to the European monarchies, by the emergent industrial and capitalist economy. A classic statement of this theory, as it applies to Brazil, is Emília Viotti da Costa, "Political Emancipation." The same theoretical perspective informs the works of Carlos G. Mota and Fernando A. Novais, as the full title of the latter's *Brasil e Portugal na crise do antigo sistema colonial (1777–1808)* attests. A major concern in Maxwell's *Conflicts* is to show not only how Great Britain's evolution into an industrial state fundamentally altered Portugal's trading relationship with Great Britain but how it changed the economic balance within the Portuguese Empire itself.

147. Maxwell, *Conflicts*, p. 114.

148. George Stanton, quoted in Burns, "Enlightenment," pp. 262–63.

CHAPTER 2

1. Boxer, *Golden Age*, pp. 323–24.

2. See "Quadro da situação política da Europea, apresentado ao Principe por D. Rodrigo de Sousa Coutinho," Aug. 16, 1803, in Pereira, *D. João VI*, 1: 131.

3. By 1806 products from the New World formed 62.4 percent of Portuguese exports to Europe, North Africa, and the United States; see Alden, "Late Colonial Brazil," p. 651, table 12.

4. Livermore, *History of Portugal*, pp. 386–96; and Serrão, *História*, 7: 18–21.

5. Decree of Nov. 26, 1807, with the accompanying instructions to the newly appointed regents, printed in *Correio*, 1 (June 1808): 5–8.

6. Manchester, "Transfer."

7. See Varnhagen, *História geral*, 5: 34; Fleiuss, *História*, pp. 64–65; Calo-

geras, *History of Brazil*, p. 57; Calmon, *História do Brasil*, 1: lvii–lviii; Carneiro da Cunha, "Fundação," 3: 135; Poppino, *Brazil*, p. 179; Burns, *History of Brazil*, pp. 100–101; and Bethell, "Independence," p. 171.

8. That contemporaries perceived the new state of affairs in Brazil to be the logical outcome of D. Rodrigo's ideas is clear from verse written in 1815, quoted in Gonçalves dos Santos, *Memórias*, 1: 346.

9. Luccock, *Notes on Rio*, p. 573.

10. Ibid., p. 568.

11. Decree of Nov. 26, 1807. D. João's accompanying instructions to the regents voiced the hope "that I may speedily return to these my kingdoms." That the pledge to return was sincere is evident from the guilt he expressed to the British envoy in Oct. 1820 over his failure to fulfill this promise; see FO, 63/229, Edward Thornton to Viscount Castlereagh, British foreign secretary, no. 54, Rio, Oct. 25, 1820.

12. *Correio*, 1 (Sept. 1808): 255–68; and Manchester, *British Preeminence*, p. 80.

13. *CL*, 1: 1–2; *Correio*, 1 (Aug. 1808): 253–54; and Manchester, "Transfer," pp. 164–67.

14. *CL*, 1: 7–8; *Correio*, 1 (Aug. 1808): 421–22. On the limited nature of the ban on manufacturing, see Novais, *Brasil e Portugal*, pp. 268–85.

15. The Real Acadêmia dos Guardas Marinhas was transferred from Lisbon to Rio with the court in 1808; see *Subsídios*, 14: 61–64.

16. See *CL*, 1: 4–8, 10–14, 15–19, 35–39, 129–32. Also created were the Real Fábrica de Polvora, the Intendência de Polícia, and the Erário Régio; see *CL*, pp. 39–40, 43, 86–107.

17. See *CL*, 1: 42; and Werneck Sodré, *História da imprensa*, pp. 23, 34. See Bruno Lobo, "Ensino da medicina."

18. These were 10 percent taxes on urban rents (*décima urbana*) and on sales and rentals of real property; a 5 percent tax on the internal sale of slaves; new taxes on cotton and tobacco; a tax on freshly slaughtered beef; and a playing cards monopoly; see *CL*, 1: 61–62, 78–80; 2: 258–65; and *LB* (1808), pt. 1, pp. 91–92. On the bank, see *CL*, 1: 158–66; and Melo Franco, *História do Banco*, pp. 4–45.

19. See Glover, "Beresford."

20. *CL*, 2: 516–35.

21. Included in the nineteen are two *juizes de crime* (criminal judges) for Rio de Janeiro. One *comarca*, one *juiz conservador das matas* (judge for the forests), and four *intendências de ouro* (gold intendants) were abolished in this period; see *CL*, 1: 75, 77–78, 108, 228, 230, 301, 305–7, 408, 430, 441, and 2: 56, 58, 62, 125, 131, 133.

22. Manchester, *British Preeminence*, pp. 86–91.

23. The economic impact of the opening of the ports in Jan. 1808 was not immediate. In 1805–6, a commercial downturn began to affect the Portuguese world and was intensified by the disruption following the French invasion of Portugal. Not until 1810 did the trade of Rio de Janeiro and Salvador ports recover to the level of 1805. The composition of that trade had altered, imports now exceeding exports. The New World economies seem to have expanded sharply only after 1810, the trade through Salvador port growing by about 70 percent between 1810 and 1815. See Magalhães Godinho, *Prix et monnaies*, p. 277; Gonçalves dos

Santos, *Memórias*, 1: 347; and tables 2.4, 2.18, and 2.21 in Lugar, "Merchant Community," pp. 76, 106, 112.

24. Luís Joaquim dos Santos Marrocos to Francisco José dos Santos Marrocos, Rio, Nov. 17, 1812, in "Cartas de Marrocos," p. 111.

25. D. Rodrigo had in 1808 been created count of Linhares, by which title he is best known in Brazilian history.

26. See letters from Rio, Aug. 29 and Nov. 17, 1812, in "Cartas de Marrocos," pp. 97, 110–11.

27. Opinion of Silvestre Pinheiro Ferreira, dated Rio, Apr. 22, 1814, in Pinheiro Ferreira, *Idéias políticas*, pp. 21–22.

28. Letter from Rio, Nov. 21, 1812, in "Cartas de Marrocos," p. 112.

29. See the article by Jacome Ratton, one of the principal merchants in Portugal before 1808, "Pensamentos patrioticos imperio luso," printed in *Investigador Portuguez*, 15 (1816): 1–13, and reprinted as an annex to Daupias d'Alcochete, "Lettres de Ratton," pp. 219–28.

30. See Lord Castlereagh to Viscount Strangford, British envoy at Rio, no. 35, London, Nov. 22, 1813, and Lord Strangford to Lord Castlereagh, no. 9, Feb. 20, 1814, as transcribed in Webster, *Independence*, 1: 170–73. See also Manchester, *British Preeminence*, pp. 102–4.

31. See Henry Chamberlain, British chargé d'affaires, to Lord Castlereagh, no. 102, Rio, Oct. 4, 1817, in Webster, *Independence*, 1: 186; and Anna, "Buenos Aires Expedition."

32. Less than a third of the titled nobility had accompanied the court to Rio in 1807. Of those who remained in Portugal, several had collaborated with the French invaders; see Serrão, *História*, 7: 33–39, 231–34.

33. A number of French royalist émigrés were to be found at court and in the officer corps. On life at court, see Oliveira Lima, *Dom João VI*, 1: 110–15; and Wanderley Pinho, *Salões e damas*, pp. 15–23.

34. FO, 63/229, E. Thornton to Lord Castlereagh, no. 60, Rio, Nov. 18, 1820.

35. A census in 1821 recorded a population of 79,321, of whom 36,182 were slaves; see table 1 in Karasch, "Rio de Janeiro," p. 138.

36. A vivid, if naive, picture of life in Rio de Janeiro at this period is presented in John Luccock, who lived there in 1808 and again from 1813 to 1817; see *Notes on Rio*, pp. 30–37, 244–63, 546–602. A recent study of the city in the period is Karasch, "Rio de Janeiro." For equivalent works in Portuguese, see Gonçalves dos Santos, *Memórias*; and Nizza da Silva, *Estratificação social* and *Cultura e sociedade*.

37. Vasconcelos, "Memorias," p. 7. The author graduated from Coimbra in 1805.

38. A typical issue of *O Correio Braziliense* resembled a small unbound book of 120 to 140 pages. It usually contained commentaries on current news items, articles discussing questions of topical interest in the arts and sciences, and less often, translations. Six issues composed a volume, of which there were 29 in total. Over its fourteen-and-a-half-year existence the *Correio* was produced by three London printers. Its closest modern parallel would be the *New Republic* in the United States or the *New Statesman* in England, in their vintage years.

39. In its first years the *Correio* contained as much information and comment on the affairs of Portugal as it did on Brazil, one reason for the readership it gained in Portugal itself.

40. "The Correio Braziliense, and the Patriota, had circulated widely, and diffused among the people more just knowledge of themselves and the world"; see Luccock, *Notes on Rio*, p. 573. *O Patriota*, published in Rio de Janeiro, appeared only in 1813 and 1814.

41. Hipólito José, born on Mar. 25, 1774, matriculated at Coimbra late in October 1792, which means that if he came directly from the New World he must have sailed no later than July of that year; see Dourado, *Hipólito da Costa*, 1: 32–33.

42. For evidence that Hipólito José never lived in Rio de Janeiro, see ibid., pp. 22, 32.

43. See Costa Pereira, *Diário*.

44. Article entitled "Sobre o novo imperio do Brazil," *Correio*, 1 (June 1808): 57.

45. These conclusions are based on a close reading of the first four years of the *Correio*, but key evidence can be found in 2 (June 1809): 637–42; 5 (July 1810): 120–24; and 6 (Mar. 1811): 228–40.

46. That Hipólito José had as early as 1798 ceased to identify Rio Grande do Sul as his *pátria,* and suffered considerable guilt in consequence, is apparent from his diary entries for Oct. 27 and Nov. 22, 1798; see Costa Pereira, *Diario*, pp. 42, 50.

47. Hipólito José did sometimes come close to referring to Brazil as a "nation," when making comparisons with a true nation such as Great Britain; see, for example, *Correio*, 11 (Sept. 1813): 491.

48. Hipólito José's changing attitude to Brazilian independence is visible from the titles of his monthly commentaries in early 1822. See *Correio* 28 (Jan.): 57, "Conserving the Union Between Brazil and Portugal"; (Apr.): 425, "The Cortes' Proceedings Towards Brazil"; and (June): 699, "Portugal's Actions Towards Brazil." The psychological break came in the April 1822 issue, when he stopped commenting on debates in the Cortes and recommended calling a legislative assembly in Brazil itself; see pp. 441, 441–59. See also his letter to Vicente José Ferreira Cardoso da Costa, Sept. 20, 1822, printed in "Correspondencia relativa," pp. 437–39.

49. See his vehement refutation of the statement by Abbé du Pradt that Portugal would have lost Brazil if the Crown had not moved to Rio in 1808 and that should the King ever return to Lisbon he would leave independence established in the countinghouses of Rio; *Correio*, 19 (Sept. 1817): 270–87.

50. *Correio*, 10 (May 1813): 681. Capitalization and emphasis follow the original text, which is the final sentence of an article entitled "Brazil: Decree Which Grants the Intendant of Police the Despotic Power to Arrest Whom He Pleases."

51. *Correio*, 3 (Aug.–Dec. 1809): 175–82, 303–11, 371–83, 518–36, 621–34; and 4 (Jan. and May 1810): 77–85, 453–59.

52. For a succinct, well-written analysis of Whiggism in this period, see Mitchell, *Holland House*. See also Herrick, "Hipólito da Costa."

53. The *Correio* did condemn slavery, but remarked that "immediate abolition would be the senseless act of a mad man as long as [slavery] not only forms part of the property of the Country but is also linked to the existing social system"; 29 (Nov. 1822): 574.

54. See, for example, *Correio*, 10 (Feb. 1813): 202–3.

55. For references to the *Correio* in private letters, see J. Ratton to António de Araújo de Azevedo, count of Barca, London, May 6, 1816, in Daupias d'Alcochete,

"Lettres de Ratton," p. 210. On the pamphlets published in Lisbon, see Dourado, *Hipólito da Costa*, 1: 295–313.

56. L. J. dos Santos Marrocos remarked about the new periodical, which lasted until 1819, "Here I have seen brochures [*papelinhos*] printed in London, and of them all I have enjoyed most the *Investigador Portuguez*"; see letter from Rio, Oct. 28, 1811, in "Cartas de Marrocos," p. 42. In June 1813, the government in Rio circularized the governors of the major provinces, urging them unofficially to encourage subscriptions to the *Investigador Portuguez*; see Dourado, *Hipólito da Costa*, 2: 315–28.

57. See Dourado, *Hipólito da Costa*, 2: 388–410.

58. Letter from Rio, Nov. 16, 1813, in "Cartas de Marrocos," p. 172. The newspapers were, in London, *O Correio*, *O Investigador Portuguez*, and *O Portuguez*; in Lisbon, *A Gazeta de Lisboa*, *O Telegrafo*, and *O Mercurio Lusitanico*; and in Rio de Janeiro, *A Gazeta do Rio de Janeiro* and *O Patriota*.

59. In the prospectus dated March 1811 for the *Investigador Portuguez*, its editors acknowledged that a monthly journal "accurately reporting political events" and providing "information on Literature and Sciences" and their advances "seems not only justifiable but of the greatest necessity. Extraordinary changes, a new order in public affairs demand a profound investigation of the origin, condition, and truth of facts, along with judicious assessment and complete fairness in expressing them"; see 1 (July 1811): 1.

60. Letter from Rio, Feb. 23, 1816, in "Cartas de Marrocos," p. 268.

61. See *Investigador Portuguez*, 41 (Jan. 1815): 474; and Serrão, *História*, 7: 110.

62. See *Correio*, 19 (Aug. 1817): 139–45; and Manchester, *British Preeminence*, pp. 102–4.

63. *CL*, 2: 425. See also Pereira, *D. João VI*, 3: 222–27.

64. Luccock, *Notes on Rio*, p. 569.

65. *CL* 1: 242, and 2: 158.

66. Between 1816 and 1820 five *comarcas* were created and one abolished, and nine posts of *juizes de fora* were created and one suppressed.

67. For a detailed review of the population and economy of Portugal between 1808 and 1820, see Serrão, *História*, 7: 238–42, 257–79.

68. Approval of a pension requested by a surgeon at the royal infirmary at Lisbon consumed two and a half years, from Sept. 1816 to Apr. 1819; see Clayton, "Vilanova Portugal," pp. 159–60.

69. "The abuses of this government are great and manifest," the regents being "peculiarly objects of contempt and dislike"; see FO, 63/231, Edward M. Ward, British chargé, to Lord Castlereagh, no. 7, Lisbon, Sept. 2, 1820.

70. See Serrão, *História*, 7: 112; and Gonçalves dos Santos, *Memórias*, 2: 68, 74.

71. See the discussion in Street, *Artigas*, pp. 284–87, 295–98; and also Hann, "Río de la Plata," pp. 221–47.

72. Hann, "Río de la Plata," pp. 265–94.

73. These were mainly ships built in the United States, financed and manned by American citizens; see Beraza, *Corsarios*, pp. 143–289.

74. FO, 63/229, E. Thornton to Lord Castlereagh, no. 60, Rio, Nov. 18, 1820. Arnold Clayton's "Vilanova Portugal" is the only analytical, if perhaps over kind, study of the man.

75. Piteira Santos, *Revolução*, pp. 176, 178; and Serrão, *História*, 7: 274.

76. See Post, *Subsistence Crisis*, pp. xi, 1, 25, 27, 141, 167.
77. See Mota, *Nordeste*, pp. 11–18; and Noya Pinto, "Transformações econômicas," pp. 130–33.
78. Johnson, "Money, Prices, and Wages," p. 244.
79. Felisberto Caldeira Brant Pontes, future marquess of Barbacena, to Custódio Pereira de Carvalho, Salvador, Nov. 27, 1819, in *Economia açucareira*, pp. 31–32.
80. Letter from Rio, Apr. 10, 1815, in "Cartas de Marrocos," p. 223.
81. Instituto Histórico e Geográfico Brasileiro, Rio, Senador Nabuco Collection, Lata 363, Pasta 3, Francisco Gomes de Campos, future baron of Campo Grande, to José Tomás Nabuco de Araújo, Rio, Mar. 20, 1854. See also Burns, "Enlightenment," pp. 264–65.
82. See Muniz Tavares, *Revolução*, pp. lxxxv, 70–82. The author, a Pernambucan priest born in 1793, was certainly a Freemason and probably involved in the events described. In 1803 a British merchant who was a Mason was aided in escaping from Salvador, where he was being held on smuggling charges, by Freemasons in the city; see Lindley, *Voyage*, pp. 208–9.
83. See the sources mentioned in Calmon, *História do Brasil*, 4: 1428–29; and the discussion in Serrão, *História*, 7: 14–15. A Brazilian-born officer, José Joaquim de Lima e Silva, recorded in his personal notebook that he first entered a regular lodge at the level of apprentice in 1813, being admitted to higher grades in a lodge of Pernambuco in 1815; see Vilhena de Moraes, *Gabinete Caxias*, pp. 105–6.
84. Government spies reported that lodge meetings often took place in gambling houses or at dinner parties, see the report of Joseph Tremeau, Rio, June 19, 1818, quoted in Clayton, "Vilanova Portugal," p. 235; and "Memórias históricas da revolução de Pernambuco," in *DH*, 107: 233–34.
85. See Muniz Tavares, *Revolução*, pp. lxxxv–lxxxvi, on the activities in the four lodges in Pernambuco, organized by 1816 under a Grand Provincial Lodge.
86. On what is generally known as the "Conspiracy of Gomes Freire," see the judicious discussion in Serrão, *História*, 7: 121–26.
87. See Muniz Tavares, *Revolução*, pp. lxxxviii–xciv.
88. Antônio Carlos Ribeiro de Andrade to J. B. de Andrada e Silva, Pernambuco, Apr. 11, 1817, in *DH*, 101: 126–27.
89. The best sources on the 1817 rising are Muniz Tavares, *Revolução*; Mota, *Nordeste*; and the documentation contained in *DH*, vols. 101–9.
90. In Rio Grande do Norte, Paraíba do Norte, Ceará, and the *comarca* of Alagoas, elements loyal to the Crown put down the revolt. In Pernambuco a close naval blockade and military defeat caused the disintegration of the rebel regime even before a military expedition from Rio had reached Recife.
91. See letter of Vicente Ferreira Correia to Pedro José de Oliveira, Goiana, Mar. 7, 1817, in *DH* 107: 180; and letter of Luís de Albuquerque Maranhão to Matias Martins de Carvalho, Quartel, Mar. 26, 1817, in *DH*, 104: 83. For variations in the wording of the slogans, see letter to Hilario da Costa Rumeo, Alagoa [nova], Apr. 23, [1817], in *DH*, 101: 115; letter of João de Olanda de Albuquerque Maranhão to André de Albuquerque Maranhão, n.p., Apr. 12, 1817, in *DH*, 101: 117; letter of João Lopes Cardoso Machado, Recife, June 15, 1817, in *DH*, 102: 9; and letter of José Alexandre de Sousa Gurgel do Amaral Coutinho, Boa Vista, July 13, 1817, in *DH*, 102: 74.

92. Letter of Manuel Joaquim Paiva to Joaquim Manuel Carneiro da Cunha, n.p., Apr. 19, 1817, in *DH*, 101: 136–37.

93. Proclamation of the Provisional Government of Pernambuco, Mar. 15, 1817, in ibid., pp. 27–28. The individuals mentioned in this proclamation—Vieira, Vidal, Dias, and Camarão—were the principal figures in the rebellion fought by the Pernambucanos from 1645 to 1654 against the Dutch, who had conquered northeastern Brazil in 1630.

94. See *DH*, 101: 9–11, 17–18; and 104: 21, 50–66.

95. Letter to Antônio de Morais e Silva, in *DH*, 104: 31.

96. Manifesto, in *DH*, 105: 104. As shown by the comment "Note how the term *pátria* was incorporated into the system, and how the connotation became regional" in *Nordeste* (p. 87), C. G. Mota's study of the rising fails to understand not only the meaning of the *pátria* but the role it played in the rebellion. The work contains only one other reference to the *pátria*, on p. 151.

97. The main agent was Padre José Inácio de Abreu e Lima, "Padre Roma," sent to Alagoas and Bahia, where he was captured and summarily shot. Mota, *Nordeste*, p. 56, states that an envoy was sent to Buenos Aires but provides no evidence for this claim.

98. Proclamation of the Paraíba Provisional Government, Apr. 1, 1817, in *DH*, 101: 81. In a private letter a leading member of the Pernambucan regime did suggest that the provinces involved in the revolt form a single republic, but with a new capital to be built in the interior, presumably to assure perfect equality between the constituent parts; see letter of Padre João Ribeiro, Mar. 31, 1817, quoted in Quintas, "Agitação," p. 220.

99. See, for example, the *Preciso*, the formal justification for the revolt, issued at Pernambuco, in *DH*, 105: 97–99.

100. See the wording of the proclamation to the Bahians transcribed in Muniz Tavares, *Revolução*, pp. 192–93.

101. See the wording of the Pernambucan *Preciso* and the proclamation of the Paraíba do Norte rebel government, Mar. 17, 1817, in *DH*, 101: 30–31, and 105: 97. See also Hind, "Internal."

102. "The City of Rio alone produced full seven thousand volunteers, and 200,000,000 Reis, or £60,000 sterling," and "this burst of national sentiment thrilled me to my very soul"; see Luccock, *Notes on Rio*, p. 557.

103. See the letter of João Osório de Castro Sousa Falcão to T. A. de Vilanova Portugal, Recife, Jan. 20, 1818, in *DH*, 102: 74; and see the proclamations issued by the governors of Olinda diocese and that by the provisional government, Mar. 8, 1817, in *DH*, 101: 9–11, 17–18.

104. Specific causes for this resentment were the continued economic dependence of Pernambuco on Portugal and the dominant position held in the trade of Recife by merchants from Portugal; see Lugar, "Merchant Community," pp. 122–23.

105. See Muniz Tavares, *Revolução*, pp. cliii–cliv; and on what is termed "primitivism," consult A. D. Smith, "Nationalism," pp. 45–46.

106. Muniz Tavares, *Revolução*, p. clv.

107. That among the most enthusiastic supporters of the rising were free mulattoes and blacks, who saw in it an opportunity to end color discrimination, is clear; see, for example, ibid., pp. cclxv, 262, 291.

108. Denunciation made at Alagoa-nova, Apr. 1817, in *DH*, 101: 188–89; and

decrees of the Provisional Government of Pernambuco, Mar. 8 and 9, 1817, in ibid., pp. 11–12, 13.

109. See the declaration before the town council of Alagoas and the message to the king, Alagoas, Mar. 31, 1817, in ibid., pp. 76–80.

110. Letter dated Pernambuco, Mar. 12, 1817, in ibid., pp. 19–20.

111. *Correio*, 19 (July 1817): 105.

112. *Correio*, 23 (Sept. 1819): 267.

113. "It was no more than a riot in a city, which is a drop of water in the sea in respect to the totality of Brazil"; *Correio*, 23 (July 1819): 58.

114. The *Correio* remarked that "the marriage of the Prince Royal creates important linkages with one of the most considerable courts of Europe"; 23 (Aug. 1819): 199. See also Oliveira Lima, *Dom João VI*, 3: 899–913.

115. Street, *Artigas*, pp. 306–10.

116. To João Anselmo Correia, June 2, 1820, quoted in Clayton, "Vilanova Portugal," p. 227. Vilanova Portugal was referring specifically to the constitutionalist revolution then triumphant in Spain.

117. That public opinion did exist and did have influence is clear from a report by João Paulo Bezerra to the King, Rio, May 8, 1817: "What is beyond dispute is that spirit of the conversation at the common tables at the eating houses [*casas de pasto*] is horrible"; see *DH*, 101: 205.

118. See *Correio*, 19 (July 1817): 107; and the investigation of the destruction of the royal flag at Pilar and the removal of the royal arms from the front of the parish church at Limeiro, in *DH*, 107: 56–68; and 102: 183–86.

119. Royal Commission to Desembargador Bernardo Coutinho Alvares de Carvalho, Rio, Aug. 6, 1817, in *DH*, 104: 12–13.

120. See *DH*, 105: 117; and Muniz Tavares, *Revolução*, p. cclxiv. On Portugal, see Serrão, *História*, 7: 125.

121. *Correio*, 19 (Sept. 1817): 313.

122. Letters to the king and T. A. de Vilanova Portugal, Apr. 11 and 14, 1818, *DH*, 104: 4–5, 6–10. A decree forbidding the opening of further prosecutions had been issued on Feb. 6, 1818.

123. See Clayton, "Vilanova Portugal," pp. 230–37; three letters of a spy sent to Pernambuco, Jan. 15, Feb. 25, and Mar. 20, 1818, in *DH*, 107: 245–65; and Pereira, *D. João VI*, 3: 304–97.

124. Fernandes Tomás, *Revolução*, pp. 24–25.

125. Letter to L. do Rêgo Barros, Rio, June 17, 1820, quoted in Clayton, "Vilanova Portugal," p. 228. See *Correio*, 19 (July 1817): 106.

126. See Fernandes Tomás, *Revolução*, pp. 61–62; Piteira Santos, *Revolução*, pp. 110–17, 170–73, 177–81; and Gonçalves dos Santos, *Memórias*, 2: 192.

127. See Mota, *Nordeste*, pp. 174–81.

128. Gonçalves dos Santos, *Memórias*, 2: 116–17.

129. In these years, 49 Brazilian-born students took their degrees. The corresponding numbers for 1811–15 had been 55 and 6; see Barman and Barman, "Prosopography."

130. See Piteira Santos, *Revolução*, pp. 117–19; Serrão, *História*, 7: 266; and "Relatório sobre o estado e administração do Reino," presented in Feb. 1821, in Fernandes Tomás, *Revolução*, p. 61.

131. FO, 63/228, E. Thornton to Lord Castlereagh, Separate, *Secret and Confidential*, Rio, May 31, 1820; and also no. 23, May 5, 1820.

132. FO, 63/229, E. Thornton to Lord Castlereagh, no. 32, Rio, July 26, 1820; Separate, *Secret and Confidential*, Rio, July 31; Separate, *Secret and Confidential*, Rio, Aug. 12; and no. 42, Rio, Aug. 22; and see also Clayton, "Vilanova Portugal," pp. 239–44.

133. The following paragraph is based on FO, 63/229, E. Thornton to Lord Castlereagh, nos. 53–62, Rio, Oct. 19–Dec. 10, 1820.

134. See Serrão, *História*, 7: 360–64.

CHAPTER 3

1. Three early and still indispensable studies are Silva Lisboa, *Historia*; Pereira da Silva, *Historia*; and Varnhagen, *Independência*. Also important are Oliveira Lima, *Independência*; and Monteiro, *Independência*. More recent works include Buarque de Holanda, *História*; Mota, *1822*; and Rodrigues, *Independência*. The only modern works in English on independence in Brazil are the essays edited by Russell-Wood, *Colony to Nation*; and Bethell, "Independence."

2. Ferreira Reis, "O Grão-Pará," p. 165.

3. See Piteira Santos, *Revolução*, pp. 67–71.

4. F. C. Brant Pontes, future marquess of Barbacena, to C. Pereira de Carvalho, Salvador, Jan. 29, 1821, in *Economia açucareira*, p. 200. The British consul at Salvador reported that "information of the Establishment of a Revolutionary Government was received here last week and appears to have given, with few exceptions, satisfaction to every class of the population of the city"; see FO, 63/230, William Pennell to Lord Castlereagh, no. 17, Salvador, Dec. 8, 1820.

5. See Piteira Santos, *Revolução*, pp. 61–66.

6. J. A. Fragoso to D. João VI, Rio, Dec. 31, 1820, in Pereira, *D. João VI*, 3: 319–20. To conservatives, the Spanish Constitution of 1812 epitomized political subversion.

7. The following account is based principally on the dispatches written from Oct. 1820 to Mar. 1821 by the British envoy, who played an active role in the consultations; see FO, 63/229, nos. 53–62, and 63/237, nos. 1–14.

8. FO, 63/229, E. Thornton to Lord Castlereagh, no. 55, *Secret*, Rio, Oct. 28, 1820.

9. Ibid., nos. 54 and 60, Rio, Oct. 25 and Nov. 18, 1820. In fact, as early as 1814, the then British envoy remarked that sending D. Pedro to Portugal "is out of the question. Your Lordship may be persuaded that the Court will never accede to it"; see Lord Strangford to Lord Castlereagh, no. 9, Rio, Feb. 20, 1814, in Webster, *Independence*, 1: 173. In 1820 Thornton failed to appreciate that his strong advocacy of this plan was counterproductive, since the king found suspect any project favored by Great Britain.

10. FO, 63/229, E. Thornton to Lord Castlereagh, no. 60, Rio, Nov. 18, 1820; and see Clayton, "Vilanova Portugal," pp. 245–50.

11. Quoted in Clayton, "Vilanova Portugal," p. 262. From 1714 to 1837 the King of Great Britain was also ruler of Hanover, a small independent state on the Elbe in northwest Germany.

12. FO, 63/237, E. Thornton to Lord Castlereagh, no. 5, Rio, Jan. 31, 1821, noting that "within these few Days, a short Pamphlet . . . had been put into Circulation."

13. *Le roi et la famille royale de Bragance doivent-ils, dans les circonstances présentes, retourner à Lisbonne ou bien rester au Brésil?* The pamphlet, although

published anonymously, was in fact written by François Etienne Caillé de Gene, a French refugee and police spy. On the role of Vilanova Portugal in its production, see Monteiro, *Independência*, 1: 271.

14. FO, 63/237, E. Thornton to Lord Castlereagh, no. 5, Rio, Jan. 31, 1821.

15. FO, 63/229, E. Thornton to Lord Castlereagh, no. 60, Nov. 18, 1820; and 63/237, Thornton to Castlereagh, nos. 1 and 5, *Most Secret and Confidential*, Rio, Jan. 8 and Jan. 31, 1821.

16. Count of Palma to T. A. de Vilanova Portugal, Salvador, Dec. 21, 1821, quoted in Clayton, "Vilanova Portugal," pp. 147, 251–52.

17. FO, 63/237, W. Pennell to E. Thornton, Salvador, Feb. 10, and *Idade d'Ouro do Brazil* newspaper, Feb. 13 and 15, 1821, enclosed in E. Thornton to Lord Castlereagh, no. 11, Rio, Mar. 1, 1821. See also Gomes de Carvalho, *Deputados*, p. 16. The garrison of Belém do Pará had already revolted on Jan. 1, 1821, but this fact was not known in southern Brazil and exerted no influence on the course of events there.

18. FO, 63/237, E. Thornton to Lord Castlereagh, no. 13, Rio, Mar. 1, 1821. The first decree, although published on Feb. 23, was backdated to Feb. 18.

19. During Jan. and Feb. 1821 the various factions among the Crown's advisers were locked in intrigues and infighting so complex and so unscrupulous that they are hard to reconstruct. Thornton's dispatches provide only a partial (in both senses of that word) account of unfolding events.

20. FO, 63/237, E. Thornton to Lord Castlereagh, Separate, *Most Secret and Confidential*, Rio, Mar. 3, 1821; on the rising, see ibid., no. 12, Rio, Mar. 1, 1821. D. Pedro's sentiments were fiercely liberal, but it is clear that he acted in league with and was often guided by both a faction within the Crown's advisers and a more popular group favoring the constitutionalist cause. On the formation of the prince's character and his attitudes at this time, see Sousa, *Fundadores*, 2: 1–204.

21. FO, 63/237, E. Thornton to Lord Castlereagh, no. 16, Rio, Mar. 14, 1821. The decree was backdated to Mar. 7.

22. Ibid., no. 23, Rio, Apr. 3, 1821.

23. After the rising, a public subscription had raised U.S. $40,000 to U.S. $50,000 as a gift for the troops; see ibid., Separate, *Secret and Confidential*, Rio, Mar. 3, 1821.

24. For example, many of the commercial clerks born in Portugal desired the king's return to Lisbon so that Portugal might regain its former primacy in the empire, but some Brazilian-born in the same calling favored the king's departure as the first step to the achievement of a republic.

25. FO, 63/237, E. Thornton to Lord Castlereagh, Rio, nos. 22 and 26, Mar. 28 and Apr. 3, 1821.

26. "There are so many versions of this event," Thornton wrote to Castlereagh, "that I should find it difficult to give your Lordship any Account with which I could satisfy myself, and it must be left to Time to discover what were the secret Motives, that directed these Proceedings on both sides"; ibid., no. 30, Rio, May 3, 1821. Time has failed to do so; but consult Monteiro, *Independência*, 1: 322–41; and Sousa, *Fundadores*, 2: 230–58.

27. The parish electors, themselves the product of two rounds of elections, would choose the district (*comarca*) electors who would actually name the five deputies for Rio de Janeiro province.

28. Several more, while trying to escape, were drowned or suffocated in the

mud of Rio bay; see FO, 63/237, E. Thornton to Lord Castlereagh, no. 30, Rio, May 3, 1821.

29. Letter of June 19, 1822, reproduced in facsimile in Pereira, *D. João VI*, 3: 345–48.

30. Article 21 of the Bases, printed in *Documentos para a historia*, pp. 165–67.

31. Even Gomes de Carvalho, in a work otherwise hostile to the Cortes, admits this to have been the case; see *Deputados*, pp. 25–26.

32. "The Cortes are going to work, cutting up rights and Property in all directions and they had made themselves hosts of enemies on all sides," the British chargé at Lisbon commented. "There is really however such a mass of Augean filth to be cleared away that I think any foreign interference which should interrupt the nightmen in their labours is for the present to be depreciated." See FO, 63/238, E. M. Ward to Earl Clanwilliam, Private, Lisbon, Apr. 21, 1821.

33. *Documentos para a historia*, pp. 226–29.

34. See Rodrigues, *Independência*, 1: 70, 76, 80.

35. The single exception was the deputies' decision on June 14, 1821, to disallow the attempt by the Crown to raise a loan in England to cover its debts to the Banco do Brasil. Several members protested against taking any action on the subject until the deputies elected by the Brazilian provinces arrived; see the translated summary of the debate in FO, 63/238, E. M. Ward to Lord Castlereagh, no. 26, Lisbon, June 16, 1821.

36. FO, 63/237, E. Thornton to Lord Castlereagh, Separate, Rio, Jan. 31, 1821.

37. On the military rising of June 5, see ibid., no. 38, Rio, June 11, 1821. This was the last dispatch written by the British envoy before leaving for Lisbon. A very detailed account of the events of June 5 is also given in the dispatches of Wenzel, baron von Mareschal, the Austrian agent, to Prince Metternich, unnumbered and no. 5A, Rio, June 6 and June 11, 1821; partly transcribed and partly summarized in Figueira de Mello, "A correspondencia de Marschall [*sic*]," pp. 177, 181.

38. A contributing factor to the crisis was the evident intention of the prince regent's government to dismiss the senior officer of the Portuguese garrison from his post as military commander of the city; see General Jorge de Avilez Juzarte de Sousa Tavares to D. Pedro, Rio, June 6, 1821, in Pereira, *D. João VI*, 3: 330–31.

39. W. von Mareschal to Prince Metternich, nos. 5A and 8A, Rio, June 11 and July 22, 1821, in Figueira de Mello, "Correspondencia de Marschall," pp. 186, 201–2.

40. Even Gomes de Carvalho, whose work is strongly biased against the Cortes, accepts that these measures, far from being aimed at fragmenting Brazil, were necessary in the circumstances of the time; see *Deputados*, p. 26. See also FO, 63/238, E. M. Ward to Lord Castlereagh, no. 18, Lisbon, Apr. 21, 1821.

41. Of the eighteen provinces outside of Rio de Janeiro at the start of 1821, three continued with royal governors, one (Maranhão) chose its governor to be its "constitutional ruler" rather than electing a junta, thirteen installed juntas, and one (Sergipe) lost its autonomy to the junta of Bahia.

42. See letter of the junta to D. João VI, Salvador, June 21, 1821; translation enclosed in FO, 63/239, E. M. Ward to the marquess of Londonderry (formerly Lord Castlereagh), no. 38, Lisbon, Aug. 11, 1821.

43. D. Pedro to D. João VI, July 17, 1821, in *Correspondencia official*, p. 7; and see W. von Mareschal to Prince Metternich, no. 11B, Rio, Oct. 1, 1821, in Figueira de Mello, "Correspondencia de Marschall," p. 219.

44. W. von Mareschal to Prince Metternich, nos. 8A, 9D, and 9E, Rio, July 22, and Aug. 27 and 27, 1821, in Figueira de Mello, "Correspondencia de Marschall," pp. 202–5, 209, 212.

45. Letters of July 17 and Sept. 21, 1821, in *Correspondencia official*, pp. 7, 10.

46. The Austrian agent commented: "They were put together by a Mr. *Andrade*, a longtime resident of Europe and a man of much spirit; that the São Paulo government (of which he is vice president) accepted, as much as it has, the regency established by the king was due to him. These instructions, which contain several peculiar ideas . . . , do present others which can be regarded as national; and they acquire an even greater degree of importance in that they will probably be the only instructions to be drawn up from a general point of view." See W. von Mareschal to Prince Metternich, no. 15D, Rio, Nov. 16, 1821, in Figueira de Mello, "Correspondencia de Marschall," p. 235. The *Lembranças e apontamentos do governo provisorio para os senhores deputados da provincia de São Paulo*, Rio, 1822, is reprinted in Nogueira, *Obra política*, 2: 17–23.

47. Nogueira, *Obra política*, 2: 17–18, 19.

48. See Sodré, *História da imprensa*, pp. 47–48, 62; Varnhagen, *Independência*, pp. 85–86; and Rodrigues, *Independência*, 4: 52–54, 79, 142–43, 152.

49. Issue of Sept. 15, 1821, quoted in Rodrigues, *Independência*, 1: 181, 289. The reference to the "European system" reveals the influence of the political ideology which characterized the European states as corrupt and therefore competitive and bellicose (and monarchical), and the American nations as pristine and therefore cooperative and peaceful (and republican), and which accordingly held that the two systems should remain separate and distinct. This conception of the incompatibility of the two hemispheres underlay President Monroe's message to Congress at the end of 1823, later known as the Monroe Doctrine.

50. In FO, 63/237, no. 15, Rio, Mar. 14, 1821, most of which is transcribed in Webster, *Independence*, 1: 208–9, Thornton alleged that "from the origin, the revolution which took place here was conceived entirely in a Portuguese sense and absolutely brought about by Portuguese agency alone." Brazilian troops and Brazilian civilians were, he alleged, "carried away by the contagion of an enthusiasm which gave them little time to enquire into the tendency or the object of it." That the coup intended a "system of the supremacy of the mother country" and that "the Brazilians were to be brought or forced under the same system" was proved, Thornton asserted, by "the arrest of two or three distinguished individuals not accused of any crime or malversion, but suspected of being the favorers and perhaps the leaders of a Brazilian party, looking toward the independence of this country." The inspiration for this interpretation of events, which does not accord with Thornton's own dispatches, is not far to seek. Fearful that the new regime would threaten Britain's commercial privileges, Thornton gave credit to information about the rising and its goals fed to him by the merchants and bureaucrats who had most to lose under the new order. Of the three individuals briefly arrested, one was a militia officer who had attempted to suppress the February coup at Salvador, and the other two were royal advisers almost certainly privy to Vilanova Portugal's plans for casting Portugal adrift and so splitting the royal dominions in two.

51. W. von Mareschal to Prince Metternich, no. 5A, Rio, June 11, 1821, in Figueira de Mello, "Correspondencia de Marschall," p. 212.

52. See Rodrigues, *Independência*, 1: 156–58.

53. W. von Mareschal to Prince Metternich, no. 9A, Rio, Aug. 27, 1821, in Figueira de Mello, "Correspondencia de Marschall," p. 210.

54. See Mello Moraes, *História do Brasil*, 1: 200.

55. W. von Mareschal to Prince Metternich, no. 13D, Rio, Oct. 24, 1821, in Figueira de Mello, "Correspondencia de Marschall," pp. 226–27.

56. D. Pedro to D. João VI, Rio, Oct. 4, 1821, in *Correspondencia official*, p. 11.

57. W. von Mareschal to Prince Metternich, no. 9E, Rio, Aug. 27, 1821, in Figueira de Mello, "Correspondencia de Marschall," p. 212.

58. W. von Mareschal to Prince Metternich, no. 17C, Rio, Dec. 16, in ibid., p. 241.

59. Jean Baptiste Maler, consul general and chargé d'affaires of France, to the minister of foreign affairs, Rio, Nov. 15, 1821, quoted in Nogueira, *Obra política*, 1: xiv–xv.

60. As Gomes de Carvalho admits, it was the provinces, not the Cortes, which urged the creation of the new governments; see *Deputados*, pp. 121–22.

61. The military coup of Feb. 26 and the "massacre" at the Merchants' Exchange on Apr. 22, 1822.

62. See FO, 63/238, E. M. Ward to Lord Londonderry, no. 22, Lisbon, May 13, 1821.

63. Gomes de Carvalho, *Deputados*, pp. 110–11.

64. *Documentos para a historia*, pp. 241–42.

65. Gomes de Carvalho, *Deputados*, pp. 121–25. It should be noted that the new autonomy of the Brazilian provinces left not just the prince regent, but also the Lisbon regime without any effective authority over them. The creation of the post of governor of arms was almost certainly designed to give the Lisbon government some presence in the affairs of the Brazilian provinces.

66. See FO, 63/239, E. M. Ward to Lord Londonderry, no. 51 amended, Lisbon, Nov. 15, 1821. He added: "But the circumstance of their sending troops to Pernambuco, and their having in contemplation to send a force to Rio de Janeiro also, shews that they are sensible that mild measures are not sufficient to preserve the union between the two Countries." These comments epitomize Ward's lack of interest in and understanding of Brazilian affairs. In the original version of no. 51, sent on Oct. 6, he simply enclosed a translation of the new law without any comment or evaluation.

67. Varnhagen, *Independência*, pp. 65–66.

68. See translation in FO, 63/239, E. M. Ward, no. 38, Lisbon, Aug. 11, 1821; and Gomes de Carvalho, *Deputados*, p. 129.

69. See *Documentos para a historia*, p. 243. The second article of the bill ordered that on his return the prince should travel incognito in Spain, France, and England.

70. Letter of Sept. 21, 1821, in *Correspondencia official*, p. 10. When the prince regent's letter of July 17 was read to the Cortes on Oct. 10, the Cortes sent a message to the king stating that the laws passed on Sept. 29 met the complaints voiced by the prince.

71. Speech on Dec. 29, 1821, by José Lino Coutinho, quoted in Gomes de Carvalho, *Deputados*, p. 163. A graduate in medicine from Coimbra, Lino Coutinho was to make a distinguished political career in independent Brazil. He was not an incipient quisling.

72. Session of Sept. 19, 1821, reported in ibid., pp. 125–27. On Nov. 14, 1821, the Cortes decided by a large majority (69 to 26) that its permanent junta, to sit while it was not in session, should be drawn equally from deputies from Portugal and from the overseas provinces; see ibid., p. 149.

73. D. Pedro to D. João VI, Rio, Dec. 10, 1821, in *Correspondencia official,* p. 15.

74. D. Pedro to D. João VI, Rio, Dec. 14, 1821, in ibid., p. 16. This description of the reaction to the decrees is confirmed by the graphic account in W. von Mareschal to Prince Metternich, no. 17C, Rio, Dec. 12, 1821, in Figueira de Mello, "Correspondencia de Marschall," pp. 240–41.

75. On the *club de resistência,* see Drummond, "Annotacções," pp. 15–16; and on the petition campaign, see Mello Moraes, *História do Brasil,* 1: 223–24, 230–31, 241–45.

76. See W. von Mareschal to Prince Metternich, no. 17C, Rio, Dec. 12, 1821, in Figueira de Mello, "Correspondencia de Marschall," p. 241. "It has even been said that the major cause for the events which gave rise to Independence was the displeasure felt by the employees over the decree abolishing the agencies in Rio de Janeiro"; see the speech of José Martiniano de Alencar, session of June 16, 1823, in *Diario,* 1: 200.

77. See FO, 63/239, E. M. Ward to Lord Londonderry, nos. 38, 49, and 57, Lisbon, Aug. 11, Sept. 22, and Oct. 10, 1821; and Gomes de Carvalho, *Deputados,* p. 131.

78. Varnhagen, *Independência,* p. 93.

79. See José Clemente's account of his role, given in a speech made in 1841, transcribed in Mello Moraes, *História do Brasil,* 1: 259–62. On José Clemente's background, see Rodrigues, *Independência,* 4: 40–42, 72.

80. J. B. Maler to the minister of foreign affairs, Rio, Jan. 13, 1822, in Nogueira, *Obra política,* 1: xxi–xxii. See D. Leopoldina's two letters to Georg Schaeffer, Rio, n.d. [late Dec. 1821] and Jan. 8, 1822, in "Cartas ineditas," pp. 112–14.

81. According to the census of 1821, the city contained some 43,000 free and freed people. Deducting one-third or more for those underage, and a further half from this remainder (females probably rarely signing), we see that the petition bore the signatures of about half the free and freed adult males, an extraordinarily high percentage; see Karasch, "Rio de Janeiro," p. 138.

82. See the document attached to D. Pedro to D. João VI, Rio, Jan. 2, 1822, in *Correspondencia official,* pp. 17–20.

83. José Clemente recalled in 1841 that on Christmas eve, "as I well remember," he had approached the prince, who informed him of his decision; see Mello Moraes, *História do Brasil,* 1: 261. The French consul received similar information from D. Pedro at about the same date; see J. B. Maler to the minister of foreign affairs, Rio, Dec. 30, 1821, quoted in Nogueira, *Obra política,* 1: xv.

84. See his letter to D. João VI, Jan. 9, 1822, in *Correspondencia official,* pp. 20–21. The incident is generally called O Fico, from the last word in the reply: "Como é para o bem de todos e felicidade geral da nação, estou pronto: diga ao povo que fico."

85. The overbluntness of his reply may explain why a far more restrained and conditional version of his response was given in the city council's original

announcement of his decision to stay. Public pressure forced an immediate clarification.

86. See D. Pedro's letter to D. João VI, Jan. 23, 1822, in *Correspondencia official*, pp. 23–27; and his account in the form of a pseudonymous "letter" dated Jan. 21, 1822, published as a pamphlet, and reprinted in Vianna, *Jornalista*, pp. 17–29.

87. See the accounts of the crisis given by the commander of the Portuguese troops in *Correspondencia official*, pp. 131–35; and W. von Mareschal to Prince Metternich, no. 3, Rio, Jan. 14, 1822, in Figueira de Mello, "Correspondencia de Mareschal," pp. 16–20.

88. The count of Gestas to the minister of foreign affairs, Rio, Jan. 9, 1822, quoted in Nogueira, *Obra política*, 1: xvi–xvii.

89. José Bonifácio remains one of the most controversial figures in Brazilian history, the object of encomium and of denigration. Balanced assessments of his life and achievements are rare, the best biography still being Sousa, *Fundadores*, vol. 1.

90. J. B. Maler to the minister of foreign affairs, Rio, Jan. 17, 1822, in Nogueira, *Obra política*, 1: xxii.

91. J. B. Maler to the minister of foreign affairs, Rio, Jan. 17, 1822, in ibid.

92. See the ideas expressed by José Bonifácio to the Austrian agent on Feb. 23, and reported in W. von Mareschal to Prince Metternich, no. 7B, Rio, Mar. 2, 1822, in Figueira de Mello, "Correspondencia de Mareschal," pp. 38–39.

93. See the passage from this pamphlet, *O Despertador Braziliense*, quoted in Varnhagen, *Independência*, p. 91.

94. Consistent with their previous attitude, all the Brazilian deputies supported the passage of the bill; see *Correio*, 28 (Jan. 1822): 71, (Feb.): 166–67; and Gomes de Carvalho, *Deputados*, pp. 160–67.

95. Gomes de Carvalho, *Deputados*, pp. 242–45.

96. Varnhagen, *Independência*, p. 103.

97. See José Bonifácio's speech to the prince regent when presenting the São Paulo petition on Jan. 26, 1822, in *Correspondencia official*, p. 61.

98. Letters of D. Pedro to D. João VI, Rio, Feb. 12, Mar. 14, and Mar. 19, 1822, and dispatches of Joaquim de Oliveira Alvares to Cândido José Xavier Dias da Silva, Rio, Feb. 17 and Mar. 21, 1822, in ibid., pp. 62, 68–70, 209–11. See also Varnhagen, *Independência*, pp. 102–3, 109–10.

99. Nogueira, *Obra política*, 1: 136.

100. Ibid., p. 138; and decree of Feb. 16, 1822, in *Correspondencia official*, pp. 66–68.

101. The offending words in the decree ran: "I being desirous, for the general benefit of the United Kingdom and of the people of Brazil, to prepare and arrange beforehand the constitutional system which they merit and I have sworn to give them"; see ibid., pp. 66–67.

102. The only provinces not to elect a *junta provisória* in accord with the law of Sept. 29 were Rio de Janeiro and São Paulo. Minas Gerais and Mato Grosso elected *juntas provisórias* but did so later, after they had declared for the prince regent. In Pernambuco the ruling junta had been chosen according to a special law for that province passed by the Cortes on Sept. 9.

103. Varnhagen, *Independência*, pp. 107–9, 226.

104. Dispatches to D. Pedro from the junta of Pernambuco, Recife, Mar. 18, and from that of Pará, Belém, June 11, 1822, in *Correspondencia official*, pp. 235–37, 373; and J. B. de Andrada e Silva to the junta of Maranhão, Rio, Sept. 5, 1822, in Nogueira, *Obra política*, 1: 189–90.

105. Goiás and Mato Grosso also supported the prince regent, but due to their isolation they played no role in the ensuing struggle.

106. Seckinger, *Brazilian Monarchy*, pp. 60–62; Street, *Artigas*, p. 336; and Hann, "Río de la Plata," pp. 348–50.

107. See W. von Mareschal to Prince Metternich, no. 9C, Rio, Mar. 16, 1822, in Figueira de Mello, "Correspondencia de Mareschal," p. 50; and Varnhagen, *Independência*, pp. 110–11.

108. See the correspondence and documents printed in *Correspondencia official*, pp. 277–308; on the reaction in Rio, see W. von Mareschal to Prince Metternich, no. 11B, Rio, Apr. 11, 1822, in Figueira de Mello, "Correspondencia de Mareschal," pp. 57–58.

109. See W. von Mareschal to Prince Metternich, no. 8, Rio, Mar. 5, 1822, in Figueira de Mello, "Correspondencia de Mareschal," pp. 43–44. D. Pedro to D. João VI, Rio, Mar. 14, 1822, in *Correspondencia official*, p. 68; and Drummond, "Annotacções," p. 16.

110. *Documentos para a historia*, pp. 275–76. The report of the special commission on commercial relations had been published on Mar. 15.

111. Ibid., pp. 279–80; and Gomes de Carvalho, *Deputados*, pp. 227–32, 235–42.

112. Boehrer, "Flight," pp. 498–99.

113. Ibid., pp. 499–500; and Gomes de Carvalho, *Deputados*, pp. 256–63.

114. See W. von Mareschal to Prince Metternich, no. 12, Rio, Apr. 20, 1822, in Figueira de Mello, "Correspondencia de Mareschal," pp. 58–59.

115. In his letter to D. João VI, Apr. 28, 1822, the clause "I have sought and tried to be . . . *Defender* of the *innate* rights of the peoples" reveals his familiarity with the Radicals' schemes; see *Correspondencia official*, p. 72.

116. *Revérbero Constitucional Fluminense*, Apr. 30, 1822, quoted in Varnhagen, *Independência*, pp. 114–16.

117. Gomes de Carvalho, *Deputados*, pp. 283–98.

118. *Documentos para a historia*, pp. 312–24.

119. Gomes de Carvalho, *Deputados*, pp. 341–43.

120. The deputies drew back from authorizing criminal charges against the bishop of São Paulo; see *Documentos para a historia*, pp. 324–25.

121. Reaction to the report, issued on Mar. 18, was at first favorable, since it did recognize the legitimacy of Brazil's complaints against the September decrees, but further study revealed the limited nature of its proposed concessions; see W. von Mareschal to Prince Metternich, no. 14A, Rio, May 17, 1822, in Figueira de Mello, "Correspondencia de Mareschal," pp. 61–62.

122. See W. von Mareschal to Prince Metternich, no. 14A, Rio, May 17, 1822, in ibid., pp. 62–63.

123. See the letter of D. Pedro to J. B. de Andrada e Silva, Apr. 3, 1822, quoted in Sousa, *Fundadores*, 1: 193–94.

124. W. von Mareschal to Prince Metternich, unnumbered, Rio, May 26, 1822, in "Correspondencia de Mareschal," pp. 69–70; and see the documents included

in D. Pedro to D. João VI, Rio, June 19, 1822, in *Correspondencia official*, pp. 277–308.

125. "Should another consul nominated by Lisbon appear," the instructions continued, "this should not prevent you from continuing as consul for the Kingdom of Brazil"; see the decree nominating Antônio Manuel Correia da Câmara, May 24, and his instructions, May 30, 1822, printed in *Archivo diplomatico*, 5: 223–24.

126. See the governing junta to D. João VI, Recife, June 10, 1822, in *Correspondencia official*, pp. 253–67; and the account in Drummond, "Annotacções," 19–20.

127. Rodrigues, *Independência*, 1: 234–38.

128. At its first meeting on June 1 the council was composed of the two delegates hurriedly elected by the electors of Rio province and a deputy to the Lisbon Cortes named from the Banda Oriental and recently arrived in Rio. See W. von Mareschal to Prince Metternich, nos. 16B and 17, Rio, June 3 and 15, 1822, in Figueira de Mello, "Correspondencia de Mareschal," pp. 72–75, 80–83; and the decrees and documents included in D. Pedro to D. João VI, Rio, June 19, 1822, in *Correspondencia official*, pp. 92–96.

129. See the decree in *Correspondencia official*, p. 96.

130. Mello Moraes, *História do Brasil*, 1: 202–3; and Varnhagen, *Independência*, p. 123.

131. Varnhagen, *Independência*, pp. 270, 288, 316.

132. "Ata da reunião de 26 de junho de 1822," printed in Dias Tavares, *A Independência*, pp. 175–81.

133. Varnhagen, *Independência*, p. 270.

134. See W. von Mareschal to Prince Metternich, no. 22, Rio, Aug. 10, 1822, in Figueira de Mello, "Correspondencia de Mareschal," pp. 89–90.

135. J. B. de Andrada e Silva to F. C. Brant Pontes, future marquess of Barbacena, in *Archivo diplomatico*, 1: 5, 7–8; and to Manuel Rodrigues Gameiro Pessoa, future viscount of Itabaiana, in ibid., 3: 6–7.

136. This manifesto is identified by Mareschal as being written by José Bonifácio; see the dispatch to Prince Metternich, no. 22, Rio, Aug. 10, 1822, in Figueira de Mello, "Correspondencia de Mareschal," pp. 92–93; it is also included in Nogueira, *Obra política*, 1: 287–93. The weight of evidence seems to indicate that it was in fact written by Joaquim Gonçalves Ledo; see Rodrigues, *Independência*, 1: 146, 294.

137. Nogueira, *Obra política*, 1: 303.

138. See W. von Mareschal to Prince Metternich, no. 23A, Rio, Aug. 19, 1822, in Figueira de Mello, "Correspondencia de Mareschal," p. 94.

139. Varnhagen, *Independência*, pp. 134–35.

140. Letter of Sept. 1, 1822, in the Arquivo do Setor de História, Museu Paulista, transcribed in Rodrigues, *Independência*, 5: 284–85.

141. See Drummond, "Annotacções," p. 40.

142. See Sousa, *Fundadores*, 3: 433–34. This incident is based on the narrative of Padre Belchior de Oliveira Pinheiro. Unfortunately, his eye-witness account is of questionable authenticity. The narrative first surfaced in 1922, and the printed work from which it was allegedly drawn—a pamphlet published at Paris in 1826—has never been found; see Rodrigues, *Independência*, 1: 296.

CHAPTER 4

1. Recognition of the Grito de Ipiranga as the declaration of national independence was not immediate. Sept. 7 was not included by the decree of Dec. 21, 1822, among the days of grand gala at the imperial court. Only on Sept. 5, 1823, did a resolution of the Constituent Assembly declare "the Seventh of this month, the Anniversary of Brazilian Independence, a National Festival;"; see Nogueira, *Obra política*, 1: 115–16; and *Diario*, 1: 722.

2. See W. von Mareschal to Prince Metternich, no. 27A, Sept. 25, 1822, in Figueira de Mello, "Correspondencia de Mareschal," p. 101.

3. See Mello Moraes, *História do Brasil*, 1: 232. In his notes to Varnhagen, *Independência*, p. 136, Vianna produces evidence to show that the date was really Sept. 12.

4. *Correio*, 29 (Nov. 1822): 549. The letter appeared in the penultimate issue of the periodical, which Hipólito José da Costa closed down in Jan. 1823. His own death followed in Sept., and this quotation marks our farewell to a principal architect of Brazilian nationhood.

5. See W. von Mareschal to Prince Metternich, no. 29, Oct. 2, 1822, in Figueira de Mello, "Correspondencia de Mareschal," p. 107.

6. W. von Mareschal to Prince Metternich, nos. 32A and 32B, Rio, Oct. 19, 1822, in ibid., pp. 111–15; and see the *edital* (edict) of Sept. 21, 1822, transcribed in Mello Moraes, *História do Brasil*, 2: 452–53.

7. F. C. Brant Pontes, future marquess of Barbacena, to J. B. de Andrada e Silva, London, Nov. 20–30, 1822, in *Archivo diplomatico*, 1: 219–20; and M. R. Gameiro Pessoa, future viscount of Itabaiana, to J. B. de Andrada e Silva, Paris, Dec. 26, 1822, in ibid., 3: 75–76.

8. D. Pedro had been admitted as a Mason early in Aug. He was selected grand master at the end of Aug. or start of Sept. and formally installed early in Oct.; see Mello Moraes, *História do Brasil*, 1: 232–37.

9. See W. von Mareschal to Prince Metternich, no. 32A, Rio, Oct. 19, 1822, in Figueira de Mello, "Correspondencia de Mareschal," p. 111; and Rodrigues, *Independência*, 1: 262. The formal meetings to recognize and acclaim D. Pedro as emperor were composed of the town councillors and the local notables.

10. The government did, on Sept. 18, introduce a new coat of arms and national emblems for Brazil; see Nogueira, *Obra política*, 1: 100–101. On José Bonifácio's role, see W. von Mareschal to Prince Metternich, no. 27A, Rio, Sept. 25, 1822, in Figueira de Mello, "Correspondencia de Mareschal," p. 103; and Sousa, *Fundadores*, 1: 230–31.

11. See H. Chamberlain, consul-general, to George Canning, foreign secretary, no. 20, Feb. 10, 1823, in Webster, *Independence*, 1: 217; and W. von Mareschal to Prince Metternich, no. 32B, Oct. 19, 1822, in Figueira de Mello, "Correspondencia de Mareschal," p. 114. The British consul-general, who was absent on leave when D. João VI departed for Lisbon, returned to Rio in the middle of 1822 nominally as consul-general but in reality as British diplomatic agent.

12. See W. von Mareschal to Prince Metternich, nos. 32A and 39B, Oct. 19 and Dec. 3, 1822, in Figueira de Mello, "Correspondencia de Mareschal," pp. 111, 135. For examples of recognition with the precondition, see *Câmaras Municipais*, 1: 196, and 2: 16, 61, 158.

13. See the *portaria* (circular) dated Nov. 11, 1822, sent to all authorities, in Nogueira, *Obra política*, 1: 400.

14. Varnhagen, *Independência*, pp. 158–70; and W. von Mareschal to Prince Metternich, nos. 33A, 34, 35, and 37A [no. 36 missing], Rio, Oct. 29 and 30, and Nov. 4 and 27, 1822, in Figueira de Mello, "Correspondencia de Mareschal," pp. 116–25.

15. W. von Mareschal to Prince Metternich, no. 39A, Rio, Dec. 3, 1822, in Figueira de Mello, "Correspondencia de Mareschal," p. 131. See also Schubert, *Coroação*.

16. Grant of Dec. 1, 1822, transcribed in Nogueira, *Obra política*, 1: 400.

17. D. Pedro's claim to grant these honors was based on the full delegation made to him by his father in Apr. 1821 of his powers as grand master of the orders; see Pereira, *D. João VI*, 3: 385.

18. Decree of Dec. 1, 1822, in Nogueira, *Obra política*, 1: 108–10.

19. See W. von Mareschal to Prince Metternich, no. 41B, Rio, Dec. 18, 1822, in Figueira de Mello, "Correspondencia de Mareschal," pp. 139–40.

20. Hilton, "United States," pp. 123–24; G. Canning to H. Chamberlain, no. 1, London, Nov. 18, 1822, in Webster, *Independence*, 1: 213; and M. R. Gameiro Pessoa, future viscount of Itabaiana, to J. B. de Andrada e Silva, Paris, Dec. 26, 1822, in *Archivo diplomatico*, 3: 75–76.

21. Nogueira, *Obra política*, 1: 274–75.

22. Ibid., p. 114.

23. Instructions to F. C. Brant Pontes, future marquess of Barbacena, Rio, Aug. 12, 1822, in *Archivo diplomatico*, 1: 11.

24. J. B. de Andrada e Silva to F. C. Brant Pontes, future marquess of Barbacena, Rio, Oct. 4 and Nov. 3, 1822, in ibid., pp. 15, 19.

25. J. B. de Andrada e Silva to A. M. Correia da Câmara, Rio, Sept. 13, 1822, in ibid., 5: 243; and see the letters later exchanged between Correia da Câmara and Sir Thomas Cochrane, in ibid., pp. 270–72, 289–90.

26. Since the acquisition of hard cash aroused Cochrane's most unscrupulous —if resourceful—characteristics, the Empire of Brazil paid most heavily for his services, the final and exorbitant claims not being settled until the 1880's, but however high the cost, Brazil's independence owed much to the "First Admiral." See Tute, *Cochrane*; Cecil, *Speculation*; and Cochrane's own account, *Narrative*.

27. Varnhagen, *Independência*, pp. 318–25; Girão, *Ceará*; and Pereira da Costa, *Cronologia*, 2: 266–342.

28. W. von Mareschal to Prince Metternich, nos. 6, 7, and 8A, Rio, Mar. 11 and 17 and Apr. 4, 1823, in "Correspondência de Mareschal, jan./abril [*sic*] 1823," pp. 178–79, 181, 184.

29. Varnhagen, *Independência*, pp. 276–77.

30. Ibid., pp. 278–79.

31. Ibid., p. 280.

32. Ibid., pp. 335–36, 349–50.

33. W. von Mareschal to Prince Metternich, no. 9B, Rio, Aug. 27, 1821, in Figueira de Mello, "Correspondencia de Marschall," pp. 207–8; Seckinger, *Brazilian Monarchy*, p. 60; Street, *Artigas*, p. 335; and Hann, "Río de la Plata," pp. 341–48.

34. Gomes de Carvalho, *Deputados*, pp. 274–77.

35. Street, *Artigas*, pp. 334–38; and Nogueira, *Obra política*, 1: 93, 158.

36. To A. M. Correia da Câmara, Rio, May 30, 1822, in *Archivo diplomatico*, 5: 234.

37. See the article in *Revérbero Constitucional Fluminense*, Feb. 3, 1822,

quoted in Seckinger, *Brazilian Monarchy*, p. 62. In the Banda Oriental a minority of the population were Brazilian or Portuguese by birth. Possession of Colônia do Sacramento by the Portuguese Crown from 1680 to 1777 could be used to support a claim to the area on historical grounds. In fact, neither of these claims seems to have been employed at this period to justify annexation. No state likes to relinquish territories under its control, and certainly renunciation by the Empire of its claims to the Banda Oriental might have adversely affected the cause of independence.

38. See W. von Mareschal to Prince Metternich, no. 1A, Rio, Jan. 30, 1823, in "Correspondência de Mareschal, jan./abr. 1823," pp. 159–60.

39. Hann, "Río de la Plata," pp. 350–51; Street, *Artigas*, pp. 337–38; and Seckinger, *Brazilian Monarchy*, p. 63.

40. See W. von Mareschal to Prince Metternich, no. 12A, Rio, Apr. 26, 1823, in "Correspondência de Mareschal, jan./abr. 1823," p. 194.

41. *Fallas do throno*, p. 3.

42. The Austrian agent reported on Feb. 10 and Mar. 17, 1823, that 43 and 53 deputies were present at Rio; see "Correspondência de Mareschal, jan./abr. 1823," pp. 168, 182. The first of six sessions for the verification of powers was held on Apr. 17; see *Diario*, 1: 1–19.

43. The total number of seats in the assembly reached 102, Bahia and Mato Grosso each being assigned an additional deputy. However, since elections were never held in Pará, Maranhão, Piauí, Sergipe, and Cisplatine provinces, or for the extra Mato Grosso seat, only 89 seats were filled. Since 2 deputies were each elected to represent two provinces and a further 14 never took their seats, only 73 deputies were elected and seated. To fill these 16 vacancies, 11 runners-up in the elections were seated as substitute deputies. In addition 5 deputies, late in taking their seats, were during their absence replaced by substitutes. One of the substitutes was elected to the new, extra seat given in Aug. 1822 to Bahia, thus reducing to 88 the total number of men who sat in the assembly.

44. On the Constituent Assembly, see Rodrigues, *Assembléia Constituente*.

45. See W. von Mareschal to Prince Metternich, nos. 6, 8A, and 12B, Rio, Mar. 11, and Apr. 4 and 26, 1823, in "Correspondência de Mareschal, jan./abr. 1823," pp. 179, 186, 198.

46. Ibid.

47. *Fallas do throno*, pp. 15–16. The constitutions of 1791 and 1792 were French. The speech itself was composed by the Emperor; see W. von Mareschal to Prince Metternich, no. 13, Rio, May 5, 1823, in "Correspondência de Mareschal, jan./abr. 1823," p. 202.

48. For the debate on the interim regulations of the assembly, governing the opening ceremonies, see session of Apr. 30, 1823, in *Diario*, 1: 6–7.

49. The addition was originally proposed by Luís Inácio Andrada Lima, a deputy from Pernambuco province; see sessions of May 5 and 6, in ibid., pp. 22, 27–31.

50. Antônio Carlos, José Bonifácio, and their nephew, José Ricardo da Costa Aguiar, who usually voted with them; see ibid., p. 25.

51. Ibid., p. 108.

52. See W. von Mareschal to Prince Metternich, no. 15B, Rio, May 14, 1823, in "Correspondência de Mareschal, jan./abr. 1823," p. 210.

53. Ibid., pp. 209–10.

54. Speech of José de Sousa e Melo, session of May 7, 1823, in *Diario*, 1: 40.

55. See sessions of May 9 and 26, 1823, in ibid., pp. 44–45, 124.

56. Articles 1, 2, 3, 6, 22, and 26; session of Sept. 2, 1823, in ibid., pp. 703–4.

57. Speech of Manuel Jacinto Nogueira da Gama, future marquess of Baependí, session of May 26, 1823, in ibid., p. 130.

58. Speech of J. M. de Alencar, session of June 16, 1823, in ibid., p. 221.

59. Speech of Antônio Ferreira França, session of Oct. 11, 1823, in ibid., 2: 226.

60. Speech of J. J. Carneiro de Campos, future marquess of Caravelas, session of June 16, 1823, in ibid., 1: 222.

61. Sessions of May 27 and Oct. 11, 1823, in ibid., 1: 142; and 2: 227.

62. Speeches of Francisco Muniz Tavares, sessions of May 22 and June 19, 1823, in ibid., 1: 100, 247.

63. Speech of J. M. de Alencar, session of June 19, 1823, in ibid., pp. 245–46; see also pp. 260–61, 289.

64. Speech of A. C. Ribeiro de Andrada Machado, session of June 19, 1823, in ibid., p. 253.

65. Ibid., pp. 294, 297.

66. Ibid., p. 210. Five of the seven committee members signed. Neither José Bonifácio nor Antônio Luís Pereira da Cunha, future marquess of Inhambupe (identified by Mareschal as a leader of the "middle" party in his dispatch no. 15B, May 15), signed the report. Antônio Carlos, who at times reverted to his original radical views, strongly favored the bill; see session of June 25, 1823, in ibid., pp. 294–95; and W. von Mareschal to Prince Metternich, no. 19A, Rio, July 15, 1823, in "Correspondência de Mareschal, jul./ago. 1823," p. 315.

67. W. von Mareschal to Prince Metternich, no. 18A, Rio, July 1, 1823, in "Correspondência de Mareschal, jul./ago. 1823," p. 308.

68. In Portuguese the term was "*poder moderador*," often translated as "moderating power." See speech of J. J. Carneiro de Campos, future marquess of Caravelas, session of June 26, 1823, in *Diario*, 1: 299–300.

69. In fact, the theory had already been briefly stated by the same speaker on June 23: "The supreme guardian authority, or Regulating Power, which in monarchies is inseparable from the monarch, [and] destined to prevent the perturbing of the Public Order and the disarray of the political machinery, is the extreme recourse and last instance in the constitutional system, and is only used when no other ordinary and regular means is available to avoid imminent damage to the State"; see ibid., p. 279.

70. See W. von Mareschal to Prince Metternich, no. 19C, July 19, 1823, in "Correspondência de Mareschal, jul./ago. 1823," pp. 319–20.

71. See sessions of July 2 and 7, 1823, in *Diario*, 1: 335, 373.

72. Since Austria did not recognize the Imperial title, the agent continued to refer to D. Pedro as His Royal Highness; see W. von Mareschal to Prince Metternich, no. 19C, Rio, July 19, 1823, in "Correspondência de Mareschal, jul./ago. 1823," pp. 319, 323; and *Organizações*, p. 38.

73. W. von Mareschal to Prince Metternich, nos. 20 and 22, Rio, July 2 and Aug. 5, 1823, in "Correspondência de Mareschal, jul./ago. 1823," pp. 325, 334.

74. Sessions of July 21 and 22, 1823, in *Diario*, 1: 435, 437–39.

75. Sessions of July 22, 23, 24, and 26, in ibid., 448–49, 452–57, 459–62, 469–71, 473–79. The Austrian envoy reported that article 3, denying the Emperor

any power of veto, passed by 4 votes; W. von Mareschal to Prince Metternich, no. 21A, Rio, July 31, 1823, in "Correspondência de Mareschal, jul./ago. 1823," p. 327.

76. Serrão, *História*, 7: 392–93.

77. W. von Mareschal to Prince Metternich, no. 21A, Rio, July 31, 1823, in "Correspondência de Mareschal, jul./ago. 1823," p. 327.

78. W. von Mareschal to Prince Metternich, no. 19C, Rio, July 19, 1823, in ibid., p. 321.

79. See Drummond, "Annotacções," pp. 65–69.

80. W. von Mareschal to Prince Metternich, nos. 25, 26, and 27, Rio, Aug. 23, 26, and 30, 1823, in "Correspondência de Mareschal, jul./ago. 1823," pp. 342–47.

81. Barbosa Lima Sobrinho, "Imprensa."

82. See the speech by J. M. de Alencar, session of July 22, 1823, in *Diario*, 1: 441.

83. W. von Mareschal to Prince Metternich, no. 30, Rio, Sept. 20, 1823, in "Correspondência de Mareschal, set./dez. 1823," pp. 309–10; see also Varnhagen, *Independência*, pp. 198–204.

84. Speech by Venâncio Henriques de Resende, session of Oct. 10, 1823, in *Diario*, 2: 228; and W. von Mareschal to Prince Metternich, no. 27, Rio, Aug. 30 in "Correspondência de Mareschal, jul./ago. 1823," p. 347, and no. 37G, Rio, Nov. 19, 1823, in "Correspondência de Mareschal, set./dez. 1823," p. 357. No significant research has been carried out on these alleged schemes.

85. The assembly met in secret session on this subject on Aug. 20 and 21; see *Diario*, 1: 616; and W. von Mareschal to Prince Metternich, nos. 25 and 27, Rio, Aug. 23 and 30, 1823, in "Correspondência de Mareschal, jul./ago. 1823," pp. 342, 345–46.

86. See articles 44, 113–114, 121, and 142, in *Diario*, 1: 690–95.

87. W. von Mareschal to Prince Metternich, nos. 34H and 37A, Rio, Oct. 21 and Nov. 19, 1823, in "Correspondência de Mareschal, set./dez. 1823," pp. 335–36, 340–41. The laws signed by the Emperor included the reform of the provincial government, the regulation of the sanction of laws, the abolition of the former Council of Delegates, the repeal of the 1818 royal decree banning secret societies, a ban on deputies' accepting government positions, and a list of the laws and decrees promulgated after D. João VI left Brazil which were to continue in force.

88. "Disgracefully, in our country we see our chief [of state] every day attacked directly and indirectly by those infamous editors of the *Tamoyo*"; see the unpublished newspaper article, written under a pseudonym by D. Pedro I, answering an article in O *Tamoyo*, Oct. 21, 1823, transcribed in Vianna, *Jornalista*, p. 97.

89. Sessions of Nov. 8 and 10, 1823, in *Diario*, 2: 387–88, 392–93.

90. *Organizações*, p. 10.

91. The dispatches of the Austrian agent provide an excellent contemporaneous commentary on the unfolding crisis from the presentation of the draft constitution to the demise of the Constituent Assembly; see "Correspondência de Mareschal, set./dez. 1823," pp. 306–61.

92. W. von Mareschal to Prince Metternich, no. 37G, Rio, Nov. 19, 1823, in ibid., p. 354. At the end of July the Austrian agent precisely foresaw the course of events: "What would be more prudent and more advantageous would be to keep the Assembly but to impose limits on it . . . ; but given the character of the Prince, one ought rather to anticipate a coup de main than a plan which requires foresight

and perseverance"; see idem, no. 21A, Rio, July 31, 1823, in "Correspondência de Mareschal, jul./ago. 1823," p. 328.

93. W. von Mareschal to Prince Metternich, no. 37F, Rio, Nov. 19, 1823, in "Correspondência de Mareschal, set./dez. 1823," p. 347. Even though in his earlier dispatches Mareschal had often favored D. Pedro I's dissolving the assembly and granting a constitution, the Austrian envoy now lamented the assembly's fate and viewed the future in deeply pessimistic terms. This change in attitude derived in part from a visible exasperation with the Emperor and his conduct and in part from a high regard for José Bonifácio and his talents.

94. The two, both deputies from Minas Gerais, were Padre Belchior Pinheiro de Oliveira, a cousin of the Andradas, and Joaquim José da Rocha. Also arrested and deported was a deputy from Bahia, Francisco Gê Acaiába de Montezuma. The deportees were allowed to take their families with them. The sixth deputy arrested, Nicolau Pereira de Campos Vergueiro, was released. See the accounts in Drummond, "Annotacções," pp. 72–86; and Sousa, Fundadores, 1: 283–87.

95. W. von Mareschal to Prince Metternich, no. 38B, Rio, Nov. 25, 1823, in "Correspondência de Mareschal, set./dez. 1823," pp. 371–74. Of the 10 full members of the Council of State, 9 graduated from Coimbra between 1786 and 1797, the median year being 1792. These 9 were born between 1760 and 1774, the median year being 1768. The 3 honorary members (and the full member who had not attended Coimbra) were fully a decade younger; the 3 were all Coimbra graduates, the median year of their degrees being 1804. Seven of the 10 and 2 of the 3 had served in the Constituent Assembly. See Barman and Barman, "Prosopography."

96. W. von Mareschal to Prince Metternich, nos. 39 and 41, Rio, Dec. 6 and 20, 1823, in "Correspondência de Mareschal, set./dez. 1823," pp. 376, 383.

97. Speech of J. M. de Alencar, session of Nov. 11–12, 1823, in Diario, 2: 397.

98. O Typhis Pernambucano, Jan. 22 and 29, 1824, transcribed in Caneca, O Typhis, pp. 67–70, 72–73. This weekly periodical, published at Recife from Dec. 1823 to Aug. 1824, was representative of Nativist thought and outlook. The odd title is a misrendering of Tiphys, name of the pilot of the boat in which Jason and his companions sought the Golden Fleece.

99. Speech of Augusto Xavier de Carvalho, Nativist deputy from Pernambuco, session of June 16, 1823, in Diario, 1: 217.

100. Issue of Jan. 22, 1824, in Caneca, O Typhis, p. 67.

101. The eighteenth province, Rio de Janeiro, had no administrative autonomy. Of the 17 nominees, 8 had graduated from Coimbra and 2 others had matriculated there. The oldest was 69 and the youngest 28, with most in their 40's or 50's. Four of the 17 either refused the appointment or never took office as president. See Barman and Barman, "Prosopography."

102. Session of May 23, 1823, in Diario, 1: 128. On Sept. 25, 1823, the minister of finance reported that, far from the imperial government's receiving revenues from the provincial governments, it was they who urgently needed financial support; see Castro Carreira, Historia financeira, p. 95.

103. The following account is based mainly on Barbosa Lima Sobrinho, "A Confederação do Equador." Well constructed and well documented, this article tends to favor the case of the Pernambucans. Brandão's Confederação do Equador is a lengthy panegyric, most useful for the documentation it reprints. No separate study in English exists of this episode.

104. Act of election transcribed in the issue of Jan. 29, 1824, in Caneca, *O Typhis*, p. 77.

105. The electors argued that, because they had appealed to the Emperor against the nomination in Jan., the installation could not legally take place until D. Pedro I had given his decision on their appeal.

106. Issue of June 10, 1824, in Caneca, *O Typhis*, p. 186.

107. See ibid., p. 187. The wording of this and other articles makes clear that resentment against Rio de Janeiro's hegemony contributed strongly to the rising.

108. Proclamation of July 2, 1824, reprinted in Brandão, *Confederação do Equador*, pp. 205–7.

109. Issue of Aug. 5, 1824, in Caneca, *O Typhis*, p. 246.

110. Frei Caneca and seven others were executed at Recife, Ratcliffe and two others at Rio de Janeiro, and the remaining five at Fortaleza, Ceará.

111. Pimenta Bueno, *Direito público*, pp. 481–505.

112. *Organizações*, p. 11.

113. At the meeting of the Recife *câmara municipal*, which on June 6, 1824, refused to accept the new constitution, Frei Caneca, the editor of the *Typhis Pernambucano*, submitted an opinion: "Since His Imperial Majesty is not the nation, does not possess sovereignty, or commission from the Brazilian nation to authorize draft constitutions and present them, this project does not derive from a legitimate source"; see Caneca, *O Typhis*, p. 272.

114. See sections 1–4 of article 6 for the precise conditions in these cases. Under section 5, conditions for naturalization were to be fixed by law; see Pimenta Bueno, *Direito público*, pp. 481–82.

115. Article 117; see ibid., pp. 495–96.

116. The age of majority was 25, but those who were married, military officers, graduates, or ordinary clergy could vote from age 21.

117. Ibid., p. 191. Considerable inflation had occurred between the promulgation of the Constitution and the moment Pimenta Bueno wrote, but the point remains valid. The draft constitution debated by the Constituent Assembly tried to deal with the problem of inflation and regional disparities in wealth by defining the income required to vote as equal to "the value of 150 *alqueires* of manioc flour at the average price in their own parish"; see article 123, in *Diario*, 1: 694.

118. Pimenta Bueno, *Direito público*, p. 491. The idea of two classes of citizens, the "active" with the right to vote and the "passive" lacking it, derived from the French constitution of 1791. Under article 93, "those who cannot vote in the primary assemblies of the parishes cannot be members or vote in the nomination of any elected authority, national or local."

119. Article 94; see ibid., p. 492.

120. The qualifications for these positions were not the same, since they were defined separately in articles 45 (Senate), 75 (provincial councils), and 95 (Chamber of Deputies). An income of 400 milreis for deputies and 800 for senators was required, but only "decent substance" for provincial councillors. Members of the Senate had to be at least 40 years of age and provincial councillors at least 25, but no specific age was fixed for deputies. Naturalized citizens and non-Catholics could not become deputies, but no such ban applied to the Senate and provincial councils. The wording of article 45 did not specifically prevent freedmen from becoming senators, although such a choice was in practice unlikely to occur. See ibid., pp. 466–67, 486, 489, 492.

121. Under article 97, the actual system of elections was to be fixed by ordinary law. Article 96 specified that no birth, residence, or domicile qualification was required of candidates for elective office. See ibid., p. 492.

122. The Conselhos Gerais, established in all the provinces save Rio de Janeiro, were permitted to deal only with matters of provincial concern, being forbidden to discuss topics national, inter-provincial, or fiscal in nature; see articles 72–73, 81–83, and 165–66; in ibid., pp. 488–89, 500. The draft constitution discussed by the Constituent Assembly did not concede to the provinces any body with legislative power; see article 209, in *Diario*, 1: 698.

123. The provincial councils' resolutions could be put into effect provisionally by the imperial government if the General Assembly was not then in session; see articles 84–88. In respect to the General Assembly, the Senate was to be half as large as the Chamber of Deputies, the size of which was to be fixed by law; see articles 14–17, 40–42, 51, and 97, in Pimenta Bueno, *Direito público*, pp. 483, 485–86, 490–91, 492.

124. Ibid., p. 482.

125. Ibid.

126. By sections 13 and 14 of article 179, "the law will be equal for all, both to protect and to punish, and will reward according to the merit of each one," and "every citizen can hold public appointments, civil, political, or military, without any distinction save that of his talents and virtues"; see ibid., p. 503. The equivalent "equal protection" clause was not added to the Constitution of the United States until 1868.

127. *Diario*, 1: 299–300. The concept of a regulating power originated with Benjamin Constant de Rebecques, a French politician and writer who drafted the Napoleonic constitution of 1815. J. J. Carneiro de Campos, future marquess of Caravelas, had advocated the regulating power in the Constituent Assembly. As a member of the Council of State, he now played a major role in drafting the Constitution.

128. Pimenta Bueno, *Direito público*, pp. 482, 492.

129. Article 101; see ibid., pp. 492–93.

130. Article 102; see ibid., p. 493.

131. An Imperial veto would not be overridden unless the vetoed bill was passed unaltered by the two succeeding legislatures. Since a legislature lasted four years, a delay of at least five and as much as eight years would ensue; see articles 18 and 64–67, in ibid., pp. 483, 488.

132. It could only hear appeals authorized by law, judge cases involving abuse of office for a limited range of public officials, and resolve questions of conflicting jurisdiction in respect to courts of appeal inferior to it; see ibid., p. 500.

133. Ibid., pp. 483, 499, 500.

134. Section 2 of article 47; see ibid., p. 486.

135. See Hunshe, *Rio Grande do Sul*.

136. In May 1824 the United States extended recognition by receiving the emperor's envoy. However, the action of the United States had no positive influence on the policies of the European monarchies.

137. On Portuguese policy toward Brazil after May 1823, see Corrêa de Sá, *D. João VI*, pp. 115–42.

138. See Manchester, *British Preeminence*, pp. 192–94; and Platt, *British Trade*, p. 29.

139. The aims and course of British policy from Aug. 1823 to Sept. 1825 can be traced in the Foreign Office dispatches transcribed in Webster, *Independence*, 1: 226–88.

140. Instructions to the count of Vila-Real, Lisbon, Oct. 12, 1824, and attached Contre-Projêt, in Pereira, *D. João VI*, 3: 371–79. On the British foreign secretary's response to this threat, see G. Canning to H. Chamberlain, London, Nov. 10, 1824, in Webster, *Independence*, 1: 246–48.

141. Honório José Teixeira to D. João VI, Lisbon, Feb. 11, 1825, in Pereira, *D. João VI*, 3: 379–81.

142. Seckinger, *Brazilian Monarchy*, pp. 66–72; and Street, *Artigas*, pp. 337–47.

143. Seckinger, *Brazilian Monarchy*, p. 72.

144. The British decision was announced by the foreign secretary, G. Canning, to the British consul-general at Rio, H. Chamberlain, on Jan. 15, 1825. "It is hopeless that the Conferences in London should be revived to any advantage. . . . What has been begun in London must, in order to be finished within any reasonable period of time, be pursued at Lisbon and Rio de Janeiro." The British were motivated not only by the approaching deadline on the 1810 treaty but by their decision to recognize the republics of Mexico, Gran Colombia and Argentina. See Webster, *Independence*, 1: 255–57.

145. See Manchester, *British Preeminence*, pp. 200–203, for a general account. The negotiations leading up to the treaty can be studied from the British and Brazilian viewpoints respectively in Webster, *Independence*, 1: 262–88; and *Archivo diplomatico*, 6: 61–152. See also the enlightening letters of A. L. Pereira da Cunha, future marquess of Inhambupe, to Antônio Teles da Silva, future marquess of Resende, Rio, Apr. [*sic*, July] 27 and Aug. 20, 1825, in "Correspondencia de Resende," pp. 160–64, 170–72.

146. Russia delayed until 1827 and Spain until 1834. The United States had exchanged envoys with Brazil in May 1824, but this recognition was of no assistance (if anything, it was a drawback) in persuading the European monarchies to acknowledge the legitimacy of the new Empire.

CHAPTER 5

1. J. B. Andrada e Silva, noting with acerbic amazement the creation of "19 Viscounts and 22 Barons," commented that "João, in the amplitude and security of his autocratic power, never gave birth so profusely." See his letter to A. M. Vasconcelos de Drummond, Talance, Jan. 1826, in "Cartas Andradinas," p. 14.

2. FO, 13/23, H. Chamberlain to G. Canning, no. 33, Rio, May 6, 1826.

3. *Fallas do throno*, pp. 123–25.

4. Not all the 152 legislators, it should be emphasized, were physically present at the opening session. All but one senator and two deputies either did take their seats at some point during 1826 or were substituted.

5. Article 9, 10, and 12; see Pimenta Bueno, *Direito público*, p. 482.

6. Article 14, sections 8, 9 (quoted), 10, 11, 13, 14, and 16; see ibid., p. 483.

7. Article 102, sections 8 and 9; see ibid., pp. 492–93.

8. The single exception, under article 27, was when a legislator was apprehended committing a crime that carried the death penalty. See also articles 17 and 26; ibid., pp. 483–84.

9. Article 98 and 101, sections 1 and 3; see ibid., pp. 492–93.

10. Afonso Taunay, *Senado*, p. 22. The electors, of whom there were less than 5,000, were selected by the voters in parish meetings. The number of electors in each province was fixed by the imperial instructions of Mar. 26, 1824.

11. Sir Charles Stuart to G. Canning, no. 9, Private, Rio, Sept. 9, 1825, in Webster, *Independence*, 1: 286.

12. D. Pedro I to Domitila de Castro Canto e Melo, marchioness of Santos, Rio, Dec. 13, 1827, in Rangel, *Marginados*, p. 283. "I intend that my brother Miguel and I," the emperor avowed, "will be the last ignoramuses of the Bragança family"; see C. B. Ottoni, *Autobiographia*, p. 43.

13. Sir C. Stuart to G. Canning, no. 9, Private, Rio, Sept. 9, 1825, in Webster, *Independence*, 1: 286. In May 1824 a delegation sent from Recife to explain Pernambuco's conduct and objections to the appointed president was subjected at a public audience to brusque and humiliating language by the emperor, conduct which only strengthened the province's determination to resist; see the comment in *O Typhis Pernambucano*, June 24, 1824, in Caneca, *O Typhis*, p. 201; and the account in Barbosa Lima Sobrinho, "Confederação do Equador," pp. 80–82.

14. Sir C. Stuart to G. Canning, no. 9, Private, Rio, Sept. 9, 1825, in Webster, *Independence*, 1: 286; and W. von Mareschal to Prince Metternich, no. 38B, Rio, Nov. 25, 1823, in "Correspondência de Mareschal, set./dez. 1823," p. 374.

15. "D. Pedro I by the Grace of God and by the Constitution Emperor," rather than "D. Pedro I by the Grace of God and by the Unanimous Acclamation of the Peoples Emperor." The distinction was important, since the second invoked the doctrine of popular sovereignty and the first did not. See Sir C. Stuart to G. Canning, no. 9, Private, Rio, Sept. 9, 1825, in Webster, *Independence*, 1: 287.

16. The passage directly continued: "if the experience of the past did not cause him to qualify his arbitrary notions by a constant reference to the benefits of a constitutional government, and to temper his natural violence by so much discretion." Sir C. Stuart to G. Canning, no. 9, Private, Rio, Sept. 9, 1825, in ibid., p. 286.

17. W. von Mareschal to Prince Metternich, no. 39, Rio, Dec. 6, 1823, in "Correspondência de Mareschal, set./dez. 1823," p. 378. Gomes da Silva's memoirs show that he was not such a fool as his nickname would imply. What made him intensely disliked, "odious to all the Parties" (as Mareschal phrased it), was his entire devotion to D. Pedro I and his total willingness to serve and please him. It was Gomes da Silva who drew up the decree dissolving the Constituent Assembly. See Gomes da Silva, *Memórias*, pp. 38, 44–45, 48–49, 82–83, 89. On o Chalaça's ability as a journalist, see Vianna, *Jornalista*, pp. 169–70.

18. On the relationship in general, see Rangel, *D. Pedro I*. In 1825 the British envoy used the emperor's "friend Senhora Domitilla de Castro," who had "from the beginning taken a warm interest in the success of the negotiation," to persuade D. Pedro I to change the wording of his ratification of the treaty with Portugal; see Sir C. Stuart to G. Canning, no. 9, Private, Rio, Sept. 1825, in Webster, *Independence*, 1: 287. The next year, the British chargé reported that the newly named Brazilian consuls at Liverpool and New York had each made large gifts to D. Domitila in order to secure their posts; see FO, 13/23, H. Chamberlain to G. Canning, *Separate and Confidential*, attached to no. 54, Rio, May 6, 1826.

19. Opinion of José da Silva Carvalho expressed to A. M. Vasconcelos de

Drummond in London, Christmas 1830, as reported in an autobiographical fragment printed in "Cartas Andradinas," pp. 87–88.

20. Arquivo do Museu Imperial, Petrópolis, Pedro de Orléans e Bragança Collection, Catalogo B, Maço 12, document 588, undated draft, transcribed in Vianna, *D. Pedro I e D. Pedro II*, pp. 26–27.

21. One individual was chosen by the electors in six provinces, two in four, seven in three, and thirteen in two. The base list from each province contained three times as many names as the province had seats to be filled in the Senate; see Afonso Taunay, *Senado*, pp. 168–84.

22. Out of 112 individuals on the Senate base lists 56 were Luso-Brazilians. The lists also included 19 military officers and 16 clerics; 3 of the former and 3 of the latter had attended Coimbra; see Barman and Barman, "Prosopography."

23. Thirty-five of 56 Luso-Brazilians, 10 of 19 military officers, 6 of 16 clerics, and 2 of 26 men who were local notables or belonged to other social categories. Of the 23 elected by more than one province, the 21 Luso-Brazilians were nominated, but not the remaining 2, both leading Nativists.

24. By a legal stratagem, D. Pedro I managed to name five men as senators from provinces which had not elected them to their base list. The election returns included all those who had received votes, whether or not on the base list. When choosing the senators D. Pedro first struck out from the relevant base list anyone who was dead (only 2 cases) or had already been chosen by him for another province (31 cases). The gaps on the base list he filled from the candidates next proximate in votes on the return. For four provinces, D. Pedro chose five senators from the names so added. The marginal increase in support that the emperor thus secured in the Senate was outweighed by the damage done to his reputation by the stratagem, confirming doubts about his trustworthiness as a constitutional monarch. See Afonso Taunay, *Senado*, pp. 24–27.

25. Two other former ministers who were not named were included on the base list for Rio de Janeiro province only because of D. Pedro I's stratagem mentioned above. Neither of the two was Luso-Brazilian or favored by the emperor.

26. Twenty-one senators out of 50, almost all Luso-Brazilians or military officers, held titles when nominated. One further senator, a Luso-Brazilian who had served as minister, was granted a title in 1826. The British consul-general believed that a massive number of titles were granted in Oct. 1826 to cover up D. Domitila's advancement to the rank of marchioness of Santos, a typical example of how the personal influenced the political in D. Pedro I's conduct; see FO, 13/24, H. Chamberlain to G. Canning, no. 103, Rio, Oct. 18, 1826.

27. Articles 36 and 37; see Pimenta Bueno, *Direito público*, p. 485.

28. Since 1 of the 15 senators had been elected deputy from two provinces, the number of seats thus vacated was actually 16. A further 8 vacancies resulted from causes such as death and failure to appear. All but 2 of these vacancies were filled by the candidate closest in votes from the relevant province.

29. The chamber contained 21 priests and 26 men who were local notables or had other occupations; and most of the Nativist deputies belonged to these categories. Since support for an ideology rather than objective factors such as education or profession identifies the Nativists, the total given for them is approximate.

30. When early in 1826 the government summarily deported a French journal-

ist whose writings had given offense, the British consul-general reported that the liberal members of the forthcoming General Assembly were much concerned; see FO, 13/22, H. Chamberlain to G. Canning, no. 17, Rio, Apr. 13, 1826.

31. The phrase appears in a political manifesto published by an elderly Nativist in 1860; see T. B. Ottoni, *Circular*, p. 69.

32. 1816–20, 49; 1821–25, 51; 1826, 2. See Barman and Barman, "Prosopography."

33. *Annaes do parlamento brasileiro*, 1826, 4: 65.

34. "News of events in Rio de Janeiro recently arrived," *O Censor Provincial* of Coimbra reported on Jan. 18, 1823, "and the Brazilians resident here have for the most part left Coimbra, threatened as they were by some *europeus* [Portuguese] or simply being afraid." In Apr. 1822 a Brazilian student published a single number of *O Brasileiro em Coimbra*, "the publication of which was the cause for riotous persecution of the Brazilian students," in the words of a report to the king dated June 30, 1823 (attached to the copy of the newspaper in the Biblioteca Municipal of Coimbra).

35. Early in 1823 the Brazilian students at Coimbra wrote a common letter to a member of the Constituent Assembly, reporting their mistreatment and asking him to propose the foundation of a university in Brazil. On June 14, 1823, the deputy presented a motion to this effect in the assembly, saying that "in these bitter circumstances, looking fixedly on the Pátria for which they yearn, they decided to make me agent of their loyal sentiments and authorized me by the letter which I here present"; see speech by José Feliciano Fernandes Pinheiro, future viscount of São Leopoldo, in *Diario*, 1: 212.

36. *Fallas do throno*, pp. 123, 124.

37. Seckinger, *Brazilian Monarchy*, pp. 28, 70–72; and Street, *Artigas*, pp. 344–50.

38. *Fallas do throno*, p. 125.

39. Values for 1823–25 compared to those for 1816–20; see table 2.28a in Lugar, "Merchant Community," p. 124.

40. See Peláez and Suzigan, *História monetária*, pp. 47–51, where the annual rate of inflation is computed at roughly 9 percent and that of the decline in the milreis at 8 percent. Other factors adversely affecting the Brazilian export economy included the 1825 slump in Great Britain and the 1826 drought in northeastern Brazil.

41. *Fallas do throno*, p. 124. Nov. 15, 1825, was the date of Portuguese ratification of the treaty made in Aug. with Brazil.

42. Castro Carreira, *Historia financeira*, pp. 58–60.

43. See Pereira, *D. João VI*, 3: 381–84; and FO, 13/22, H. Chamberlain to G. Canning, no. 10, Rio, Jan. 7, 1826.

44. Even the British government was concerned about the impact on Brazilian public opinion of rumors about such a secret pact between D. Pedro I and his father; see FO, 13/21, Foreign Office to H. Chamberlain, no. 5, London, Jan. 12, 1826.

45. Castro Carreira, *Historia financeira*, pp. 114–15; and FO, 13/23, H. Chamberlain to G. Canning, no. 66, Rio, July 5, 1826.

46. Manchester, *British Preeminence*, pp. 203–5.

47. *Fallas do throno*, p. 124.

48. On the death of D. João VI and the ensuing crisis in Brazil and Portugal, see Oliveira Lima, *Dom Pedro e Dom Miguel*, pp. 11–59.

49. *Fallas do throno*, p. 125.

50. FO, 13/23, H. Chamberlain to G. Canning, nos. 30 and 40, Rio, May 5 and 23, 1826.

51. See the proclamation issued on July 12, 1826, by D. Isabel Maria, the regent of Portugal, quoted in Serrão, *História*, 7: 400–401.

52. Ibid., pp. 395–96. 53. *Fallas do throno*, p. 125.

54. Ibid. 55. Ibid., p. 129.

56. *Annaes do Parlamento*, 1826, 2: 84.

57. See, for example, Arquivo Nacional, Rio, Seção dos Arquivos Particulares, Caixa 777, Pacote 1, the viscount of Nazaré to the emperor, Nov. 19, 1825.

58. *Annaes do Parlamento*, 1826, 2: 84, 206–7.

59. The Senate, as might be expected, proved to be an essentially conservative body, which from the start failed to initiate much legislation.

60. As a Nativist deputy, a veteran of the Constituent Assembly, expressed it with typical hyperbole: "We must guard the Constitution before it totally collapses." Speech of Padre Custódio José Dias, session of May 9, in *Annaes do Parlamento*, 1826, 1: 34.

61. Speech of José Bernardino Batista Pereira de Almeida, session of May 17, 1826, in ibid., p. 64.

62. Speech of Lúcio Soares Teixeira de Gouveia, session of May 12, 1826, in ibid., p. 61.

63. Laws of Aug. 11 and Oct. 15, 1827, *LB* (1826–29), pp. 77–79, 109–18.

64. Laws of Oct. 15, 1827, ibid., pp. 112–28.

65. See Flory, *Judge and Jury*, pp. 49–68.

66. FO, 13/24, H. Chamberlain to G. Canning, *Private and Confidential*, Rio, Aug. 19, 1826.

67. A treaty made in May 1827 by the Argentine envoy at Rio recognizing Brazilian sovereignty over the Banda Oriental aroused such popular fury in Buenos Aires that it had to be repudiated. See Seckinger, *Brazilian Monarchy*, pp. 147–48; and Street, *Artigas*, pp. 351–52.

68. FO, 13/23, H. Chamberlain to G. Canning, no. 45, Rio, May 28, 1826.

69. D. Leopoldina regarded D. Domitila as worse than Madame de Pompadour and Madame de Maintenon; see her letter to G. Schaeffer, São Cristóvão, Oct. 8, 1826, in "Cartas ineditas," pp. 125–26.

70. Armitage, *History of Brazil*, 1: 264–66, as amplified by Sousa, *Fundadores*, 3: 687–93.

71. See the private letters of the marquess of Resende, Brazilian minister in Vienna and Paris, to D. Pedro I, 1827–29, in "Correspondencia de Resende," pp. 177–355.

72. See *British and Foreign State Papers*, pp. 609–12.

73. See ibid., pp. 1008–24; and Manchester, *British Preeminence*, pp. 206–10.

74. Oliveira Lima, *Dom Pedro e Dom Miguel*, pp. 125–29.

75. See Serrão, *História*, 7: 404–5.

76. This recognition was confirmed in June by a vote of a meeting of the Three Estates of the Realm; see ibid., pp. 405–9.

77. The marquess of Resende to D. Pedro I, London, Aug. 7, 1828, in "Correspondencia de Resende," pp. 245–48.

78. FO, 13/24, H. Chamberlain to G. Canning, *Private and Confidential*, Rio, Aug. 19, 1826. Bank notes and copper coinage in circulation almost doubled between 1825 and 1827; see table II.4 in Peláez and Suzigan, *História monetária*, p. 49.

79. The third deputy was also a Coimbra graduate, but having graduated in 1809 he belonged to the youngest and transitional group of the Luso-Brazilians.

80. N. P. de C. Vergueiro, the nominee, was a political oddity. A native of Portugal, and an 1801 graduate of Coimbra, he had settled in São Paulo province, married there, and gained such local confidence that he was elected to the Lisbon Cortes, to the Constituent Assembly, and to the Senate base list by two provinces; see Forjaz, *Vergueiro*.

81. By May 1828 D. Pedro I had been forced to accept that as long as the marchioness of Santos remained in Rio de Janeiro he had no hope of securing a new bride from the royal families of Europe. The favorite was made to withdraw to her native province of São Paulo; see D. Pedro I's letters to her, Rio, May 13 and 22, 1828, in Rangel, *Marginados*, pp. 359, 367. She returned to Rio de Janeiro and her former status from Apr. to Aug. 1829; see Rangel, *D. Pedro I*, pp. 219–34.

82. Gomes da Silva denied that any such "secret cabinet" existed; see *Memórias*, pp. 83–86.

83. *Fallas do throno*, pp. 143–44, 154.

84. In the first group were the laws abolishing the *provedor-mor de saúde*, the *físico-mor* and *cirurgião-mor*, and the *seladores da alfândega*, and replacing the *desembargo do paço* and the *mesa de consciência e ordens* by the Supreme Tribunal of Justice. In the second were laws relating to the press, imprisonment without warrant, and gold and diamond contraband; regulating the provincial councils; and reforming the municipal councils; see *LB* (1826–29), pp. 236–56, 258–60, 271–87, 305, 310–26, 329–30.

85. FO, 13/24, H. Chamberlain to G. Canning, *Private and Confidential*, Rio, Aug. 19, 1826.

86. On the June mutiny, see Armitage, *History of Brazil*, 1: 319–23.

87. Seckinger, *Brazilian Monarchy*, pp. 146–50; and Street, *Artigas*, pp. 348–66.

88. For a good discussion of the deputies' attitudes toward the war, see Hann, "Río de la Plata," pp. 407–25.

89. See *Relação alfabetica*; and Arquivo Histórico do Itamaratí, Rio, Correspondência, 251-2-13, Antônio da Silva Júnior and Vicente Ferreira da Silva to the minister of foreign affairs, Lisbon, 1828; and 251-2-15/16, Antônio da Silva Caldeira and Antônio Joaquim Ribeiro de Faria to the minister of foreign affairs, Porto, 1828.

90. Arquivo Histórico do Itamaratí, Rio, Correspondência, 251-2-12, A. da Silva Jr., Brazilian consul, to the marquess of Aracatí, Lisbon, Aug. 25, 1828.

91. See FO, 13/24, H. Chamberlain to G. Canning, Separate and Private, Rio, Aug. 30, 1826.

92. Oliveira Lima, *Dom Pedro e Dom Miguel*, pp. 218, 249; and Wasth Rodrigues, "Fardas," p. 33.

93. Sousa, *Fundadores*, 6: 48–49, and 9: 172–74.

94. Vianna, *Jornalista*, pp. 154–64; and João Loureiro to Manuel José Maria da Costa e Sá, Rio, June 17, 1829, in "Cartas de Loureiro," p. 325.

95. The *Precursor das Eleições*, which appeared in Sept. 1828, complained:

"In the last election six hundred and thirty-three citizens received votes to be deputies." A third of the 21 names belonged to the Coimbra bloc, with Bernardo Pereira de Vasconcelos heading the list. Evaristo Ferreira da Veiga was also one of those recommended. See Vianna, *Imprensa*, pp. 36, 39–40.

96. Letter of Dec. 15, 1828, in "Cartas de Loureiro," p. 282.

97. See T. B. Ottoni, *Circular*, pp. 62–63; and C. B. Ottoni, *Autobiographia*, pp. 37–38.

98. Sousa, *Fundadores*, 4: 797.

99. No study exists of this able if unpopular man, who played an important role in Brazilian politics from Dec. 1821 until his death in 1854.

100. On the other hand, only Russia and the Vatican among the European powers recognized D. Miguel as lawful king of Portugal; see Serrão, *História*, 7: 410–13.

101. Letter of Feb. 11, 1829, in "Cartas de Loureiro," p. 303; and see Serrão, *História*, 7: 415–16.

102. Due to lack of investor confidence, the loan had to be issued at a huge discount, its face value being £769,200; see Castro Carreira, *Historia financeira*, pp. 148–52, 657–58.

103. Arquivo do Museu Imperial, Petrópolis, Pedro de Orléans e Bragança Collection, Catalogo B, Maço 12, document 588, undated draft, transcribed in Vianna, *D. Pedro I e D. Pedro II*, pp. 25–27.

104. Document of Mar. 17, 1829, in the Arquivo Nacional, Rio, transcribed in "Arquivo histórico 1," p. 101.

105. Ibid., p. 114.

106. Serrão, *História*, 7: 417–21.

107. The marquess of Santo Amaro was sent on a mission to Europe in Apr. 1830. Part of his instructions included "requesting help from England and France in the event of the Chamber of Deputies being dissolved in order to control the provinces"; see letter of D. Pedro I to Miguel Calmon du Pin e Almeida, future marquess of Abrantes, Boa Vista, Sept. 26, 1830, transcribed in Vianna, *D. Pedro I e D. Pedro II*, p. 75; and instructions of the duke of Broglie to the count of Saint Priest, Paris [1833], quoted in Rangel, *No rolar do tempo*, p. 149.

108. Expenditures were set at 13,900,000 milreis and revenue at 13,300,000 milreis. Of the budgeted revenue no less than 5,300,000 milreis was termed "extraordinary" (mainly borrowing); see Castro Carreira, *Historia financeira*, pp. 150–51.

109. See Gomes da Silva, *Memórias*, pp. 130–31.

110. *Fallas do throno*, p. 173.

111. A pamphlet, which voiced the opposition's views and which was published immediately after D. Pedro I ceased to reign, stated that his goal was a coup d'état "which since 1829 had been waiting in the wings"; see *Historia da revolução*, p. 19.

112. Letter of Aug. 25, 1830, in "Cartas de Loureiro," p. 354.

113. This was F. C. Brant Pontes, marquess of Barbacena. His career from 1821 to 1827 is indicative of the narrowness of the political community in these years: he led the abortive resistance to the rising at Salvador on Feb. 10, 1821; was one of the five men arrested in Rio after the Feb. 27, 1821, coup there; acted as Brazil's first agent in London; sat in the Constituent Assembly; was granted a title of nobility on Oct. 12, 1825; served as minister from Nov. 1825–Jan. 1826;

was named a senator on Jan. 26, 1826; and commanded the Brazilian army at the battle of Itazuingó in 1827.

114. Gomes da Silva, *Memórias*, pp. 139–51.

115. Sousa, *Fundadores*, 6: 69. The new chamber included 14 Luso-Brazilians, 9 military officers, 33 from the Coimbra bloc, 14 priests, and 45 others (mostly local notables). The number of Nativists can be estimated at well over 30. Compared to the 1826 chamber, the number of Luso-Brazilians fell from 24 to 14 and the number of priests from 21 to 14.

116. See the marquess of Resende to J. B. de Andrada e Silva, n.p. [Paris], n.d. [Sept. 1830], in "Correspondencia de Resende," pp. 396–98; and the fragment of Vasconcelos de Drummond's autobiography attached to "Cartas Andradinas," pp. 87–88.

117. See the agonized discussions held in the Council of State on Nov. 6, 1830, as to the course of action to be followed, in "Arquivo histórico 2," pp. 143–71.

118. Castro Carreira, *Historia financeira*, pp. 155, 183–84.

119. Article 10 of the law of Nov. 24, 1830, *LB* (1830), pt. 1, p. 53.

120. See Pimenta Bueno, *Direito público*, p. 482.

121. Vianna, *Imprensa*, pp. 121–31, 540–49, 597–613; and Armitage, *History of Brazil*, 2: 95–96.

122. Vianna, *D. Pedro I e D. Pedro II*, pp. 63–110; and Armitage, *History of Brazil*, 2: 81–83, 264–92.

123. Armitage, *History of Brazil*, 2: 93–94.

124. *Historia da revolução*, p. 16.

125. These street battles occurred on the nights of Mar. 13 and 14; see ibid., pp. 20–23, 31.

126. Documentary supplement to ibid., pp. 2–4.

127. Arquivo Histórico do Itamaratí, Rio, Correspondência, 251-1-3, remarks made in France and reported in José Joaquim da Rocha, Brazilian envoy, to Francisco Carneiro de Campos, minister of foreign affairs, no. 2, *Confidential*, Paris, Dec. 16, 1831.

128. All were senators, all had been ministers, and all were Luso-Brazilians.

129. The commander of the police force was replaced, and it was believed that the commander of the Rio garrison was about to be replaced by a military officer trusted by the emperor. In addition, a battalion from Santa Catarina had disembarked at Rio on Apr. 5. There was a general expectation that a decree suspending the constitutional guarantees was about to be issued. See *Historia da revolução*, pp. 35–39.

130. The *juizes de paz* of the capital presented the demand; see Armitage, *History of Brazil*, 2: 129; and *Historia da revolução*, pp. 40–41.

131. *Historia da revolução*, p. 43.

132. *Fallas do throno*, p. 211. D. Pedro later wrote that he abdicated "at 3 ½ A.M. on the 7th, because at that time there was no remedy other than either submitting to the demands of the armed forces and of a people in anarchy, who wanted the ministry I had dismissed as incompetent and liable (as I feared) to betray me, or abdicating to save my honor and to avoid breaching the provision of the Constitution by which I was conceded the right freely to appoint and dismiss ministers of state"; document transcribed in Vianna, *D. Pedro I e D. Pedro II*, p. 40.

CHAPTER 6

1. D. Pedro I and his family, escorted by many of the foreign envoys, left his country palace and at 7:30 A.M. embarked on a British warship in Rio harbor; see *Historia da revolução*, p. 46.

2. C. B. Ottoni, *Autobiographia*, p. 46.

3. By article 122, the regent was the ruler's closest relative aged 25 or over; see Pimenta Bueno, *Direito público*, p. 496.

4. Article 123 and 124; see ibid.

5. See the proclamation urging moderation by Antônio Borges da Fonseca, editor of *A República*, the main Exaltado periodical, in *Historia da revolução*, p. 14.

6. Of those few who placed loyalty to D. Pedro I above devotion to Brazil the most prominent were João Carlos Augusto de Oeynhausen, marquess of Aracatí, a councillor of state, senator, and former minister; A. Teles da Silva, marquess of Resende, then envoy in Paris; and Vicente Navarro de Andrade, baron of Inhomerim, personal physician to D. Pedro I. All three were Portuguese-born and belonged to the court circle.

7. *Fallas do throno*, pp. 211–13.

8. Ibid., p. 212. He was replaced as *comandante das armas* by his brother, José Joaquim de Lima e Silva, future viscount of Magé; see *Historia da revolução*, p. 50.

9. *LB* (1830–31), pp. 280–82.

10. João Loureiro, who was not only Portuguese but an ardent partisan of D. Miguel as king, naturally put a cynical interpretation on this universal goodwill: "All the parties are behaving with decorum and restraint, in the hopes of winning the regency elections for their own"; see letter of June 14, 1831, in "Cartas de Loureiro," p. 371.

11. Under section 2 of article 14, the General Assembly also defined the powers held by regents belonging to the imperial family; see Pimenta Bueno, *Direito público*, pp. 61–62, 483.

12. Article 130 mentioned the nomination of a guardian by a testamentary will only; see ibid., p. 497. See also *LB* (1830–31), p. 356; and Calmon, *História de D. Pedro II*, p. 60.

13. *LB* (1830–31), pp. 317–18.

14. *Fallas do throno*, p. 208; and letter of June 14, 1831, in "Cartas de Loureiro," p. 373. Moniz was in fact named as regent in place of and at the suggestion of his cousin, Manuel Odorico Mendes, also from Maranhão, who had played a leading role in the opposition to D. Pedro I and in the events of Apr. 7; see Sousa, *Fundadores*, 9: 191–94.

15. Only six Brazilians graduated from Coimbra from 1826 to 1830, and a law passed on Aug. 30, 1834, rendered graduates of foreign law schools thenceforth ineligible for appointment to the judiciary and law faculties in Brazil; see *LB* (1834), pt. 1, p. 31.

16. See the testimony of Francisco Inácio de Carvalho Moreira, baron of Penedo, transcribed in Nabuco de Araujo, *Estadista*, 1: 11.

17. Letter of Mar. 31, 1832, in "Cartas de Loureiro," p. 397.

18. Sousa, *Fundadores*, 9: 275–76.

19. The title of an 1840 political cartoon, "The Shoemaker Elector," repro-

duced in Flory, *Judge and Jury*, p. 48, exemplifies the political activities of the small folk. The role played by the press in politics is aptly illustrated by J. Loureiro's comment in 1832: "In Minas and São Paulo disorders had begun to appear, incited by the seditious ideas furnished by the journals of Rio"; letter of Jan. 14, 1832, in "Cartas de Loureiro," p. 390.

20. Sousa, *Fundadores*, 9: 270–74; and Rambo, "Carioca Press," pp. 79–81.

21. The appeal made by a Ceará politician to a colleague in Rio illustrates both the problem faced and the remedy employed: "I am convinced that the only way to reduce the infighting is to found a Masonic lodge; will you please get the Grand Orient . . . to grant authority to install one, and send it here as quickly as possible." Two sets of Masonic lodges, pro- and antiregime, existed. See José Ferreira Lima Sucupira to J. M. de Alencar, Fortaleza, Mar. 28, 1833, in "Correspondência de Alencar," pp. 195–96.

22. Coffee exports in Rio province doubled between 1826 and 1833 and more than tripled between 1826 and 1839; see Ferreira Soares, *Notas estatísticas*, p. 208.

23. Peláez and Suzigan, *História monetária*, pp. 59–65; and Castro Carreira, *Historia financeira*, pp. 183–99.

24. As in Pará on May 25 and June 2, in Maranhão on Sept. 12, and in Goiás on Aug. 14, 1831; see Ferreira Reis, "Grão-Pará," pp. 103–5, 156; and "Mato Grosso," pp. 189–90.

25. Quintas, "Nordeste," pp. 202–4, 222–24; and Rambo, "Carioca Press," pp. 20, 28–29, 111.

26. The motto of a leading Nativist newspaper in Minas Gerais, *O Sentinela do Serro*, ran thus: "The purpose of every political association is the preservation of natural and inalienable rights; these rights are liberty, security, property, and resistance to oppression." See Pinheiro Chagas, *Teófilo Ottoni*, p. 190.

27. See Rambo, "Carioca Press," p. 95.

28. Bethell, *Slave Trade*, pp. 75–78.

29. Quintas, "Nordeste," pp. 202–4, 222–24.

30. Castro Carreira, *Historia financeira*, pp. 153, 183, 187; and *LB* (1830–31), pp. 516–21.

31. *LB* (1830–31), pp. 296–99; and see letter of June 18, 1831, in "Cartas de Loureiro," p. 373.

32. The best accounts of this crisis are in Sousa, *Fundadores*, 7: 131–61; and in Pereira Castro, "Experiência republicana," p. 17.

33. The best biography of Feijó is probably Sousa, *Fundadores*, 7; but see also Egas, *Feijó*; Ellis Jr., *Feijó*; and Azevedo, *Feijó*.

34. As might be expected, these clubs were organized in Pernambuco, Bahia, and São Paulo before they appeared in Rio de Janeiro; see Rambo, "Carioca Press," pp. 108–9.

35. Vianna, *Imprensa*, pp. 149–54.

36. Wanderley Pinho, "Bahia," pp. 276–78; and Seckinger, "Politics of Nativism."

37. The society's name indicated that it opposed any change to the existing form of the Constitution. The newspaper's name, that of one of the first Portuguese settlers in Brazil, suggested that the movement was nationalistic in outlook. No adequate study of the Caramurú party exists; but see Rambo, "Carioca Press," pp. 110–11.

38. The Moderados' belief in an imminent restoration is evident from the dispatches of José Joaquim da Rocha, Brazilian envoy at Paris from 1831 to 1834; see Arquivo Histórico do Itamaratí, Rio, Correspondência, 225-1-3/4.

39. *LB* (1830–31), pp. 359–87; and Berrance de Castro, *Milicia cidadã*, pp. 17–31.

40. When the local *promotor público* (district attorney) or *juiz municipal* was to be appointed, the town council presented a list of three names from which the provincial president would select the new official; see *LB* (1832), pp. 192–93; and Flory, *Judge and Jury*, pp. 114–15.

41. *Sete de Abril*, Aug. 5, 1835, quoted in Flory, *Judge and Jury*, pp. 122, 231.

42. This group received the pejorative nickname of O Maromba; see Pereira Castro, "Experiência republicana," p. 38.

43. *Relatorio*, 1832, quoted in Sousa, *Fundadores*, 8: 102.

44. Ibid., 7: 200.

45. See "Tentativa de golpe de estado de 30 de julho de 1832 (a revolução dos três padres)," in ibid., 8: 99–129.

46. Ibid., p. 115.

47. He would in the 1850's receive the titles of viscount and marquess of Paraná; see Teixeira Filho, "Honório Hermeto."

48. *LB* (1832), pp. 106–7.

49. It should be noted that these military triumphs gave D. Pedro for the first time personal credibility in terms of the Napoleonic vision of the nation.

50. See Rambo, "Carioca Press," pp. 174–76; and *Times* (London), Sept. 3, 1835.

51. The last decree signed by Costa Carvalho printed in *LB* (1833) is dated July 9, and the first without his signature is July 15. The possible connection between the resolution to banish the former Emperor and the withdrawal of the regent has not previously been noted. The anonymous biography of Costa Carvalho in Sisson, *Galeria*, 1: 54, states that he withdrew because of sickness, not signing any documents after July 18.

52. Virtually nothing has been written on the nature and organization of this conspiracy; even the date on which Antônio Carlos left Brazil is not clear.

53. See Rambo, "Carioca Press," pp. 184–89; Vianna, *História imperial*, pp. 56–57; and João Antônio Rodrigues de Carvalho to J. M. de Alencar, Rio, Dec. 19, 1833, in "Correspondência de Alencar," pp. 274–75.

54. Vianna, *D. Pedro I e D. Pedro II*, pp. 46–49.

55. *Times*, Oct. 4 and 19, 1833.

56. The 1834 chamber contained no less than 24 priests, half of whom were committed Nativists. A further 13 deputies were strong Nativists, so that the group numbered at least 25 in a body of 104. Of the 6 senators named between 1832 and 1835, 4 were priests.

57. D. Miguel's removal was arranged by the convention of Evora Monte signed on May 26; Sousa, *Fundadores*, 4: 1143–44.

58. *Organizações*, p. 51; and Sousa, *Fundadores*, 7: 220, 222–25.

59. *Organizações*, p. 51.

60. Articles 4, 7, and 15; see Pimenta Bueno, *Direito público*, pp. 506–7, 509. Had the original project for constitutional reform been enacted unchanged or had the coup of July 30 succeeded and a new constitution been promulgated, the Chamber of Deputies would have been given these same powers.

61. These and further powers were specified in article 10; see ibid., pp. 507–8.
62. *Organizações*, p. 51.
63. By the law of Oct. 3, 1834, the provincial assembly every two years elected a list of six persons who would act, in order of election, as vice president if need arose; see *LB* (1834), p. 55.
64. To the 1834 chamber had been elected 37 Coimbra bloc deputies, 7 Luso-Brazilians, 5 graduates of the two Brazilian law schools, and 4 military men.
65. Letter of Sept. 20, 1834, in "Cartas de Loureiro," p. 426.
66. Manuel do Nascimento Castro e Silva to J. M. de Alencar, Rio, June 3, 1835, in "Correspondência de Alencar," p. 47.
67. José Mariano de Albuquerque to J. M. de Alencar, Fortaleza, Feb. 6, 1833, in ibid., p. 305.
68. Letter of July 10, 1834, in "Cartas de Loureiro," p. 425.
69. The social, economic and cultural diversity of the Brazilian provinces makes difficult any generalization about this under-studied subject. Indicative, as case studies, are Boiteaux, "Partidos politicos," pp. 909–11; and Leitman, "Ragamuffin War," pp. 54–70.
70. Article of Oct. 12, 1835, quoted in Sousa, *Fundadores*, 7: 249.
71. The nature and organization of this coalition has yet to be investigated by historians; but see ibid., pp. 237–40.
72. Articles 27 and 28 of the Ato Adicional followed almost word for word the original system of presidential elections in the U.S. Constitution; see Pimenta Bueno, *Direito público*, pp. 511–12.
73. Of the other provinces in the north and northeast, Pará was won by its bishop, Piauí by Lima e Silva, and the remaining four by Holanda Cavalcanti; see Sousa, *Fundadores*, 7: 244–45.
74. Francisco Alvares Machado de Vasconcelos to J. da Costa Carvalho, future marquess of Mont'Alegre, Rio, July 25, 1835, in Moraes, "Reminiscencias historicas," p. 93.
75. M. do N. Castro e Silva to J. M. de Alencar, Rio, June 3, 1835, in "Correspondência de Alencar," p. 47; and Sousa, *Fundadores*, 7: 227–29.
76. This crisis is graphically reported in the letters to J. M. de Alencar from Joaquim Inácio da Costa Miranda, Rio, Aug. 28, and Oct. 3 and 14, 1835; and from M. do N. Castro e Silva, Rio, Aug. 11 and 30, Sept. 27, and Oct. 18, 1834, in "Correspondência de Alencar," pp. 48–55, 78–87, 177–78 (the letter of Sept. 27 is wrongly attributed to Vicente Ferreira de Castro e Silva).
77. Ferreira Reis, "O Grão-Pará," pp. 89–112; and João Batista Gonçalves Campos to J. M. de Alencar, [Belém do] Pará, Nov. 19, 1833, in "Correspondência de Alencar," pp. 427–29.
78. Bethell and Carvalho, "Brazil," pp. 702–3.
79. Spalding, *Revolução farroupilha*, pp. 12–28; and on the economic causes of the revolt, see Leitman, "Ragamuffin War," pp. 77–152.
80. Proclamation of Colonel Bento Gonçalves da Silva, reprinted in Spalding, *Revolução farroupilha*, p. 96.
81. Not all were so deceived. On Oct. 8, 1834, João Loureiro wrote: "It seems to me that I can tell you right now that he [Feijó] will be judged a better minister than regent"; in "Cartas de Loureiro," p. 429.
82. On the regent's offering of posts to leading members of the Coimbra bloc, such as J. da Costa Carvalho, the former regent, see Arquivo Nacional, Rio, Seção

dos Arquivos Particulares, Codice 607, vol. 7, D. A. Feijó to the marquess of Barbacena, Rio, Dec. 10, 1835; and João Loureiro's comment—"but these did not wish to accept the offers from him"—in letter of Nov. 25, 1835, in "Cartas de Loureiro," p. 433.

83. See Sousa, *Fundadores*, 7: 246–47.

84. The text of Feijó's speech to the Cortes in Apr. 1822 is printed in Ellis Jr., *Feijó*, pp. 51–55; the key passages are on pp. 54–55.

85. The memorandum or notes are transcribed in Sousa, *Fundadores*, 7: 286–88; and see letter of Nov. 25, 1835, in "Cartas de Loureiro," p. 443. Feijó's reluctance to accept the regency, which grew as the election returns revealed his failure to win the northern provinces, may have been due to his conviction that he would not command the common consent of the *pátrias* that was indispensable for governing.

86. The words quoted were used by Feijó in the Speech from the Throne delivered on May 3, 1836; see *Fallas do throno*, p. 261.

87. Bethell and Carvalho, "Brazil," pp. 703–4.

88. Arquivo Nacional, Rio, Seção dos Arquivos Particulares, Codice 607, vol. 7, to the marquess of Barbacena, Rio, Dec. 10, 1835.

89. *Fallas do throno*, pp. 261–62.

90. See Sousa, *Fundadores*, 5: 158–60, 167–69, 175–79; and Holub, "Bernardo Pereira de Vasconcelos."

91. The speech openly attacked the papacy over its refusal to accept Padre Antônio Maria de Moura, nominated by the government two years before, as the new bishop of Rio de Janeiro; see Sousa, *Fundadores*, 7: 262–72.

92. To J. M. de Alencar, Rio, Mar. 29, 1836, in "Correspondência de Alencar," p. 230.

93. "I tell you, it has been for me a major sacrifice, my remaining as minister; because those men, realizing that Feijó would not dismiss the ministry, have resorted to every kind of stratagem and insult to see if the ministers, driven to distraction, would not resign their portfolios, leaving the Regent to their mercies. The session has been taken up with insults, with speechifying, with disputes, and as of today, nothing has been accomplished"; see M. do N. Castro e Silva to J. M. de Alencar, Rio, Aug. 23, 1836, in ibid., p. 63.

94. Castro Carreira, *Historia financeira*, pp. 206–8, 215.

95. Flory, *Judge and Jury*, pp. 159–62.

96. See Leitman, "Ragamuffin War," pp. 33–35; and Tasso Fragoso, *Revolução farroupilha*, pp. 89–92.

97. See J. I. da Costa Miranda to J. M. de Alencar, Rio, May 12, 1837, in "Correspondência de Alencar," p. 112.

98. To J. M. de Alencar, Rio, June 1, 1837, in ibid., p. 236.

99. Arquivo Nacional, Rio, Seção dos Arquivos Particulares, Codice 630, minute of letter of Antônio Pedro da Costa Ferreira, future baron of Pindaré, to Feijó, Rio, Aug. 23, 1837; and Sousa, *Fundadores*, 7: 289–91.

100. To Bento Gonçalves da Silva, Rio, Jan. 20, 1835, quoted in Sousa, *Fundadores*, 7: 237.

101. *Fallas do throno*, p. 281.

CHAPTER 7

1. Melo Franco, *Partidos*, pp. 29–31; Oliveira Torres, *Democracia coroada*, pp. 288–89; Oliveira Lima, *Independência*, p. 352; and Nabuco de Araujo, *Estadista*, 1: 31.

2. See M. do N. Castro e Silva to J. M. de Alencar, Rio, Oct. 18, 1837, in "Correspondência de Alencar," pp. 69–70. On Feijó's choice of Araújo Lima and his reasons, see, for example, Sousa, *Fundadores*, 7: 291, 295; and 8: 146.

3. Vasconcelos, Miguel Calmon du Pin e Almeida, and Joaquim José Rodrigues Torres all held degrees from Coimbra, and Sebastião do Rêgo Barros studied there three years before leaving hastily in 1823 due to the harassment of Brazilian-born students. After gaining his *baccalaureat ès sciences* at Paris, he obtained a doctorate in mathematics from Hamburg University. Antônio Peregrino Maciel Monteiro held his *baccalaureat ès sciences, licence ès sciences,* and doctorate in medicine from Paris. Rodrigues Torres studied in Paris in the late 1820's, and Miguel Calmon spent the mid-1820's in France and England.

4. Sousa, *Fundadores*, 5: 102.

5. Despite his key role in politics stretching from 1821 to his death in 1870 and the availability of his personal papers in the Instituto Histórico e Geográfico Brasileiro, Rio, there is a lack of good studies of Pedro de Araújo Lima, viscount and marquess of Olinda; but see Camara Cascudo, *Marquez de Olinda*.

6. FO, 13/154, William Gore Ouseley, British envoy, to Viscount Palmerston, foreign secretary, no. 71, Rio, Sept. 18, 1839; and Rangel, *Textos e pretextos*, pp. 33–35.

7. The diary kept by Araújo Lima during his tour of Italy in late 1824 reveals his intellectual tastes and outlook; see Instituto Histórico e Geográfico Brasileiro, Rio, Olinda Collection, Lata 214, Pasta 61.

8. See Ibid., Lata 208, Pasta 34, undated speech probably given at the conferring of degrees at the Escola Militar in Sept. 1846; Barata, *Escola Politécnica*, p. 61; and C. B. Ottoni, *Autobiographia*, p. 117.

9. Baron of Fort Rouen to the minister of foreign affairs, Rio, Oct. 17, 1837, quoted in Rangel, *No rolar do tempo*, p. 130.

10. Count of Saint Priest to the minister of foreign affairs, Rio, Sept. 7, 1833, quoted in ibid., p. 128.

11. See Sousa, *Fundadores*, 5: 132–34.

12. Ibid., pp. 158–59.

13. Annual report presented by Joaquim Vieira da Silva e Sousa, an 1822 graduate of Coimbra, quoted in Vieira Fazenda, "Periodo regencial," pp. 46–47.

14. Sousa, *Fundadores*, 5: 159–60.

15. Quoted in ibid., p. 202.

16. See his speech of Aug. 25, 1832, in *Recordações do Antonio Pereira Rebouças*, 1: 108–19; and Rodrigues, *Brazil and Africa*, pp. 67–71.

17. Kent, "African Revolt in Bahia"; and S. J. Stein, *Vassouras*, p. 145.

18. The law had been enacted to comply with the terms of the slave trade treaty signed with Great Britain in 1826.

19. Bethell, *Slave Trade*, pp. 390–92.

20. Sousa, *Fundadores*, 5: 167.

21. *Chronista*, Mar. 15, 1838, in an article discussing the need for a university in Rio.

22. See *LB* (1836), pt. 1, pp. 21–24, and pt. 2, p. 29; (1837), pt. 1, p. 30, and pt. 2, pp. 15, 50; 1° *centenario do Jornal do Commercio*, pp. 387–88; and FO, 13/ 153 and 154, W. G. Ouseley to Lord Palmerston, nos. 15 and 71, Rio, Mar. 23 and Sept. 18, 1839.

23. Escragnolle Doria, *Collegio*, pp. 13–17.

24. "Discurso recitado por occasião da abertura das aulas do collegio D. Pedro Segundo, aos 25 de março de 1838 por Bernardo Pereira de Vasconcellos," transcribed in Sousa, *Fundadores*, 5: 282–85.

25. See R. D. Anderson, *Education in France*, pp. 8–14.

26. Declaration of the municipal council of Salvador, Nov. 7, 1837, transcribed in Osório, *Itaparicá*, pp. 211–23.

27. Quoted in Wanderley Pinho, "Bahia," p. 282.

28. The revolt took its name from one of its leaders, Dr. Francisco Sabino da Rocha Vieira.

29. João Francisco Cabussu to J. M. de Alencar, [Salvador,] Apr. 11, 1838, in "Correspondência de Alencar," p. 332. See also the sources cited in Holub, "Brazilian Sabinada."

30. Statement in the 7 *de Novembro* newspaper, quoted in Wanderley Pinho, "Bahia," p. 283.

31. *Chronista*, Jan. 25, 1838. This newspaper, which characterized itself on Jan. 27, 1838, as being "not ministerial, but instead governmental," was edited by Firmino Rodrigues Silva, Justiniano José da Rocha, and Josino do Nascimento Silva, all three later to be leading Conservative party journalists and politicians. If the Conservative party did exist from Sept. 1837, as is commonly postulated, then the fact should be patent from the columns of O *Chronista*. The newspaper's contents do not present politics in terms of a Conservative party or indeed of any party.

32. On the elections to the new chamber, see M. do N. Castro e Silva to J. M. de Alencar, Rio, Nov. 11, 1836, in "Correspondência de Alencar," pp. 66–67.

33. Annual report presented in 1835 by J. V. da Silva e Sousa, quoted in Vieira Fazenda, "Periodo regencial," p. 46.

34. Article 1 of the Ato Adicional, which laid down that "the authority of the legislative assembly of the province shall not extend to the said court nor to its muncipality," spared Brazil the political tensions which, in the case of Argentina, for example, arose from the same city being both the national and a provincial capital. Only in 1882 did Argentina follow the Brazilian precedent. By article 5 of the Ato the meeting place of the first provincial assembly of Rio province was designated by the national government. Its choice, the city of Niterói, was confirmed as capital of Rio province by the new provincial assembly; see Pimenta Bueno, *Direito público*, pp. 506–7.

35. See Ferreira Soares, *Notas estatísticas*, pp. 28, 45, 60, 72, 74, 89, 99, 108, 119, 209, 215.

36. Respectively, Rodrigues Torres and Paulino José Soares de Sousa, married to Anna and Maria, daughters of João Alvares de Azevedo.

37. "Discurso autobiográfico," pp. 279, 280–81. Honório Hermeto's correspondent in Rio was the Portuguese-born João Maria Colaço de Magalhães Velasques Sarmento, future viscount of Condeixa; see *Nobreza*, 2: 534.

38. The ethnic and social origins of only the military have been studied in detail; see ch. 2 of McBeth, "The Politicians v. the Generals." Not only were

many of the leading merchants in the export-import trade Portuguese-born, but they often retained their citizenship and on retirement usually went back to their native land. An example of a leading planter who was Portuguese-born is Manuel Antônio Ribeiro de Castro, baron of Santa Rita; see his obituary in the *Jornal do Commercio*, June 19, 1854.

39. *Chronista*, Jan. 25, 1838.

40. Wanderley Pinho, "Bahia," p. 281.

41. *Chronista*, June 9, 1838. Already, on Sept. 10, 1837, Bento Gonçalves da Silva, the captured head of the rebels, had escaped from prison in Bahia and by Dec. was back in Rio Grande do Sul; see Spalding, *Revolução farroupilha*, pp. 124, 145–46.

42. See Flory, *Judge and Jury*, pp. 159–61.

43. See Pimenta Bueno, *Direito público*, pp. 186–87.

44. Such was particularly the case when the president was a native of the province. In Sept. 1837, of the eighteen presidents six were born in that province and one, born in France, was married and domiciled in the province he administered. Three presidents were military men engaged in the suppression of rebellion. Three presidents were senators and five were elected deputy from the province over which they presided.

45. *Chronista*, May 26, 1838.

46. *Chronista*, Jan. 12 and Oct. 12, 1838. Six other candidates obtained 2,770 votes among them.

47. *Chronista*, June 5, 1838.

48. The 41 other laws largely involved personal questions, such as the grant of retirement with pay, approval of pensions to military for long service or disability, grants of naturalization, and similar matters. The 7 laws of substance were concerned with financial and military matters; see *LB* (1838), pt. 1, pp. 23, 41, 42, 49, 58, 60, 64.

49. *Organizações*, pp. 70–71.

50. The 1838 chamber contained 45 members of the Coimbra bloc, 4 Luso-Brazilians, and 4 men with French degrees. There were 19 graduates of the two Brazilian law schools. The chamber also included 7 military men, 6 bureaucrats, 11 priests, and 4 landowners. There were at least 16 Nativist deputies.

51. FO, 13/152, W. G. Ouseley to Lord Palmerston, no. 2, Rio, Jan. 18, 1839.

52. Ibid., no. 24, Rio, Apr. 17, 1839.

53. Ibid., nos. 17 and 26, Rio, Mar. 23 and Apr. 26, 1839.

54. See FO, 13/152 and 154, W. G. Ouseley to Lord Palmerston, nos. 24 and 67, Rio, Apr. 17 and Sept. 13, 1839. In the cabinet named in Apr. 1839 three men, all novices, held two ministries each. Its fourth member, named minister of war in May, was the count of Lajes, who had held the post under D. Pedro I and Feijó— at no time with conspicuous success.

55. See FO, 13/154, W. G. Ouseley to Lord Palmerston, no. 64, Rio, Aug. 9, 1839; and Tasso Fragoso, *Revolução farroupilha*, pp. 129–41.

56. FO, 13/155, William Watson, vice-consul, to Lord Palmerston, no. 11, Maranhão, May 20, 1839; and Ferreira Reis, "Grão-Pará," pp. 158–62.

57. FO, 13/155, W. Watson to Lord Palmerston, no. 17, Maranhão, Aug. 19, 1839, enclosing copies of W. Watson to W. G. Ouseley, nos. 5 and 6, Maranhão, July 15 and Aug. 15, 1839. The revolt was named after Manuel Francisco dos Anjos Ferreira, o Balaio (the Straw basket), which referred to his trade.

58. "I cannot completely share," the envoy continued, "the alarm and despondency which I occasionally hear expressed. The immense and increasing commerce and produce of Brazil, and particularly of this Capital and Province, the material interests shared by so many persons of intelligence both Foreigners and Brazilians and the physical improvements and progress of the country, are among the chief sources of hope for the ultimate extrication of the Empire from its present difficulties. I speak of course of the probabilities for a time, only perhaps a few years." See FO, 13/154, W. G. Ouseley to Lord Palmerston, no. 71, Rio, Sept. 18, 1839.

59. Flory, *Judge and Jury*, pp. 165–67; and Sousa, *Fundadores*, 7: 310–23.

60. Sousa, *Fundadores*, 5: 237.

61. Letter of Nov. 29, 1839, in "Cartas de Loureiro," p. 444.

62. Baron of Fort Rouen to the minister of foreign affairs, Rio, Dec. 7, 1839, quoted in Calmon, *História de D. Pedro II*, pp. 123.

63. Quoted in Escragnolle Doria, *Collegio*, p. 32.

64. Installing the emperor's portrait in a government building, usually the presidential palace, provincial assembly, or town hall, served to give the monarch a visual identity, an important consideration since most people were not literate. The portrait also served on such days of official court gala as the emperor's birthday as a substitute for the monarch, to which individuals bowed as though actually at court.

65. *Chronista*, Jan. 25, 1838.

66. *Chronista*, June 21, 1838. The style of this article suggests that it was written by J. J. da Rocha.

67. D. Pedro II suffered from the juvenile form of the disease which ceases at puberty. His last recorded attack was in Mar. 1840; see Calmon, *História de D. Pedro II*, pp. 8–9, 126–27.

68. See ibid., pp. 89–91.

69. Opinion of the viscount of Santo Amaro in Nov. 1838, as reported by the viscount of Itabaiana to the marquess of Resende, Boulogne, Jan. 4, 1839, in "Correspondencia de Resende," p. 490.

70. Entry for Jan. 3, 1838, in the diary of François, prince of Joinville, son of Louis Philippe of France, in Lacombe, "Diário inédito," p. 184. In Dec. 1839 the British envoy, commenting on a rumor that "the Emperor is not quite free from some mental affection, or defect of intellectual faculties," reported that D. Pedro II was extremely shy and emotionally very immature but that none of this was "decided evidence of deficiency of intellect"; see FO, 13/154, W. G. Ouseley to Lord Palmerston, *Private and Secret*, Rio, Dec. 19, 1839.

71. Pimenta Bueno, *Direito público*, p. 496.

72. Sousa, *Fundadores*, 3: 1157.

73. Calmon, *História de D. Pedro II*, pp. 116–17; and Sousa, *Fundadores*, 5: 287.

74. V. F. de Castro e Silva to J. M. de Alencar, Rio, Apr. 5, 1836, in "Correspondência de Alencar," p. 179.

75. On this whole subject, see Sousa, *Fundadores*, 8: 140–46.

76. The views of the French envoys at Rio on the Andrada brothers and on A. F. de P. e Holanda Cavalcanti de Albuquerque, future viscount of Albuquerque, are summarized in Rangel, *No rolar do tempo*, pp. 110–25; and *Textos e pretextos*, pp. 11, 19–20 respectively. See Arquivo Nacional, Rio, Seção dos Arquivos

Particulares, Codice 112, vol. 4, P. J. Soares de Sousa, future viscount of Uruguaí, to Francisco Peixoto de Lacerda Werneck, future baron of Patí do Alferes, Niterói, Mar. 1838.

77. *O Parlamentar*, Dec. 12, 1838, as reported in *Chronista*, Dec. 15, 1838. See Padre Geraldo Leite Bastos to J. M. de Alencar, Rio, July 26 [1837]; and M. do N. Castro e Silva to Alencar, Rio, Oct. 18, 1837, in "Correspondência de Alencar," pp. 70, 431.

78. "I cannot go against the demands of my conscience, for I am convinced that it will be a calamity for Brazil should he [Holanda Cavalcanti] be Regent"; see M. do N. Castro e Silva to J. M. de Alencar, Rio, Feb. 13, 1838, in "Correspondência de Alencar," pp. 73–74. A minority of Nativists, similarly repelled, supported Feijó, who came in fifth among the candidates for Regent in 1838.

79. FO, 13/153, W. G. Ouseley to Lord Palmerston, no. 56, *Confidential*, Rio, July 20, 1839.

80. FO, 13/154, W. G. Ouseley to Lord Palmerston, no. 71, Rio, Sept. 18, 1839.

81. The passage of the law of interpretation would not of itself, it should be stressed, centralize power but would permit the amendment of the criminal procedure code in that sense.

82. Decree of Jan. 10, 1840; see *Fallas do throno*, p. 313.

83. The minutes and statutes of the club are transcribed in Sousa, *Fundadores*, 8: 253–63.

84. Also belonging to the club were Francisco de Paula Cavalcanti de Albuquerque, future viscount of Suassuna, like his brother a senator, and three Nativists: Senator A. P. da Costa Ferreira, future baron of Pindaré; José Mariano de Albuquerque, a deputy; and Padre Carlos Peixoto de Alencar, a deputy.

85. No satisfactory biography of Senator Alencar exists, but see his entry in Studart, *Diccionario*, 2: 156–58; and the information in his son's biography, Meneses, *José de Alencar*, pp. 17–59, 163–73.

86. Sousa, *Fundadores*, 8: 256–57.

87. Ibid., p. 259.

88. See the study of Aureliano in Vianna, *História imperial*, pp. 31–148.

89. *Fallas do throno*, pp. 318, 320. The third member, Francisco Gê Acaiába de Montezuma, a Coimbra graduate, joined the secret club on May 9. Of him, Honório Hermeto later remarked scornfully that he "does not sell himself, he's only for rent."

90. Sousa, *Fundadores*, 8: 260.

91. Ibid., pp. 260–63. Alencar's proposal for a Council of State "composed of one member from each province" was in essence an attempt to institutionalize the traditional duality of El Rei Nosso Senhor and the individual *pátria*.

92. *Fallas do throno*, p. 320.

93. Ibid.; and Sousa, *Fundadores*, 8: 155–56.

94. Arquivo Nacional, Rio, Seção dos Arquivos Particulares, Codice 112, vol. 4, P. J. Soares de Sousa, future viscount of Uruguaí, to F. P. de Lacerda Werneck, future baron of Patí do Alferes, Rio, July 15, 1840; and Sousa, *Fundadores*, 7: 157–58.

95. Sousa, *Fundadores*, 8: 162–63.

96. *Fallas do throno*, p. 328, note 2.

97. Ibid., pp. 327–32. Although the signature of F. de P. Cavalcanti de Albuquerque, senator from Pernambuco, is not on the petition, he was actively involved in this meeting and so has been added to the seventeen senators who signed.

98. Unanimous in favor were the deputies from Goiás, Mato Grosso, and Espírito Santo, but these were only four in total. The eighteen senators came from Pernambuco (four of six); Minas Gerais (four of ten); Ceará and Rio de Janeiro (two of four each); Maranhão (two of two); Goiás, Mato Grosso, and Espírito Santo (one of one each); and Bahia (one of six).

99. On D. Pedro II's role in the affair, see the judicious discussion in Sousa, *Fundadores*, 8: 185–95.

100. *Fallas do throno*, p. 329.

101. Ibid., p. 334.

102. Limpo de Abreu was unusual. Born in Portugal, he had been brought to Brazil as an infant and raised there. He graduated from Coimbra in 1820. Marriage into a family of notables in Minas Gerais linked him to the Nativists of that province. See Almeida Magalhães, *Abaeté*.

103. See annotation by D. Pedro II to the text of Franco de Almeida, *Furtado*, and included as note 13 in the 2d ed. of that work, p. 27.

104. "Where is the coherence of ideas of the men who composed the former cabinet? What did Sr. Aureliano have in common with the Srs. Andrada? What did the Srs. Holanda have in common with Sr. Limpo de Abreu? How could a parliamentary government be formed of men of such diverse ideas, who had always been utterly hostile?"; speech by Manuel Nunes Machado, session of Aug. 12, 1841, in *Perfís Parlamentares*, p. 68.

105. *Annaes do Parlamento*, 1840, 2: 399–400, quoted in *Organizações*, p. 80.

106. The son of the former regent Francisco de Lima e Silva, Luís Alves had first distinguished himself in suppressing the Apr. 1832 rising in Rio city, at the orders of Feijó. In the present century he has been made the presiding saint (no lesser word will suffice) of the Brazilian army, its "Patron." The future duke of Caxias has been the subject of several hagiographic biographies, beginning in 1878 with Pinto de Campos, *Vida do grande cidadão*. Of the more recent works, the best are Vilhena de Morais's *O duque de ferro* and *Novos aspectos*.

107. Spalding, *Revolução farroupilha*, pp. 178–86.

108. *Annaes do Parlamento*, 1840, 2: 399–400, quoted in *Organizações*, p. 80.

109. Only six of the eighteen provinces were unaffected—Maranhão, Piauí, Pernambuco, Alagoas, Goiás, and Santa Catarina. In an equivalent period of time, the Regresso ministry of 1837 removed four presidents.

110. In Apr. 1841 *O Brasil* reported that the cabinet had in eight months transferred 43 *juizes de direito*; see Flory, *Judge and Jury*, pp. 184, 242. Analysis of the decree books in Arquivo Nacional, Rio, Seção dos Ministérios, Series IJ[1] and IJ[4], show that some 65 changes were made, one-third of them in Dec. 1840.

111. Mello e Matos, *Paginas*, pp. 46–48; and the account in Flory, *Judge and Jury*, pp. 168–70, which is written from the cabinet's viewpoint.

112. On the Paraíba do Norte elections, see *Chronista*, Jan. 27, 1838.

113. J. I. da Costa Miranda to J. M. de Alencar, Rio, Apr. 12, 1837, in "Correspondência de Alencar," pp. 110–11.

114. See the fragmentary diaries of D. Pedro II for Aug. 27 and Dec. 2–5, 1840, transcribed in Vianna, *D. Pedro I e D. Pedro II*, pp. 113–21; and Vianna, *História imperial*, pp. 70–72.

115. T. B. Ottoni, *Circular*, pp. 151–52.

116. Filler, "Liberalism," pp. 90–98.

117. Vianna, *História imperial*, pp. 72–73.

118. This was P. J. Soares de Sousa; see Soares de Souza, *Uruguaí*. Cândido José de Araújo Viana, future viscount of Sapucaí, had been minister of finance from 1832 to 1834 and one of D. Pedro II's tutors in 1839 and 1840.

119. *LB* (1841), pt. 1, pp. 75–96.

120. Soares de Souza, *Uruguaí*, p. 104.

121. Thus Honório Hermeto was named president of Rio de Janeiro province on Dec. 1, 1841.

122. See the extremely enlightening letter from H. H. Carneiro Leão, future marquess of Paraná, to P. J. Soares de Sousa, future viscount of Uruguaí, quoted in ibid., pp. 121–22.

123. See Filler, "Liberalism," pp. 107–8, 196–97.

124. Arquivo do Museu Imperial, Petrópolis, Pedro de Orléans e Bragança Collection, Maço 105, document 5074, Joaquim Cândido Soares de Meirelles to D. Pedro II, Jan. 25, 1842.

125. Ibid.

126. Filler, "Liberalism," pp. 46–47.

127. *Fallas do throno*, pp. 351–56.

128. As Filler points out, the rebels almost certainly received early information about the government's decision to impose a permanent ban; see "Liberalism," pp. 107–8.

129. The character and career of Rafael Tobias de Aguiar are acutely analyzed in ibid., pp. 86–93, 97–100.

130. See ibid., p. 159; and Evangelista, *Lorena*, pp. 77–79. An attempt to start a rising in Ceará failed through lack of support; see Meneses, *José de Alencar*, p. 59.

131. One leading conspirator, Teófilo Ottoni, did manage to escape the government's roundup and reach Minas Gerais, where he played a major role in the rising; see Filler, "Liberalism," pp. 207, 210–12.

132. The new steamship line allowed the government to move troops in one day to the province of São Paulo and later to bring them back to meet the Minas Gerais rising; see ibid., pp. 119, 165, 215.

133. Ibid., pp. 116–17.

134. Quoted in ibid., pp. 110–11, 202.

135. See James, "Obedience and Dissent."

136. Filler, "Liberalism," p. 204.

137. These vivid, revealing letters are printed in full in Vilhena de Moraes, *Caxias em São Paulo*, pp. 83–84.

138. Filler, "Liberalism," pp. 121–22, 212–13.

139. Ibid., pp. 208–9.

140. T. B. Ottoni, *Circular*, pp. 178–79.

CHAPTER 8

1. See Barman and Barman, "Law Graduate," p. 436.

2. In 1840 over 200 students were enrolled at the two law schools, three-quarters of them at the Olinda faculty. Each school had nine full professors, of

whom five in each case held degrees from Coimbra or other European law schools, and four were graduates of the law school in question. By 1850, enrollment in the law schools had risen to over 500 students, 70 percent of them at Olinda. See ibid.

3. These three adjectives were used in May 1862 by the marquess of Olinda, when presenting his cabinet to the Chamber of Deputies, to describe two novice ministers; see *Annaes do Parlamento*, 1862, 1: 108, quoted in *Organizações*, p. 131.

4. See Francisco José de Matos to J. M. de Alencar, Ceará [Fortaleza], July 13, Aug. 7, Sept. 7 and 30, and Nov. 7, 1842, in "Correspondência de Alencar," pp. 120–27; and José Antônio Marinho, *História*, pp. 52–55, 331–33.

5. Arquivo do Museu Imperial, Petrópolis, Pedro de Orléans e Bragança Collection, Maço 116, document 5571, transcribed in Vianna, *Vultos*, pp. 149–53. The passage comes from a collective offer of resignation which the cabinet ministers presented on Nov. 15, 1851, to D. Pedro II. The document is basically an analysis of the emergence of political parties after 1840, composed by men principally responsible for that development. P. J. Soares de Sousa, future viscount of Uruguaí, was a minister in both 1842 and 1851. For a vivid if highly partisan account of the resulting purge, see Marinho, *História*, pp. 298–327.

6. See Bernardo Jacinto da Veiga, president of Minas Gerais, to F. Rodrigues Silva, Ouro Prêto, Oct. 31, 1842; and P. J. Soares de Sousa, future viscount of Uruguaí, to the F. Rodrigues Silva, Rio, Nov. 15, 1842, both quoted in Mascarenhas, *Jornalista*, pp. 65, 66. Official *chapas* had been used in the *eleições do cacête* in 1840.

7. As a senator, Feijó had to be tried by the upper house on the criminal charge brought against him; see Sousa, *Fundadores*, 7: 354–60.

8. Writing to F. Rodrigues Silva on Oct. 11, 1842, J. J. da Rocha reported that "Aureliano has been defeated four times in less than two weeks"; quoted in Mascarenhas, *Jornalista*, pp. 73–75.

9. See Manchester, *British Preeminence*, pp. 289–93; and Bethell, *Slave Trade*, pp. 228–35.

10. Soares de Souza, *Uruguaí*, pp. 155–57; and Vianna, *História imperial*, pp. 91–97.

11. See the letters written during 1843 by J. J. da Rocha to F. Rodrigues Silva, quoted in Mascarenhas, *Jornalista*, pp. 96–104; and Arquivo do Museu Imperial, Petrópolis, Pedro de Orléans e Bragança Collection, Catalogo B, Maço 27, document 970, H. H. Carneiro Leão, future marquess of Paraná, to D. Pedro II, undated (but after June 1843).

12. The budget law passed on Oct. 21, 1843, reduced the subsidies to the provinces by one-third from the existing level for 1843–44, reduced them by a further third in 1844–45, and abolished them entirely in 1845–46; see *LB* (1843), pt. 1, pp. 67, 77–78.

13. Arquivo do Museu Imperial, Petrópolis, Pedro de Orléans e Bragança Collection, Catalogo B, Maço 27, document 970.

14. Annotation by D. Pedro II to the text of Franco de Almeida, *Furtado*; see note 21 on p. 33.

15. On the fall of the cabinet, see Vianna, *História imperial*, pp. 97–104.

16. Almeida Torres was to become viscount of Macaé and Alves Branco, viscount of Caravelas.

17. Decree no. 342, *LB* (1844), pt. 2, p. 8.

18. J. J. da Rocha to F. Rodrigues Silva, Rio, Mar. 21, 1844, and Rio, undated [Apr. 1844], quoted in Mascarenhas, *Jornalista*, pp. 112–13, 116–18.

19. On June 20, 1844, *O Brasil* reported that 52 *juizes de direito* had been shifted since the cabinet took office; quoted in Flory, *Judge and Jury*, pp. 184, 242. The decree books in Arquivo Nacional, Rio, Seção dos Ministérios, Series IJ[1] and IJ[4], show that some 90 changes were made between Feb. and Sept. 1844. See also Mello e Matos, *Paginas*, pp. 116–20.

20. Drawing up a *chapa* was never an easy business. To reconcile the claims of ambitious politicians and the legitimate interests backing them required considerable knowledge and ingenuity. Since the individuals who drew up a *chapa* obviously acquired enormous influence in that particular province, *chapas* were usually the product of complex maneuverings between the political leaders in the province, the president, and the ministers and politicians in Rio. The *chapa* was to remain the key element in the new organization of politics. The greatest achievement of any politician was to *furar a chapa*, to secure election despite not being on the slate, a feat not often accomplished.

21. Soares de Souza, *Uruguai*, p. 171.

22. The nearest equivalent to a party machine had been the Sociedades Defensoras da Liberdade e Independência Nacional, which flourished from 1831 to 1834; see Sousa, *Fundadores*, 6: 108–12.

23. In the 1842 elections, because of the support that Holanda Cavalcanti had given to the Majority campaign, the cabinet made an alliance with the Nativist faction in Pernambuco province. Thereafter most of the Cavalcanti clan rallied to the Conservatives, their Nativist opponents switching to the Liberal party.

24. The experience of France under Napoleon III shows that in the nineteenth century manipulation of the electoral system by a government did not necessarily make that government dependent on local interests or render it incapable of action in the localities.

25. See the letters of M. do N. Castro e Silva, when minister of finance, to J. M. de Alencar, Jan. 2, 1835, to Apr. 14, 1837, in "Correspondência de Alencar," pp. 42–69.

26. On Alagoas, see Craveiro Costa, *Sinimbu*, pp. 112–21; and Mello e Matos, *Paginas*, p. 122. On Santa Catarina, see Boiteaux, "Partidos politicos," pp. 917–23; and Instituto Histórico e Geográfico Brasileiro, Rio, Lata 382, Pasta 2, João José Coutinho to J. T. Nabuco de Araújo, Destêrro [Florianópolis], Oct. 26, 1856.

27. Article written in 1856 by the editor of *O Cruzeiro do Sul*, quoted in Boiteaux, "Partidos politicos," p. 918. In 1845 the British consul at Recife reported to the foreign secretary that "it is difficult even for a resident to arrive at the objects of the two parties which divide this Province and I must therefore entreat Your Lordship's forbearance if I fail to convey a clear apprehension of them in my correspondence"; see FO, 13/229, H. Augustus Cowper to Earl Aberdeen, Recife, July 14, 1845.

28. J. J. da Rocha to F. Rodrigues Silva, Rio, undated [ca. Mar. 1843], quoted in Mascarenhas, *Jornalista*, p. 93.

29. Speech of July 9, 1841, which also contained the statement that "the government headed by the Regulating Power is always legitimate"; quoted in Rodrigues, *Parlamento*, p. 41.

30. Leitman, "Ragamuffin War," pp. 32–36; and Spalding, *Revolução farroupilha*, pp. 66–79.

31. By the 1827 treaty British goods imported into Brazil paid no more than 15 percent ad valorem duty, a right previously enjoyed by several other nations under the most-favored-nation clause of their respective commercial treaties with Brazil.

32. This surplus was achieved not by any considerable reduction in expenditures but by a notable increase in revenues. See Fig. 1, p. 166, and Castro Carreira, *Historia financeira*, pp. 223, 252, 260.

33. Soares de Souza, "Praia Grande," pp. 95–103.

34. S. J. Stein, *Brazilian Cotton*, pp. 10–12.

35. The regularity and punctuality which the new steamship gave to written correspondence transformed the nature of communication, as the change in the nature of the letters sent by Pedro Antunes de Alencar Rodovalho to J. M. Alencar from 1831 to 1833 and those sent from 1843 to 1845 shows; see "Correspondência de Alencar," pp. 149–66.

36. At the end of 1845, 1 seat was vacant. Two new seats had been created since 1831, bringing the total Senate to 52. Of the 17 surviving senators, 3 were to die in 1846 and 4 in 1847, and others never attended sessions. The 17 members of the Coimbra bloc, much younger, thus effectively constituted the largest group and commanded a majority in the Senate.

37. The competition was proposed at the second anniversary meeting on Nov. 27, 1840; see *Revista do Instituto Geográfico e Histórico Brasileiro*, tomo 2 (1840), p. 642. The winning essay, written by Karl F. L. von Martius, a Bavarian scientist who had come to Brazil with D. Leopoldina in 1817, is translated in Burns, *Perspectives*, pp. 21–41.

38. Sacramento Blake, *Diccionario*, 2: 371–83, and 3: 433–35.

39. Law no. 387 of Aug. 19, 1846, *LB* (1846), pt. 1, pp. 13–39.

40. See the percipient analysis of the Liberal quinquennium in Beiguelman, *Pequenos estudos*, pp. 49–54.

41. Dispatches of Eugene Ney, count of Ney, to the minister of foreign affairs, Mar. 24, Apr. 4, and May 26, 1844, quoted in Rangel, *No rolar do tempo*, pp. 171–76.

42. Calmon, *História de D. Pedro II*, pp. 307–8.

43. *Organizações*, p. 99.

44. Nabuco de Araujo, *Estadista*, 1: 127.

45. See Calogeras, *Politica exterior*, 3: 461–590.

46. Bethell, *Slave Trade*, pp. 247–66, 269–71, 282–84.

47. Bento da Silva Lisboa, baron of Cairu, as reported in Lord Howden to Lord Palmerston, Jan. 12, 1847, quoted in ibid., p. 290.

48. *Almanak administrativo*, p. 79.

49. See *Annuario politico*, p. 369; and Flory, *Judge and Jury*, p. 185.

50. Bethell, *Slave Trade*, pp. 290–95.

51. Calmon, *História de D. Pedro II*, pp. 358–59.

52. Bethell, *Slave Trade*, pp. 293–94, where the date of the next session is misstated as Jan. 1, 1850. The majority was formed of a coalition of convinced anti-slavers and supporters of the trade.

53. See Carneiro, *Insurreição praieira*; and Quintas, *Sentido social*.

54. Carneiro, *Insurreição praieira*, pp. 165–67.

55. See Bethell, *Slave Trade*, pp. 315–19.

56. Ibid., pp. 325–31.

57. Ibid., pp. 313–14, 334–40, 343.

58. Ibid., pp. 339–43, 353.

59. Dispatch of Henry Southern, no. 14, Rio, Feb. 13, 1852, quoted in ibid., p. 359, note 3.

60. The five known landings of slaves after Feb. 1852 represented the last efforts, easily suppressed, of a doomed interest; see ibid., pp. 367, 370, 373–74.

61. The adoption of a forward policy against Rosas had led in Oct. 1849 to the resignation of Olinda. He was replaced by P. J. Soares de Sousa, future viscount of Uruguaí, who with great skill organized an alliance with Rosas's enemies in both Uruguay and Argentina itself; see Soares de Souza, *Uruguaí*, pp. 243–413.

62. Ibid., pp. 434–37.

63. Law no. 563, July 4, 1850; law nos. 557, 559, and 560, June 26 and 28, 1850; law no. 602, Sept. 19, 1850; and law no. 582, Sept. 5, 1850; see *LB* (1850), pt. 1, pp. 240–41, 243, 244, 248, 271–72, 314–40; and Weinstein, *The Amazon Rubber*, pp. 32–57.

64. Law no. 556, June 25, 1850; decree no. 801, July 2, 1851; law no. 601, Sept. 19, 1850; and law nos. 518 and 537, Jan. 31 and May 15, 1850; see *LB* (1850), pt. 1, pp. 4, 23–26, 57–239; and *LB* (1851), pt. 2, pp. 180–93.

65. See decree nos. 987 and 1030, June 12 and Aug. 7, 1852; and law nos. 642 and 670, July 12, Sept. 11, 1852, *LB* (1852), pt. 1, pp. 5–7, 48–49; and pt. 2, pp. 153–55 and 337–44; law nos. 608 and 630, Aug. 16 and Sept. 18, 1851, *LB* (1851), pt. 1, pp. 7, 56–58; and law no. 599, Sept. 14, 1850, and decree no. 828, Sept. 29, 1851, *LB* (1850), pt. 1, pp. 299–301; and (1851), pt. 2, pp. 259–75.

66. Speech of Sept. 4, 1852, in *Fallas do throno*, p. 467.

67. An official "estimate" published in the report of the minister of the interior for 1856 gave a population of over 7,000,000; see *Relatorio*, p. 95. Since the census of 1872, itself an undercount, recorded over 10,000,000 Brazilians, the 1856 figure is too small. A private estimate published in 1854 suggested a population of 8,100,000; see Nunes de Sousa, "Estatistica."

68. Decree nos. 797 and 798, June 18, 1851, authorized by law no. 586, Sept. 6, 1850; see *LB* (1850), pt. 1, p. 282; and (1851), pt. 2, pp. 161–68.

69. See decree no. 907, Jan. 29, 1852, *LB* (1852), pt. 2, p. 19; and Melo, "Guerra dos Maribondos."

70. Meneses, *José de Alencar*, pp. 111–19.

71. *Qualquer homem de casaca poderia ser por êle chamado ao ministério*; see Lery Santos, *Pantheon fluminense*, p. 15. For use of the term in a rural setting, see the complaint of Felipe Tiago Borges against Alexandre José Almeida, printed in *O Estandarte*, Mar. 28, 1856; copy in Arquivo do Museu Imperial, Petrópolis, Pedro de Orléans e Bragança Collection, Maço 123, document 6141.

72. Gonçalves Dias was a graduate of Coimbra, the sonnet being written during the poet's first winter at that university. However, because men who graduated from Coimbra after 1834 could not serve as judges, they were not fully *bachareis*. See Henriques Leal, *Pantheon maranhense*, 3: 15–22.

73. See Hallewell, *Books in Brazil*, pp. 36–90.

74. See Barman and Barman, "Law Graduate," p. 436.

75. C. B. Ottoni, *Autobiographia*, p. 34; Alfredo Taunay, *Memórias*, pp. 69–71; and Egas, *Galeria*, 1: 225.

76. For those who could not qualify for or afford the four faculties there existed the Escola Militar, which provided both a military and a technical education, and

the Church seminaries. On the first, see Barata, *Escola Politécnica*, pp. 45–62; on the clergy and their training during the reign of D. Pedro II, see Boehrer, "The Church," pp. 121–30.

77. Barman and Barman, "Law Graduate," pp. 432–50.

78. See ibid.; and Pang and Seckinger, "Mandarins."

79. See Kidder and Fletcher, *Brazil and the Brazilians*, pp. 321–24.

80. Instituto Histórico e Geográfico Brasileiro, Rio, Saraiva Collection, Lata 272, Pasta 24489, João Lins Vieira Cansanção de Sinimbu, future viscount of Sinimbu, to José Antônio Saraiva, Salvador, Jan. 8, 1858.

81. Arquivo do Museu Imperial, Petrópolis, Pedro de Orléans e Bragança Collection, Maço 116, document 5771, collective resignation offered by the cabinet, Nov. 15, 1851; transcribed in Vianna, *Vultos*, p. 151.

82. Arquivo Histórico do Itamaratí, Rio, Visconde de Cabo Frio Archive, Arquivo 1, Gaveta 1, Maço 11, Custódio Teixeira Leite, future baron of Aiuruoca, to Joaquim Tomás do Amaral, future viscount of Cabo Frio, Rio, May 13, 1853.

83. See Marinho, *História*, p. 53.

84. This was the argument used by Francisco de Sales Torres Homem, a former radical politician, in the articles he wrote in the *Correio Mercantil* in Feb. 1853.

85. "The abnormal and violent state of the country in relation to personal security"; see speech of J. T. Nabuco de Araújo, minister of justice, session of July 13, 1854, *Annaes do Parlamento*, 1854, 3: 120.

86. Instituto Histórico e Geográfico Brasileiro, Rio, Senador Nabuco Collection, Lata 382, Pasta 3, José Maurício Fernandes Pereira de Barros to J. T. Nabuco de Araújo, Rio, Apr. 7, 1854.

87. See Curtin, *Atlantic Slave Trade*, p. 234; Bethell, *Slave Trade*, pp. 388–95; and *Jornal do Commercio*, July 11, 1850.

88. Merrick and Graham, *Population*, pp. 50–63.

89. Meneses Martinho, "Organização do trabalho"; and Arquivo Nacional, Rio, Seção dos Arquivos Particulares, Codice 112, vol. 3, the baron of Patí do Alferes to the baron of Muritiba, Montealegre, Rio, Nov. 25, 1858.

90. See Cavalcanti, *Eça de Queiros*, pp. 56–60.

91. See the short discussion in Silva Bruno, *História*, 2: 140–44. This topic is an almost untouched field for research.

92. Arquivo Nacional, Rio, Seção dos Arquivos Particulares, Codice 112, vol. 4, João Carneiro do Amaral to F. P. de Lacerda Werneck, future baron of Patí de Alferes, Rio, Nov. 12, 1839.

93. See S. J. Stein, *Vassouras*, pp. 21–25, 92–101.

94. See Castro Carreira, *Historia financeira*, p. 678; and Lahmeyer Lobo, *História*, 1: 266.

95. Between 1841–42 and 1851–52, coffee exports rose by about 85 percent in both weight and value, whereas the other agricultural exports increased by less than half in weight and one-quarter in value; Ferreira Soares, *Notas estatísticas*, pp. 28, 45, 60, 72, 74, 89, 99, 108, 119, 209, 215. See also Leff, *Underdevelopment*, 1: 84–86.

96. Between 1841–42 and 1851–52 rubber exports almost tripled in both weight and value; Ferreira Soares, *Notas estatísticas*, p. 89. See also Instituto Histórico e Geográfico Brasileiro, Rio, Institute Collection, Lata 111, Pasta 1, S. Ferreira Soares, "Apontamentos sobre a estatistica financial da provincia do Rio Grande de São Pedro do Sul," Nov. 26, 1852.

97. See Instituto Histórico e Geográfico Brasileiro, Rio, Mauá Collection, Lata 513, Pasta 8, the baron of Mauá to Ricardo José Ribeiro, Rio, Jan. 8, 1864.

98. Ferreira Soares, *Notas estatísticas*, pp. 319–20.

99. From 1837 to 1845 transfer payments to the provinces were included in the annual budget; see LB (1836), pt. 1, p. 53; (1837), pt. 1, pp. 73–74; (1838), pt. 1, p. 41; (1840), pt. 1, pp. 19–20, 73–74; (1841), pt. 1, pp. 55, 59; and (1843), pt. 1, pp. 67, 77–78.

100. See Chaia, *Financiamento escolar*, pp. 71–72.

101. Arquivo Histórico do Itamaratí, Rio, Visconde de Cabo Frio Archive, Arquivo 1, Gaveta 1, Maço 11, C. Teixeira Leite, future baron of Aiuruoca, to J. T. do Amaral, future viscount of Cabo Frio, Rio, May 13, 1853.

102. Arquivo Histórico do Itamaratí, Rio, Barão de Penedo Archive, Arquivo 2, Gaveta 2, Maço 7, Eusébio de Queirós Coutinho Matoso Câmara to F. I. de Carvalho Moreira, future baron of Penedo, Rio, June 12, 1853.

Bibliography

The sources, both archival and printed, cited in this work have been kept as spare as possible, with English-language sources being preferred. The archives cited in this work are the Arquivo Nacional and the Instituto Histórico e Geográfico Brasileiro at Rio de Janeiro, the Arquivo do Museu Imperial at Petrópolis, and the British Foreign Office series 13 and 63, available on microfilm at the University of California, Berkeley. The archives used in the research for this study are stated in Barman and Barman, "Prosopography." In respect to the printed literature in English, consult Francis A. Dutra, *A Guide to the History of Brazil, 1500–1822: The Literature in English* (Santa Barbara, Calif., 1980), which is broader in its time coverage than the title would suggest. The principal printed sources consulted are as follows:

Alden, Dauril. "Late Colonial Brazil, 1750–1808," in Leslie Bethell, ed., *The Cambridge History of Latin America*, vol. 2, pp. 601–60. Cambridge, Eng., 1984.
———. *Royal Government in Colonial Brazil, with Special Reference to the Administration of the Marquis of Lavradio, Viceroy, 1769–1779.* Berkeley, Calif., 1968.
Almanak administrativo, mercantil, e industrial . . . para o anno de 1851. Rio, 1851.
"Almanak de Lisboa—1807," *Revista do Instituto Histórico e Geográfico Brasileiro*, 290 (supplement, Jan.–Mar. 1971): 1–246.
"Almanak histórico da cidade do Rio de Janeiro, 1794," *Revista do Instituto Histórico e Geográfico Brasileiro*, 266 (Jan.–Mar. 1965): 218–90.
Almeida Magalhães, Bruno de. *O visconde de Abaeté.* São Paulo, 1939.
Anderson, Benedict. *Imagined Communities: Reflections on the Origins and Spread of Nationalism.* London, 1983.
Anderson, Robert D. *Education in France, 1848–1870.* Oxford, 1975.
Anna, Timothy E. "The Buenos Aires Expedition and Spain's Secret Plan to Conquer Portugal, 1814–1820," *Americas*, 34, no. 3 (Jan. 1978): 356–80.
Annaes do parlamento brasileiro. Camara dos Srs. Deputados [1826–1889]. Rio.
Annuario politico, historico e estatistico do Brasil, 1847. Rio, n.d.
Antonil, André João [João Antônio Andreoni]. *Cultura e opulência do Brasil por suas drogas e minas.* Ed. Andrée Mansuy. Paris, 1968.

Archivo diplomatico da Independencia. 6 vols. Rio, 1922–25.

Armitage, John. *A History of Brazil from the Period of the Arrival of the Braganza Family to the Abdication of Don Pedro I.* 2 vols. London, 1836.

Arnade, Charles W. *The Emergence of the Republic of Bolivia.* New York, 1970.

"Arquivo histórico," *Revista Brasileira de Ciências Políticas,* 7, no. 1 (Jan.–Mar. 1973): 101–18.

"Arquivo histórico," *Revista Brasileira de Ciências Políticas,* 7, no. 2 (Apr.–June 1973): 143–71.

"Autos de exame e averiguação sobre o autor de uma carta anonima escrita ao juiz de fora do Rio de Janeiro, Dr. Baltazar da Silva Lisboa," *Annaes da Biblioteca Nacional,* 60 (1938): 259–313.

Azevedo, Vitor de. *Feijó, vida, paixão, e morte de um chimango.* São Paulo, 1942.

Barata, Mario. *Escola Politécnica do Largo do São Francisco, berço da engenharia brasileira.* Rio, 1976.

Barbosa Lima Sobrinho, Alexandre José de. "A ação da imprensa em torno de Constituinte, o *Tamoio* e a *Sentinella,*" in Octaciano Nogueira, ed., *A Constituinte de 1823,* pp. 7–77. Brasilia, 1973.

———. "A Confederação do Equador do centenário ao sesquicentenário," *Revista do Instituto Histórico e Geográfico Brasileiro,* 306 (Jan.–Mar. 1975): 33–112.

Barman, Roderick J., and Jean Barman. "The Prosopography of the Brazilian Empire," *Latin American Research Review,* 13, no. 2 (1978): 78–97.

———. "The Role of the Law Graduate in the Political Elite of Imperial Brazil," *Journal of InterAmerican Studies and World Affairs,* 18, no. 4 (Nov. 1976): 423–50.

Bauss, Rudy. "Rio Grande do Sul in the Portuguese Empire: The Formative Years," *Americas,* 39, no. 4 (Apr. 1983): 519–35.

Beiguelman, Paula. *Pequenos estudos de ciência política.* São Paulo, 1967.

Beraza, Augustín. *Los corsarios de Artigas (apartado de los tomos XV y XVI de la "Revista Historica").* Montevideo, 1949.

Berrance de Castro, Jean. *A milícia cidadã: A Guarda Nacional de 1831 a 1850.* São Paulo, 1977.

Bethell, Leslie. *The Abolition of the Brazilian Slave Trade: Britain, Brazil and the Slave Trade Question, 1807–1869.* Cambridge, Eng., 1970.

———. "The Independence of Brazil," in Leslie Bethell, ed., *The Cambridge History of Latin America,* vol. 3, pp. 157–96. Cambridge, Eng., 1985.

Bethell, Leslie, and José Murilo de Carvalho. "Brazil from Independence to the Middle of the Nineteenth Century," in Leslie Bethell, ed., *The Cambridge History of Latin America,* vol. 3, pp. 679–746. Cambridge, Eng., 1985.

Biblioteca Nacional. *Documentos Históricos.* Vols. 101–9: *Revolução de 1817.* Rio, 1953–55.

Biblioteca Nacional. *Documentos Históricos.* Vol. 110: *Devassa de 1801 em Pernambuco.* Rio, 1955.

Boehrer, George C. A. "The Church in the Second Reign, 1840–1889," in Henry H. Keith and S. F. Edwards, eds., *Conflict and Continuity in Brazilian Society,* pp. 113–40. Columbia, S.C., 1969.

———. "The Flight of the Brazilian Deputies from the Cortes Gerais of Lisbon, 1822," *Hispanic American Historical Review,* 40, no. 4 (Nov. 1960): 497–512.

Boiteaux, José Arthur. "Os partidos politicos em Santa Catarina, primeira parte

1821–1871," in *Annaes do primeiro congresso de historia nacional*, vol. 1, pp. 901–49. Rio, 1914.

Boxer, Charles R. *The Golden Age of Brazil, 1695–1750: Growing Pains of a Colonial Society*. Berkeley, Calif, 1964.

——. *Portuguese Society in the Tropics: The Municipal Councils of Goa, Macao, Bahia and Luanda, 1510–1800*. Madison, Wis., 1965.

——. *Race Relations in the Portuguese Colonial Empire*. Oxford, 1963.

Brandão, Ulysses de Carvalho Soares. *Pernambuco d'outr'ora: A Confederação do Equador*. Recife, 1924.

Brasileiro em Coimbra. Coimbra, 1822.

British and Foreign State Papers, 1826–1827. London, 1828.

Bruno Lobo, Francisco. "O ensino da medicina no Rio de Janeiro," *Revista do Instituto Histórico e Geográfico Brasileiro*, 260 (July–Sept. 1963): 3–115.

Buarque de Holanda, Sérgio, ed. *História geral da civilização brasileira*. Vol. 3: *O processo da emancipação*. 2d ed. São Paulo, 1965.

Burns, E. Bradford. "Concerning the Transmission and Dissemination of the Enlightenment in Brazil," in A. Owen Aldridge, ed., *The Ibero-American Enlightenment*, pp. 256–81. Urbana, Ill., 1971.

——. *A History of Brazil*. 2d ed. New York, 1970.

——. *Nationalism in Brazil: A Historical Survey*. New York, 1968.

——, ed. *Perspectives on Brazilian History*. New York, 1967.

[Caillé de Gene, François Etienne.] *Le Roi et la famille royale de Bragance doivent-ils, dans les circonstances présentes, retourner a Lisbonne ou bien rester au Brésil?* Rio, 1820; reprinted in *O debate político no processo da Independência*. Rio, 1972.

Calmon, Pedro. *História de D. Pedro II*. Vol. 1: *Infância e mocidade 1825–1853*. Rio, 1975.

——. *História do Brasil*. 7 vols. Rio, 1959.

Calogeras, João Pandiá. *A History of Brazil*. Trans. Percy A. Martin. Chapel Hill, N.C., 1939.

——. *A politica exterior do Imperio*. Vol. 3: *Da Regencia á queda de Rosas*. São Paulo, 1933.

Camara Cascudo, Luiz da. *O marquez de Olinda e seu tempo (1793–1870)*. São Paulo, 1938.

As câmaras municipais e a Independência. 3 vols. Rio, 1973.

Caneca, Frei Joaquim do Amor Divino. *O Typhis Pernambucano*. Brasília, 1984.

Cardozo, Manoel S. "Dom José Joaquim da Cunha e Azeredo Coutinho, governador interino e bispo de Pernambuco, 1798–1802," *Revista do Instituto Histórico e Geográfico Brasileiro*, 282 (Jan.–Mar. 1969): 3–45.

——. "The Internationalism of the Portuguese Enlightenment: The Role of the Estrangeirado, c. 1700–c. 1750," in A. Owen Aldridge, ed., *The Ibero-American Enlightenment*, pp. 141–207. Urbana, Ill., 1971.

Carneiro, Edison. *A insurreição praieira (1848–49)*. Rio, 1960.

Carneiro da Cunha, Pedro Octávio. "A fundação de um império liberal," in Sérgio Buarque de Holanda, ed., *História geral da civilização brasileira*, vol. 3, pp. 135–78. 2d ed. São Paulo, 1965.

Carneiro de Mendonça, Marcos. *O intendente Câmara, Manuel Ferreira da Camara Bethencourt de Sá, intendente das minas e diamantes, 1764–1835*. São Paulo, 1958.

"Cartas Andradinas," *Annaes da Biblioteca Nacional*, 14 (1886–87): 12–88.
"Cartas de João Loureiro, escriptas do Rio de Janeiro ao Conselheiro Manuel José Maria da Costa e Sá," *Revista do Instituto Histórico e Geográfico Brasileiro*, tomo 76, pte. 2 (1913): 271–468.
"Cartas de Luis Joaquim dos Santos Marrocos," *Annaes da Biblioteca Nacional*, 56 (1934): 5–459.
"Cartas ineditas da 1ª Imperatriz D. Maria Leopoldina (1821 a 1826)," *Revista do Instituto Histórico e Geográfico Brasileiro*, tomo 75, pte. 2 (1912): 109–127.
Castro Carreira, Liberato de. *Historia financeira e orçamentaria do Imperio do Brazil desde a sua fundação*. Rio, 1889.
Cavalcanti, Paulo. *Eça de Queirós, agitador no Brasil*. 2d ed. rev. São Paulo, 1966.
Cecil, Henry. *A Matter of Speculation: The Case of Lord Cochrane*. London, 1965.
Censor Provincial. Coimbra.
Chaia, Josephina. *Financiamento escolar no Segundo Império*. Marília, São Paulo, 1965.
Chronista. Rio.
Clayton, Arnold B. "The Life of Tomás Antônio de Vilanova Portugal: A Study in Government of Portugal and Brazil, 1781–1821." Ph.D. diss., Columbia University, 1977.
Cochrane, Thomas, earl of Dundonald. *Narrative of Services in the Liberation of Chili, Peru and Brazil*. 2 vols. London, 1859.
Collecção das leis brasileiras, desde a chegada da corte ate a epoca da Independencia. Vol. 1: *1808–1810*, and vol. 2: *1811–1816*. Ouro Prêto, 1834–35.
Collecção das leis do Brasil para o anno (1808–89). Rio.
Connor, Walker. "A Nation Is a Nation, Is a State, Is an Ethnic Group, Is . . . ," *Ethnic and Racial Studies*, 1, no. 4 (Oct. 1978): 377–400.
Corrêa de Sá, José d'Almeida, marquês de Lavradio. *D. João VI e a Independencia do Brasil: Os ultimos annos da seu reinado*. Lisbon, 1937.
Correio Braziliense. London, 1808–22.
"Correspondência do barão de Mareschal (em francês—julho a agosto de 1823)," *Revista do Instituto Histórico e Geográfico Brasileiro*, 314 (Jan.–Mar. 1977): 306–47.
"Correspondência do barão de Mareschal, setembro/dezembro de 1823," *Revista do Instituto Histórico e Geográfico Brasileiro*, 315 (Apr.–June 1977): 302–89.
"Correspondência do barão Wensel de Mareschal com o príncipe de Metternich Rio de Janeiro/abril [*sic*] 1823," *Revista do Instituto Histórico e Geográfico Brasileiro*, 313 (Oct.–Dec. 1976): 159–231.
"Correspondencia do marquez de Resende," *Revista do Instituto Histórico e Geográfico Brasileiro*, tomo 80 (1916): 149–525.
Correspondencia official das provincias do Brazil durante a legislatura das Cortes Constituentes de Portugal nos annos de 1821–1822. 2d ed. Lisbon, 1872.
"Correspondência passiva do senador José Martiniano de Alencar," *Anais da Biblioteca Nacional*, 86 (1966): 7–469.
"Correspondencia relativa aos successos dados em Portugal, e no Brasil, 1822–1823," *Revista do Instituto Histórico e Geográfico Brasileiro*, tomo 22 (1859): 413–39.
Costa Pereira, Hipólito José da. *Diário da minha viagem para Filadelfia (1798–1799)*. Rio, 1955.

Craveiro Costa, João. *O visconde de Sinimbu, sua vida e sua atuação na politica nacional (1840–1889)*. São Paulo, 1937.

Curtin, Philip D. *The Atlantic Slave Trade: A Census*. Madison, Wis., 1969.

Daupias d'Alcochete, Nuno, ed. "Lettres de Jacques Ratton á Antonio de Araujo de Azevedo, Comte de Barca (1812–1817)," *Bulletin des Etudes Portuguaises*, 25 (1964): 137–256.

"Devassa ordenado pelo Vice-Rei conde de Rezende, 1794," *Annaes da Biblioteca Nacional*, 61 (1939): 239–523.

Diario da Assemblea Geral Constituente e Legislativa do Imperio do Brasil. 2 vols. Rio, 1823–24.

Dias Tavares, Luís Henrique. *A Independência do Brasil na Bahia*. Brasília, 1977.

"Discurso autobiográfico pronunciado no senado pelo então visconde de Paraná no sessão de 31 de julho de 1854," *Revista do Instituto Histórico e Geográfico Brasileiro*, 236 (July–Sept. 1957): 275–84.

Documentos para a historia das Cortes Gerais da nação portuguesa. Vol. 1: *1820–1826*. 2d ed. Lisbon, 1889.

Dourado, Mecenas. *Hipólito da Costa e o Correio Braziliense*. 2 vols. Rio, 1957.

Drummond, Antonio de Menezes de Vasconcellos. "Annotacções de A. M. V. de Drummond á sua biographia publicada em 1836 na *Biographie universelle et portative des contemporaines*," *Annaes da Biblioteca Nacional*, 13 (1885–86): 2–149.

Economia açucareira do Brasil no séc. xix: Cartas de Felisberto Caldeira Brant Pontes marquês de Barbacena. Rio, 1976.

Egas, Eugenio. *Diogo Antonio Feijó*. São Paulo, 1912.

———. *Galeria dos presidentes de São Paulo*. 3 vols. São Paulo, 1925–27.

Ellis Júnior, Alfredo. *Feijó e a primeira metade do seculo XIX*. São Paulo, 1942.

Escragnolle Doria, Luiz Gastão d'. *Memoria historica commemorativa do 1º centenario do collegio de Pedro Segundo*. Rio, 1937.

Evangelista, José Geraldo. *Lorena no século XIX*. São Paulo, 1978.

Fallas do throno desde o anno de 1823 até o anno de 1889 acompanhadas das respectivas votos de graças. Rio, 1889.

Fernandes Tomás, Manuel. *A revolução de 1820*. Ed. José Tengarrinha. Lisbon, 1974.

Ferreira Reis, Arthur Cezar. "O Grão-Pará e o Maranhão," in Sérgio Buarque de Holanda, ed., *História geral da civilização brasileira*, vol. 4, pp. 71–172. 2d ed. São Paulo, 1967.

———. "Mato Grosso e Goiás," in Sérgio Buarque de Holanda, ed., *História geral da civilização brasileira*, vol. 4, pp. 173–90. 2d ed. São Paulo, 1967.

Ferreira Soares, Sebastião. *Notas estatísticas sobre a produção agrícola e carestia do gêneros alimentícios no Império do Brasil*. 2d ed. Rio, 1977.

Figueira de Mello, Jeronymo de A. "A correspondencia do barão Wenzel de Mareschal (agente diplomatico da Austria no Brasil de 1821 a 1831)," *Revista do Instituto Histórico e Geográfico Brasileiro*, tomo 80 (1916): 5–148.

———. "A correspondencia do barão Wenzel de Marschall [*sic*] (agente diplomatico da Austria no Brasil de 1821 a 1831)," *Revista do Instituto Histórico e Geográfico Brasileiro*, tomo 77, pte. 1 (1914): 165–244.

Filler, Victor M. "Liberalism in Brazil: The Regional Revolts of 1842." Ph.D. diss., Stanford University, 1975.

Fleiuss, Max. *Historia administrativa do Brasil*. 2d ed. São Paulo, n.d.

Flory, Thomas. "Fugitive Slaves and Free Society: The Case of Brazil," *Journal of Negro History*, 64, no. 4 (Fall 1979): 116–30.

———. *Judge and Jury in Imperial Brazil, 1808–1871: Social Control and Political Stability in the New State*. Austin, Tex., 1981.

Forjaz, Djalma. *O senador Vergueiro sua vida e sua epoca (1778–1859)*. São Paulo, 1924.

Franco de Almeida, Tito. *O conselheiro Francisco José Furtado, biografia e estudo de história política contemporanea*. 2d ed. São Paulo, 1944.

Freyre, Gilberto. *The Masters and the Slaves: A Study in the Development of Brazilian Civilization*. Trans. Samuel Putnam. New York, 1946.

Galloway, J. H. "Agricultural Reform and the Enlightenment in Late Colonial Brazil," *Agricultural History*, 53, no. 4 (Oct. 1979): 763–79.

Girão, Raymundo. *Pequena história do Ceará*. 2d ed. Forteleza, 1962.

Glover, Michael. "Beresford and His Fighting Cocks," *History Today*, 26 (Apr. 1976): 262–68.

Gomes da Silva, Francisco. *Memórias*. 2d ed. Rio, 1959.

Gomes de Carvalho, Manoel Emilio. *Os deputados brasileiros nas Cortes Gerais de 1821*. Porto, 1912.

Gonçalves dos Santos, Luiz [Padre Perereca]. *Memórias para servir à história do reino do Brasil*. 2 vols. Belo Horizonte, 1981.

Goulart, José Alípio. *Tropas e tropeiros na formação do Brasil*. Rio, 1961.

Gudeman, Stephen, and Stuart B. Schwartz. "Cleansing Original Sin: Godparenthood and the Baptism of Slaves in Eighteenth-Century Bahia," in Raymond T. Smith, ed., *Kinship, Ideology and Practice in Latin America*, pp. 35–58. Chapel Hill, N.C., 1984.

Hallewell, Laurence. *Books in Brazil: A History of the Publishing Trade*. Metuchen, N.J., 1982.

Hann, John H. "Brazil and the Río de la Plata, 1808–1828." Ph.D. diss., University of Texas, 1967.

Hayes, Carlton J. H. *Nationalism: A Religion*. New York, 1960.

Hemming, John. "Indians and the Frontier in Colonial Brazil," in Leslie Bethell, ed., *The Cambridge History of Latin America*, vol. 2, pp. 501–45. Cambridge, Eng., 1984.

Henriques Leal, Antonio. *Pantheon maranhense*. 4 vols. Lisbon, 1874.

Herrick, Jane. "Hipólito da Costa, the Reluctant Revolutionist," *Americas*, 7, no. 2 (Oct. 1950): 171–81.

Higgs, David. "Unbelief and Politics in Rio de Janeiro During the 1790s," *Luso-Brazilian Review*, 21, no. 1 (Summer 1984): 13–31.

Hilton, Stanley E. "The United States and Brazilian Independence," in A. J. R. Russell-Wood, ed., *From Colony to Nation: Essays on the Independence of Brazil*, pp. 109–29. Baltimore, Md., 1975.

Hind, Robert J. "The Internal Colonial Concept," *Comparative Studies in Society and History*, 26, no. 3 (July 1984): 543–68.

Historia da revolução do Brasil no dia 7 d'abril de 1831. Rio, 1831.

Hobsbawm, Eric. *Workers: Worlds of Labor*. New York, 1984.

Holub, Norman. "Bernardo Pereira de Vasconcelos o gigante aleijado (1795–1850)," *Revista do Instituto Histórico e Geográfico Brasileiro*, 296 (July–Sept. 1972): 38–52.

———. "The Brazilian Sabinada (1837–38): Revolt of the Negro Masses," *Journal of Negro History*, 54, no. 3 (Summer 1969): 275–83.

Homen de Mello, Francisco Inacio. "Documentos relativos a . . . Rio Grande do Sul," *Revista do Instituto Histórico e Geográfico Brasileiro*, tomo 42, pte. 1 (1879): 5–156.

Hoornaert, Eduardo. "The Catholic Church in Colonial Brazil," in Leslie Bethell, ed., *The Cambridge History of Latin America*, vol. 1, pp. 541–56. Cambridge, Eng., 1984.

Hunshe, Carlos Henrique Trein. *O biênio 1824–25 da imigração e colonização alemã no Rio Grande do Sul, província de São Pedro*. Pôrto Alegre, 1975.

"A Inconfidencia da Bahia em 1798," *Annaes da Biblioteca Nacional*, 43/44 (1920–21): 83–225.

James, M. E. "Obedience and Dissent in Henrican England: The Lincolnshire Rebellion, 1536," *Past and Present*, no. 48 (Aug. 1970): 3–70.

Jensen, Merrill. *The Articles of Confederation: An Interpretation of the Social-Constitutional History of the American Revolution, 1774–1781*. Madison, Wis., 1940.

Johnson, Harold B., Jr. "A Preliminary Inquiry into Money, Prices, and Wages in Rio de Janeiro, 1763–1823," in Dauril Alden, ed., *Colonial Roots of Modern Brazil, Papers of the Newberry Library Conference*, pp. 231–67. Berkeley, Calif., 1973.

Jornal do Commercio. Rio de Janeiro.

Karasch, Mary. "Rio de Janeiro: From Colonial Town to Imperial Capital (1808–1850)," in Robert J. Ross and G. J. Telkamp, eds., *Colonial Cities*, pp. 123–49. Dordrecht, Neth., 1985.

Kent, Robert K. "African Revolt in Bahia, 24–25 January 1835," *Journal of Social History*, 3, no. 4 (Summer 1970): 331–56.

Kidder, Daniel P., and James C. Fletcher. *Brazil and the Brazilians Portrayed in Historical and Descriptive Sketches*. Philadelphia, 1857.

Klein, Herbert. "The Colonial Freedman in Brazilian Slave Society," *Journal of Social History*, 3, no. 1 (Fall 1969): 30–52.

Koster, Henry. *Travels in Brazil*. Abridged ed. Carbondale, Ill., 1966.

Kuznesof, Elizabeth A. "Clans, the Militia, and Territorial Government: The Articulation of Kinship with Polity in Eighteenth-Century São Paulo," in David J. Robinson, ed., *Social Fabric and Spatial Structure in Colonial Latin America*, pp. 181–226. Ann Arbor, Mich., 1979.

Lacombe, Lourenço Luís, ed. "Diário inédito do principe de Joinville," *Anuário do Museu Imperial*, 11 (1950): 177–219.

Lahmeyer Lobo, Eulália Maria. *História do Rio de Janeiro (do capital comercial ao capital industrial e financeiro)*. 2 vols. Rio, 1978.

Leff, Nathaniel H. *Underdevelopment and Development in Brazil*. Vol. 1: *Economic Structure and Change, 1822–1949*. London, 1982.

Leitman, Spencer L. "Socio-Economic Roots of the Ragamuffin War: A Chapter in Early Brazilian History." Ph.D. diss., University of Texas, 1972. [*Raíses sócio-econômicas da guerra dos farrapos, um capítulo de história do Brasil no século xix*. Trans. Sarita Linhares Barsted. Rio, 1979.]

Lery Santos, Preslindo. *Pantheon fluminense*. Rio, 1880.

Lindley, Thomas. *Narrative of a Voyage to Brazil; Terminating in the Seizure of a British Vessel*. London, 1805.

Linz, Juan. "Early State-Building and Late Peripheral Nationalisms Against the State: The Case of Spain," in S. N. Eisenstadt and Stein Rokkan, eds., *Building States and Nations*, vol. 2, pp. 32–116. Beverly Hills, Calif., 1973.

Lipset, Seymour. *The First New Nation: The United States in Historical and Comparative Perspective.* New York, 1963.

Livermore, Harold V. *A History of Portugal.* Cambridge, Eng., 1947.

Luccock, John. *Notes on Rio de Janeiro and the Southern Parts of Brazil, Taken During a Residence of Ten Years There, 1808 to 1818.* London, 1820.

Lugar, Catherine. "The Merchant Community of Salvador, Bahia, 1780–1830." Ph.D. diss., State University of New York at Stony Brook, 1980.

Macedo, Roberto. *O barão de Rio Verde.* Rio, 1940.

Magalhães Godinho, Vitorino. *Prix et monnaies au Portugal, 1750–1850.* Paris, 1955.

Manchester, Alan K. *British Preeminence in Brazil: Its Rise and Decline.* Durham, N.C., 1933.

———. "The Rise of the Brazilian Aristocracy," *Hispanic American Historical Review,* 11, no. 2 (May 1931): 145–68.

———. "The Transfer of the Portuguese Court to Rio de Janeiro," in Henry H. Keith and S. F. Edwards, eds., *Conflict and Continuity in Brazilian Society,* pp. 149–55. Columbia, S.C., 1969.

Mansuy-Diniz Silva, Andrée. "Portugal and Brazil: Imperial Reorganization, 1750–1808," in Leslie Bethell, ed., *The Cambridge History of Latin America,* vol. 1, pp. 469–508. Cambridge, Eng., 1984.

Marinho, José Antonio. *Historia do movimento politico que no ano de 1842 teve lugar na provincia de Minas Gerais.* 2d ed. Conselheiro Lafayette, Minas Gerais, 1939.

Mascarenhas, Nelson Laje. *Um jornalista do Império (Firmino Rodrigues Silva).* São Paulo, 1961.

Mattoso, Katia M. de Queirós. *Presença francesa no movimento democrático baíano de 1798.* Salvador, 1969.

Maxwell, Kenneth R. *Conflicts and Conspiracies: Brazil and Portugal 1750–1808.* Cambridge, Eng., 1974.

———. "The Generation of the 1790s and the Idea of Luso-Brazilian Empire," in Dauril Alden, ed., *Colonial Roots of Modern Brazil, Papers of the Newberry Library Conference,* pp. 107–44. Berkeley, Calif., 1973.

McBeth, Michael C. "The Politicians v. the Generals: The Decline of the Brazilian Army During the First Empire, 1822–1831." Ph.D. diss., University of Washington, 1972.

Mello e Matos, Luis José de Carvalho. *Paginas de historia constitucional do Brazil, 1840–1848.* Rio, 1870.

Mello Moraes, Alexandre José de. *História do Brasil–Reino e do Brasil–Império.* 2 vols. Belo Horizonte, 1982.

———. *História e teoria dos partidos políticos no Brasil.* 2d ed. São Paulo, 1974.

Melo, Mario. "Guerra dos Maribondos," *Revista do Instituto Archeologico, Historico e Geographico Pernambucano,* 22, nos. 107–10 (1920): 38–47.

Melo Franco, Afonso Arinos de. *História do Banco do Brasil (primeira phase —1808–1835).* São Paulo, 1947.

Meneses, Raimundo de. *José de Alencar, literato e político.* São Paulo, 1965.

Meneses Martinho, Lenira. "Organização do trabalho e relações sociais nas firmas comerciais do Rio de Janeiro; primeira metade do século XIX," *Revista do Instituto de Estudos Brasileiros,* 18 (1976): 41–62.

Merrick, Thomas W., and Douglas H. Graham. *Population and Economic Development in Brazil. 1800 to the Present.* Baltimore, Md., 1979.

Metcalf, Alida Christina. "Families of Planters, Peasants, and Slaves: Strategies for Survival in Santana de Parnaíba, Brazil, 1720–1820." Ph.D. diss., University of Texas, 1983.

Mitchell, Leslie. *Holland House*. London, 1980.

Monteiro, Tobias do Rego. *Historia do Imperio: A elaboração da Independencia*. Rio, 1927.

Moraes, João. "Reminiscencias historicas, periodo regencial," *Revista do Instituto Historico de São Paulo*, 11 (1906): 83–105.

Morton, F. W. O. "The Conservative Revolution of Independence: Economy, Society and Politics in Bahia, 1790–1840." D.Phil. diss., Oxford University, 1974.

————. "The Military and Society in Bahia, 1800–1821," *Journal of Latin American Studies*, 7, no. 2 (Nov. 1975): 249–69.

————. "The Royal Timber in Late Colonial Bahia," *Hispanic American Historical Review*, 58, no. 1 (Feb. 1978): 41–61.

Mota, Carlos Guilherme. *Idéia da revolução no Brasil (1789–1801): Estudos das formas de pensamento*. 2d ed. Petrópolis, Rio, 1979.

————. *Nordeste 1817: Estruturas e argumentos*. São Paulo, 1972.

————, ed. *1822: Dimensões*. São Paulo, 1972.

Muniz Tavares, Francisco. *Historia da revolução de Pernambuco em 1817*. 3d ed., with notes by M. de Oliveira Lima. Recife, 1917.

Nabuco de Araujo, Joaquim Aurelio. *Um estadista do Imperio, Nabuco de Araujo, sua vida, suas opiniões, sua epoca*. 2d ed. 2 vols. São Paulo, 1936.

Newbold, Robert C. *The Albany Congress and the Plan of Union in 1754*. New York, 1955.

Nizza da Silva, Maria Beatriz. *Análise de estratificação social: O Rio de Janeiro de 1808 a 1821*. São Paulo, 1975.

————. *Cultura e sociedade no Rio de Janeiro, 1808–1821*. São Paulo, 1977.

Nobreza de Portugal e do Brasil. 3 vols. Lisbon, 1960–61.

Nogueira, Octaciano, ed. *Obra política de José Bonifácio*. 2 vols. Brasília, 1973.

Novais, Fernando A. *Brasil e Portugal na crise do antigo sistema colonial (1777–1808)*. São Paulo, 1979.

Noya Pinto, Virgílio. "Balanço da transformações econômicas no século XIX," in Carlos G. Mota, ed., *Brasil em perspectiva*, pp. 126–61. 8th ed. São Paulo, 1977.

Nunes de Sousa, Francisco. "Estatistica do Brasil," in *Almanak administrativo, mercantil e industrial . . . para o anno de 1854, supplemento*, pp. 430–31. Rio, 1854.

Oliveira Lima, Manoel de. *Dom João VI no Brasil, 1808–1820*. 3 vols. 2d ed. Rio, 1945.

————. *Dom Pedro e Dom Miguel, a querela da successão (1826–1828)*. São Paulo, n.d.

————. *O movimento da Independência e o Império brasileiro (1821–1889)*. 4th ed. São Paulo, 1967.

Oliveira Martins, F. A. *Pina Manique, o político–o amigo de Lisboa*. Lisbon, 1948.

Oliveira Torres, João Camilo de. *A democracia coroada: Teoria política do Império do Brasil*. 2d ed. Petrópolis, Rio, 1964.

Organizações e programas ministeriais regime parlamentar no Império. 2d ed. Rio, 1962.

Osório, Ubaldo. *A ilha de Itaparicá, história e tradição*. 4th ed. rev. Salvador, 1979.

Ottoni, Christiano Benedicto. *Autobiographia.* Rio, 1908.
Ottoni, Theophilo Benedicto. *Circular dedicada aos srs. eleitores de senadores pela provincia de Minas Gerais.* With an introduction by Basilio de Magalhães. Rio, 1916.
Pang, Eul-Soo, and Ronald S. Seckinger. "The Mandarins of Imperial Brazil," *Comparative Studies in Society and History,* 9, no. 2 (Apr. 1971): 215–44.
Peláez, Carlos Manuel, and Wilson Suzigan. *História monetária do Brasil.* Rio, 1976.
Pereira, Ángelo. *D. João VI, principe e rei.* 3 vols. Lisbon, 1955–56.
Pereira Castro, Paulo. "A 'experiência republicana,' 1831–1840," in Sérgio Buarque de Holanda, ed., *História geral da civilização brasileira,* vol. 4, pp. 9–67. 2d ed. São Paulo, 1967.
Pereira da Costa, Francisco Augusto. *Cronologia histórica do Estado do Piauí desde os seus tempos primitivos até a proclamação da República.* 2 vols. Rio, 1974.
Pereira da Silva, João Manuel. *Historia da fundação do Imperio brasileiro.* 7 vols. Rio, 1864–68.
Perfís parlamentares: No. 3, Nunes Machado. Ed. Vamireh Chacon. Brasília, 1978.
Pimenta Bueno, José Antônio, marquês de São Vicente. *Direito público brasileiro e analise da constitução do Império.* Rio, 1958.
Pinheiro Chagas, Paulo. *Teófilo Ottoni, ministro do povo.* 2d ed. Rio, 1956.
Pinheiro Ferreira, Silvestre. *Ideias políticas.* Rio, 1976.
Pinto de Campos, Joaquim. *Vida do grande cidadão brasileiro, Luís Alves de Lima e Silva, barão, conde, marquês e duque de Caxias.* 2d ed. Rio, 1958.
Pires de Lima, Américo. "Memória de D. Rodrigo de Sousa Coutinho (1° conde de Linhares) sobre o melhoramento dos domínios de S. Mag. e na América," *Brasília,* 4 (1949): 382–422.
Piteira Santos, Fernando. *Geografia e economia da revolução de 1820.* Lisbon, 1962.
Platt, Desmond C. M. *Latin America and British Trade, 1806–1914.* London, 1972.
Poppino, Rollie E. *Brazil, the Land and the People.* New York, 1968.
Post, John D. *The Last Great Subsistence Crisis in the Western World.* Baltimore, Md., 1977.
Potter, David M. "The Historian's Use of Nationalism and Vice-Versa," *American Historical Review,* 67, no. 4 (July 1962): 924–50.
Prado Júnior, Caio. *The Colonial Background of Modern Brazil.* Trans. Suzette Macedo. Berkeley, Calif., 1967. [*Formação do Brasil contemporâneo, colônia.* 7th ed. São Paulo, 1963.]
1° [Primeiro] centenario do Jornal do Commercio 1827–outubro–1927. Rio, 1927.
Quintas, Amaro. "A agitação republicana no nordeste," in Sérgio Buarque de Holanda, ed., *História geral da civilização brasileira,* vol. 3, pp. 207–37. 2d ed. São Paulo, 1965.
———. "O nordeste, 1825–1850," in Sérgio Buarque de Holanda, ed., *História geral da civilização brasileira,* vol. 4, pp. 193–241. 2d ed. São Paulo, 1967.
———. *O sentido social da revolução praieira (ensaio de interpretação).* Recife, 1946.
Rambo, Marion H. "The Role of the Carioca Press During the Triune Regencies, 1831–1835." Ph.D. diss., University of Virginia, 1973.

Ramos, Donald. "Social Revolution Frustrated: The Conspiracy of the Tailors in Bahia, 1798," *Luso-Brazilian Review*, 13, no. 1 (Summer 1976): 74–90.

Ramos de Carvalho, Laerte. *As reformas pombalinas na instrução pública*. São Paulo, 1952.

Rangel, Alberto. *D. Pedro I e a marquesa de Santos*. 3d ed. Rio, 1968.

———. *Marginados: Anotações às cartas de D. Pedro I a D. Domitila*. Rio, 1974.

———. *No rolar do tempo (opiniões e testemunhas respigardos no archivo do Orsay-Paris)*. Rio, n.d.

———. *Textos e pretextos (incidentes da chronica brasileira á luz de documentos conservados na Europa)*. Tours, 1926.

Recordações da vida parlamentar do advogado Antonio Pereira Rebouças. 2 vols. Rio, 1870.

Relação alfabetica dos estudantes e mais individuos riscados da universidade por ordens regias de 29 de abril, e 23 de julho de 1828 e 28 de marco de 1820. Coimbra, 1829.

Relatorio do ministerio do Imperio. Rio, 1856.

Rizzini, Carlos. *Hipólito da Costa e o Correio Braziliense*. São Paulo, 1957.

Rocha Pitta, Sebastião da. *História da América Portuguesa desde o ano mil quinhentos do seu descobrimento até o mil e setecentos e vinte quatro*. Belo Horizonte, 1977.

Rodrigues, José Honório. *A Assembléia Constituente de 1823*. Petrópolis, Rio, 1974.

———. *Brazil and Africa*. Trans. Richard A. Mazarra and Sam Hileman. Berkeley, Calif., 1965.

———. *Independência: Revolução e contra-revolução*. 5 vols. Rio, 1975.

———. "The Influence of Africa on Brazil and of Brazil on Africa," *Journal of African History*, 3, no. 1 (1962): 49–67.

———. *O parlamento e a consolidação do Império, 1840/1861*. Brasília, 1982.

Russell-Wood, A. J. R. *The Black Man in Slavery and Freedom in Colonial Brazil*. New York, 1982.

———. "A Brazilian Student at the University of Coimbra in the Seventeenth Century," in Frederick W. Hodcroft et al., eds., *Mediaeval and Renaissance Studies on Spain and Portugal*, pp. 192–209. Oxford, 1981.

———. "Colonial Brazil: The Gold Cycle, c. 1690–1750," in Leslie Bethell, ed., *The Cambridge History of Latin America*, vol. 2, pp. 547–600. Cambridge, Eng., 1984.

———. *Fidalgos and Philanthropists: The Santa Casa de Misericordia of Bahia, 1550–1755*. London, 1968.

———, ed. *From Colony to Nation: Essays on the Independence of Brazil*. Baltimore, Md., 1975.

Sacramento Blake, Augusto Victorino Alves. *Diccionario bibliographico brazileiro*. 7 vols. Rio, 1883–1902.

Santos, Lúcio José dos. *A Inconfidência Mineira, papel de Tiradentes na Inconfidência Mineira*. Belo Horizonte, 1972.

Santos Vilhena, Luiz dos. *Recopilação de noticias soteropolitanas e brasilicas*. 3 vols. Salvador, 1921–1935.

Schubert, Guilherme. *A coroação de D. Pedro I*. Rio, 1973.

Schwartz, Stuart B. "The Manumission of Slaves in Colonial Brazil: Bahia, 1684–1745," *Hispanic American Historical Review*, 54, no. 4 (Nov. 1974): 603–35.

————. *Sovereignty and Society in Colonial Brazil: The High Court of Bahia and Its Judges, 1609–1751*. Berkeley, Calif., 1973.

Seckinger, Ron. *The Brazilian Monarchy and the South American Republics, 1822–1831: Diplomacy and State Building*. Baton Rouge, La., 1984.

————. "The Politics of Nativism: Ethnic Prejudice and Political Power in Mato Grosso, 1831–34," *Americas*, 32, no. 4 (Apr. 1975): 393–416.

Serrão, Joaquim Veríssimo. *História de Portugal*. Vol. 6: *O despotismo iluminado (1750–1807)*, and vol. 7: *A instauração do liberalismo (1807–1832)*. Lisbon, 1982, 1984.

Seton-Watson, Hugh. *Nations and States: An Enquiry into the Origins of Nations and the Politics of Nationalism*. London, 1977.

Shafer, Boyd C. *Nationalism: Its Nature and Interpreters*. Washington, D.C., 1971.

Silva Bruno, Ernani. *História do Brasil—geral e regional*. Vol. 2: *Nordeste (Maranhão–Piauí–Ceará–Rio Grande do Norte–Paraíba–Pernambuco–Alagoas)*. São Paulo, 1967.

Silva Lisboa, José da, visconde de Cairu. *Historia dos principais successos politicos*. 4 vols. Rio, 1826–30.

Simon, William Joel. *Scientific Expeditions in the Portuguese Overseas Territories (1783–1808) and the Role of Lisbon in the Intellectual-Scientific Community of the Late Eighteenth Century*. Lisbon, 1983.

Sisson, Sebastião Augusto, ed. *Galeria dos brasileiros ilustres (os contemporaneos)*. 2 vols. 2d ed. São Paulo, 1948.

Smith, Alan G. R. *The Emergence of a Nation State: The Commonwealth of England, 1529–1660*. London, 1984.

Smith, Antony D. "Nationalism: A Trend Report and Bibliography," *Current Sociology*, 21, no. 3 (1973): 3–185.

Smith, Carleton S. "Two Copies of the First Book Published in Brazil, at the New York Public Library," in *Homage to a Bookman: Essays on Manuscripts, Books, and Printing, Written for Hans P. Krauss on His 60th Birthday, Oct. 12, 1967*, pp. 187–95. Berlin, n.d.

Snyder, Louis L. *The Meaning of Nationalism*. New Brunswick, N.J., 1954.

Soares de Souza, José Antônio. *A vida do visconde do Uruguaí (1807–1866) (Paulino José Soares de Sousa)*. São Paulo, 1944.

————. "Da vila real da Praia Grande à imperial cidade de Niterói," *Revista do Instituto Histórico e Geográfico Brasileiro*, 303 (Apr.–June 1976): 3–165.

Sousa, Octavio Tarquinio de. *História dos fundadores do Império do Brasil*. 10 vols. Rio, 1957.

Spalding, Walter. *A revolução farroupilha*. 2d ed. São Paulo, 1980.

Stein, Robert. "The Free Men of Colour and the Revolution in Saint Domingue, 1789–1792," *Social History*, 14, no. 27 (May 1981): 7–28.

Stein, Stanley J. *The Brazilian Cotton Manufacture*. Cambridge, Mass., 1957.

————. *Vassouras: A Brazilian Coffee County, 1850–1900*. Cambridge, Mass., 1957.

Street, John. *Artigas and the Emancipation of Uruguay*. Cambridge, Eng., 1959.

Studart, Guilherme, barão de Studart. *Diccionario bio-bibliographico cearense*. 3 vols. Fortaleza, 1910–15.

Subsídios para a história maritima do Brasil, vol. 14. Rio, 1955.

Tasso Fragoso, Augusto. *A revolução farroupilha (1835–1845)*. Rio, 1939.

Taunay, Afonso d'Escragnolle. *O senado do Imperio*. São Paulo, n.d.

Taunay, Alfredo d'Escragnolle, visconde de Taunay. *Memórias*. Rio, 1960.
Teixeira Filho, Henrique Carneiro Leão. "Honório Hermeto Carneiro Leão, marquês de Paraná, do berço de Jacuí ao fastígio do poder, 1809–1856," *Revista do Instituto Histórico e Geográfico Brasileiro*, 236 (July–Sept. 1957): 285–306.
Tilly, Charles, ed. *The Formation of National States in Western Europe*. Princeton, N.J., 1975.
Times. London.
Tute, Warren. *Cochrane: A Life of Admiral the Earl of Dundonald*. London, 1965.
Varnhagen, Francisco Adolfo de, visconde de Pôrto Seguro. *História da Independência do Brasil*, 4th ed. Ed. Helio Vianna. São Paulo, n.d.
――――. *História geral do Brasil*. 5 vols. 7th ed. São Paulo, n.d.
Vasconcelos, Antonio Luiz de Brito Aragão e. "Memorias sobre o estabelecimento do Imperio do Brazil, ou novo Imperio lusitano," *Annaes da Biblioteca Nacional*, 43/44 (1920–21): 1–48.
Vianna, Helio. *Contribuição à história da imprensa brasileira (1812–1869)*. Rio, 1945.
――――. *D. Pedro I e D. Pedro II, acréscimos às suas biografias*. São Paulo, 1966.
――――. *D. Pedro I, jornalista*. São Paulo, 1967.
――――. *Estudos de história imperial*. São Paulo, 1950.
――――. *Vultos do Império*. São Paulo, 1968.
Vieira Fazenda, José. "Aspectos do periodo regencial," *Revista do Instituto Histórico e Geográfico Brasileiro*, tomo 77, pte. 1 (1914): 41–65.
Vilhena de Moraes, Eugenio. *Caxias em São Paulo, a revolução de Sorocaba*. Rio, 1933.
――――. *O duque de ferro*. Rio, 1933.
――――. *Gabinete Caxias e a amnistia aos bispos na "questão religiosa": A attitude pessoal do Imperador*. Rio, 1930.
――――. *Novos aspectos da figueira de Caxias*. Rio, 1937.
Viotti da Costa, Emília. "The Political Emancipation of Brazil," in A. J. R. Russell-Wood, ed., *From Colony to Nation: Essays on the Independence of Brazil*, pp. 43–88. Baltimore, Md., 1975. [A revised translation of "Introdução ao estudo da emancipação política," in Carlos G. Mota, ed., *Brasil em perspectiva*, pp. 64–125. 8th ed. São Paulo, 1977.]
Wallerstein, Immanuel E. *The Modern World System: Capitalist Agriculture and the Origins of the European World Economy in the Sixteenth Century*. New York, 1974.
Wanderley [de Araújo] Pinho, José. "A Bahia, 1808–1856," in Sérgio Buarque de Holanda, ed., *História geral da civilização brasileira*, vol. 4, pp. 242–311. 2d ed. São Paulo, 1967.
――――. *Salões e damas do segundo reinado*. 2d ed. Rio, n.d.
Wasth Rodrigues, J. "Fardas do Reino Unido e do Império," *Anuário do Museu Imperial*, 11 (1950): 5–52.
Webster, Charles K., ed. *Britain and the Independence of Latin America, 1812–1830*. 2 vols. London, 1938.
Weinstein, Barbara. *The Amazon Rubber Boom, 1850–1920*. Stanford, Calif., 1983.
Werneck Sodré, Nelson. *História da imprensa no Brasil*. Rio, 1966.

Index

In this index an "f" after a number indicates a separate reference on the next page, and an "ff" indicates separate references on the next two pages. A continuous discussion over two or more pages is indicated by a span of page numbers, e.g., "pp. 57–58." Passim is used for a cluster of references in close but not consecutive sequence. Italic page numbers indicate a map or figure.

Portuguese names are indexed under the last surname, regardless of common usage in Brazil. Concepts in Portuguese are usually indexed under their English equivalent, with a cross-reference under the Portuguese term.

Index